ADVANCED CORPORATE FINANCE

Editors

CHANDRASEKHAR KRISHNAMURTI
Associate Professor
Auckland University of Technology, New Zealand

S.R. VISHWANATH
Assistant Professor
Institute of Management Technology, Nagpur

PHI Learning Private Limited
Delhi-110092
2022

₹595.00

ADVANCED CORPORATE FINANCE
Chandrasekhar Krishnamurti and S.R. Vishwanath

ISBN-978-81-203-3611-7 (Print Book)
ISBN-978-93-5443-486-0 (e-Book)

Published by Asoke K. Ghosh, PHI Learning Private Limited, Rimjhim House, 111, Patparganj Industrial Estate, Delhi-110092 and Printed by Mudrak, D-61, Sector 63, Noida, U.P.-201301.

Contents

PART III: LIABILITY AND RISK MANAGEMENT

PART V: STRUCTURING INCENTIVES

PART VI: CREATING VALUE THROUGH CORPORATE RESTRUCTURING

PART VII: COORDINATION AND CONTROL

Preface

Modern finance theory hypothesizes that value creation is the central objective of corporations. For many years, business students have been taught that companies can create value by choosing positive net present value projects. Traditional capital budgeting is based on the premise that capital investments are now-or-never propositions. It assumes that managers invest and then wait to see what happens. It does not consider the possibility that managers can wait and then invest. In other words, the discounted cash flow is based on questionable assumptions. Likewise, modern corporations are structured in such a way that managers act on behalf of owners. Due to agency conflicts, they may exhibit value destroying behaviour. One way to motivate them is to design an incentive compensation plan which makes them behave like owners. This book examines these and many such issues.

The goal of the book is to develop the theoretical and practical tools essential to a Chief Financial Officer (CFO). The theme is how the CFO can create value through financial, strategic and operating decisions. Readers build the knowledge and skill critical to the CFO's responsibilities of evaluating investment decisions; proposing, assessing, and implementing financing decisions; and managing risk. The book introduces advanced valuation techniques and provides a rigorous understanding of what creates value and why.

The book is organized into seven major parts.

Part I provides a rationale for value-based management as the overriding objective of the firm and also highlights how CFOs can increase value by fine tuning financial policies.

Part II introduces real options, a *new methodology* for valuing corporate investments. It reviews the assumptions behind the discounted cash flow methodology and suggests an alternative framework for valuation. Most corporate investments allow a great deal of flexibility (e.g. the right to abandon, expand or add technologies) to the managers. This flexibility is best described as a series of options. In this part, the focus is on the analysis of this type of corporate investment decisions under uncertainty. It begins with a discussion on financial options and applies the insights gained from it to capital investments.

Part III explores old and new financial instruments, and highlights the objective and methods of active risk management. One of the roles of a CFO is to estimate funding requirement to support the company's strategy and maintain contact with capital markets and financial institutions to obtain necessary funding at acceptable prices. This part shows how managers figure out what type of capital is necessary and how to manage risks associated with the particular type of capital.

Part IV examines structuring and financing problems and opportunities associated with large scale, stand-alone projects. In this part, project finance is discussed, with particular emphasis on how firms structure, value, and finance large, green-field projects such as telecommunications systems, toll roads, manufacturing plants, and mines. Interestingly, many of the largest projects have encountered financial distress. Many well-known projects such as the Euro Tunnel, Euro Disneyland, Iridium have all been restructured. Project Finance is usually restricted to large scale, capital intensive projects and often involves a high proportion of debt finance (60%–90%) provided by a group of lenders. Toll roads, tunnels, bridges, ports and power projects are general candidates for project financing. The Eurotunnel project in France, Hub power project in Pakistan, Petrozuata in Venezuela are some of the prominent project finance transactions.

Part V on Structuring Incentives deals with agency problems facing several well-known firms, and how finance managers can address these problems by designing incentives that align the interests of the managers with those of the shareholders. One of the most important tools that owners and managers have is the design and implementation of the ownership and governance structure of organizations, and performance measurement and reward systems. This part provides a general framework for analyzing incentive schemes. The objective is to understand how incentive strategy affects individual, team and company performance, and to show the readers a way to think about organizational problems and their solutions. This part also covers design of stock option plans and the EVA compensation system.

Part VI on Corporate Restructuring reviews some of the most popular restructuring methods and presents empirical evidence on these. It explores the technical difficulties and incentive aspects created by high leverage; the relationship between capital structure and capital costs; and interactions between a firm's financial and its business strategies. In the 1980s and 1990s, a large number of firms in the USA undertook leveraged recaps and buyouts to deal with the 'free cash flow' problem, which refers to the managers' tendency to waste free cash flow on unprofitable projects. In this part we have developed an understanding of when high leverage is appropriate and the incentives created by high leverage.

Part VII tries to integrate the contents of the book since good corporate governance is essential for effective implementation of policies.

End-of-the-chapter exercises wherever applicable have been included for the benefit of students and instructors. Moreover, a list of Harvard Business School Cases have been prepared to be used along with the book. Instructors may use these cases for instruction to enhance the effectiveness of the book.

Module 1

Esty, Benjamin and Craig F. Schreiber, Service Corporation International, *Harvard Business School Case No.* 9-296-080, March 18, 1996.

Fruhan, William, Microsoft/Intuit, *Harvard Business School Case No.* 9-295-121, May 24, 1995.

Module 2

Luehrman, Timothy and William A. Teichner, Arundel Partners: The Sequel Project, *Harvard Business School Case No.* 9-292-140, June 12, 1992.

Luehrman, Timothy, Peter Tufano, and Barbara Wall, MW Petroleum (A), *Harvard Business School Case No.* 9-295-029, November 7, 1994.

Module 3

Fruhan, William, STMicroelectronics N.V., 2003 Convertible Bond Offering, *Harvard Business School Case No.* 9-204-092 October 15, 2003.

Tufano, Peter and Cameron Poetzscher, Times Mirror Co. PEPS Proposal Review, *Harvard Business School Case No.* 9-296-089, April 19, 1996.

Cossin, Didier and Dinos Constantinou, Preparing for the Google IPO: A Revolution in the Making, *International Institute for Management Development Case No.* IMD185, November 26, 2004.

Kester, Carl, Enrique Ostale, and Charles M. La Follette, Compania de Telefonos de Chile, *Harvard Business School Case No.* 9-293-015, August 13, 1992.

Muelbroek, Lisa and Puja Malhotra, Risk Management at Apache, *Harvard Business School Case No.* 9-201-113, April 16, 2001.

Module 4

Luehrman, Timothy and Andrew D. Regan, Texas High-Speed Rail Corporation, *Harvard Business School Case No.* 9-293-072, January 21, 1993.

Esty, Benjamin and Mathew Mateo Millet, Petrolera Zuata, Petrozuata C. A., *Harvard Business School Case No.* 9-299-012, September 23, 1998.

Module 5

Hall, Brian and Carleen Madigan 'Gerald Weiss' Stock Options, *Harvard Business School Case No.* 9-899-258, April 19, 1999.

Hall, Brian and Jonathan P. Lim, Massachusetts Financial Services, *Harvard Business School Case No.* 9-902-132, January 17, 2002.

Desai, Mihir, Masako Egawa and Yanjun Wang, The Continuing Transformation of Asahi Glass: Implementing EVA, *Harvard Business School Case No.* 9-205-030, October 5, 2004.

Module 6

Esty, Benjamin and Tara L. Nells, USG Corp., *Harvard Business School Case No.* 9-297-052, December 5, 1996.

Jensen, M.C., Willy Burkhardt and Brian Barry, Wisconsin Central Ltd. Railroad and Berkshire Partners (A): Leveraged Buyouts and Financial Distress, *Harvard Business School Case No.* 9-190-062, November 20, 1989.

Ruback, Richard, R.J.R. Nabisco, *Harvard Business School Case No.* 9-289-056, May 15, 1989.

Esty, Benjamin and Jason S. Auerbach, Bankruptcy and Restructuring at Marvel Entertainment Group, *Harvard Business School Case No.* 9-298-059, September 16, 1997.

Module 7

Kester, Carl and Robert W. Lightfoot, Koito Manufacturing Ltd., *Harvard Business School Case No.* 9-291-027, April 9, 1991.

Dyck, Alexander, The Hermitage Fund: Media and Corporate Governance in Russia, *Harvard Business School Case No.* 9-703-010, October 17, 2002.

This book has been designed to give a global perspective to readers especially the Indian students. It draws as much from research done in the USA as from elsewhere. It provides numerous examples from around the world to maintain a global focus.

This book is meant to be used by students of finance in a typical MBA programme in Indian universities/management schools as also in other parts the world. It can also be used for CFA and such other professional programmes in finance.

It can also be profitably used by practitioners who want to upgrade their knowledge of corporate finance.

Any constructive suggestion for improving the contexts will be highly appreciated.

Chandrasekhar Krishnamurti
S.R. Vishwanath

About the Contributors

Al Ehrbar (Stern Stewart & Co., New York, USA)

Al Ehrbar is Senior Vice President at Stern Stewart & Co. A leading business and financial journalist, he has been senior editor at *Fortune* magazine, editor and publisher at *Corporate Finance* magazine, and senior economics writer at the *Wall Street Journal*. He is the recipient of numerous awards for journalist excellence and has authored the book *EVA: Economic Value Added—The Real Key to Creating Wealth.*

Atul Gupta (Bentley College, Massachusetts, USA)

Atul Gupta is the Robert and Julia Dorn Professor of Finance at Bentley College. His research papers have been published in *Financial Management, Journal of Banking and Finance, Journal of Financial Research, Journal of Financial Services Research* and *Journal of Monetary Economics.*

Chandrasekhar Krishnamurti (Auckland University of Technology, New Zealand)

Chandrasekhar Krishnamurti is Associate Professor at the College of Business, Auckland University of Technology. He has held teaching positions at Monash Business School, Australia; National University of Singapore; Nanyang Business School, Singapore; Indian Institute of Science, India. He has a PhD in Finance from University of Iowa, USA. Professor Krishnamurti has a wealth of teaching, research and consulting experience having worked in the USA, India and Singapore, and is especially interested in market microstructure, risk management using derivatives, emerging markets and international finance. He has been a consultant for Financial Institutions Reform and Expansion (FIRE) project funded by USAID and administered by Price Waterhouse LLP, USA, and has utilized his wide-ranging research expertise to conduct studies in Nasdaq, New York Stock Exchange, Paris Bourse, and stock exchanges in emerging countries. Professor Krishnamurti writes a regular (*MoneyGuru*) column for *Lycos Asia's Finance Portal* (sg.finance.lycosasia.com) covering topics of interest to individual investors.

Professor Krishnamurti's main areas of research are in Corporate Finance and Market Microstructure. His secondary research interests include Emerging Markets, International Finance and Risk Management. Professor Krishnamurti has conducted executive training in Derivatives and Risk Management, Investment Strategies for Individual Investors. He has published in major international journals such as *Financial Management, Journal of Banking and Finance, Journal of Financial Research, Quarterly Journal of Business and Economics* (USA), *The ICFAI Journal of Applied Finance* (India), *Research in International Business and Finance* (USA), and *Managerial Finance* (UK). He has presented his research at major conferences around the world.

Laurence Booth (Rotman School of Management, University of Toronto, Canada)

Laurence Booth is the CIT Chair in Structured Finance at the Rotman School of Management, University of Toronto. His research has been published in *Journal of Finance, Journal of Financial and Quantitative Analysis, Journal of Financial Research, Journal of Applied Corporate Finance* among others. His research interests are in static and inter-temporal micro-financial economics and capital market theory.

Petko Kalev (Monash Business School, Australia)

Petko Kalev has a masters degree in Statistics and a PhD from University of Melbourne. He has taught in the Department of Statistics at the University of Melbourne, Department of Econometrics, and Business Statistics at Monash Business School. His research interests are in initial public offerings, term structure of interest rates, and volatility modelling. He teaches Empirical methods in Finance at the doctoral programme college of Business level.

Ravishanker Mateti (Charlton College of Business, University of Massachusetts, USA)

Ravishanker Mateti is on the faculty of Charlton College of Business, University of Massachusetts at Dartmouth, USA. He holds masters degrees in Management and Economics, and a PhD in Finance from University of Connecticut, Storrs. His teaching and research interests are in the area of Derivatives, Risk Management and Financial Engineering.

P.V. Viswanath (Lubin School of Business, Pace University, USA)

P.V. Viswanath is Professor of Finance and is New York Stock Exchange Scholar at Lubin School of Business, Pace University. He teaches both undergraduate and graduate students, and also serves as a consultant to the financial industry in the areas of Margin Policy and Dividend Policy. He has been a financial consultant to start-up businesses also. He received his PhD in finance from University of Chicago. His papers have appeared in *Journal of Finance, Journal of Financial and Quantitative Analysis, Financial Management, Journal of Law and Economics, Journal of Risk and Insurance, Journal of Futures Markets, Journal of Money, Credit and Banking,* and *Advances in Financial Planning and Forecasting*. He has presented his research in many conferences around the world.

S.R. Vishwanath (Institute of Management Technology, Nagpur, India)

S.R. Vishwanath is Assistant Professor at Institute of Management Technology, Nagpur, India. Earlier he worked as a consultant with Tata Management Training Center in Pune, India. His first book *Corporate Finance: Theory and Practice* is now in second edition. He has also edited a book on *Mergers, Acquisitions and Corporate Restructuring*. He has held academic positions at several top tier business schools in India.

PART I

INTRODUCTION

CHAPTER

1

An Overview of Value-Based Management*

LEARNING OBJECTIVES

After reading this chapter, you should be able to:

- Give a rationale for shareholder wealth maximization.
- Highlight the drivers of value.
- Provide a framework for value creation in companies.

INTRODUCTION

Heightened competition in product and capital markets, and pressure from shareholder groups are forcing corporations to choose value maximizing strategies. Many corporations have announced their commitment to shareholder value maximization. But believing is not the same as achieving. This chapter provides an overview of value-based management concepts and tools.

Many corporate executives still focus on quarterly earnings figures as a key driver of stock market values. Although no one can discount the importance of quarterly earnings numbers or the impact on the stock market of earnings surprises, they are not the fundamental driver. The stock market values are driven by real corporate performance as compared to market benchmarks. The key relationship is whether the money entrusted to

* This chapter is contributed by Laurence Booth.

the corporate management earns a higher return than the owners can get elsewhere. Focussing on this key relationship differentiates the Value Manager from other managerial styles. Implementing a 'value managerial' system can be accomplished by two main metrics: a sales operating margin, **turnover metric** and a more traditional return on investment, **reinvestment rate metric**. Both the metrics are simply ways of expressing the underlying determinants of market value. The most critical decision facing a firm is whether to adopt a value-based managerial system rather than a particular set of decision tools.

WHAT DRIVES SHAREHOLDER VALUE?

The discussion of finance topics involves both normative and positive statements, and it is important to be aware of their distinction. **Normative** statements refer to what *ought* to be and are usually derived from an assumption about how the world behaves. This is most evident in standard economics topics, where assumptions about human and corporate behaviour are made to derive supply and demand curves, which are then used to explain how prices are determined. *Financial theory* is an application of these standard economic models to explain how prices in the capital market are determined. As such, financial economists use essentially the same tools as their colleagues in other areas of economics to predict how, for example, equity prices *ought* to be determined, and, how as a result, corporate management *ought* to behave. In contrast, *positive* statements refer to *what is, was or will be*, it is commonly referred to as an appeal to the facts.*

The above distinction between positive and normative statements is important, since it turns out that many heated arguments in finance, as in many areas of business, are in reality arguments over assumptions, not facts, that is, they are arguments over what *ought* to be. This is as true of shareholder value analysis, as it is of any other area of finance. In this chapter, the author will discuss the normative principles that underlie shareholder value analysis, and some of the positive evidence in its support.

The Normative Justification for Creating Shareholder Value

It is a normative statement that Creating Shareholder Value (CSV) is the correct goal of the firm. Figure 1.1 demonstrates the dynamics and the conflicts between different stakeholders in the firm. The firm is the rectangular box with the managers inside the box in control of the firm's operations. The firm buys labour, capital (both debt and equity) from

* The above definitions are from Lipsey, R.G., *An Introduction to Positive Economics*, 2nd ed., Weidenfeld and Nicolson, 1969, p. 4.

investors, intermediate goods from suppliers and uses up what we commonly refer to as free goods, such as the right to emit pollutants and use social services provided by the State. The firm then creates its product, which it sells to consumers and in the process creates free goods, such as, for example, by increasing the level of education in the community by retraining its workforce. All of this production, in turn, occurs under the watchful eye of governments (all levels) and is subject to societal pressure from other members of the community.

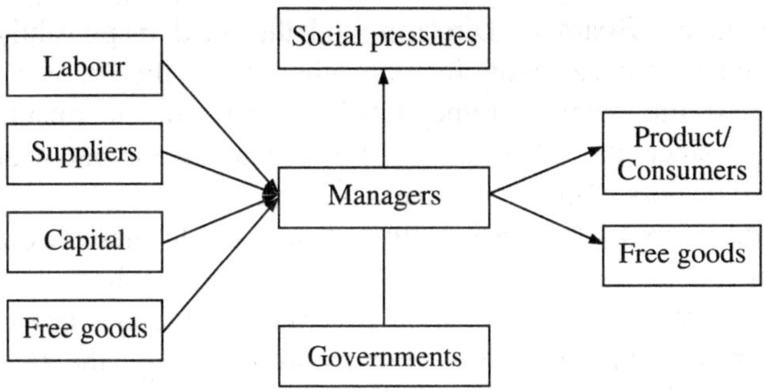

Figure 1.1 Creating shareholder value.

All of these stakeholders have some claims on the firm. How this tangle of claims on the firm subsequently gets resolved in terms of the firm's objectives depends on both the legal structure of the country and the state of the markets in which the firm operates. Finance, as we understand it, has largely developed in countries with a common Anglo-Saxon legal heritage that places the ownership of the firm's common equity as the primary determinant of elections to the Board of Directors, who then have a fiduciary responsibility to act in their interests. The corollary of this legal principal is that the stockholders are primarily interested in the maximization of their wealth and ergo the market value of the firm's common stock price. Hence, the focus of this essay is on CSV.

The economic justification for CSV as the overriding objective of the firm primarily comes from an assumption implicit in most of the finance literature that all the markets in which the firm operates are perfectly competitive. This means that if the firm's employment is increased or decreased, that the employees in Figure 1.1 are indifferent. If they are hired, then they are just getting market wages, and if they are laid off, then they can immediately get equivalent jobs elsewhere. Similarly, suppliers and consumers can switch to other firms, and taxes to all layers of government will be the same regardless of the firm's operations. As a result, the welfare of all other stakeholders in the firm is unaffected by the firm's operations, so that maximizing the welfare of the stockholders causes no welfare losses to these other stakeholders. The implicit assumption underlying most of the shareholder value literature is, therefore, that there are no other stakeholders in the firm, except the stockholders! Or put in another way, the normative statement that CSV should be the objective of the firm is based on the assumption that all markets are perfectly competitive.

The perfect market assumption is valid for small businesses in practically every country around the world, since they do not affect the functioning of other markets. However, for large businesses it is more questionable. In many of the less diversified European economies, the impact of certain large firms is critical for the functioning of their economies. As a result, there is 'worker' representation on the Board of Directors and the legal responsibility of the board is to take into account factors other than the interests of the stockholders.* At the other extreme, CSV has become the mantra of the corporate USA, since the USA has by far and away the most diversified economy and the most competitive markets.†

Canada, for example, has historically sat in between these two extremes. The large number of interlocking ownership structures has made hostile takeovers scarcer than in the USA, while governance structures have generally resulted in more captive, less active, boards. Additionally, the fact that the Canadian equity has largely been trapped in Canada due to foreign ownership restrictions in tax sheltered plans, as well as the dividend tax credit, has meant that the Canadian firms could pay less attention to their shareholders. Of interest is that the overall Canadian equity market has consistently underperformed than that of the USA.

Tables 1.1 and 1.2 give the average rates of return earned in the US and Canadian markets on equities, government bonds, treasury bills, and the consumer price index. Although the Canadian fixed income returns have been higher than those in the USA, the equity rates of return have lagged behind those in the USA. There are a variety of potential reasons for the poorer performance of the Canadian equity market, but the greater emphasis in the USA on CSV is certainly a potential factor. As the North American Free Trade Agreement (NAFTA) has opened up the market for goods and services, we are seeing more competition among firms. Consequently, the Canadian market structure is moving closer to the US model. Similarly, as the international capital market becomes more integrated, it will intensify the pressure on the Canadian firms to pay more attention to CSV.

However, before discussing how to create shareholder value, it is important to point out how not to create shareholder value. From Figure 1.1, we find that there are many ways in which the overall value of the firm's operations (largely the firm's revenues) can be allocated. This means that one

---

* This is also justified by the illiquid state of the equity markets and the low reliance put on equity financing.

† However, even in the USA, some states require that the Board of Directors consider factors other than the interests of the shareholders, for example, hostile takeovers.

way to create shareholder value is simply to transfer the existing value to the shareholders, at the expense of these other claimants. For example, the firm can skimp on pollution controls and increase contamination of the environment, leaving others to clean up its mess. The equity holders can also engage in activities that shift wealth from the bond holders to the equity holders, as often occurs during times of financial distress.

Table 1.1 Canadian Estimates

	TSE300	Canadas	T. Bills	CPI
1926–1956				
AM	12.71	4.00	0.84	1.59
GM	10.44	3.87	0.62	1.47
Volatility	21.90	5.32	0.57	4.96
1957–1997				
AM	11.24	8.13	7.51	4.59
GM	10.05	7.62	7.44	4.54
Volatility	15.96	10.79	3.94	3.32

Table 1.2 The US Estimates

	S&P500	Treasuries	T. Bills	CPI
1926–1956				
AM	13.05	3.38	1.14	1.54
GM	10.11	3.27	1.14	1.40
Volatility	24.47	4.85	1.20	5.39
1957–1997				
AM	12.88	7.26	5.81	4.45
GM	11.67	6.72	5.77	4.40
Volatality	16.18	11.09	2.76	3.12

Finally, many corporate financing strategies are tax motivated and merely transfer wealth from all tax payers to the firm's shareholders. There is no theoretical justification in economics to support CSV when it is simply a transfer of wealth from other claimants on the firm to the common shareholders. The reason for this is simply that the society as a whole is no better off. The economic justification for CSV is based on the efficiency gains of more productive operations and a better reallocation of resources.* This

* This point needs emphasizing, since the author has spent many hours discussing the ethical issues surrounding CSV with business ethicists and environmentalists who are extremely hostile to the concept.

result stems from having managers become 'value' managers, where they treat corporate resources as they would if they were the owners.*

PROBLEMS WITH ACCOUNTING EARNINGS

It may surprise some, but stock market value is not created by accounting games to dress up the financial statements. This is not to deny that accounting statements are important, they obviously are, but the fact is that the stock market looks far into the future when assessing value. Consider the stock prices in Table 1.3 taken at random from quotes from *Financial Post* on 1 August, 1998. The quotes are for the first 10 common equity issues for each letter from A to J. The *first* column is the stock price, the *second* the dividend yield and the *third* the implied annual dividend. The *fourth* column then values this dividend assuming that it goes on forever with a 5% discount rate. That is, the stock is treated as if it were a perpetuity preferred share. The *final* column gives that part of the share price that is not accounted for by the perpetuity values of the current dividend.

Table 1.3 Stock Market Horizons

Stock	Price	Dividend yield	Dividend	Perpetuity	Growth%
AGF	25.75	1.10	0.283	5.66	78.0
BC Gas	30.60	3.70	1.13	22.60	26.0
CAE	11.50	1.40	0.161	3.22	72.0
Dennings	3.50	2.90	0.102	2.04	42.0
EL Fin	285	0.2	0.570	11.4	96.0
Fahnstck	26.75	1.6	0.428	8.56	68.0
GSW(A)	14.05	1.4	0.197	3.94	72.0
Hammersn	6.95	4.2	0.292	5.84	16.0
Intrawest	29.60	0.5	0.148	2.96	90.0
Jannock	15.5	3.2	0.496	9.92	36.0
Average					**60.0**

The final column of Table 1.3 makes for interesting reading. For BC Gas and Hammersen, the growth components of the current stock price are relatively low at 26% and 16% respectively, which is what you would expect given their operations. However, for the other eight firms future growth

* The crux of the CSV movement is that the modern corporation separates ownership from control. As a result, the incentive structure facing senior management in large corporations leads them to mismanage corporate resources since they are not immediately answerable to the owners.

accounts for 36–96% of the share price. This implies that shareholders are looking well beyond the company's current performance in valuing their shares. This in turn raises problems as well as opportunities. BC Gas is primarily a regulated gas distributor and oil pipeline in British Columbia, where the bulk of its operations are regulated by the BC Utilities Commission to ensure a fair return to the common shareholders. This means that there are few surprises in its quarterly financial statements and any that there are, are likely to result in changes by the BCUC, so as not to have a significant long-term effect on the shareholders. This is the main reason why *growth* accounts for such a small part of BC Gas' stock price. It also means that the market does not react very much to BC Gas' quarterly results: there simply is not much *news* in them. In contrast, for the other firms a large amount of the stock price comes from future growth prospects, which are very hard to predict. It is inevitable when valuing these *growth* companies that every piece of information is scrutinized in some detail to see whether the firm's performance is still on target. In this state of scarce and limited information, one of the most reliable sources is obviously the firm itself through its quarterly statements. If these results are below the market expectations, without any accompanying information to explain the discrepancy, investors will extrapolate the impact into the future. The result will be an immediate impact on the stock price, with a greater effect felt for those firms with a greater *growth* component in their stock price. It is one of the ironies of finance that it is the fact that the market values operations very far into the future that causes it to react violently to short-term results.

This result has strong implications for corporate finance. *First*, there is no doubt that earnings management pays off. The market does not like surprises and the management of quarterly earnings can prevent dramatic market revaluations in response to what the firm may correctly estimate to be temporary phenomena.* On the other hand, it does not mean that the market is dumb and can be permanently fooled by the manipulation of financial statements. What the market is interested in is the underlying ability of the firm to generate real, not accounting earnings. This is a normative statement however. A large amount of research over the last 30 years has gone into determining whether it is also a positive statement. The author will not review all the evidence on how the market reacts to accounting versus real decisions. Instead, the author will discuss the two classic accounting issues that have been examined extensively: the use of First in, First out (FIFO)/Last in First out (LIFO) inventory valuation and purchase versus pooling accounting for mergers and takeovers, and the how the market values research and development (R&D) expenditures. Inventory valuation is a classic test of

* By earnings management, the author means minor revenue recognition and expenditure scheduling along with recognition of gains and losses on asset disposals, which can smooth earnings without significant long term effects.

whether the market values accounting earnings or cash, since in the USA whichever inventory method is used for, the financial statements also has to be used for tax purposes.

During the inflationary 1970s using FIFO for valuing inventory persistently underpriced the cost of goods sold since the last items produced invariably cost more. This resulted in not only higher accounting earnings, but also higher taxes and consequently less cash.* In contrast, LIFO inventory valuation, priced the cost of goods sold with the last units produced, which although reduced the accounting earnings, also reduced taxes leading to stronger cash flow.

Biddle and Lindahl (1982) found that the US firms switching to LIFO saw their stock price increase, despite lower accounting earnings, with the magnitude of the price gains increasing with the size of the tax gains. Several other US studies have found similar effects that the market looks through cosmetic accounting issues to focus on underlying cash. Accounting for mergers is a similar test of whether the market values a particular accounting method, when in this case the choice should have no real effect at all. If one firm buys another, the difference between the purchase price and the (revalued) assets of the purchased company is called goodwill. In purchase accounting, this goodwill is recorded as an asset and written off against future income, usually over the next 40 years, thereby reducing the accounting earnings. Moreover, until 1993 in the USA, as is still the case in most countries, writing off goodwill had no tax implications. Even though writing off goodwill is a classic non-cash charge in the income statement, firms in the USA frequently paid extra just to be able to get the transaction classified as a pooling of interests. In AT&T's acquisition of NCR, Davis (1996) points out that AT&T incurred extra costs of almost $ 500 million to ensure that the takeover could be treated as a pooling. Similarly in Canada, where it is harder to avoid purchase accounting, Royal Bank's proposed takeover of Bank of Montreal, as well as the share exchange ratio, seems to have been heavily influenced by the desire to account for the transaction as a pooling of interests.

However, contrary to the predictions of the 'accounting earnings model', Davis shows that the market does not reward firms for using pooling rather than purchase accounting and that "there is no evidence that paying to pool is a justifiable or profitable use of firm resources". Quite the contrary, Davis concludes that 'purchased goodwill' is valued in the market and that the extensive US practises that he discloses, whereby goodwill is buried with other assets in defiance of SEC guidelines, does not help stock prices. While a critical assessment of how the market values what are primarily financial statement issues shows that the market can see through some major accounting changes, what about real cash effects in the financial statements? A classic case

---

* In Canada, most firms use FIFO, which is why an additional 3% inventory write off was allowed for tax purposes.

here is how to treat research and development expenditures. Clearly, R&D is an investment, it is undertaken to produce new investments and products, and to generate future cash. However, in almost all the cases, R&D expenditures are immediately written off, rather than capitalized. The result is that a reduction in 'worthwhile' R&D helps immediate accounting earnings at the expense of the firm's future prospects. If the market is indeed fixated on accounting earnings, we would expect to see high R&D firms with depressed earnings and stock prices.

Testing the impact of R&D on market values is difficult since R&D expenditures are frequently hidden in a firm's financial statements. However, Table 1.4 contains 34 firms in *Financial Post* database that reported R&D expenditures for every year from 1988–1997. Without being *scientific*, the firms ranked by R&D expenditures as a percentage of total revenues also tend to have the highest price to book ratios. There are problems with using price to book ratios, but note that ISG and Develcon Electronics have negative accounting earnings, whether measured by the 10-year average Return On Equity (ROE) or the 10-year average Earnings Before Interest and Taxes (EBIT) profit margin. These low earnings are partly the result of very large R&D expenditures (40% and 12.4% of sales, respectively), but the market prices their stock at almost seven times and four times the book value, respectively. In contrast, low R&D firms such as MacMillan Bloedel, Domco, Celanese Canada, and Potash Corporation of Saskatchewan are also low price to book companies, even though their accounting earnings are much higher. Clearly, for all these firms the market is looking beyond the accounting earnings to arrive at prices based on other factors.

Table 1.4 R&D and Stock Prices

	Price/Book	R&D	EBIT(%)	ROE
BioChem Pharma Inc.	6.980	40.137	9.856	0.089
I.S.G. Technologies, Inc.	5.811	29.611	–28.287	–50.481
CAE Inc.	3.367	15.358	3.536	3.696
Northern Telecom Limited	2.540	12.634	7.351	9.675
Cognos Incorporated	4.289	12.493	7.010	7.777
Develcon Electronics Ltd.	3.920	12.414	–25.818	–69.245
Corel Corporation	3.511	11.810	10.477	1.182
Newbridge Networks Corporation	6.025	10.243	21.986	20.663
Draxis Health Inc.	4.800	8.466	54.286	14.565
Canadian Marconi Company	1.144	8.294	7.984	6.213
International Verifact Inc.	4.167	7.988	–6.974	–8.770
Mitel Corporation	2.078	7.891	1.678	–1.621
Geac Computer Corporation	3.122	7.835	9.089	8.304
BCE Inc.	1.550	7.020	15.196	9.981

WHAT DOES THE MARKET VALUE?

Again a discussion of what drives market values gets deep into normative and positive statements, but key insights can be gained from how professional valuators approach the problem. Most texts point out that accounting earnings are not cash, since they cannot be spent. Further, since investors normally invest cash in the firm, they are interested in getting cash back. The standard finance answer to what the market values is, therefore, simple: **future cash flows**. As a result, the Discounted Cash Flow (DCF) approach is the recommended valuation method in every finance textbook and the basis for most *fairness opinions* in professional valuations. However, defining and calculating cash flow is somewhat controversial, since there are several definitions circulating in the investment community.

In a famous article, Hunt (1975), after coming back from a visit to Ireland, wrote about Professor Finagle's three laws of information.

1. The information we have is not what we want
2. The information we want is not what we need
3. The information we need is not available

Hunt discusses Finagle's laws in the context of what investment analysts want from a firm's financial statements. What they have are the financial statements with 'accounting earnings' the bottom line. However, what analysts need for their valuations are not accounting earnings, but cash flow, the actual cash generated from the firm's operations. Most analysts start by simply adding back non-cash charges to obtain what is commonly referred to as **cash flow**.* In the context of the two accounting problems discussed earlier, dealing with cash flow removes the problem of amortizing goodwill, since the goodwill that is disclosed and deducted from accounting earnings is then added back to get the cash flow, thereby neutralizing its deduction. In the same way, the analyst would also add back depreciation, deferred income tax, amortization of bond discounts, and all other write-offs disclosed in the income statement that do not involve cash. Cash flow is a huge improvement over accounting earnings, and focussing on it, rather than earnings largely removes the need to avoid purchase accounting. However, it is not what analysts wanted, even in 1975. What they wanted was to undo as many of the accounting policies as possible to get to the true cash generated by the firm's operations. Adding back non-cash items was a start but of no help, for example, in undoing the inventory accounting adjustments involved with FIFO and LIFO. However, note that if a firm uses FIFO for cost of goods sold, the most recent goods produced end up in inventory, as a result inventory

---

* The *Financial Post*'s FP analyst database and software defines cash flow as net income plus non-cash charges. Others call this measure cash flow from operations, for example RBC-DS in their Foundations publication.

increases faster than with LIFO. One way of offsetting this accounting treatment is to subtract from cash flow the increase in non-cash Net Working Capital (NWC).* When we do this we get what is generally referred to as Cash Flow from Operations (CFO).

Firms that overstate earnings by using FIFO would then see the resulting increased inventory reducing their NWC and their CFO that also picks up other accounting games. Premature recognition of sales can boost sales, but instead of getting cash the firm may just get a doubtful long-dated receivable. Similarly, offering discounts to major customers to book credit sales near the end of the year may boost sales and earnings, but would also increase receivables and NWC. As a result, focussing on CFO, instead of accounting earnings, nullifies most revenue recognition games. Similarly, overtrading by a firm by stretching its accounts payable will also show up in a lower CFO.† Focussing on CFO undoes most of the pure accounting changes used by firms to try and disguise their true operating results. In Hunt's terminology, this is generally what analysts want, however, it is still not what they need. The reason for this is that firms can still control and possibly manipulate their capital expenditures. One firm with a large CFO may also have a very large capital expenditure (capex) programme and thus be short of cash, whereas another firm with similar CFO could have very limited capex. Hunt argued that the capex needed to maintain the firm's operations should be subtracted from the CFO to get the true cash generating ability of the firm. The result is what Hunt called the **firm's funds position**, and which is now more commonly referred to as Free Cash Flow (FCF).

Free cash flow is normally defined as of the form:

$$\text{FCF} = \text{Net income} + \text{Non cash items} - \frac{\text{Increased NWC}}{\text{Capex}}$$

It captures whether or not the firm actually generated cash from its operations, after adjusting the earnings for non-cash items the need to reinvest in NWC and the new capital expenditures to maintain the firm's operations. In principle, the idea is simply to see whether the firm's operations generated cash that could either be returned as a dividend or equity buyback to the stockholders, or be used to fund an expansion of its operations and/or acquisition of other firms. Hunt's definition of FCF is the standard definition and is commonly used in security valuation.‡ However, when companies are being valued by professional valuators one final adjustment is needed, this is to adjust for the firm's financing. While we started off with net income, which

---

* Financial analysts generally define NWC as current assets minus spontaneous liabilities, that is, payables and accruals. All interest-bearing short-term financing is ignored.

† *Financial Post* in FP Analyst defines CFO in this way.

‡ RBC-DS and *Financial Post* both define FCF as above, less dividends. The only distinction is that Financial Post subtracts all capex, whereas RBC-DS subtracts 'maintenance' capex.

is owned by the stockholders, we subsequently added back depreciation, as well as subtracting out capex and changes in NWC, both of which involve financing from all of the investors in the firm, both debt and equity.

To be consistent we, therefore, need to adjust the firm's earnings for financial charges resulting from different financing decisions. This is accomplished by adding back the after-tax interest charges using the firm's marginal tax rate. The resulting definition of FCF is that which is normally used for valuation purposes. This 'valuation' definition of FCF has the unique advantage of abstracting from how the firm financed its operations. This is needed in valuing firms, since conventionally the firm as a whole is valued and then the debt subtracted out to get the equity value as the residual. The reason for this is that how to finance an acquisition is determined after the total value is calculated. FCF is still not a perfect measure. It is difficult to pick up firms that are deliberately running down their fixed assets, and, thus, overstating their earnings and FCF. To pick this up the analyst needs to look at turnover ratios and actually get out and kick tyres. However, FCF is the best available measure of the firm's ability to generate cash. It is the valuation analogue to the measure of cash normally recommended for use in standard capital expenditure analysis.

A firm value is then determined by projecting FCF over a fixed time horizon, usually five or ten years. At the end of this time period a terminal value is forecasted based usually on a multiple of EBIT, a perpetuity FCF multiple or a premium to book value. The resulting stream of inflows is then discounted back to get a current value of the firm's operations using an appropriate weighted average cost of capital.* The value of any 'redundant' assets such as surplus marketable securities not needed to generate the FCF stream, is then added to this value and the values of any non-debt liabilities, e.g. unfunded pension liabilities or other warranty/legal liabilities subtracted.

A summary of the components of FCF are presented here.

1. **Plus non-cash items:** Depreciation, goodwill amortization, deferred income taxes, bond discount amortization, foreign exchange adjustments, earnings of non-consolidated firms, and any other non-cash items.

   Why: No cash involved; they hide the true cash generated by the firm.

2. **Minus changes in NWC:** Largely additional receivables and inventory net of payables and accruals.

   Why: Increased credit sales and premature revenue recognition show up in increased receivables, inventory accounting differences show

* The weighted average cost of capital (WACC) is defined as where E/V and D/V are the equity and debt financing proportions, and K_e, and $K_d(1 - T)$ are the costs of equity and debt financing respectively, and where the cost of debt is on an after-tax basis, the same as the equity cost.

up either in the income statement or in the inventory plus producing for inventory costs just as much as producing for goods sold for cash, payables are sometimes manipulated.

3. **Minus capex:** Subtract all capex, but not 'diversifying' investments unrelated to existing operations.

   Why: Adding depreciation (wearing down of capital) without subtracting capex overstates cash generated.

4. **Plus financial charges:** Add back after-tax interest charges using the marginal tax rate.

   Why: Two otherwise identical firms will have different FCF if they have been financed differently.

WHAT ARE THE 'VALUE DRIVERS' BEHIND THE FCF APPROACH?

A variety of different models are offered by consultants for predicting FCF, all of which emphasize slightly different 'value drivers.' However, all internally consistent models can be reduced to the free cash flow model as discussed in the previous section.* The author likes to forecast and analyse FCF by breaking it out into its four major components: (i) operating cash flow, (ii) tax benefits, (iii) NWC and (iv) capex, and then making them all dependent on future sales growth. Anyone familiar with cash flow forecasting for a non-financial company† will know that getting the sales growth rate right is the key to a successful forecast and as a result the key driver for forecasting FCF.

The most difficult numbers to analyse are the non-investment components of FCF. Adding back the after-tax interest charges to net income is equivalent to regarding the firm as wholly equity financed. This leads to focussing on EBIT. However, this number reflects the deduction of non-cash charges like depreciation and amortization, so a better number is to back up the income statement to Earnings Before Interest, Tax, Depreciation and Amortization (EBITDA), which is generally referred to as operating income. Taxes are always complicated, so it is frequently easiest to analyse them separately, if possible. The EBITDA is then treated as fully taxable, giving the key number as EBITDA ($1-T$), where T is the corporate tax rate. Expressing this as a percentage of sales revenue then gives the after-tax operating margin [EBITDA ($1-T$)/Sales]. Although the after-tax operating margin is the

* A good discussion of this can be found in J. Fred Weston et al., *Mergers, Restructuring and Corporate Control*, Prentice Hall, Englewood Cliff, NJ, 1990.

† The following comments do not apply to natural resource stocks, where the direction of commodity prices is obviously the key.

conceptually correct measure, in practice a before-tax measure is often used[*] simply because marginal tax rates do not vary much across companies, once you adjust for the different depreciation rates that give rise to deferred taxes.[†]

The advantages of focussing on operating margins over more conventional measures are several. *First*, they can be used in comparisons across firms with different capital structures. Firms with a large amount of debt financing, for example, generally have lower net margins simply because of the large amount of interest. *Second*, firms with newer fixed assets generally have larger depreciation charges and, as a result, lower earnings. *Finally*, EBITDA removes the effect of the non-cash charges like goodwill, which are buried in the amortization numbers.[‡] Since amortizations are generally not tax deductible, not deducting them from EBITDA in the first place is the same as subsequently adding them back. However, for depreciation, there is value in the fact that for tax purposes, firms are allowed to deduct Capital Consumption Allowances (CCA or tax depreciation). In Canada, the value of the tax shield from CCA is calculated from a simple formula based on the fact that capital consumption allowances are calculated on a declining cost basis.[§] The tax value from existing and future depreciable assets is also increased by the value of any tax loss carry forwards. Analysing the tax shield value of a firm's operations is frequently difficult, since some firms hide the information in their statements. However, depending on the firm's past and the immediate future, these tax shields can be a significant component of value.

The final two components of FCF are NWC and capex so that if the tax benefits of FCF are analysed separately, FCF can be forecast as of the form.

$$\text{FCF}_t = MS_0(1 + g) - (i + c)gS_0 \tag{1.1}$$

where M is the after-tax operating margin [EBITDA (1–T)/Sales], i and c the forecast NWC and capex expressed as a percentage of sales respectively, and the forecast sales level is just the current sales (S_0) level times one plus the forecast sales growth rate.[**] The key to understanding this equation is that the operating margin is earned on the total sales level, whereas extra NWC and capex are only needed to support the incremental sales. Equation (1.1) captures

[*] RBC-DS, for example, in its Foundations reports the pretax EBITDA/Sales ratio as one of the firm's key financial ratios.

[†] Some like to separate the operating margin into the gross margin and the fixed cost ratio to capture the effects of operating leverage. However, the accounting treatment of fixed costs frequently does not allow this.

[‡] Operating margins also ignore income from other investments. The value of other income is added to firm value with 'redundant' assets. CCA′ $*$ $A(k\%\ *)$.

[§] The formula is where the value of the CCA shield determined by the CCA rate ($*$), the discount rate (k), and the amount of undepreciated assets (A).

[**] See Laurence Booth, An application of valuation principles: Peoples jewellers purchase of zales, in R. Rupert (ed.) *Canadian Investment Banking Review*, McGraw Hill Ryerson, 1992.

the key value drivers in a firm's operations. The operating margin captures the contribution of each dollar of sales. Unlike the net profit margin it is uncontaminated by the way in which the firm is financed (interest), by the allocation of non-cash charges like goodwill which are largely arbitrary, or the existence of extraordinary write-offs and income. The NWC and capex ratios then take into account the extra investment needed to support sales growth. They are simply the inverses of their respective turnover ratios. As such, they capture the efficiency of the firm's operations. Firms that use their resources efficiently will have high turnover ratios, so that i and c will be relatively low, increasing the FCF and firm value. On the other hand, firms with lax working capital management and excessive capital expenditures will find themselves short of cash.

Using this equation to forecast allows the components of FCF either to be forecast based on target ratios and a forecast sales growth, or actual planned dollar values, for example for capex, with others as fixed ratios. Either way sensitivity analysis with respect to FCF and firm value is relatively easy and clear cut. This modelling of FCF also points out directly that sales growth usually hurts FCF, since for most firms i and c are larger than M, that is, sales growth usually results in immediate capex and NWC expenditures at the expense of limited increases in after-tax EBITDA.* Some analysts do not like this formulation of FCF since it does not immediately highlight profitability. Instead it focuses on turnover ratios and profit margins. However, in Appendix A it is shown that we can easily reformulate the FCF equation in terms of profitability and reinvestment rates,

$$\text{FCF}_t = IC_0 \text{ ROI } (1 - b)\ (1 + b\,\text{ROI}) \tag{1.2}$$

where ROI is EBIT(1–T) divided by the average invested capital (IC), and reflects the return on all the capital invested in the firm; and the 'plowback' or retention rate (b) is the incremental change in invested capital as a percentage of EBIT(1 – T). Intuitively, $IC_0\text{ROI}(1 + b\text{ROI})$ is the forecast after, tax EBIT, based on the prior invested capital, return on investment and growth rate, and $-bIC_0\text{ROI}(1 + b\text{ROI})$ is the amount reinvested and, thus, subtracted to get FCF. The advantage of this approach is that instead of focussing on operating margins, we are focussing on incremental investment and profitability, which for finance people is usually more intuitive. Equation (1.2) for the firm as a whole is equivalent to the familiar equity share valuation formula, which uses the return on equity and the earnings retention

* The firm's break-even growth rate can be calculated by setting FCF = 0 and solving for g. This formula ignores the CCA tax advantages, but clearly points out that a firm's FCF grows faster with higher NWC and capex turnovers (low i and c) and higher operating margins. The idea that there is a sales growth rate that the firm can grow at without needing external funds was popularized by Higgins, R.C. How Much Growth Can a Firm Afford, *Financial Management*, Fall, 1977. For most firms, $M < i$, c.

rate. The intuition in both the cases is the same: FCF increases with the profitability of the firm and the firm's reinvestment rate. The '*b* ROI' growth term is normally referred to as the firm's sustainable growth rate, since it is the long run growth rate that flows from the firm's profitability and reinvestment rates.

Equation (1.2) is also useful, since whether or not this additional growth is valuable depends on whether the additional invested capital can be invested in the firm at a rate higher than the firm's Weighted Average Cost of Capital (WACC). Although, all of corporate finance uses this same critical concept, by focussing on profitability rates it is explicit in this formulation. In contrast, in the previous sales-oriented model, the idea of an investment hurdle rate is implicit. It is buried in the operating margin and turnover rates, rather than being explicit. For example, suppose the free cash flows in Eq. (1.2) go on forever and that the firm's ROI and plowback rates are some long run average value. These are, of course, unrealistic assumptions, but they generate some interesting insights, since the value of the firm becomes,

$$V = \frac{IC_0\text{ROI}}{K} + \frac{bIC_0}{k-g}\,\frac{\text{ROI}-K}{k} \tag{1.3}$$

where the growth rate in the firm's FCF is the sustainable growth rate. This is a minor variant of the famous Miller and Modigliani* 'investment opportunities' equation that is the basis of most valuation models. The first part of the equation is just the return from the current level of invested capital discounted in perpetuity. This is frequently called the **present value** of existing operations since it just reflects the value of current operating income stretched into perpetuity. The second part reflects the present value of the reinvested income (bIC_0ROI) for each subsequent period, since the income is valued at the sustainable growth rate, g and discounted back at the weighted average cost of capital (k). This present value of future investments is then multiplied by the ROI minus the WACC, which represents the ability to earn more than the firm's overall cost of capital. The second part is, therefore, commonly referred to as the present value of future growth opportunities.

Breaking the value of the firm into these two parts, existing and future growth opportunities allows for a simple two by two description of corporate values as in Figure 1.2. Similar to the famous Boston Consulting Group Growth share matrix, a firm with very high value from existing and future opportunities is a 'star,' possibly Microsoft, while a firm with low current and low future opportunities value is a 'dog'. In between, are the two interesting cases, a firm with low current value, but high future opportunities would be a 'turn around' in the BCG matrix, but in finance we think of these as growth

* See M. Miller and F. Modigliani , Dividend Policy Growth and the Valuation of Shares, *Journal of Business*, October, 1961.

stocks, like Yahoo. Finally, the high existing but low future opportunities would be the standard 'cash cow', like tobacco companies. The above stereotyping of corporate value flows from the basic valuation equation and adds some character to the prior discussion about the forecasting future (FCF). However, difficult as it is to project FCF, this cannot be done in isolation; it has to flow from an understanding of the business and its prospects. Although, professional valuators may carefully assess the future FCF, such an exercise requires a large amount of effort and skill. In this respect, the growth share matrix by reducing the complexities of valuation to four simple quadrants may be a more realistic way in which investors actually view different stocks as 'stories'. The growth share matrix also completes the discussion started with Table 1.3.

	PV future opportunities		
PV existing opportunities		High	Low
	High		
	Low		

Figure 1.2 A finance growth share matrix.

From Table 1.3 we saw that the perpetuity value of the current dividend for BC Gas was a large part of its share price. From Figure 1.2, we can see that BC Gas is essentially a cash cow; regulators should award BC Gas its cost of capital implying that there are very limited growth opportunities. In practice, incentive regulation and some non-regulated business add some limited growth opportunities. From Table 1.3, as the proportion of valuing flowing from growth opportunities increases, the investors turn more towards genuine stars and growth stocks, while placing less and less reliance on the value of current opportunities.

VALUE DRIVERS: ANOTHER PERSPECTIVE*

Value is created when the Net Present Value (NPV) of a strategy is positive at the time of implementation.

Value created by strategy
= PV of incremental cash flows due to new investment
– PV of investment in fixed assets and Working capital
+ PV of residual value

From our knowledge of capital budgeting, we know that the NPV is a function of valuation parameters or *value drivers* such as sales growth rate, operating profit margin, tax rate, fixed capital investment, working capital investment, cost of capital and the duration of the project. These value drivers are affected by operating decisions such as product mix, promotion, advertising, distribution, customer service, investment in inventory, capacity expansion, etc. The value is enhanced if the same returns are achieved for lower level of investment or higher returns for the same level of investment.

The value of the strategy can be enhanced by

1. acceleration of cash flows (leads to higher NPV),
2. increase in level of cash flows,
3. a reduction in risk associated with cash flows (volatility) and, hence, indirectly, the firm's cost of capital, and
4. increasing the residual value of the business.

The total shareholder value is the sum of NPV of all projects undertaken by the firm. This special characteristic of NPV (i.e. additivity) provides us some useful insights into the following value creation:

- Whenever a loss-making project is terminated, the value of the firm goes up.
- Whenever a firm accepts a positive NPV project, the value of the firm goes up.
- Whenever a firm acquires another firm for a price greater than the PV of the expected cash flows, the value of the firm drops.

Market-based assets such as customer and channel partner relationships also contribute to the four drivers of value. For instance, faster response to marketing efforts and earlier brand trials accelerate cash flows while brand extensions and development of new users enhance cash flows. The important point is that shareholder value is driven by both *tangible* and *intangible* assets.

* This section on value drivers has been inserted by editors to preserve the overall theme of the book.

SUSTAINABLE GROWTH

We define sustainable growth for those companies which have target payout ratio and capital structure as the annual percentage increase in sales that is consistent with the firm's established financial policies. Let

p = the profit margin on existing and new sales
d = the target payout ratio
$(1 - d)$ = retention ratio
L = target debt-equity ratio
S = Sales at the beginning of the year
ds = increase in sales during the year

The increase in sales is preceded by an increase in asset base. The increase in asset base can be financed by retained earnings, new debt or new equity. If we assume that the firm is unable or unwilling to sell new equity, the option reduces to retained earnings or new debt. Since the firm has a target debt-equity ratio to maintain, the increase in debt has to be proportional to the increase in retained earnings. So under stable conditions, increase in sales is determined by retained earnings.

Increase in sales = Addition to retained earnings + Increase in debt

$$\text{Sustainable growth } g' = \frac{\text{Change in equity during the period}}{\text{Beginning equity}}$$

$$= \text{(Retention rate * Earnings)/Beginning equity}$$
$$= \text{Retention rate * (Earnings/Beginning equity)}$$
$$= \text{Retention rate * ROE}$$

But

$$\text{ROE} = \frac{\text{PAT}}{\text{Equity}}$$

$$= \frac{\text{PAT}}{\text{Sales}} * \frac{\text{Sales}}{\text{Assets}} * \frac{\text{Assets}}{\text{Equity}}$$

i.e.,

$$g' = \text{Retention rate} * \frac{\text{PAT}}{\text{Sales}} * \frac{\text{Sales}}{\text{Assets}} * \frac{\text{Assets}}{\text{Equity}} \tag{1.4}$$

Sustainable growth is a function of return on assets, retained earnings and financial leverage.

$$g' = \text{retention rate} * \text{ROE}$$

$$g' = (1-d)\left[\text{ROA} + \frac{D}{E}\{\text{ROA} - i(1-T)\}\right] \tag{1.5}$$

where

i = interest rate on debt

T = tax rate

D/E = debt-equity ratio

ROA = EBIT $(1 - T)$/Book value of total capital

Sustainable growth can be increased by injecting debt which will increase the actual return on equity as long as ROA is greater than the after-tax cost of debt by an amount

$$\frac{D}{E}[\text{ROA} - i(1 - T)]$$

But the systematic risk of the stock and, hence, expected return increase with leverage.

According to the Capital Asset Pricing Model (CAPM),

$$\text{Expected return} = R_f + \beta_L[E(R_M) - R_f] \tag{1.6}$$

The relationship between levered and unlevered beta is of the form

$$\beta_L = \beta_U\left[1 + (1 - T)\frac{D}{E}\right] \tag{1.7}$$

(i.e. leverage increases beta)

where

β_U = unlevered beta of the stock (equity beta when the company has no debt)

β_L = levered beta of the stock (equity beta when the company has debt)

Given the beta at the current level of debt β_L, the unlevered beta of the stock can be calculated as

$$\beta_U = \left[\frac{\beta_L}{1 + (1 - T)D/E}\right] \tag{1.8}$$

The new beta, after increasing leverage, can be estimated using Eq. (1.7). The new beta can be plugged in the CAPM to arrive at the new expected return.

After quantifying the change in required return (cost of equity) due to increase in beta and actual return due to injecting debt, the percentage change in value can be calculated as

$$\text{Percentage change in value} = \left[\frac{\text{PV of increased return}}{\text{PV of existing return}} - 1\right] * 100$$

If we assume that the stream of returns is a growing perpetuity, PV of returns reduces to [Return/$k - g$], where k = cost of equity, g = sustainable growth in equity.

It should be noted that the increase in actual return should be more than the increase in expected return (cost of equity) for the value to increase. We will apply our new found knowledge to two situations and figure out what creates value and why*. Consider two companies. The first company has an investment opportunity with 25% ROE in amounts sufficient to produce 10% sustainable growth rate in sales for 10 years. The second company has an investment opportunity with 10% ROE in amounts sufficient to produce 10% sustainable growth rate in sales for 10 years. Both the companies have 20% cost of equity. The market value of the two hypothetical companies is shown in Tables 1.5 and 1.6.

Table 1.5 Market Price of Company A

Beginning of year	PV of investment $	ROE	PAT	RR†	Retained earnings	Div.	PV@20%
1	1000	25%	250	40%	100	150	125
2	1100		275		110	165	114.6
3	1210		302.5		121	181.5	105
4	1331.0		332.8		133.1	199.7	96.3
5	1464.1		363		146.4	219.6	88.3
6	1610.5		402.6		161.1	241.5	80.9
7	1771.6		442.9		177.2	265.7	74.2
8	1948.7		487.2		194.9	292.3	68.0
9	2143.6		535.90		214.4	321.3	62.3
10	2357.9		589.5		235.8	353.7	57.1
11	2593.7					2593.7	418.8
						Total =	$ 1290.5

† RR = retention rate

Table 1.6 Market Price of Company B

Beginning of year	PV of investment $	ROE	PAT	RR†	Retained earnings	Div.	PV@20%
1	1000	10%	100	100%	100	0	0
2	1100		110		110	0	0
3	1210		121		121	0	0
4	1331.0		133.1		133.1	0	0
5	1464.1		146.4		146.4	0	0
6	1610.5		161.1		161.1	0	0
7	1771.6		177.2		177.2	0	0
8	1948.7		194.9		194.9	0	0
9	2143.6		214.4		214.4	0	0
10	2357.9		235.8		235.8	0	0
11	2593.7					2593.7†	418.8

† Market price at the end = Book value

* William Jr., Fruhan, How fast should your company grow, *Harvard Business Review*, Jan-Feb, 1984.

At the end of 10 years, the stock is expected to sell at the book value of \$ 2593.70. In other words, ROE = cost of equity.

The second company retains all the profits it generates (i.e. retention rate is 100%) to produce a growth of 10% p.a. The theoretical market price for the second company is shown in Table 1.6. The PV of cash returned to stockholders \$ 1290.5 is \$ 290.5 more than the initial investment of \$ 1000 for shareholders in company A. So the *M/B* ratio of company A is greater than 1. The PV of cash returned to stockholders \$ 418.9 is lower than the initial investment of \$ 1000 for shareholders in company B. So the *M/B* ratio of company B is less than 1. The moral of the story is that how fast a company *can* grow and how fast a company *should* grow are two different things. Growth is desirable if expected ROE is greater than the cost of equity and if the spread can be maintained. If not, growth will destroy value. The value creation model shown in Figure 1.3 depicts the concept.

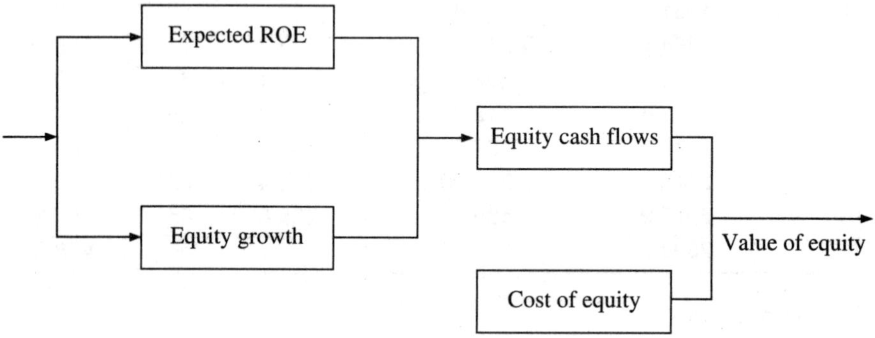

Figure 1.3 Value creation model.

From Tables 1.5 and 1.6, we note the following:

- Market price/Book value = 1290.5/1000 = 1.29 for company A
- Market price/Book value = 418.8/1000 = 0.42 for company B

The value creation model presented earlier has three components: (i) profitability, the spread between cost of equity and return on equity, (ii) the advantage horizon during which the firm generates abnormal returns, and (iii) reinvestment.

In any industry group, more profitable firms—those able to generate higher earnings per rupee of earnings—should have higher *M/B* ratios. Conversely, firms that are unable to generate positive abnormal returns should sell for lower *M/B* ratios.

$$\text{ROE} > K_e, \quad M/B > 1$$

$$\text{ROE} < K_e, \quad M/B < 1$$

$$\text{ROE} = K_e, \quad M/B = 1$$

The period for which a firm can maintain a positive (ROE – K_e) spread is called **advantage horizon**. The greater the abnormal return, the longer the advantage horizon, the sooner the abnormal returns, the higher the *M*/*B* ratio*.

The market value of equity can be obtained by discounting equity cash flows at an appropriate discount rate.

$$M = \left[\frac{\text{ECF}}{1+k} + \frac{\text{ECF}}{(1+k)^2} + \cdots\right] \tag{1.9}$$

If we assume that cash flows and discount rate are constant, the series reduces to a perpetuity.

$$M = \frac{\text{ECF}}{k}$$

Further, if we assume that ECF = Net income, i.e. retention is zero, then

$$M = \frac{\text{Net income}}{k}$$

But, Net income = ROE * Book value of equity. Hence,

$$M = \frac{\text{ROE} * B}{k}$$

or

$$\frac{M}{B} = \frac{\text{ROE}}{k}$$

Thus, market-to-book ratio is a function of ROE and cost of equity. If all the earnings are returned to shareholders and earnings are constant, then

$$M = \frac{\text{ROE} * B}{1+k} + \frac{\text{ROE} * B}{(1+k)^2} + \cdots \tag{1.10}$$

Divide both the sides by *B*. Then we obtain

$$\frac{M}{B} = \frac{\text{ROE}}{1+k} + \frac{\text{ROE}}{(1+k)^2} + \cdots \tag{1.11}$$

Add and subtract *k* from each of the terms

$$\frac{M}{B} = \frac{(\text{ROE} + k) - k}{1+k} + \frac{(\text{ROE} + k) - k}{(1+k)^2} + \cdots \tag{1.12}$$

* William, Fruhan Jr., Financial strategy: Studies in the creation , *Transfer and Destruction of Shareholder Value*, Irwin, Homewood, IL, 1979.
Esty, Benjamin C., Note on Value Drivers, *HBS Case Study No. 9-297-082*, April 7, 1997.

The first term (ROE – k) is the abnormal earnings and the second term, k, is the normal earning.

It can be proved that the present value of this series is of the form:

$$PV = 1 + (\text{ROE} - k)\left(\frac{1}{k}\right) - \left\{\frac{1}{k(1+k)^n}\right\} \tag{1.13}$$

This model assumes that retention is zero. Allowing for different rates would yield a more realistic model.

$$M = \frac{D_1}{k - g} = \frac{(\text{Net income} * \text{Payout})}{k - g}$$

But

Payout = (1 – Retention) = 1 – r

g = Sustainable growth rate = ROE * r

Net income = ROE * B

$$M = \frac{\text{ROE} * B * (1 - r)}{k - (r * \text{ROE})}$$

$$\frac{M}{B} = \frac{\text{ROE} * (1 - r)}{k - (r * \text{ROE})} \tag{1.14}$$

If a firm pays out all its earnings as dividends, r is zero. Those firms that generate positive abnormal returns can increase the value by retaining a larger fraction of earnings and invest in business.

Equations (1.12) and (1.14) can be combined as of the form

$$\frac{M}{B} = \frac{1 + (\text{ROE} * r)}{1 + k} + \frac{\text{ROE}(1 - r)}{k - r * \text{ROE}}\left[1 - \frac{(1 + r * \text{ROE})}{(1 + k)^n}\right]$$

Thus, M/B is a function of ROE, the retention rate and the advantage horizon, n.

Competitive Advantage Period (CAP) is defined as the time period for which the company earns returns in excess of the cost of capital*. Over time competitive pressures drive returns to the cost of capital. Although a company's competitive advantage period is affected by a multitude of internal and external factors, only a few key factors such as current return on capital,

---

* Michael Mauboussin, and Paul Johnson, Competitive advantage period (CAP): The neglected value driver, *CS First Boston Research*, January, 1997.

rate of industry change and barriers to entry have a significant bearing. Companies with high *P/E* multiples tend to have a long competitive advantage period and those with low *P/E* multiples tend to have low CAP. The CAP of some companies in the Food Industry is given here in tabular form:

(in years)

Company	1982	1989
Campbell Soup	4	20
CPC International	10	15
H.J.Heinz	5	13
Hershey Foods	6	20
Kellogg	18	19
Average	8.6	17.4

HOW DO THESE MODELS HELP CREATE SHAREHOLDER VALUE?

The discussion in the previous section is a brief overview of how professional valuations are done to determine the firm value, and how this links with corporate stereotyping. By breaking out the standard FCF definition into its components, we can then understand the valuation drivers underlying a shareholder value creation. Since the 'creating shareholder value' concept moved out of academia into the business world, a small (?) cottage industry has developed to help companies implement management procedures aimed at CSV. Knowing how the market values companies is only the first step to CSV, the critical second step is implementing internal control procedures to encourage managers actually create value. This is what is commonly referred to as changing the corporate culture by creating 'value managers'. However, creating value managers requires that managerial performance be judged by the correct criteria, and what the previous sections have shown is that not only are there a variety of ways for defining FCF, but there are also a variety of performance tools that result.

In principle, choosing the wrong tool or implementing only part of the FCF formula can produce results that destroy shareholder value, rather than increase it. This has lead to considerable controversy as to how to implement shareholder value creation. The 'grand-daddy' of shareholder value creation is EVA* or economic value added. EVA makes similar types of adjustments to net income as mentioned earlier, but then explicitly subtracts a full capital charge (cost of capital times book value of assets) from operating income to

* This is a trademark of Stern-Stewart.

estimate EVA. If EVA is implemented on a pro forma basis, then it is identical to the valuation Eq. (1.4), as such it is fully consistent with the traditional textbook implementation of financial valuation models. Competitor measures include total business return from Boston Consulting Group, Cash flow ROI from Holt Value Associates and Shareholder Value Added (SVA) from the LEK/Alcar group (Myers 1997). Differentiating between the effectiveness of these different measures and traditional net income or residual income measures has proven extremely difficult.

The standard approach has been to examine the relationship between the chosen measure, such as EVA, and subsequent stock market performance. However, both Kramer and Pushner (1997) and Chen and Dodd (1998) find that the relationship is weak at best and very similar across different measures. To a large extent this should not be a surprise as seen from Table 1.3 and Figure 1.1, for many firms the stock market value is very dependent on future prospects. What this means is that the current annual statements, even extensively restated to get free cash flow or EVA, are not as important as the growth opportunities built into the stock price, and it is variation in these expectations that account for most of the subsequent stock market performance. However, even if most of these measures are very highly correlated and only loosely related to subsequent stock market performance, it does not mean to say that the choice between them is arbitrary. What is most important is not the measure of CSV, but the cultural change created by switching to a value management culture. Here the critical influence is the management compensation plan and ensuring that compensation is tied to value creation, not destruction. At its most basic, CSV has the following message: the market values firms that

- increase the productive use of their assets by increasing turnover ratios,
- increase profit margins, and as a result
- increase profitability.

Increasing sales growth rates create shareholder value

- as long as the reinvestment of invested capital is expected to earn returns that exceed the firm's cost of capital, and
- conversely firms without such opportunities *destroy* shareholder value by reinvesting and should instead return the money to shareholders through dividend increases or share buybacks.

These statements are largely motherhood statements in finance, but it is remarkable how often they are not reflected in managerial policies within the firm and the corporate culture, and as a result do not help create value.*

* Appendix B summarizes some of the implications for CSV.

CONCLUDING REMARKS

Indeed, half the companies that have adopted a VBM metric have met with mediocre success. Many have formally abandoned. This is not to say the metrics have no use. Companies such as Siemens, Dow Chemical, Lloyds have created enormous value for shareholders by following VBM principles*. One reason why VBM efforts fail is cultural resistance in organizations. VBM efforts require great deal of time, patience, effort and money to derive tangible results. Making some accounting changes alone will not help†. Quite often companies should be willing to make major operational and strategic changes. The steps involved in implementing a VBM programme are as follows‡:

1. Conduct a strategic audit of existing strategy.
2. Calculate current value using DCF methods as well as calculate the cost of capital for each unit/business.
3. Assess strategic landscape by defining factors for and barriers to success.
4. Build framework foundation by determining position and goals as well as evaluating mission and goals.
5. Formulate and select value maximizing strategies.
6. Implement plans.
7. Embrace change.

APPENDIX A: RECONCILING THE METRICS

Definitions:

Invested capital (IC): Shareholder's equity plus all interest-bearing debt, net of surplus 'cash'.

Net working capital: Current assets minus current liabilities, plus all interest-bearing debt, minus surplus cash.

ROI: Earnings before interest and tax, after tax at the firm's marginal rate, divided by invested capital or EBIT $(1 - T)/IC$.

Incremental capex: Total capex minus depreciation and amortization (DA), new invested capital: incremental capex plus incremental NWC.

Plowback rate (*b*)**:** New invested capital divided by EBIT $(1 - T)$.

---

* Philippe, Haspeslagh, Tomo Noda, and Fares Boulos, Managing for value: It's not just about the numbers, *Harvard Business Review*, July-August, 2001.

† See the chapter on EVA for a description of accounting changes made to arrive at economic value added.

‡ A good book on the topic is Norton, George III, *Valuation: Maximizing Corporate Value*, John Wiley, New York, 2003.

Then,

$$\text{FCF} = \text{Net Income} + \text{Interest } (1 - T) + DA - \frac{\text{Increased NWC}}{\text{Capex}}$$

Adding back the after-tax interest (1 – T), to net income gives EBIT(1 – T), and then subtracting depreciation and amortization from increased NWC/ Capex gives new invested capital. If new invested capital is then defined as the 'plowback' or retention rate of EBIT(1 – T), and ROI defined as EBIT (1 – T) divided by the average invested capital, the FCF at time t is then,

$$\text{FCF}_t = IC_0\text{ROI}(1 - b)$$

Further, if we back up one period, the invested capital at t is just the invested capital at t – 1, plus the incremental FCF from t – 1 that has been reinvested, that is,

$$\text{FCF}_t = IC_0\text{ROI } (1 - b)\ (1 + b\text{ROI})$$

The key determinants of future FCF are the ROI, and the plowback (retention) rate, which together determine the sustainable growth rate.

APPENDIX B: KEY PERFORMANCE TOOLS—SALES-ORIENTED MODEL

- Sales growth rate
- Operating margins
- Incremental investment rates
- NWC
- Capex

Balachandran, Nagarajan and Rappaport (1986) introduced the concept of the 'threshold' operating margin on new sales consistent with CSV. Assuming that new sales of one dollar causes incremental investment in both NWC and capex of f and generate new after-tax operating profits of M, then if the sales are in perpetuity and the firm discounts the stream of cash at k, the incremental return is M/f, and the threshold margin fk. For example, suppose incremental investment is 50% of sales, and the operating margin is 10%, then an additional $ 1 mm in sales requires $ 0.50 mm in incremental invested capital and generates $ 0.1 mm in after-tax EBIT. Further, suppose the firm's cost of capital (discount rate) is 15%, should the firm expand sales?

Since the incremental return is 20% (0.10/.5) and exceeds the 15% cost of capital, the sales expansion is a good idea. Alternatively, since the 10% operating margin exceeds the 7.5% (0.10 * 0.15) threshold margin, using the operating margin approach we can also see that the sales expansion is a good idea. Creating value then involves increasing sales, increasing operating margin, reducing investment intensity and/or reducing the cost of capital.

APPENDIX C: KEY PERFORMANCE TOOLS—ROI-ORIENTED MODEL

- ROI
- Reinvestment rates
- FCF growth rate
- Sustainable growth *b*ROI

The 'standard' finance model emphasizing investment rates and future profitability. Creating shareholder value then involves increasing ROI in existing investments, and increasing reinvestment rates, when expected ROI exceeds the firm's cost of capital. This approach has the advantage of the most direct link between ROI and the cost of capital, but falls into the standard ROI trap that the firm should increase value by increasing ROI. The problem is that the ROI, like all return measures, can be maximized by simply cutting investment and only investing in very profitably projects that equal or exceed the current ROI. As a result, high ROI firms frequently under invest, since accepting lower ROI projects causes their ROI to fall and are rejected, even though the project's ROI exceeds the firm's cost of capital.

The 'standard' finance model is not recommended for small, junior, companies with high R&D levels, limited short-term profit potential and large sales potential.* The ROI metric is best applied to mature corporations, where increased efficiency and better asset utilization are the keys to generating higher FCF. In contrast, the sales model is best suited to smaller innovative companies.

EXERCISES

1. Tata Steel, one of the largest steel companies in the world, is a 92 year-old steel company that manufactures steel and steel-related products. It has an installed capacity of 2.7 m tones of saleable steel at its plant in Jamshedpur, India. It manufactures a wide range of products that include bars and rods, sheets, hot rolled strips, hot rolled coils, structurals and semi-finished products. Tata Steel's corporate strategy involves focus on the company's core business of steel making and disinvestments from businesses such as cement that until 1997–98 contributed about 5% of turnover. Since 1980, Tata Steel has adopted various expansion and modernization programmes to enhance capacity as well as efficiency. The analyst forecast of free cash flow for Tata Steel is presented in Exhibit 1. Estimate the value of Tata Steel's shares for as of 1996 and for all the forecast years. Estimate the impact of

* Technically, such firms 'look' like call options, and increasingly people are trying to apply real option pricing theory to value them.

EXHIBIT 1

Forecast of Free Cash flow for Tata Steel (INR million)

	1996	1997	1998	1999	2000	2001	2002	2003	2004	2005	2006	2007	2008	2009	2010
EBIT	8452.7	10080.8	11312.5	18339.1	29871.1	38.437.2	43137.3	44042.4	44884.9	45651	46325.4	46889.8	47324.6	47607.7	47714.1
Less: Tax	0	1300.4	1459.3	2365.7	3853.4	4958.4	5564.7	5681.5	5790.1	5889	5976	6048.8	6104.9	6141.4	6155.1
NOPAT															
Depreciation	2976.1	3300	3500	4000	5000	6000	6000	6000	6000	6000	6000	6000	6000	6000	6000
Capex	–8000	–8000	–13000	–11500	–10000	–6000	–6000	–6000	–6000	–6000	–6000	–6000	–6000	–6000	–6000
Inc. W.C	–4957.2	–1647.8	–1415.5	–3549.3	–4601.2	–3461.9	–2272.4	–1399.9	–1471.7	–1547.2	–1626.8	–1710.4	–1798.6	–1891.3	–1989
FCFF															
Sales growth		12.40%	10.4	23.7	28	14.3	8.2	4.7	4.7	4.7	4.7	4.7	4.8	4.8	4.8
EBIT margin		16.60%	16.9	22.1	28.1	31.7	32.9	32.1	31.2	30.3	29.4	28.4	27.4	26.3	25.1
Net margin		10.30%	10.5	16.7	22.6	25.2	26.4	25.8	25.2	24.5	23.7	23	22.1	21.3	20.3
WACC	18.90%	18.90%	18.90%	18.90%	18.90%	18.90%	18.90%	18.90%	18.90%	18.90%	18.90%	18.90%	18.90%	18.90%	18.90%
Debt	52393														
No. of shares (m)	400														

Source: C S First Boston

improvement in NOPAT margin, reduction in capital expenditure, working capital, and WACC on Tata Steel's share price. Assume a terminal growth rate of 9% and a discount rate of 16%.

2. Stock prices reflect a *competitive advantage period* during which the company earns returns in excess of cost of capital.

$$V = \text{value of the firm} = \frac{\text{NOPAT}}{\text{WACC}} + \frac{\mu(\text{ROIC} - \text{WACC}) * \text{CAP}}{\text{WACC} * (1 + \text{WACC})}$$

where

μ = annualized new investment in working capital and fixed assets net of depreciation (estimated by dividing the present value of projected net capital additions by CAP).

$$\text{ROIC} = \text{Return on invested capital} = \frac{\text{NOPAT}}{\text{Invested capital}}$$

$$\begin{aligned}\text{Invested capital} &= \text{Cash} + \text{Inventory} + \text{Property, plant and equipment}\\ &\quad + \text{Accounts receivable} - \text{Accounts payable}\end{aligned}$$

Gather some data and estimate the competitive advantage period implied by stock prices of companies of your interest.

3. Analysts use a number of metrics for stock picking. Some of the popular ones are *EV*/*IC*, *P*/*B* and *P*/*E* multiples.

$$\frac{EV}{IC} = \frac{(\text{ROIC} - G)}{(\text{WACC} - G)}$$

where

EV = enterprise value or value of the company

IC = invested capital

G = growth rate in invested capital, NOPAT and FCFF

$$\frac{P}{B} = \frac{\text{ROE} - G}{K_e - G}$$

$$\frac{P}{E} = \frac{(1 - r)}{K_e - (\text{ROE} * r)}$$

where

r = retention ratio

K_e = cost of equity

Consider two all equity financed companies with the following characteristics:

	Company X	Company Y
Book value of equity		
Investment ($, m)	1000	1000
Net income ($, m)	250	100
ROE (%)	25	10
K_e (%)	14	14
No. of shares (in millions)	1000	1000

Calculate the intrinsic value of shares for various sustainable growth rates like 0%, 5%, and 8%. What is the optimal sustainable growth rate (or alternatively, payout ratio) for the two companies? Also calculate *P/E* and *P/B* ratio. See if these metrics are correlated with value creation.

4. One of the measures of value is the total shareholder return (dividend yield + capital gains yield). A company is approving a five-year plan under which the stock price is expected to increase from $ 45 to $ 87 per share during the five-year period. The dividend yield on the company's stock is 2.5%. The cost of equity for the company is 16%. Is the company creating value?

5. A company has three business units. The relevant data for these divisions are presented as follows:

	ROE	K_e (%)	Growth(%)	Book equity ($, m)
A	25	19	8	25
B	20	20	12	5.5
C	10	17	4	20.0

Estimate the economic value of the business units and EV/Book Value ratios for all the units.

6. Return on equity, ROE can be calculated as

$$\text{ROI} + [\text{ROI} - (1 - T)r]\,\frac{D}{E}$$

where

ROI = Return on investment = NOPAT/Assets

r = cost of debt

T = tax rate

D/E = debt-equity ratio

The following data is available for two divisions. Calculate ROE.

	A	B
ROI(%)	14.8	15.1
r(%)	7	8
T(%)	40	40
D/*E*	100	67

7. A company neither creates nor destroys value when NOPAT equals capital charge. That is, NOPAT = WACC (assets). The break-even sales margin is the margin at which the economic profit is zero. The following data is available for two divisions of a company:

	A	B
Pre-tax sales margin	18	15
Sales/Assets	1.4	1.68
WACC (%)	11.5	15
Tax rate (%)	40	40

Calculate the break-even profit margin. Which of these divisions are profitable? Why?

[*Hint:* NOPAT = EBIT(1 – *T*). At the break-even profit margin level, EBIT(1 – *T*) = Assets * WACC. Divide both the sides by sales.]

REFERENCES

1. Biddle, G. and F. Lindahl, Stock Price Reactions to LIFO Adoptions: The Association between Excess Returns and LIFO Tax Saving, *Journal of Accounting Reserach,* **20**(2, Autumn): 551–588, 1982.
2. Davis, M., The Purchase vs Pooling Controversy: How the Stock Market Responds to Goodwill, *Journal of Applied Corporate Finance,* **9**(Spring): 50–59, 1996.
3. Hunt, P., Funds Position: Keystone in Financial Planning, *Harvard Business Review*, May-June, 1975.
4. Myers, R., Measure for Measure, *CFO Magazine*, November, 1997.
5. Kramer, J. and G. Pushner, An Empirical Analysis of Economic Value Added as a Proxy for Market Value Added, *Financial Practice and Education*, **7-1**, Summer, 1997. Chen S. and J. Dodd, Usefulness of Operating Income, Residual Income and EVA: A Value Relevance Perspective,' Paper presented at the 1998 *AAA Annual Meeting.*

6. Balachandran, B., N. Nagarajan and A. Rappaport, Threshold Margins for Creating Shareholder Value, *Financial Management*, **15**(1, Spring): 68–77, 1986.

SUGGESTED FURTHER READING

Esty, B., Service Corporation International, *Harvard Business School Case No.* 9-296-080, July, 1996.

Fruhan, William, Microsoft/Intuit, *Harvard Business School Case No.* 9-295-121, November, 2001.

PART II

REAL OPTIONS

CHAPTER

2

Real Options*

LEARNING OBJECTIVES

After reading this chapter, you should be able to:

- Highlight different types of financial options.
- Bring out an analogy between financial options and real options.
- Highlight the different types of real options.
- Introduce valuation of real options.

INTRODUCTION

Managers often overrule the NPV-based recommendations in capital budgeting on strategic grounds. Does it mean that the NPV approach is flawed? The standard Discounted Cash Flow (DCF) methodology assumes that managers make an investment decision and then see how the market evolves. In many situations managers can wait and then make a decision. The latter is an option to defer or time the investment decision. Pharmaceutical companies, for example, frequently enter into agreements with small biotechnology companies and universities for research and development. The traditional DCF methodology does not work well in the case of such projects because of prolonged development and uncertainty in cash flows. For gaining access to research, the pharmaceutical company makes an up-front payment and a series of progress payments. These contingent payments give the pharmaceutical company the right but not the obligation to make further investments. Such investments are best evaluated as options (Nichols 1994).

* This chapter is contributed by S.R. Vishwanath.

Consider a project that has a best outcome of $ 13 million and a worst outcome of $ 9 million. Each of these outcomes are equally likely to occur (probability is 0.5). The expected value of the project, the weighted average of outcomes, is $ 11 million. i.e. (13 * 0.5 + 9 * 0.5) = 11.

The discounted value at a discount rate of, say, 10% is 11/1.10 = $ 10 million.

If the initial investment is $ 9.5 million, then the NPV is $ 10 million – $ 9.5 million = $ 0.50 million.

Based on the NPV, most managers would go ahead with the project. But NPV does not deal with the management's ability to time the project. Suppose the management has the option to wait for one year at which time they can decide to invest. If the demand for the product turns out weak, the management can decide not to invest as it does not make sense to invest $ 9.5 million and receive $ 9 million a year later. However, if the product turns out to be successful, the project would yield $ 13 million for an investment of $ 9.5 million. The NPV in this case is $ 3.5 million. Since there is a 50–50 chance of a good outcome (NPV 3.5 million) and a bad outcome (do not invest; 0 NPV in year 1), the expected value is (0.5 * 3.5 + 0.5 * 0) $ 1.65 million. The present value at year 0 is $ 0.96 million. The moral is: *there is a value attached to the option to defer*. By not considering the option, the managers will miss out on a chance to add value by waiting. The NPV rolls up outcomes from alternate states of the world into one number, which fails to capture the manager's ability to avoid downside outcomes.

FINANCIAL OPTIONS

An option gives the holder the right, but not the obligation, to buy or sell a designated asset (e.g. stock, currency, commodity) at a predetermined price. There are two types of options. A **call** option gives the holder the right to buy the underlying asset by a certain date for a certain price. A **put** option gives the holder the right to sell the underlying asset by a certain date for a certain price. The contract price is known as **strike price** or exercise price; the date in the contract is known as **expiration date**. The *American* options can be exercised at any time up to maturity and the *European* options can be exercised only at maturity. The asset underlying the option contracts could be stocks, stock indices, foreign currency, debt instruments, commodities, etc. For stock options, the underlying asset is stock. Each contract is for a fixed number of units of the underlying asset. In the case of equity options it is 100 shares. The buyer of the option pays the seller a premium for enjoying the right (but not the obligation). The call options have value if the price of the underlying asset is more than the exercise price because the holder of the contract can exercise his option to purchase and sell the asset for a higher price in the market. If the price of the asset is less than the exercise price, the option expires worthless and the buyer of the option loses his premium. That is,

$$\text{Value of call option on the expiration date} = \text{Max } [S - X, 0].$$

Assume that on 6 January, 2003 you have purchased a call option to buy 100 shares of Hindustan Lever, a Unilever group company in India, at a strike price of INR 180. Each option has a premium of INR 5. The options expire on 30 January, 2003. At the time of entering into the contract, the buyer has to pay a premium of INR 5 * 100 for each contract. The value of the call option for various exercise prices is given in a tabular form.

(in INR)

Exercise price	Spot price	Premium	Value of call option
180	170	5	–5
180	175	5	–5
180	180	5	–5
180	185	5	0
180	190	5	5
180	195	5	10

The option is worthless as long as the strike price exceeds the exercise price by an amount equal to the premium paid. The pay-off can be plotted as shown in Figure 2.1.

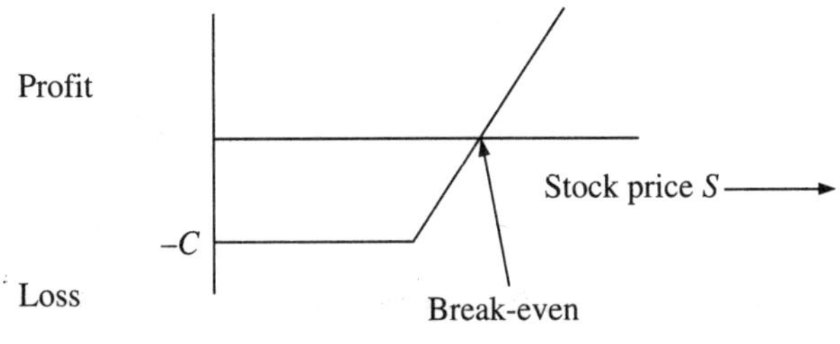

Figure 2.1 Pay-off to a long call option position.

The maximum that an option holder loses is the premium paid whereas the upside potential is unlimited. The value of the option increases one-to one for any increase in price above the break-even price. Since each option is for 100 shares, the strike price, exercise price and premium have to be multiplied by 100 to arrive at the aggregate pay-off. If the holder of the option decides to exercise the option, he should pay Rs 180 * 100 (i.e. exercise price * 100 shares). Those options worth exercising are called *in-the-money* and those that are not, are considered as *out-of-the-money*.

The pay-off from the perspective of a seller is given in Figure 2.2.

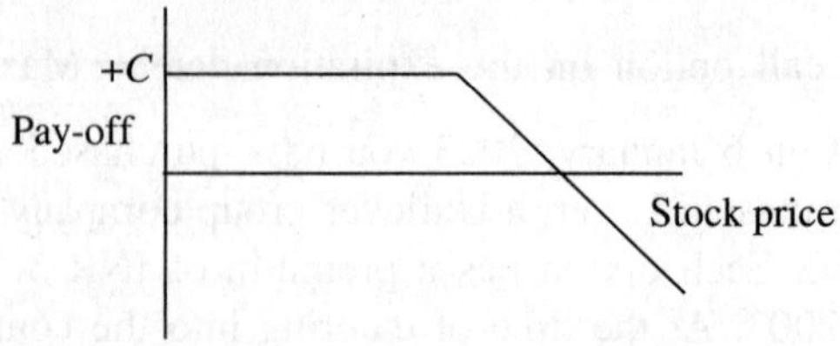

Figure 2.2 Pay-off from the perspective of a seller.

Note that the seller (writer) of the call option gets the premium as long as the strike price is lower than the exercise price. While the upside is fixed, the downside is unlimited. Also note that the pay-offs are mirror images—what the buyer gains, the seller loses and vice versa. That is, they sum to zero.

A put option, as opposed to a call option, gives the holder an option to sell a fixed amount of the underlying asset at a fixed price. As in the case of a call option, the buyer of the put option pays a premium to the seller. A put option has value if the stock price is less than the exercise price. That is, the holder can purchase in the open market at a lower price and deliver it to the seller at the (higher) exercise price.

The value of put option on the expiration date = P = max $(0, X - S)$

The pay-off to a *long* put option position is given in Figure 2.3.

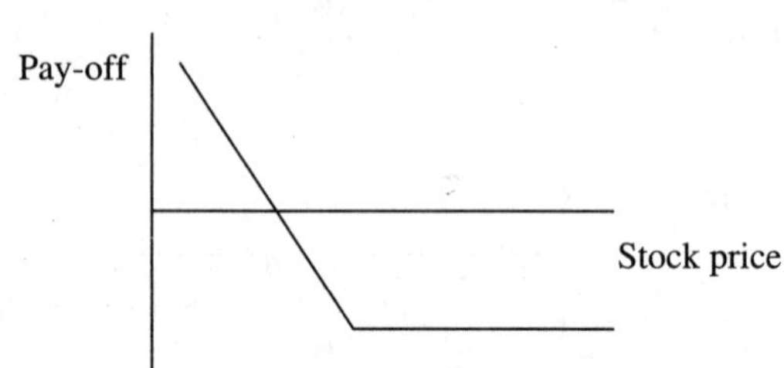

Figure 2.3 Pay-off to a long put option position.

Note that the buyer of the put option makes money if the ending spot price of the underlying asset is lower than the exercise price. Likewise, the pay-off to the writer of a put option is given in Figure 2.4.

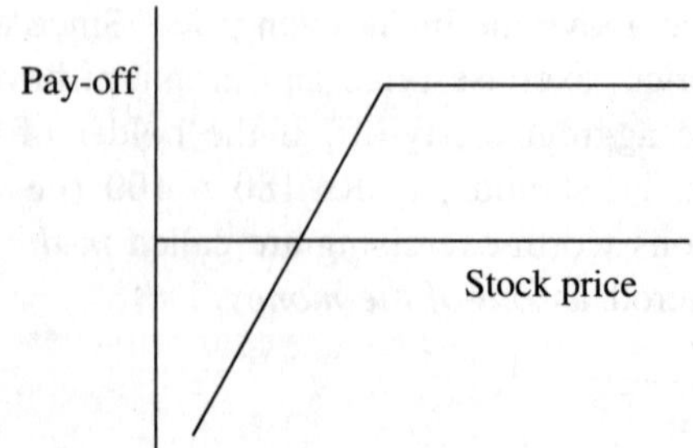

Figure 2.4 Pay-off to the writer of a put option.

Like call options, the pay-off for the put option holder and writer sums to zero. An investor may combine these four positions to create a number of options strategies. For example, one may buy the underlying asset and sell a call option on the same asset. This strategy is known as *covered call write.* A hypothetical option value table for gold is given here. Assume that the Spot price = $ 596 per oz. The options are traded at the following prices (per oz). Each contract is for 100 troy oz.

Option Price

Exercise Price	Call	Put
575	14.5	22.5
605	8.0	—

The $ 575 call is 'in the money' as it allows an investor to buy $ 596 of gold for only $ 575. The profit from exercising the call is $ 21 (ignoring premium). The $ 605 call is 'out of the money' for obvious reasons. Yet, it has value. The call option premium is $ 8 as given in the table. Why? As gold prices are volatile, the spot price may exceed the exercise price at a future date before expiration. Financial options have a few other properties. As mentioned earlier there are two types of options—American and European. The American-type options can be exercised before expiration whereas the European-type options can be exercised only upon maturity. Since the American options have all rights that the European options have and the right to exercise early, an American option is at least as valuable as the European option*. The option values cannot be negative. They can at worst be zero since options provide the right but not the obligation to exercise.

Six variables affect option values. They are: asset price, exercise price, maturity, volatility, risk-free rate of interest and dividends (in the case of stocks). The impact of an increase in any of these variables on the European-type call and put option values is given in Table 2.1.

Table 2.1 The Impact of Changes in the Values of Underlying Variable on Option Values

Variable	Call	Put
Asset price	↑	↓
Exercise price	↓	↑
Maturity	↑	?
Volatility	↑	↑
Interest rates	↑	↓
Dividends	↓	↑

* The American options are more valuable than the European options if the right to exercise early is valuable.

The value of the call option increases as the asset price increases because a higher current asset price makes it more likely that on the expiration date, the market price of the asset will be above the exercise price. Likewise, lower asset prices make the put option more valuable.

A higher exercise price makes a call option less valuable and a put option more valuable.

If the variability of asset prices is high, then the chances of large gains are also high. The holder of the option contract benefits from upside potential but has a limited downside (equal to the premium). So increases in volatility have a favourable impact on option prices.

Similarly, a longer time to maturity has a favourable impact on option prices because the probability of ending up in-the-money becomes larger. At the same time, the present value of the exercise price decreases. In the case of call options, the decrease in the present value of the exercise price augments the positive time effect of increaseu uncertainty and the value goes up. For a European put option, the net impact of these two effects is not known; the former increases the value of the option whereas the latter decreases.

An increase in the risk-free rate of interest lowers the present value of the exercise price paid on the expiration date. For a call option this means a lower payment (in the present value terms) for the asset if the option is exercised and the call option is, therefore, worth more. The converse is true of put options.

An increase in dividends reduces the future asset prices, which reduces the profit opportunity for the holder of a call option. Consequently, the value of a call option reduces with increases in dividends. The opposite is true for put options.

Assume that you have purchased a European call option and sold a European put option on the same asset (S) with the same exercise price X and expiration date. The investment required to establish this position is the difference between call and put values. That is, $C - P$.

The pay-off to this position is $S-X$. On the expiration date, if the spot price is less than the expiration price, the call option expires worthless and the put option will be exercised against the position. Consequently, the pay-off will be negative.

Consider another investment in which an investor borrows the present value of X to purchase the asset. The investment required is equal to

$$S - \frac{X}{(1+r)^T}$$

and the pay-off to this position on the expiration date, T, is $S-X$ since the investor owns the asset (S) and owes X.

As the pay-off to these two investment positions is the same, their initial investment must also be the same to prevent arbitrage opportunities.

$$C - P = S - \frac{X}{(1+r)^T}$$

This property is known as **put call parity**. Having discussed the types and properties of options, we move on to a more important question, viz. how are options priced? For example, how did the market price the call option on HLL stock mentioned earlier at INR 5? In the 1970s, Fischer Black and Myron Scholes derived an equilibrium model of option pricing. They proved that it is possible to construct a portfolio involving positions in the stock and the risk-free asset whose returns exactly replicate the return to the option. They also show how the composition of the portfolio must constantly change such that the replication is maintained. Consider an option on a stock. The pay-off from the option depends on the price of the underlying security.

Assume that a stock is currently trading at \$ 50. Further, assume that the stock can rise to \$ 55 or fall to \$ 45 after one period. That is, the stock can take on only two values*. A call option trading on this stock at an exercise price of \$ 50 must have a value of \$ 3.5714. Let us see why. If the stock finishes in the 'high' state (i.e. \$ 55), the option has a value of \$ 5. The option is worthless if the ending spot price is \$ 45 as it is cheaper to borrow in the open market. The option position can be replicated by purchasing 50 shares by borrowing \$ 2142.86 at a risk-free rate of 5%.

The current value of this position = Value of 50 shares of stock \$ 2500 (i.e.50 ∗ 50) – borrowed amount \$ 2142.86.
= \$ 357.14

Let us verify whether the portfolio has the same pay-off as the option. If the stock closes at \$ 55, the value of the stock position = \$ 50 ∗ 55 = \$ 2750 and the amount to be repaid = \$ 2142.86 ∗ 1.05 = \$ 2250. So the net position is \$ 500. If the stock closes at \$ 45, the stock value would be \$ 2250 and the amount to be repaid is also \$ 2250. So the net position is zero. Since the pay-off to this position is the same as that of the call option, their initial values should be the same. That is, the call option should sell for \$ 357.14. Let us generalize it now.

Let the stock price in the two States of the world be S^+ and S^- and the end of the period option values be C^+ and C^-, respectively. The ratio of the number of shares in the replicating portfolio to the number of shares underlying the option contract, called **hedge ratio**, h is given by

$$h = \frac{C^+ - C^-}{S^+ - S^-}$$

In the example, S^+ and S^- are \$ 55 and \$ 45, respectively. Likewise C^+ and C^- are Rs 5 and 0, respectively.

---

* This is based on Courtadon and Merrick (1983). Also see Mason and Merton (1985), Cox, Ross and Rubinstein (1979). Any standard text on options/derivatives would discuss the binomial model in great detail.

$$h = \frac{5-0}{55-45} = \frac{1}{2}$$

That is, 50 shares should be purchased when each option contract is for 100 shares. If *B* is the amount to be borrowed at *r*%, then

$$B = \frac{100}{1+r}[hS^- - C^-]$$

$$= \frac{100}{1.05}\left[\frac{1}{2}(45) - 0\right] = \$2142.86$$

Obviously, the binomial option-pricing model looks unrealistic because it considers only two States of the world. If the time period between the two stock price movements is a minute or a second, the characterization is not that unrealistic. The Black–Scholes model assumes a more general diffusion process.

The Black–Scholes option-pricing model uses five variables (for non-dividend paying stocks), viz. X, S, T, r and σ^2 to give a rupee value for the European call option where X = exercise price, S = stock price, T = time for expiration, r = risk-free rate of return and σ^2 = variance of returns.

According to the model, the value of the call option = $SN(d_1) - Ke^{-rt}\,\mathrm{N}\,(d_2)$ where

$$d_1 = \frac{\ln(S/K) + (r + \sigma^2/2)t}{\sigma\sqrt{t}}$$

$$d_2 = d_1 - \sigma\sqrt{t}$$

Ke^{-rt} is the PV of the exercise price in the continuous form; d_1 and d_2 are the calculated and cumulative normal distribution functions, $N(d_1)$ and $N(d_2)$ corresponding to the standardized normal variables are estimated. The Black–Scholes formula does not incorporate dividend payments. The modified version of the Black–Scholes incorporating continuous dividend payments is given as (see Merton 1973):

$$\text{Option value} = Pe^{-\ln(1+d)T}\,N(z) - Xe^{-\ln(1+r)T}\,N(z - \sigma\sqrt{t})$$

where

P = stock price
X = strike price
T = expiration term (years)
d = annualized dividend yield
σ = annual stock price volatility
r = risk-free interest rate

$$z = \frac{\ln(P/X) + (\ln(1+r) - \ln(1+d) + \sigma^2/2)T}{\sigma\sqrt{T}}$$

$N(\ )$ = Cumulative normal distribution function

The annualized yield on treasury security maturing on the option's expiry date is taken as the risk-free rate. The dividend yields are measured as the annualized yield over the past one, two or three years.

A call option should be exercised if the stock price exceeds the strike price at expiration. That is if $S > X$. For the sake of convenience, let us express it as a ratio. The option has value if $S/X > 1$. If S/X is less than 1, the option should not be exercised as it is out of money.

The variability (per unit of time) of returns is measured by variance. Multiplying the variance per unit of time by the amount of time to maturity gives the cumulative variance. The higher the cumulative variance, the more valuable is the option. The Black–Scholes value of a European call option as a % of value of underlying asset is available in a table form to make our life simple. A portion of the same is given in Table 2.2.

Table 2.2 The Black–Scholes Call Option Value (%)

Share price/PV of exercise price	Annual σ * Square root of time 0.25	0.5	0.75	1.0
0.5	0	3	10	19
0.6	0	5	14	24
0.7	1	8	18	28
0.8	3	12	22	32
0.9	6	16	26	35
1.0	10	20	29	38

Consider the following data:

Stock price = \$ 50
Annual volatility = 25 %
R = 5 %
Exercise price = \$ 60
T = 4 years
PV of exercise price = $60/(1.05)^4 = 49.36$
Share price/PV(X) = $50/49.36 = 1.01$
$\sigma(\sqrt{4})$ = $25\% * 2 = 50\%$

The cell at the intersection of row 6 and column 2, 20%, gives the call option value as % of the value of underlying asset.

Option value = 20% of stock price = 0.2 * \$ 50 = \$ 10.

REAL OPTIONS

The underlying asset in the case of real option is a real asset. Real options are implicitly held by companies. The example of a business that had the option to defer the investment is one type of real option. The first account of a real option is found in the writings of Aristotle (Copeland and Keenan 1998a). Thales, a sophist philosopher, divined from some tea leaves that there would be a bountiful olive harvest in the next season. He bought the right to rent olive presses from the owners of the olive presses for a normal rent. When the bountiful harvest arrived others did not have the required pressing capacity. So Thales rented the presses to them at above the market rate and pocketed a profit. What Thales had purchased is an option but not the obligation to rent the press. If the harvest were to be poor, he could walk away by losing a small 'premium'.

Professor Stewart Myers of MIT coined the term 'real option' in an article published in 1984. In his words:

> *Strategic planning needs finance. Present value calculations are needed as a check on strategic analysis and vice versa. However, standard discounted cash flow techniques will tend to understate the option value attached to growing profitable lines of business. Corporate finance theory requires extension to deal with real options.**

Types of Real Options

There are six categories of real options. They are as follows:

1. Timing option
2. Growth option
3. Abandonment option
4. Option to expand scale
5. Option to switch inputs and outputs
6. Option to contract scale

The first step in real options analysis is to recognize them. Exhibit 2.1 presents a small list of real options by sector.

Timing option

Capital projects are like call options in the sense that both involve the right but not the obligation to acquire an asset at a specified price on or before a certain date. The analogy between project characteristics and call option is given in Exhibit 2.2. The amount spent on the project is the exercise price. The present value of cash flows from the project is the stock price. The length of time the company can defer the investment decision without losing the investment opportunity corresponds to the time to maturity. The uncertainty in the project's cash flows corresponds to the standard deviation of returns.

* Myers, Stewart, Finance Theory and Financial Strategy, *Interfaces*, Jan–Feb, 1984.

EXHIBIT 2.1

Typical Real Options by Sector

Aerospace	Valuing options in customer contracts
Banking and securities	Valuing real estate leases
Automotive	Decisions to modify new car designs
Chemicals	Timing of investment
Energy	Timing the development of oil and gas fields/ Switching inputs
Pharmaceuticals	Growth options embedded in R&D projects

Source: Copeland and Keenan 1998b

EXHIBIT 2.2

Project Characteristics and Option Variables

Project characteristic	Call option
Expenditure required to acquire the asset	X Exercise price
PV of cashflows	S Stock price
Length of time decision may be deferred	t Time to expiration
Riskiness of underlying operating assets	σ^2 Variance of returns from stock
Time value of money	r_f Risk-free rate of return

The cash flows lost due to competitors who have fully committed corresponds to dividends.

The impact of increasing the variables on the value of the option has been discussed earlier. We extend it to real options. The impact of an increase in option variables on the value of the real option is shown in Exhibit 2.3. Like financial options, the value of timing option can be found using the option value tables.

Recollect that the NPV of a project = PV of cash flows – Initial investment

$$= S - X$$

The timing option enables the managers to defer investment for a certain period of time without losing the opportunity. In other words, the managers would always want to spend later rather than sooner. If an investment can be deferred for one year, one could put the investment in a bank for one year and withdraw it when the time is ripe to invest. That is, the investment X would be invested at r_f for one year.

So, the amount now is the present value of X discounted at r_f. PV (X) = $X/(1+ r_f)^t$.

EXHIBIT 2.3

The Impact of Changes in Option Variables on the Value of Real Option

Variable	Value of real option
Increase in the PV of the project	Increase
A higher investment cost	Decrease
A longer time to maturity	Increase
Increase in uncertainty (Volatility of cash flows)	Increase
Increase in risk-free rate	Increase
Increases in cash flow lost	Decrease

Since our objective is to refine NPV to incorporate other option variables such as r_f, t and σ let us redefine NPV as S – PV(X). As with financial options this can be expressed as a ratio: S/PV(X)

Cumulative variance = $\sigma^2 t$ (cumulative volatility is the square root of cumulative variance).

We can use these two values to estimate the value of the option as per cent of value of underlying assets. An illustration follows.

An oil company has an investment opportunity to develop some reserves. The PV of future cash flows is currently \$ 100 million. They can lock into the investment now by incurring an expenditure of \$ 80 million. Alternatively, they may wait for two years by paying an up-front fee of \$ 6 million and then make an investment of \$ 90 million to develop the reserves. Based on the volatility of price of oil, the annual standard deviation of returns for the oil field is 35%*. Interest rates are 8%.

The value of the first alternative is \$ 20 million. That is NPV = \$ 20 million.
The value of the second alternative is: X = 90, S = 100.

$$\text{PV (exercise price)} = \frac{90}{1.08^2} = 77.6$$

$$\frac{\text{Value of operating assets}}{PV(X)} = \frac{100}{77.6} = 1.3$$

$$\sigma(\sqrt{t}) = 0.35 * \sqrt{2} = 0.50$$

Look for the corresponding row and column. The option value is 31% of asset

* It is not correct to estimate the volatility of the cash flows from the oil project on the basis of volatility of oil prices. It can at best give a first-cut measure. Estimating volatility will be discussed later in this chapter.

value = 0.31 * 100 = $ 31 million.

$$\text{NPV} = 31 \text{ million} - \text{Fees} = 31 - 6 = \$\, 25 \text{ million.}$$

The value of flexibility, therefore, is $ 25 million – $ 20 million = $ 5 million. Obviously, it makes sense to wait and then invest.

Timing options are important in all natural resource extraction industries, real estate development, farming and paper products.

Growth option

A growth option is characterized by an early investment (in R&D say) which leads to a chain of inter-related projects opening up future new generation products and processes, access to new market, oil reserves, etc. Any investment that creates new investment opportunities can be characterized as a growth option. Companies derive their value from two sources: assets in place and the present value of growth opportunities. Stock markets realize it when pricing securities. The estimated value of the growth option for some well-known American companies is presented in Exhibit 2.4 (see Kester 1984).

EXHIBIT 2.4

Value of Growth Option Reflected by Stock Prices

Company	M.V of equity ($, m)	Estimated value of growth options ($, m)*	% of market value represented by growth options
Motorola	5250	3850–4410	73–84
Apple Computer	2000	1340–1604	67–80
Digital Equipment	5690	3790–4550	67–80
IBM	72,890	36,457–51,030	50–70
Union Carbide	4350	2483–3230	57–74
Goodyear	2520	520–1320	21–52
General Foods	2280	167–1012	7–44

As can be seen from the exhibit up to 80% of Motorola's market value in 1984 came from future growth opportunities.

Just as a package of bond and warrants are valued separately, the option component embedded in projects should be evaluated separately and then added to the value obtained from the DCF methodology. Assume that a project is expected to lead to a second-generation investment.

* Range of growth option values are estimated by subtracting the high and low value of capitalized earnings (at discount rates ranging from 15% to 25%) from the market value of equity.

The NPV of the entire proposal may be written as

$$\text{NPV} = \text{NPV (phase 1)} + \text{Call value of phase 2}$$

To evaluate the growth options embedded in projects:

1. Segregate discretionary expenditure and its associated cash flows from phase 2 project from phase 1.
2. Find the NPV of phase 1 using the traditional DCF approach.
3. Discount the discretionary spending to the present using an appropriate *risk-free rate*. If the discretionary spending that leads to phase 2 project is \$ 300 million to be made in the third year, discount it to the present by using a three-year risk-free rate. This constitutes X.
4. Find the present value of cash flows (net of inflows and *routine* expenditure on working capital and fixed assets) using WACC. This is S.
5. Find $S/\text{PV}(X)$.
6. Estimate cumulative volatility ($\sigma\sqrt{t}$). t is three years in this case. Estimation of σ is discussed at a later stage in this chapter.
7. Find the value of the call option and add it to the NPV of phase 1.

Most capital investments are phased investments which are compound options. That is, an option on an option. When there are multiple stages in expansion, each stage represents an option on the next stage as given in Figure 2.5.

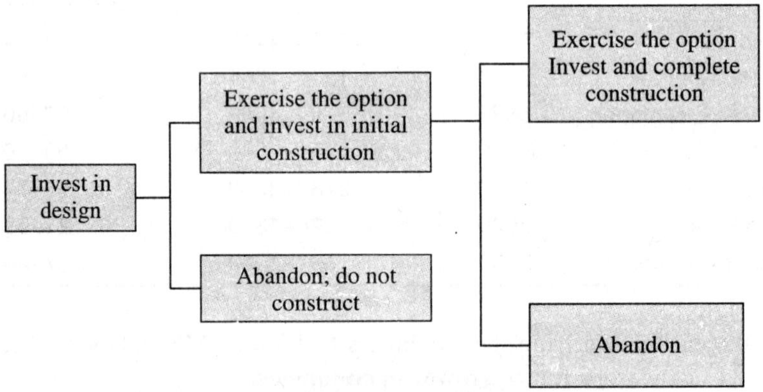

Figure 2.5 Projects as compound options.

So it is inappropriate to treat projects with multiple stages of expansion as simple call options. These are call options on call options or call options on put options, or put options on put options and so on. Since compound options are more complex, we do not discuss them here*.

* Interested readers may refer to Rubinstein M., Double Trouble, *RISK*, January, 1992.

Abandonment option

If the market conditions deteriorate severely, the management can abandon operations and realize resale value of project assets in second-hand markets. Abandonment options are important in capital-intensive industries, financial services and new product introduction in uncertain markets.

In a competitive industry with overcapacity, the management has to continuously consider whether to stay or get out. The actual decision depends on the value of the project below which the management may choose to abandon and the value above which extension could take place. Consider an example. A mining company is considering opening up a gold mine with an investment of $ 4 million for two years. Expected cash flows are $ 2 million in each of the two years. At a discount rate of 10%, the NPV is negative. The management does not buy this analysis. Gold prices are very volatile. The revenues from the project move up or down when the gold prices fluctuate.

The NPV analysis is based on the assumption that the company will continue digging even if revenues are low and the company makes a loss. The company might choose to abandon if the gold price goes down in both the years. The NPV does not recognize this possibility. Let us look at another example. A mining company is considering a two-year project. The project requires investments of $ 50 million now and after one year. There is a 70% chance that the project will be a winner. The company's management can learn more about the quantity of ore present in the mine and the direction of prices in the next one year. There is an 80% chance that the project evolves in the same direction in the subsequent year as the previous year. The discount rate for the project is 10%. The cash flows from the project are given as follows:

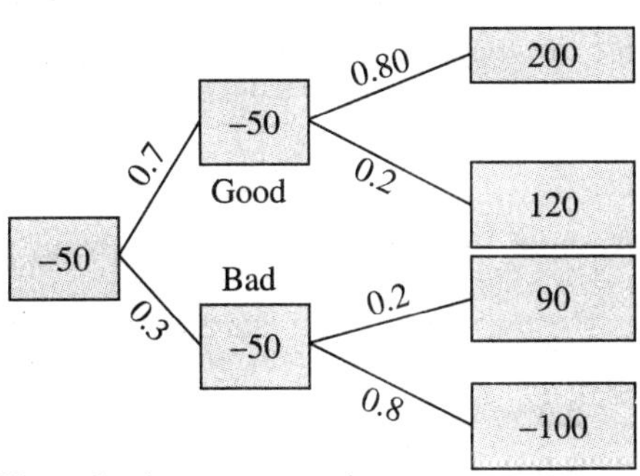

The traditional NPV analysis suggests that

$$\text{NPV} = -50 + \frac{-50}{1.10} + \frac{0.7(0.8 * 200 + 0.2 * 120) + 0.3(0.2 * 90 - 0.8 * 100)}{(1.10)^2}$$

$$= \$ -4.38 \text{ million}$$

So the project should be rejected. Assume that the managers can abandon the project after one year. They will go ahead with the project only if the results are favourable.

$$NPV = -50 + \frac{0.7(-50)}{(1.1)} + \frac{0.7(0.8 * 200 + 0.2 * 120) + 0.3(0)}{(1.1)^2}$$

$$= \$\,20 \text{ million}$$

The managers can go ahead with the project. Abandonment options exist in most businesses and are more valuable when uncertainty is high. An option to abandon is a *put* option. The value of the put option can be found by replicating the pay-off from the put option. It is possible to construct a portfolio consisting of a fraction of the project (Δ) and lending an amount B at the risk-free rate r that replicates the pay-off on the put (Sachdeva and Vandenberg (1993). Also see Robichek and Van Horne (1967)). Let the pay-offs from the project be $V_{1,1}$ and $V_{1,2}$, and $P_{1,1}$ and $P_{1,2}$ in the two states of the world.

The pay-offs from the replicating portfolio are of the form:

$$P_{1,1} = \Delta V_{1,1} + B(1 + r)$$

$$P_{1,2} = \Delta V_{1,2} + B(1 + r)$$

Solve for Δ and B, we get

$$\Delta = \frac{(P_{1,1} - P_{1,2})}{(V_{1,1} - V_{1,2})}$$

$$B = \frac{P_{1,1} - \Delta V_{1,1}}{(1 + r)}$$

Since the pay-offs from the portfolio are identical to the pay-offs on the put, the current price of the put must be equal to the current value of the portfolio. Then

$$P_0 = (\Delta)\ (V_0) + B$$

Let us look at an example. A project has the following pay-offs in one year:

Probability	Cash flow ($)
0.5	120
0.5	80

Its expected value today at a discount rate of 20% is \$ 83.33 (V_0). The risk-free rate is 8%. Then

$$\Delta = -1$$

$$B = \frac{0 - (-1)(120)}{(1 + 0.08)} = \$\,111.11$$

Therefore, the value of the put option = –1(83.33) + 111.11 = $ 27.28.

Natural resource investments: a special case

Natural resource investments like mining and oil exploration are uniquely suited for real options analysis. The owner of a mine, for example, has the option to defer exploration, close or reopen or even abandon a mine. The owner of the mine has the right to acquire the output of the mine (e.g. copper) at a fixed exercise price (the variable cost of production). When the output prices are low and the fixed costs of operating the mine are high, it might be prudent to shut down the mine, at least temporarily till the output prices bounce back.

Assume that you have a two-year right to mine a copper deposit. The mine is known to have 8 million pounds of copper[*]. The development of the mine involves a cash outlay of $ 1.25 million and the development itself is expected to take one year at the end of which the owner can mine or subcontract extraction to a third party by paying an extraction cost. Assume that the extraction costs are 85 cents per pound. The owner can then sell the output to another party at the spot price one year from now. The sequence of activities is shown in a time line in Figure 2.6.

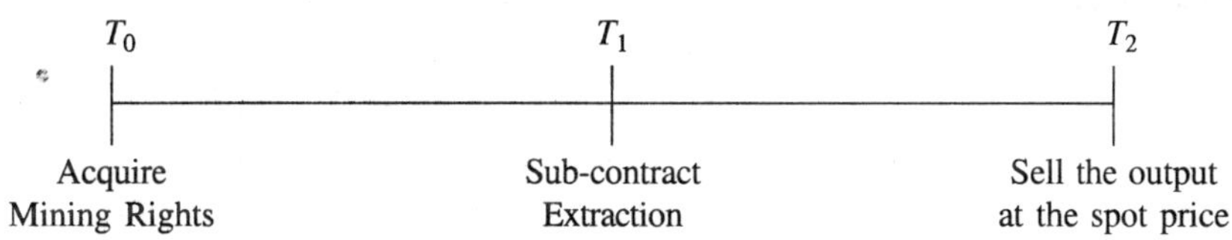

Figure 2.6 Time line depicting the sequence of activities in copper mining.

Percentage changes of copper prices follow a normal distribution with a mean of 7% standard deviation of 20%. Current price of copper is 95 cents per pound. The required rate of return for the project is 10% and the risk-free rate is 5%.

$$\text{The NPV of the project} = -1.25 + \frac{8[E(S_1) - 0.85]}{1.1}$$

where

$E\ (S_1)$ = Expected spot price of copper one year from now

The expected spot price $E\ (S_1) = S_0 e^{\mu T} = 0.95e^{0.07} = 1.0189$

Thus, NPV = –0.022. This analysis ignores the fact that the owner can abandon the project after the development if the spot price is less than 85 cents. This is a one year call option on copper with a strike price of 85 cents.

* This example is based on an unpublished note by Professor Campbell Harvey, Duke University.

The value of the call option can be estimated as of the form:

$$\text{Value of call} = S_0N(d_1) - Ke^{-rt}N(d_2) = 0.95N(d_1) - 0.85e^{-0.05}N(d_2)$$

where

$$d_1 = \frac{\ln(S_0/K) + r_f + \sigma^2/2}{\sigma\sqrt{t}} = \frac{\ln(0.95/0.85) + 0.05 + 200}{0.20} = 0.906$$

$$d_2 = d_1 - \sigma\sqrt{t} = 0.706$$

Call option value = $ 0.162

The 'true' NPV = –1.25 + (8)* (0.162) = $ 0.046

In many natural resource investments like oil exploration, there are two sources of uncertainty—the quantity of oil in the ground and the price of oil. Options that derive their value from two or more sources of uncertainty are called **rainbow options**. Using the simple option-pricing model to value such options can lead to biased estimates of value.

Other options

If price or demand change, the management can change the output mix of the facility. Such options are termed option to switch (output). These are important in those cases where the good is sought in batches or subject to uncertain demand. Examples are consumer electronics, toys, specialty paper. Likewise, the management may have the option to switch inputs as in the case of oil, electric power and agricultural crops. In the case of power projects, for example, the management can choose the technology in such a way that the flexibility to switch between alternate fuels is retained. This flexibility though comes at a price, can be advantageous depending on the relative prices of fuels and their volatility. The management can switch to cheaper alternative when the situation warrants.

ESTIMATING VOLATILITY

One of the inputs to the option-pricing model is the variance of returns. In the case of equity options, the standard deviation of stock returns in the immediate past (say, six months or three months) is used to estimate the value of volatility. Another approach is to estimate the volatility 'implied' by past option prices. That is, given all parameters and the option price, one may find out volatility by trial and error. In the case of real options, the underlying asset

* There are 8 million of these options and the development cost $ 1.25 million.

is the project. How should volatility be estimated since the project's returns are unobservable? There are at least three alternatives:

1. Estimate the volatility of a stock market index and take it as a proxy for volatility of project returns. Companies can have higher or lower volatility than a broad-based index. Further, cash flows from projects within companies are probably more volatile. What is more, volatility of an index gives the value of volatility of *equity price*. What we need is the volatility of *project returns*. In sum, the volatility of a stock market index is only a rough estimate.
2. Calculate the implied volatility of the options on the company's stock and take it as a proxy for the project's variance.
3. Use spreadsheets (or sophisticated packages like Crystal Ball) to simulate project's cash flows and estimate the standard deviation of the project's returns.

MANAGING REAL OPTIONS

The value of the real option depends on the underlying variables like the present value of operating cash inflows, outflows, time to maturity, volatility of cash flows, risk-free rate of interest and cash flow lost due to competition. The value of the option can be (and should be) managed by increasing the PV of cash in flows, decreasing the PV of cash outflows, increasing the uncertainty in cash flows, extending the opportunity's duration, and reducing the value lost by waiting to exercise. One may reduce the value lost by waiting, for example, by erecting entry barriers to competitors (e.g. locking in key customers). Likewise, raising prices or reducing expenses can increase the PV of cash inflows*. As mentioned previously, the value of an option can be expressed as a function of two metrics $S/PV(X)$ and $\sigma\sqrt{t}$. The value of option increases if either (or both) increases. A company may classify projects on an option space as shown in Figure 2.7 (see Luehraman 1988a, b).

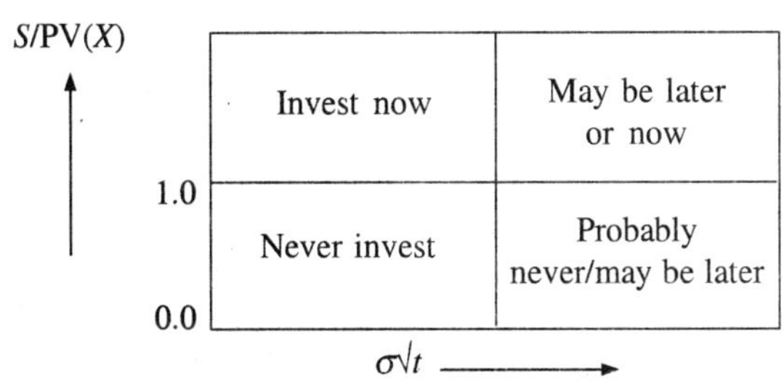

Figure 2.7 Classifying projects on an option space.

---

* It might not be possible to increase prices unless the product has unique features. To add unique features, one may have to invest in capital equipment, marketing and so on. This raises X. That is, altering one variable may have an impact on others. So, one should ascertain the *net* impact on the option value.

Those projects that have low volatility but high $S/\text{PV}(X)$ should be exercised immediately. That is, the company must invest immediately. Those projects that have low volatility *and* low value-to-cost ratio should never be exercised. Those projects with moderately high volatility and value-to-cost ratio may be harvested now and those with negative NPV, positive value-to-cost ratio and moderately high volatility may be exercised at a later date when conditions warrant. In sum, a manager is required to proactively cultivate a company's projects. Proactive cultivation needs constant monitoring and support to promising projects. Assume that a company has a portfolio of projects of which some have negative NPV. Conventional capital budgeting suggests that they should be discarded. That is incorrect. The principal insight gained from real options analysis is that these projects should be actively cultivated if they have a high cumulative volatility.

CONCLUDING REMARKS

In this chapter, the author described the pitfalls of using the traditional DCF approach to value capital projects. The DCF methodology breaks down when investments have option-like characteristics. Capital projects, like options, could have asymmetric pay-offs in the sense that the upside might be unlimited while the downside is limited to the initial investment made. It is possible for a project to have many options. One should evaluate them individually and add them up*. The following points need to be remembered while executing a real options analysis:

- The estimate of option's volatility has a significant impact on the final value. Due care should be taken in estimating volatility.
- Projects should not be valued using option-pricing theory when they do not have option-like characteristics! Assume, for example, you have the option to buy something for 90% of its value at any time. Is this an option? Obviously not. You would buy the asset irrespective of when the option is exercised because the option enables you to purchase something for a discount.
- Real options can be classified as exclusive and shared. Exclusive options are unique to the holder. Value arising out of patents is an example. Shared options, on the other hand, are not unique to a company. As the name suggests, they are collectively held by the industry.
- Real options are also of two types—simple and compound. Compound options are options on options.

The real challenge in real options analysis is not concerned so much with the tools and techniques but with preparing the organization to make a shift

* This ignores the interaction between the options.

to new ways of thinking. Airbus Industrie, Merck and several other organizations have started implementing the real options analysis.

REFERENCES

1. Copeland, T. and P. Keenan, How Much is Flexibility Worth, *The McKinsey Quarterly*, 2, 1998a.
2. ———, Making Real Options Real, *The McKinsey Quarterly*, 3, 1998b.
3. Courtadon, G. and J. Merrick, The Option Pricing Model and the Valuation of Corporate Securities, *Midland Corporate Finance Journal*, Autumn, 1983.
4. Cox, J., S., Ross, and M., Rubinstein, Option Pricing: A Simplified Approach, *Journal of Financial Economics*, September, 1979.
5. Kester, C.W., Today's Options for Tomorrow's Growth, *Harvard Business Review*, March-April,1984.
6. Luehrman, T., Strategy as a Portfolio of Real Options, *Harvard Business Review*, Sep-Oct, 1998b.
7. Mason, S. and R.C. Merton, The Role of Contingent Claims Analysis, in Edward Altman, and Marti Subrahmanyam (ed.), *Recent Advances in Corporate Finance*, Richard D Irwin, 1985.
8. Merton, R., Theory of Rational Option Pricing, *Bell Journal of Economics and Management*, June, 1973.
9. Nichols, N., Scientific Management at Merck: An Interview with CFO Judy Lewent, *Harvard Business Review*, Jan-Feb, 1994.
10. Robichek, A. and J. Van Horne, Abandonment Value and Capital Budgeting, *Journal of Finance*, March, 1967.
11. Sachdeva, Kanwal and Pieter Vandenberg, Valuing the Abandonment Option in Capital Budgeting—An Option Pricing Approach, *Financial Practice and Education*, Fall, 1993.

SUGGESTED FURTHER READING

Amram, M. and N. Kulatilaka, Real Options: Managing Strategic Investment in an Uncertain World, *Harvard Business School Press*, Boston, 1999.

———, Disciplined Decisions: Aligning Strategy with Financial Markets, *Harvard Business Review*, Jan–Feb, 1999.

———, Uncertainty: The New Rules for Strategy, *Journal of Business Strategy*, March, 1999.

———, Strategy and Shareholder Value Creation: The Real Options Frontier, *Journal of Applied Corporate Finance*, **13**. (2, Summer), 2000.

Brennan, M. J. and E. Schwartz, A New Approach to Evaluating Natural Resource Investments, in Joel Stern and Donald Chew Jr (ed.), *The Revolution in Corporate Finance*, Blackwell, 1992.

Colwell, D., T. Henker and J. Ho, Real Options Valuation of Australian Gold Mines and Mining Companies, *Working Paper*, University of New South Wales, Undated.

Copeland, T., The Real-Options Approach to Capital Allocation, *Strategic Finance*, October, 2001.

Copeland, T. and V. Antikarov, Real Options: A Practitioner's Guide, Texere LLC, 2001.

Damodaran, A., The Promise of Real Options, *Journal of Applied Corporate Finance*, **13**(2), 2000.

Dixit, A., Investment and Hysterisis, *Journal of Economic Perspectives*, Winter, 1992.

Dixit, A. and R. Pindyck, The Options Approach to Capital Investment, *Harvard Business Review*, May-June, 1995.

Edelson, M., Real Options: Valuing Managerial Flexibility, *HBS Case No.* 9-294-109, March, 1994.

Fernandez, P., Valuing Real Options: Frequently Made Errors, *Working Paper*, IESE Business School, June, 2001.

Grenadier, S. and A. Weiss, Investment in Technological Innovation: An Option Pricing Approach, *Journal of Financial Economics*, **44**, 1997.

Gompers, P., Penelope's Personal Pocket Phones, *HBS Case No.* 9-299-004, April, 1999.

Imai, J. and M. Nakajima, A Real Option Analysis of an Oil Refinery Project, *Financial Practice and Education*, Fall/Winter, 2000.

Kemna, A.G.Z, Case Studies on Real Options, *Financial Management*, Autumn, 1993.

Kulatilaka, N. and N. Venkataraman, Strategic Options in the Digital Era, *Business Strategy Review*, **12**(4), 2001.

Leslie, K. and M. Michaels, The Real Power of Real Options, *The McKinsey Quarterly*, 3, 1997.

Luchman, T., P. Tufano and B. Wall, MW Petroleum (A), *Harvard Business School Case No.* 9-295-029, November, 1994.

Luehrman, T., Capital Projects as Real Options: An Introduction, *Harvard Business School Case No* 9-295-074, March, 1995.

———, Investment Opportunities as Real Options: Getting Started on the Numbers, *Harvard Business Review*, July-August, 1998 a.

Luehrman, T., and W. A. Techner, Arundel Partners: The Sequel Project, *Harvard Business School Case No.* 9-292-140, June, 1992.

Mauboussin, M., Get Real: Using Real Options in Security Analysis, *C S First Boston Research*, June, 1999.

McDonald, R. and D. Siegel, The Value of Waiting to Invest, *Quarterly Journal of Economics*, 101. 1986.

Meulbroek, L., Real Options Valuation when Multiple Sources of Uncertainty Exist, *HBS Case No.* 9-201-106, March, 2001.

Moel, A. and P. Tufano, When are Real Options Exercised? An Empirical Study of Mine Closings, *Review of Financial Studies*, Spring, 2002.

Paddock, J., D. Siegel and J. Smith, Option Valuation of Claims on Physical Assets: The Case of Offshore Petroleum Leases, *Quarterly Journal of Economics*, August, 1988.

Smit, H.T.J., Investment Analysis of Offshore Concessions in the Netherlands, *Financial Management*, **26**, 1997.

Trigeorgis, L. and S. Mason, Valuing Managerial Flexibility, *Midland Corporate Finance Journal*, Spring, 1987.

Trigeorgis, Lenos, Real Options and Interactions with Financial Flexibility, *Financial Management*, Autumn, 1993.

EXERCISES

1. The current price of a stock is \$ 100; strike price is \$ 110; standard deviation of returns is 30%, interest rates are 8% and time to expiration is two years. Calculate the value of the call option.
2. How would your answer change if the strike price increases to \$ 140, maturity to 5 years?
3. A company has the following projects. Calculate NPV and then classify them on the basis of exercise decision (exercise now and so on).

Variable	A	B	C	D
S (\$, m)	100	100	100	100
X (\$, m)	90	90	110	110
T (Years)	0.0	2.0	0.0	1.0
σ per year	0.30	0.30	0.30	0.30
R_f = 6%				

4. The cash flows and probabilities from an investment are given below. Calculate the NPV assuming no abandonment. Assume a discount rate of 20%. Also calculate the value of abandonment. The risk-free rate is 10%*.

Period 0		1		2		3
	Prob.	Cash flow	Prob.	Cash flow	Prob.	Cash flow
					0.7	150
			0.2	140		
					0.3	100
	0.4	160				
					0.4	100
			0.8	80		
					0.6	70
−103.31					0.4	100
			0.5	100		
					0.6	70
	0.6	90				
					0.8	80
			0.5	50		
					0.2	40

5. The cash flows from a project are given as follows.

(in $, m)

Year	0	1	2	3	4	5	6
Cash flow	(125)	9.0	10.0	11.0	11.6	12.1	12.7
Terminal value							191.0

The project is expected to lead to a second-generation project whose cash flows are given as follows:

Year	0	1	2	3	4	5	6
Cash flow				(382)	23.1	25.4	28.0
Terminal value							419.3

* See Sachdeva, Kanwal and Pieter Vandenberg, Valuing the Abandonment Option in Capital Budgeting—An Option Pricing Approach, *Financial Practice and Education*, Fall 1993 for answer.

The cost of capital is 12%. Risk-free rate is 5%. Calculate the NPV of the project. Is the project worthwhile? Estimate the value of the second stage project as an option assuming annual volatility of 40%. What is the true NPV of the project?

6. A company is in the process of bringing out a breakthrough drug to the market. The company will have to invest $ 10 million to bring the product to market. The cash flow forecasts from the product are given below:

($, m)

Year	0	1	2	3	4	5
NOPAT	(3100)	900	3305	3185	845	0
Capex	5400	0	0	0	0	0
N.W.C	1500	0	0	0	0	(1500)

There is no terminal value.

Cost of capital = 19%. Calculate the NPV. The drug is expected to lead to a second-generation product which requires an investment of $ 100 million in the fourth year. How big should the current expected value of the second-generation drug be in order to justify the investment? Calculate the value of the first project if the project can be abandoned for $ 4 million in year 2 if the demand for the project is not high. To carry out your analysis assume that standard deviation is 50% and the risk-free rate is 10%*.

7. Given the following values, calculate the value of the option:

S = $ 3 million

X = $ 3.5 million

r = 5%

T = 5 years

Volatility = 35% p.a.

* Note that the option to abandon is a *put* option. The value of the put option can be calculated using the put-call parity relationship. $P = C + Xe^{-rt} - S$ where C is the value of the call option.

PART III

LIABILITY AND RISK MANAGEMENT

CHAPTER

3

Financing a Firm's Growth*

LEARNING OBJECTIVES

After reading this chapter, you should be able to:

- Provide an overview of convertibles.
- Introduce valuation of convertibles.
- Highlight factors responsible for financial innovation.
- Highlight the role of financial engineering in advancing a firm's corporate strategy.
- Introduce innovative instruments such as PERCS, PEPS, etc.

INTRODUCTION

One of the roles of the Chief Financial Officer is to establish contact with the capital markets and obtain capital at acceptable prices. The goal of financial strategy is to support a long-term business strategy. This chapter provides an overview of some of the recent innovations in the US capital markets.

Companies have access to a wide array of financial instruments. A standard academic discussion on financial instruments begins with the debt-equity continuum as shown in Figure 3.1.

* This chapter is contributed by Chandrasekhar Krishnamurti.

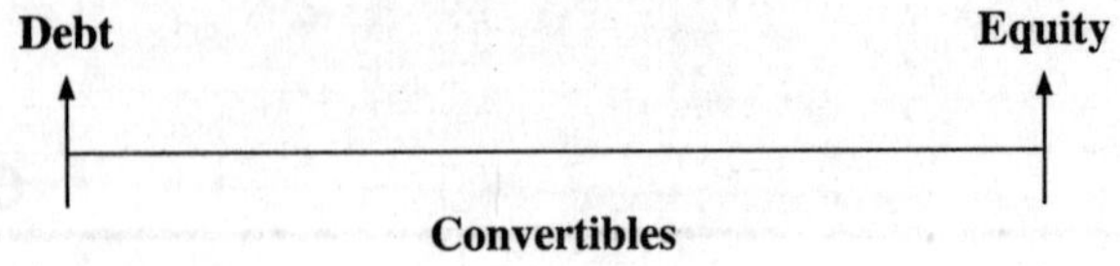

Figure 3.1 Debt-equity continuum.

At the one end of the spectrum, we have straight debt and at the other, equity. Some instruments that have both debt-like and equity-like characteristics fall in between. Some instruments fall outside the continuum. Each instrument has a different *risk-return trade-off.*

Debt instruments have a finite life unlike equity. The term to maturity is also called *tenor*. Debt can be classified as short term and long term on the basis of maturity. Short-term debt falls due within a year whereas long-term debt has longer life. 'Commercial paper' is an example of short-term debt. When companies borrow money, they undertake an agreement to make interest and principal payments at specified intervals. The interest could be fixed or floating. In the case of floating rate debt, the interest rate is reset at periodic intervals according to a predetermined formula. Debt can be issued to a small group of investors or the general investing public. Thus, debentures sold to public is a marketable claim whereas term loan from a financial institution is not.

Creditors have a general lien on the assets of the company. Secured debt, as the name suggests, provides the lender the specific charge on the issuer's assets whereas unsecured debt does not. In other words, secured debt gives a prior claim.

Convertible bonds are hybrid instruments. A convertible bond gets converted into shares of the company at a specified price after a specified period of time at one stroke or in instalments. The holder of a convert is entitled to receive interest on the convertible portion till conversion. Thus, a convert is a package of straight debt and equity option. The option to convert is usually at the discretion of the holder and will only be exercised when and if the holder finds such an exercise desirable. The features (terminology) of a convertible bond are discussed in the ensuing paragraph.

The number of shares a holder will receive on exercising the option is called **conversion ratio**[*]. The price paid to acquire the underlying shares through conversion is called **conversion price**.

---

[*] There is a class of convertibles called *death-spiral convertibles* that convert into a fixed dollar amount of common stock (equal to the convert's price). They derive their name from the fact that when stock price falls, the death-spiral owners receive more shares because of which shareholders face severe dilution. The terms of these bonds are so onerous that only companies desperately in need of cash would consider them. Some 23 companies issued death spirals and raised $ 123 million in 2001.

$$\text{Conversion ratio} = \frac{\text{Par value of security}}{\text{Conversion price}}$$

To illustrate, if the par value were to be \$ 100 and conversion price \$ 20, the investor will receive five shares.

The conversion value of a convert is the value of the bond if it is converted immediately.

$$\text{Conversion value} = \text{Market price of shares} * \text{Conversion ratio}$$

A conversion premium is the difference between the conversion price and the current market price of the stock at the time of the issue. The premium is expressed in percentage. To illustrate, if the conversion price is \$ 50 and the current market price of the stock is \$ 40, then

$$\text{Conversion premium} = \frac{50 - 40}{40} = 0.25 = 25\%$$

Although conversion premiums range from 10 to 70%, a premium in excess of 30% is considered too high to attract the traditional convertible band investors.

The *current yield* of a convert is the coupon payment on the bond expressed as the fraction of the current market price. Thus, if the coupon payment is 4% and the market price is \$ 100, the yield is 4%. The current yield is usually set higher than the dividend yield on the company's stock. The break even measures the time it would take for the added return on the convert to equal the premium paid for the security in excess of its parity.

$$\text{Break even} = \frac{\text{Convertible market price} - \text{Conversion value}}{\text{Convertible coupon} - (\text{Stock dividend} * \text{Conversion ratio})}$$

The coupon payments on convertibles are tax deductible for the issuer and the rating agencies assign varying degrees of equity content depending on the structure of the instrument. A coupon typically ranges from 4% to 6%.

Since a convertible is a hybrid instrument consisting of bond and option components, we would expect the value of the convertible to increase as the underlying stock price increased, and decrease whenever the stock price declined. Although, theoretically the price of the stock can be anything, including zero, the downside in the case of convertibles is limited because of the straight bond component that provides contractual coupon payments. This serves as an investment floor.

An example is in order. Thermo Electron had issued 4.25% convertible bonds with a face value of \$ 1000 due on 1 January 2003. The current bond price is 97.50. The current yield on the bond is 4.25/97.50 = 4.359%. The company does not pay dividends. The excess of current yield on the bond over the dividend yield, called **yield advantage**, is, therefore, 4.359%. SCI Systems issued $ 575 million of 3.00% convertibles at a premium of 26% on 10 March, 2000 due 15 March, 2007. The bond has a face value of $ 1000 convertible into 17.7841 shares of SCI.

Exhibit 3.1 gives the details of some recent convertible bond offerings.

EXHIBIT 3.1

Recent Convertible Bond Offerings

Issue date	Issuer	Coupon (%)	Maturity	Convertible price (%)	Size (m)
7 April, 1999	America Online	3.14	5/15/29	133.125	1256
9 March 2000	iBasis	5.75	3/15/05	99.875	150
23 February 2000	Level 3 comm.	6 .00	3/15/10	105	863
20 January 2000	Mail.com	7.00	2/1/05	95.75	100

Source: Morgan Stanley Dean Witter

THE WORLDWIDE MARKET FOR CONVERTIBLE BONDS

The global convertible bond market is estimated to be $ 610 billion in size with North America accounting for $ 325 billion, Europe accounting for $ 177 billion, Japan accounting for $ 77 billion and Non-Japan Asia accounting for $ 318 billion. The US convertible bond market has grown from $ 79 billion in 1991 to $ 305 billion at the end of 2003. Issuance in Europe is growing at 80% for the last few years whereas the global market is growing at 35%–40%*. Several factors are responsible for this growth. The interest rates in Europe have been falling and the equity prices are rising. When the interest rates are low, the returns from bonds and money market instruments will also be low. Investors may choose to invest in stocks. But this exposes them to the vagaries of the market. A convertible is, hence, a good alternative. Companies are taking advantage of the rising equity market by selling convertibles, thereby selling stock at a premium. There has also been a boom in the mergers and acquisitions activity in Europe. Companies are divesting non-core businesses, and convertibles/exchangeables† are often used in the transaction.

* Roundtable on Convertible Bonds, *Euromoney*, November, 1999.

† Exchangeable bonds grant the bond holder the right to exchange the bonds for the stock of a firm other than the issuer of the bond.

The US convertible bond market is dominated by high growth, high-tech, start up firms (e.g. Internet and telecom companies) whereas the European market is dominated by large-cap, blue chip companies. This trend is changing now. A large number of stable companies with investment grade rating from the US have started issuing convertibles in the recent past. During the first half of 2001, 111 deals worth $ 56 billion had been done in the US alone*. Exhibit 3.2 gives the list of top lead underwriters of convertible bonds around the world and the statistics on the global convertible bond issuance in 2006.

Why Do Companies Issue Convertible Bonds?

Often convertibles are viewed as delayed equity. If the managers of a company expect the firm's stock price to rise and investors to exercise their option of conversion, a convertible, as opposed to an outright equity issue, will result in lower dilution. Since the investor has an option of conversion, the coupon on convertibles tends to be lower than their non-convertible counterparts. For this reason, some managers consider convertibles 'cheap'. The coupon on convertibles is lower because of the valuable option (of conversion) given to the investor. The option of conversion is a sweetener attached to straight debt.

A straight debt suffers from the moral hazard problem. That is, the company's risk can be shifted from equity to debt by taking on riskier projects. Since shareholders have limited liability, they enjoy all the upside potential but lose nothing in the case of project failure. Smart bondholders realize this and demand higher coupon. The cost of moral hazard problem is borne by the share holders. Since the holders of a convertible have a choice to convert debt into equity, the agency problem is reduced.

Assume that the managers and investors of a company disagree about the risk of a company.

EXHIBIT 3.2

Top Lead Underwriters of Convertibles for the First Quarter 2006

Global convertibles	Citigroup
US	Merrill Lynch & Co
Europe, Middle East and Africa	Credit Suisse
Asia except Japan and Australia	Deutsche Bank
Japan	Nomura

Source: Thomson Financial

* Is this love, or a teenage crush?, *Euromoney*, July 2001.

Top Lead Underwriters (Global Convertibles)
1 January 2006–31 March 2006

Book runner	Proceeds ($, m)	Rank
Citigroup	4544.1	1
Morgan Stanley	3074.5	2
Merrill Lynch	2980.8	3
Deutsche Bank	2326.6	4
Credit Suisse	2172.5	5
Lehman Brothers	1847.9	6
UBS	1839.2	7
Barclays	1599.0	8
J P Morgan	1572.4	9
Nomura	692.4	10

Source: Thomson Financial

Global Convertible Bond Issuance

	1 January 2006–31 March 2006		1 January 2005–31 March 2005	
	Proceeds ($, m)	No. of issues	Proceeds ($, m)	No. of issues
US	9632.3	19	6584.1	31
Asia	3551.2	28	2275.4	16
Australia	970.8	6	338.7	4
Europe, Middle East, Africa	10460.4	17	6480.3	12
Japan	1284.1	11	976.0	9

Source: Thomson Financial

If the investors believe that the company's risk is higher than that projected by the managers, they will demand higher interest rates. The equity option in the case of a convertible bond makes the value of the convertible insensitive to risk shifting. This is because the value of the straight bond component decreases as the risk increases but the value of the equity component *increases*. Thus, the package as a whole is risk neutral. By issuing convertibles, the managers and investors come to an agreement so that the value of the instrument is insensitive to the risk of a company. Convertibles are often issued by high growth, risky firms for this reason.

At times, the managers of a company may have better information than outside investors about the company's prospects. If the company's shares are undervalued by the market, the managers of the company have a disincentive to issue equity. They may issue debt. But debt increases the probability of bankruptcy. Convertibles fall in between. Based on this analysis, we could expect convertibles to be issued by those companies that are undervalued but not to a large extent, straight debt by undervalued companies and equity by overvalued companies.

High growth firms may not find straight debt attractive as they may not have an investment-grade rating. So the interest expense will be high. Defaulting on interest payments may lead to restrictions on investment activities of the firm, which curtails growth. Equity financing will be expensive as high growth firms may have to sell equity at lower prices than that implied by growth opportunities. Those managements that have confidence in the future of the company can issue convertibles and use the call provision to force conversion when the stock price rises in the future (Brennan and Schwartz (1988)).

What is the best way to find out why managers issue convertible bonds? Ask them! This is precisely what academic surveys do. Exhibit 3.3 presents the results of one such survey[*]. The researchers asked the Chief Financial Officers of 243 companies (88 responded). Their study suggests that straight debt is considered the chief alternative to convertibles with common stock as the second choice. A large number of companies favour convertibles because of the lower coupon. Another recent survey by Graham and Harvey (2001) finds that most issuers consider convertibles delayed equity and issue them when the stock is under valued.

The Story After the Issue

Over time the stock price and, hence, conversion premium change. Holding the convertible bond enables the investor to earn interest on the bond component while at the same time retaining the option of conversion if it is desirable. Given this advantage, an investor would prefer to hold the bond rather than convert it into shares. While an investor prefers to hold the convertible bond rather than convert because of the downside protection offered by the bond, the opposite is true for the corporation. Issuers would want to force conversion so that the legal obligation to pay interest and principal is replaced by the non-contractual, more flexible commitments (dividends) to common stock.

[*] Billingsley, Randall and David Smith, Why do Firms Issue Convertible Debt?, *Financial Management*, **25**, (2, Summer): 93–99, 1996.

EXHIBIT 3.3

Rationale for Convertibles

	Factors						(in%)
	1	2	3	4	5	6	n
Lower coupon versus straight debt	48.3	25	13.3	5.6	5.6	1.2	85
Stock undervaluation so we would not issue equity	15.7	22.6	7.8	11.3	7	28	76
Stock was overvalued so we took the opportunity to lock in a favourable coupon	3.4	4.8	2.2	7	26.8	52.4	76
Delayed equity	22.5	31	20	12.7	14.1	2.4	86
Investment banker recommended it	7.9	4.8	27.8	38	18.3	7.3	82
Other firms had recently issued	2.2	11.9	28.9	25.4	28.2	8.5	83

Note: 1= Most influential, 2 = Next most influential, etc.

Issuers of convertibles face uncertainty in future capital structure of the company in the sense that the company receives equity only if the investors convert the bond into shares. To make sure that the company receives shares if and when it is desirable, i.e. to 'control' investors, issuers can do two things:

1. Insert a call option. Since the objective of the management is to maximize the value of the stock (and not the value of convertible), the bond could be called as soon as the conversion value reaches the call price. The investor is coaxed to convert because he or she gets more by converting than by holding the bond. In short, the management places a lid on the value of the convertible. Usually, investors have 30 days to decide whether to surrender the bond or to convert. The SCI Systems bond cited earlier is freely callable starting 20 March 2003 at an initial price of 101.71, and then descending to 100% of par over four years.

2. Increase dividends making conversion more attractive. At the time of the issue, the coupon on convertible is set higher than dividends on the shares (otherwise the investor will immediately convert). As long as the coupon is higher than dividends, the investor enjoys higher income simultaneously retaining the option. The issuer can induce the investors to convert by raising dividends. When dividends are sufficiently high, the bond holders voluntarily decide to convert. But conversion exposes the investor to the risk of common stock.

EDO Corporation, a manufacturer of advanced electronic, mechanical and electro-optical systems had issued $ 35 million of 7% convertible debentures in 1986. In November 2001, the company called the remaining $ 23.665 million of its outstanding debentures. The convert is redeemable at a price of $ 1000 plus accrued interest up to the redemption date. The bond is convertible into common shares of EDO at $ 22 per share or 45.4550 shares per note. One of the prime assumptions in issuing convertibles is that the company's stock price will rise in future. If, for some reason, the stock price falls after issuing the convertible, investors will not convert and straight debt remains. This situation is called 'debt overhang'. Often managers cite the debt overhang problem for not issuing convertibles. If the company issues convertibles when the chief alternative is debt, one need not crib when investors do not convert because the interest rate on convertibles is lower than that on straight debt resulting in cash savings. In fact, an issuer should rejoice. But the overhang problem is not solved. One should fix the root cause of a problem, not its consequences.

Managers are constantly under pressure to get the best immediate financing deal. This prompts them to take a short-term view. Companies implicitly hold valuable growth options. So a company's financing should be structured in such a way that financial flexibility to exercise its growth options in future is maintained. The financial plan should ensure future access to capital even if it means a higher price for capital today*. Going by this reasoning, high growth, start up firms should choose between convertibles, straight bonds and equity not just on the basis of current cost of capital and debt ratio, but also on the basis of future financing needs and the cost of capital. Even though convertibles ordinarily make sense to the high growth firms, a company with high operating leverage, high (current) debt ratio and uncertain product market conditions should issue equity even if it implies selling stock at a discount.

As pointed out above, when the share price falls, conversion becomes increasingly unlikely. When the price drop is substantial, the possibility of upside potential is remote and the instrument trades like a bond. Such converts, in the market parlance, are called **busted convertibles**. Likewise, when the share price rises substantially, the instrument increasingly resembles equity. Figure 3.2 shows the value of a convertible at various stock prices.

Designing the Features of a Convertible

At the time of the issue, a Finance Manager should decide on the features of

---

* See Willigan, Geraldine, The Case of the Expensive Expansion, *Harvard Business Review*, Jan-Feb, 1989.

the bond such as convertibility, coupon rate, call and put options, exercise price, etc. The investors pay attention to both the conversion premium and the interest on the bond. The higher the conversion premium, the less attractive is the bond. Conversely, the lower the conversion premium, the more attractive is the bond and lower can be the interest. Increasing the coupon raises the bond floor and makes the convertible more attractive, other things remaining constant. Likewise, decreasing the coupon lowers the bond floor.

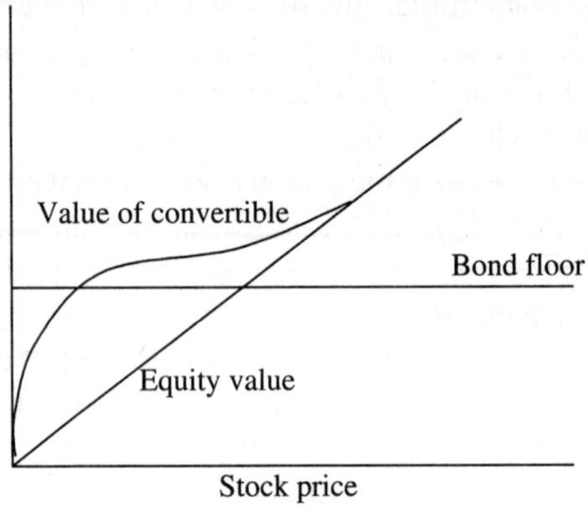

Figure 3.2 The value of convertible at various stock prices.

The higher the coupon, the lower can be the conversion premium and vice versa. The actual features of the convertible depend on the particular financing problem the company is facing and the general market conditions.

- Interest on convertibles is a tax-deductible expense. So firms with predictable taxable income could issue 'bond like' instruments to take advantage of tax deductibility of interest expense and issue equity-like instruments when the prospects of stock price rising is high.
- Companies suffering from asset substitution and risk shifting can give higher conversion, i.e. issue equity-like securities to reduce the agency cost.
- High growth companies could issue convertibles with shorter maturities and less call protection and force conversion when the stock price rises. The call schedule should be designed to provide maximum flexibility to the issuer in forcing conversion as and when it is desirable. The issuers benefit from the call feature because it gives them the opportunity to strengthen their balance sheets by replacing debt by equity.

Bonds with premium less than 10% are considered stock equivalents, those with premium ranging between 30% and 80% are considered hybrids and those with premium greater than 80% are considered bond equivalent converts. Given here is a tabular representation of a small list of issuers in different categories.

Hybrids	**Conversion Premium**
Briggs & Stratton 5% due 15 May 2006	32.342%
Genzyme 3% due 15 May 2008	35.575%
FMC 6.75% due 16 January 2005	50.073%
Stock equivalents	
El Paso Energy 1.66% due 16 August 2002	2.30%
MetLife 4% due 15 May 2003	6.5%
Bond Equivalents	
Human Genome 3.75% due 15 March 2007	92.471%
Reliant Energy 6% due 15 March 2012	130.072%

Source: Morgan Stanley

Convertible bonds often come with a hard call protection that prevents the issuer from calling the bond before a certain number of years, typically 2–5 years. Converts also come with what is known as soft call protection (provisional call) which stipulates that a bond be called only if the underlying stock price is at a pre-specified level, say 125% of the conversion price. In December 1999, Human Genome Science raised $ 200 million by issuing a 5.00% convertible subordinated note due 2006*. The note was issued at a premium of 22% to the common price of $ 58.719. The security had a provisional call protection that prohibited the company from calling the security before 20 December 2002, unless the underlying stock traded at or above $ 107.437 for 20 out of 30 consecutive trading days. The company could call the note if this condition is met but pay holders any unpaid coupons through 20 December 2002.

Exhibit 3.4 presents the details of some recent convertible bond offerings with provisional call feature.

EXHIBIT 3.4

Recent Convertible Bond Offerings with Provisional Calls

Issuer/ Issue date	Convert security	Prem at issue	Dates and terms‡	Trigger (%)	Call details†
Amazon.com 28 Jan. 1999	4.75% Due 2009	27%	Provisional until 5 Feb. 2002	150%	102.85% 30 days
Human Genome 8 Dec. 1999	5% due 2006	22%	Provisional till 20 Dec. 2002	150%	102.5% 30 day
Amkor Tech 16 March 2000	5% due 2007	22%	NCB 20 Dec. 2001 Then provisional until 20 March 2003	150%	103.571% 30 days

Source: Morgan Stanley Dean Witter

* Anand S. Iyer et al. Making the Most of Make-Whole Provisions, Morgan Stanley Dean Witter U.S.Convertible Research, March 23, 2000.

† Call price as of first call date.

‡ Not callable before

CONVERTIBLE BOND INNOVATION: DEATH-SPIRAL CONVERTIBLES

In the early 2000s, C S First Boston and Merrill Lynch, two large and well-respected investment banks, started selling a new type of convertible called **toxic convertibles**, to Hong Kong issuers*. These carry a floating conversion price. The typical formula is that at any point during the lifetime of the bonds (typically three years), the bond holder (CSFB) can look back at the last 30 days (six weeks) of trading, and pick the lowest closing prices within that period, typically over a four-day or five-day average. It can then take a portion of the bonds and convert them at a set discount to that low average price, which is typically between 7% and 10%. As a result, CSFB gets a discount on a discount. CSFB can then sell those shares in the market, locking in a profit. The bond allows CSFB to choose either the floating conversion price or the fixed conversion price, whichever is lower. It results in a near-certain profit at the expense of the issuer.

The consequence of a floating conversion price is that there is no certainty over the number of shares that could be issued if the bonds are converted. This creates a massive overhang on the market, so investors sell the shares, and as the price falls, the floating conversion price falls with it, and the potential dilution gets even worse. This is why they are known as toxic convertibles. In the case of highly geared companies, the effect can be even worse, and the bonds are sometimes known as death-spiral convertibles because the price spirals down as the dilution increases.

Death-spiral convertibles convert into a fixed dollar amount of common stock (equal to the convert's price). They derive that name from the fact that when the stock price falls, the death-spiral owners receive more shares because of which shareholders face severe dilution. The terms of these bonds are so onerous that only companies desperately in need of cash would consider them. Some 180 death-spiral issues raised approximately $ 2 billion in 2001. In 1997, Casmyn Corporation, a gold mining company, with assets in Zimbabwe and Zambia issued $ 32 million convertible preferred securities†. Unlike ordinary converts, the Casmyn convert had a conversion price set at a discount from the lowest trading price in a lookback period‡. Further, the discount and the lookback period increased over time. The lookback period and discount were 15 days and 8.5% respectively, after three months of issuance. The same increased to 60 days and 39% after 18 months of issuance. Assume that the

- face value of the convert is $ 1000;
- current stock price is $ 12.5;

---

* See http://www.webb-site.com for a study of toxic convertible issues.

† This is based on Hillion and Vermaelen, 2001.

‡ In the case of lookback options, the exercise price depends on the average price of the underlying asset for a certain number of days before the exercise unlike normal options.

- lowest price in the lookback period is $ 12.5; and
- discount is 20%.

An investor can convert the security into 1000/(0.8 * 12.5) = 100 shares. The value of the shares at a current price of $ 12.5 is $ 1250. The investor earns a 25% risk-free return. The result holds good for *any* stock price. The issuance of death spirals creates selling pressure from convert holders, who, in order to lock up a profit, short the stock and cover their position with converted common shares. The stock price in the case of Casmyn, for example, fell from $ 10 to 25 cents. Table 3.1 gives a small list of death-spiral issuers.

Table 3.1 List of Companies Issuing Death Spirals

Company	No. of issues
Swissray International	12
Cycomm International	8
CSL Lighting	7
Dynagen	7
Syquest	7
American Resources	7

Despite the potentially disastrous consequences who do companies issue death spirals? Death spirals, like ordinary convertibles, can be issued if a firm's stock is undervalued. In the case of ordinary convertibles, the conversion price is usually set near the current market price. If a company expects good news to arrive before the security holders are allowed to convert, it might be cheaper to issue death spirals with floating conversion price than ordinary convertibles with fixed conversion.

The CSFB deals typically split the bonds into two or more tranches, with the first tranche or Tranche 1 issued immediately. The CSFB usually has an option to require the next tranche to be issued on the same terms, called the additional tranche 1. That option in itself has a value, because if the share price rises after Tranche 1 is issued, then the CSFB benefits from the fact that the maximum conversion price has already been fixed. Often a third tranche, which CSFB call Tranche 2, can be issued at the option of the listed company, and this usually involves resetting the fixed conversion price based on a premium to the market price at the time of the new bond issue.

In recent deals, the CSFB has included something called the 'downside price', at a deep discount (typically 35%–40%) to the market. If the market price is at or below the downside price when bonds are presented for conversion, then the issuer has the right to redeem them instead, subject to payment of a premium (they always get their pound of flesh). However, if the issuer does not or cannot exercise that right then the conversion will proceed and the price may decline further. Note that the downside price is not actually a limit on the conversion price, because the 30-day lookback period allows the CSFB to convert at less than the downside price after the price has risen back above it.

They have also sometimes included a 'put price', at an even deeper discount (typically 50%–60%). If the market price is below this level, then the CSFB cannot convert the bonds but has the right to require redemption. If the market price reaches this level, then you can bet that the upside is limited so long as the CSFB has not called for redemption, because as soon as the price begins to recover, the conversion rights become exercisable again.

It is still possible that a share price will move upwards after the bond is issued, for example, if the earnings grow fast enough to offset the dilution of the share base, or if the issue size is relatively small compared with market capitalization, then the damage may not be as great and the overhang is smaller. Even in these circumstances, the dilution will still be a drag on the performance of the shares.

The CSFB deals usually include an option to subscribe new shares for cash worth about 15%–20% of the face value of the bonds, with an exercise price at a premium to the market price at the time the bonds and options are issued. In most cases, however, the share price falls due the overhang of the bonds, and the options are not exercised. Companies may be thinking that these options provide some kind of incentive for the CSFB not to drive the price down with rapid conversions, but history shows that the options are seldom exercised, and it is clear that the bulk of the profit comes from bond conversions.

Warrants

A warrant is an option that gives the holder the privilege of buying a specified number of shares of the company at a specified exercise price at any time on or before the expiration date. Warrants usually come as attachments to bonds to make an issue more attractive to investors. The debenture holder can exercise a warrant separately. Warrants can also be detached and separately listed on a stock exchange for trading purposes. The issuer of the warrant receives the price of the warrant at the time of the issue and the exercise price when the option is exercised. The company gets equity investment if the investor exercises the option. The uncertainty in the investor's reaction can affect further debt issuance by the company. In other words, if warrant holders do not exercise the option, the company may have to postpone further debt issuance due to inadequate equity base. A company contemplating on issuing equity to build equity may issue debentures with warrants instead of issuing straight equity if the shares are fully priced because issuing shares at a discount to the current market price will result in underpricing of *all* shares subsequently. The exercise price is determined by market conditions. An issue of warrant at a strike price lower than that expected by the company's management will not affect a growing company much in the sense that the value of the foregone capital in the present value terms will not be high.

A comparison between convertibles and warrants is in order.

- The conversion rights are inseparable in the case of convertibles. Warrants are separable from the bond and are usually listed on stock exchanges for trading.
- A warrant gives additional cash to the issuer when the holder exercises the right. A convertible does not.
- When convertibles are converted into shares, the associated debt is not repaid unlike in the case of a debt-warrant package.

Convertibles frequently come with call provision. The issuer can force conversion when the situation so demands. The warrant holders cannot be coaxed to exercise*. They may or may not exercise their option depending on what has happened to the underlying share price in the interim. The warrant holders will not exercise if the share price does not go up. So there is an element of uncertainty regarding the amount of equity the issuer gets. If cheap debt is the objective regardless of what happens to equity, a warrant with debt is a better choice.

Warrants are like exchange traded call options. But there are some differences:

- Call options are contracts between two individuals/entities whereas a warrant is a call option sold by the issuing company to the general investing public.
- When warrants are issued, the company receives the issue price.
- When warrants are exercised, the company receives the exercise price.
- When warrants are exercised, the company issues *new* shares.

In their simplest form warrants are call options. Their pay-off resembles the pay-off from a standard call option. But there is a difference. Assume that an all-equity company has S shares and W warrants outstanding. The warrants can be converted into r shares at an exercise price of x per share.

On the date of the maturity, the warrant holders will exercise if the value of the shares they receive is more than the exercise price. Upon exercise, they will receive Wr new shares for which they pay Wrx. Assume that the current market value of the company is V_0. After the exercise, the total number of shares increases to $S + Wr$ and the firm value to $V_0 + Wrx$.

$$\text{The fraction of all shares owned by the warrant holders} = \lambda = \frac{Wr}{A + Wr}$$

λ is the dilution factor of warrants.

---

* It is possible to design the package in such a way that the investor gets to exercise the warrant by turning in the bond. In other words, the package behaves like a synthetic convertible.

The value of the shares received by the warrant holders if they exercise equals to $\lambda(V_0 + Wrx)$.

Total exercise price = Wrx

So, the net value at maturity is: Max $[\lambda(V_0 + Wrx) - Wrx, 0]$.

The pay-off of a warrant can be written as a function of the company's assets V_0 if warrants are not exercised. The graph of the pay-off of a warrant looks exactly like that of a call option except that the slope is the value of dilution factor and not 1.

The price of a convertible depends on a number of factors like the underlying stock price and its volatility; time to maturity; coupon; call and put provision; dividend yield on the underlying stock and interest rates. Since convertibles are combinations of straight bonds and options, pricing them is a matter of valuing the individual components and adding them up. The value of the bond component is calculated by discounting coupon and principal payments by the prevailing yield on a comparable (similar investment rating) straight bond (or one that is issued by the same company). The value of the option component can be calculated by a standard option-pricing formula such as Black–Scholes*.

Value of a convertible bond = Straight value + Value of the call option on the stock.

Market Reaction to Security Offerings

To decide on a security, a company would want to know how the market typically reacts to a security offering. Exhibit 3.5 presents the results of academic research on market reaction to public issues. As can be seen, the market reaction to convertible offerings is more negative than non-convertible issues probably because a convertible leads to a dilution of EPS when the bond is converted.

EXHIBIT 3.5

Market Reaction to Security Offerings

(Average two-day abnormal returns and average sample size in parantheses.)

	Types of issuer	
Type of security	**Industrial**	**Utility**
Common stock	–3.14% (155)	–0.75% (403)
Preferred stock	–0.19% (28)	+.08% (249)
Straight bonds	–0.26% (248)	–0.13% (140)
Convertible bonds	–2.07% (73)	n.a.

Source: Smith 1986

* Convertibles can also be valued by the binomial option-pricing model. See Courtadon and Merrick (1983).

Securities Innovation

The last two decades have witnessed unprecedented innovation in the range of and manner in which firms issue securities. Just as engineers apply scientific principles to design new products and services, financial engineers apply principles of financial economics for the purpose of structuring, pricing and managing the risk of financial contracts.

Financial Engineering involves the design, development and implementation of innovative financial instruments and processes, and the formulation of creative solutions to problems in Corporate Finance.

Innovative instruments make financial markets more complete and efficient. For instance, greater efficiency could be achieved by reducing transaction costs. Financial markets can be made more complete by designing a new security whose contingent after-tax returns cannot be replicated by any combination of existing securities.

Financial Engineering involves three types of activities—(i) design of new financial instruments, (ii) development of new financial processes and (iii) providing creative solutions to problems in Corporate Finance. Index-linked bonds, on-line trading of securities and project finance are examples of the three activities, respectively.

WHAT DRIVES FINANCIAL INNOVATION?

Some academics consider financial innovations 'unpredictable improvements' that come into being as a result of regulatory and tax impulses (and not because of MBAs from A-rated business schools), while others consider innovative instruments and processes as attempts by companies to lessen the financial constraints they face. The factors responsible for financial innovation can be classified into 11 categories as shown in Exhibit 3.6. Financial engineering can be used not only in reducing financing costs and creating customized financial instruments, but also in advancing a company's strategic goals*. For instance, a company could control the volatility of output prices using Financial Engineering principles to differentiate its products when customers attach importance to reduced uncertainty in prices. Similarly, a company could hedge its exchange rate exposure and, hence, the volatility of the expected revenue stream to reduce the uncertainty in returns to shareholders.

---

* Tufano, Peter, How Financial Engineering Can Advance Corporate Strategy, ***Harvard Business Review***, Jan–Feb, 1996.

EXHIBIT 3.6

Factors Affecting Financial Innovation

1. Tax asymmetries that can be exploited to produce tax savings for the issuer, investors or both.
2. Transaction cost.
3. Agency cost.
4. Opportunities to reduce some form of risk or to reallocate risk from one market participant to another who is either less risk averse or else willing to bear the risk at a lower cost.
5. Opportunities to increase an asset's liquidity.
6. Regulatory and legislative changes.
7. Level and volatility of interest rates.
8. Level and volatility of prices.
9. Academic work that resulted in advances in financial theories or better understanding of the risk–return characteristics of existing class of securities.
10. Accounting benefits.
11. Technological factors and other factors.

Source: Finnerty 1988

New instruments can be classified into debt, equity, convertible or preferred stock categories. For instance, mandatory convertibles are a class of convertibles.* New securities can add value in several ways (Finnerty 1992):

Reduction in agency cost: Puttable bonds, for instance, enable investors to sell the bond back to the issuer if the issuer increases leverage beyond a certain level or when the control changes. Similarly, rating sensitive notes bear interest rates that change with the credit standing of the issuer.

Managing exchange rate and commodity price risk: Dual Currency Bonds (DCBS) are offered in one currency while the interest payments and redemption are made in another currency. The issuer offers to make interest and principal payments in some specified list of currencies. The investor has the option to choose the currency DCBs and, thus, reallocate currency risk. Likewise, commodity indexed bonds, bear coupon and principal payments are tied, to the price of a commodity to which the issuer has an exposure. The issuer's revenue declines when the price of the commodity falls. So does debt service. In other words, such bonds increase the debt capacity of the company.

Reducing transaction costs: Corporate bonds usually include a call provision that enables the issuing firm to redeem the issue before maturity by paying the

* Mandatory convertibles are discussed as separate section in this chapter.

bond holders. When the interest rates fall, the managers have the option of redeeming the issue and replacing it with a new issue. Because of the call provision, the issuer pays a premium over face value called the **call premium** that typically follows a declining schedule falling to zero a few years before maturity. Issuers are typically prohibited from redeeming the issue for a few years after the issue (call protection period).

Following two reasons are commonly cited for including the call provision:*

1. It enables managers to increase shareholder value by refunding the bond when the interest rates decline.
2. It enables companies to redeem when covenants become too restrictive.

The first reason assumes that managers have special expertise in forecasting interest rates, which is questionable. If they do, bond holders will recognize this over a period of time and price the call option accordingly. Since any gains to the issuer from refunding is a loss to the bond holder (because s/he has to accept a lower interest bond), we would expect the bond holders to demand higher interest rates on callable bonds when compared to non-callable bonds. If the higher interest payment cancels out the value of the call option, the issuer can be indifferent between paying a higher interest and including a call provision and issuing a non-callable bond. Further, lower quality bonds are more likely to have call provisions because the issuer can replace the bond when credit quality improves (because of which the interest is lower).

Most bond covenants restrict the issuer's investment and financing decisions. For instance, covenants prohibit the issuer from selling another secured bond or a merger. Due to such restrictions a firm may have to pass up a positive NPV project in future. One way to get around the covenants is to include a call provision.

Callable bonds are derivative embedded securities. A callable bond can be viewed as a non-callable bond on which the bondholder has written a call option to the issuer. From the issuer's perspective:

$$\text{Callable bond} = \text{Non-callable bond} - \text{Call option.}$$

The option embedded in the bond can be viewed as a call option (sold by the investor to the issuer) on the price of the bond with a strike price equal to the call price with an expiry date equal to the call dates. As is evident, the call option has multiple exercise dates prior to the final maturity of the option. So it is a *Bermudan style* option. The call option in the case of a callable bond is an embedded option that cannot be separated from the bond. The value of

* Alan Kraus, An Analysis of Call Provisions and the Corporate Refunding Decision, *Midland Corporate Finance Journal* , **1**, 1983.

the call option depends on the current and future levels of interest rates, slope of the term structure, volatility of interest rates, length of the call protection period, bond maturity and prepayment penalty (Pricing of Interest rate derivatives is beyond the scope of this book. Interested readers may refer to Ho and Lee (1986), Heath, Jarrow and Morton (1990), Black, Derman and Toy (1990).). Once an issuer has decided that it will include a call provision, it must then decide on the design of the call features such as the (schedule of) call price and the length of the call protection period because the required coupon (the spread over non-callables) depends on these. Intuitively, we would expect the following relationships to hold: the greater the volatility of the interest rates, the greater the spread; the steeper the term structure, the lower the spread[*]; and the shorter the call protection period, the higher is the spread. Refunding is not an easy decision. If interest rates decline after the call, the company loses; whereas if the company does not refund and the interest rates rise, the company still loses! Managers use rules of thumb to trigger a call to deal with this. For instance, one may call a bond as soon as the interest rate falls by a certain percentage points or when the savings exceed a certain minimum. Bond refunding involves significant transaction costs. In 1998, Tennessee Valley Authority issued an instrument called **Ratchet bonds**, which captures the advantages of callable bonds while at the same time eliminating the undesirable feature—transaction cost.[†] The coupon on the ratchet bond indexed to the yield on a specified treasury bond resets as long as the resulting rate is lower than the current rate. That is, ratchet bonds *ratchet* only downwards (the coupon can only decrease or remain the same). Since the coupon resets automatically, the issuer need not have to worry about the call decision or the transaction costs involved.

Reducing inflation risk: There are many securities whose cash flows are tied to an index such as a currency index or a general price index. Inflation indexed securities are designed to provide protection against increases in prices. Usually they are tied to a broad measure of prices such as the consumer price index (CPI) although the GDP deflator or a wholesale price index may be used. The choice depends on the needs of the issuer and the investor. The real return on these bonds is certain whereas in an ordinary bond, the nominal return is certain. In other words, inflation indexed bonds offer a fixed real return. There are two common types of bonds— (i) **capital indexed bonds (CIB)** and (ii) **interest indexed bonds (IIB)**. CIBs pay a fixed real coupon rate and a nominal principal that rises with inflation. Periodic coupon is calculated as the real coupon rate multiplied by inflation adjusted principal. The inflation adjusted principal itself is paid at maturity. A tabular

[*] When the term structure is negative, there is a greater likelihood of the bond being called.
[†] See Kalotay , Andrew and Leslie Abreo, Ratchet Bonds : Maximum Refunding Efficiency at Minimum Transaction Cost , *Journal of Applied Corporate Finance*, **12**, 1, (Spring), 1999.

representation of cash flows of a hypothetical five year, 5% CIB issued by the Government of India assuming a certain inflation scenario is given here in tabular form.

Year	Real coupon (1)	Inflation rate (2)	Compounded inflation (3)	Coupon payment (4) (1) * (3)	Coupon indexation (5) (4) − (1)	Redemption payment (6) =100 * (3)
1	5	6	1.06	5.3	0.3	
2	5	5	1.113	5.565	0.565	
3	5	5	1.168	5.84	0.84	
4	5	4	1.214	6.07	1.07	
5	5	4.5	1.269	6.345	1.345	126.90

Interest indexed bonds pay a fixed coupon and an indexation of the fixed principal every year. The principal repayment at maturity is, however, the nominal principal as is the case with any bond. The inflation adjustment is made to the coupon by adding the inflation rate to the coupon on the bond.

The cash flows for an IIB are given here in tabular form.

Year	Real coupon (1)	Inflation rate (2)	Coupon payment (3) = (1) + (3)	Principal indexation (4) = (2)	Redemption payment (5) 100*(3)
1	5	6	11	6	
2	5	5	10	5	
3	5	5	10	5	
4	5	4	9	4	
5	5	4.5	9.5	4.5	100

Floating rate instruments: These are debt securities whose coupon rates vary over time according to a predetermined formula. The coupon rate is pegged to a reference rate such as the Prime Rate or London Inter Bank Offered Rate (LIBOR) or T-Bill rate. The coupon rate equals the reference rate plus a mark up to reflect the credit risk of the issuer. The coupon rate is reset at regular intervals, say, three months. Thus, the coupon on floating rate instruments 'float'. The coupon is generally semi-annual. The premium over the reference rate may decline over time. For instance, the coupon might be a reference rate plus 1.05% for the first five years, 1% for the next five years and so on. There is a maximum and minimum within which the coupon can fluctuate. They can also have call and conversion features, which enable the issuer to redeem the issue on or after a pre-specified date at pre-specified prices and enable the investor to exchange the instrument to a fixed rate instrument with predetermined coupon and maturity.

Floating rate notes make coupon payments that increase with the level of interest rates, while inverse floaters make coupon payments that decrease with the level of interest rates. Inverse floaters or bull floaters have reset formulas at some fixed rate minus the reference rate. The coupon on the instrument rises when LIBOR falls. For instance, the reset formula may be 15% LIBOR. These securities attract investors who are bullish on bond prices because the coupon rate moves inversely to the market rate. Bear floaters, on the other hand, reset at a multiple of the reference rate minus some fixed rate. For instance, the reset formula could be twice the LIBOR minus 9.12%. The investors who are bearish on bond prices would be attracted to such securities because the coupon rate rises by more than the increase in the market rate.

One characteristic of inverse floaters is that their prices rise more than those on fixed rate bonds of same maturity. Likewise, when the rates rise, the investors receive lower coupon. Who would issue inverse floaters? Those companies which have a floating rate exposure (e.g. finance companies are exposed to rise in deposit rates) would want to issue an inverse floater to smooth out the cost of funds. Combining a floater and an inverse floater cancels the variable reference rate giving rise to a fixed rate liability. These instruments are becoming popular in emerging markets as well.

Variable Maturity Term Loan

Floating rate instruments and loans enable companies to exploit fall in interest rates but increase the uncertainty in debt service and cost of capital. Fixed payment, fixed maturity term loans turn out to be expensive if interest rates fall after locking into the loan. A financial innovation in the US, called **Fixed Payment Variable Maturity (FPVM) loan***, spreads the risk of interest rate fluctuation between the lender and the borrower (unlike a floating rate loan in which the entire interest rate risk is borne by the borrower) while allowing for a fixed debt service schedule. But the maturity is not fixed. In other words, a fixed payment variable maturity loan lies in between fixed rate, fixed maturity loans and floating rate, fixed maturity loans. Here is how it works: consider a company that needs a \$ 10 million loan. It can opt for the standard floating rate loan at an interest rate of prime rate plus 1%, say. As the prime rate fluctuates, the interest rate on the loan also fluctuates. The company will have to make annual payments of \$ 2 million for five years towards the principal repayment as well as variable interest payments starting from year 1 through year 5. Let us suppose the actual interest rates (Prime + 1%) turn out to be as tabulated here:

---

* Boettcher, James and Fernando Sotelino, A look at the variable maturity loan, *Harvard Business Review*, May–June, 1982.

Year	Interest (%)
1	11
2	12
3	13
4	12
5	12

Average = 12%.

The debt service would be of the following tabular form:

(in $ '000)

Year	Interest on outstanding principal	Principal	Total payment
1	11	20	31.00
2	9.60	20	29.60
3	7.80	20	27.80
4	4.80	20	24.80
5	2.40	20	22.40

This is a standard floating rate loan. The fixed annual payment under FPVM would be then

$$\frac{\text{Principal}}{\text{PVIFA}(12{,}5)} = \frac{10 \text{ million}}{3.605} = \$\,2.773 \text{ million}$$

The discount rate is the *expected average* interest rate. The company pays this fixed amount irrespective of what the actual interest rate would be. The debt service in the case of FPVM looks like as tabulated here:

Year	Amount (million)	Interest	Principal
1	2.773	X_1	P_1
2	2.773	X_2	P_2
N	2.773	X_n	P_n

The interest paid in any year depends on how rates evolve. The balance is the principal. The interest for the next year is calculated on the outstanding balance. The debt service remains fixed irrespective of what the actual interest rate is. The higher the interest rate, the greater the proportion of the fixed payment that would go towards the interest and lower the principal amortized.

As prime rate falls, the principal amortized increases; the principal decreases as prime increases. The final maturity gets lengthened if the actual interests are higher and gets contracted if the actual interest rates are lower. But the sensitivity of the tenor to changes is low unless the swings in interest rates are dramatic.

ASSET SECURITIZATION

Companies short of cash due to selling goods on credit may resort to what is known as *securitization* to realize cash. **Securitization** is a process by which illiquid assets can be transformed into liquid form and distributed to a broad range of investors through capital market. It involves packaging of loans and receivables, and the underwriting and sale of these packages to investors in the form of securities which are collateralized by the underlying assets and their associated income stream. A number of homogeneous receivables are pooled together to form a basket and then sold or 'passed through' to another institution called **Special Purpose Vehicle (SPV)**. The assets are removed from the balance sheet of the originator. The SPV then unbundles these units and sells them to the investors. These securities are called **Pass-Through Certificates** (PTC). The PTC is designed in such a way that the cash outflow in the form of interest and redemption of PTC synchronize with the aggregate inflow of interest and principal of the basket of loans.

The structure of securitization is shown in Exhibit 3.7.

EXHIBIT 3.7

Structure of Securitization

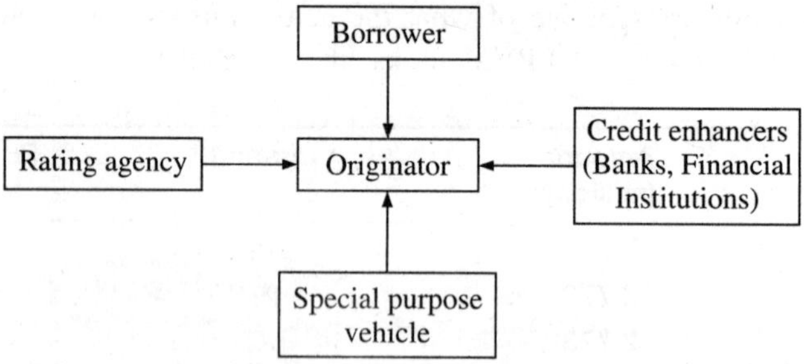

The loans or other financial claims are assigned to a SPV which in turn issues one or more debt instruments whose interest and principal payments are dependent on the cash flows coming from the underlying instruments. The asset backed instruments may take a wide range of forms. They may pay interest at fixed or floating rates; they may be short or long in term; they may have a fixed maturity or be pre-payable or callable under a variety of conditions. Some are publicly issued or privately placed; some denominated in local currency and others in foreign currency. Commercial banks, finance companies and corporations constitute the principal originators of the loans. A great majority of these instruments are held by institutional investors, such as insurance companies, mutual funds, pension funds and the like.

An Example

In 1999, the state government of Karnataka in India approached Karnataka State Financial Corporation (KSFC) to raise INR 2.3 billion on behalf of the government. The proceeds were supposed to be used to provide subsidy to small-scale units in the priority sector. Consequently, KSFC agreed to issue bonds. These bonds were taxable, unsecured, redeemable and non-convertible; had a tenor of four years and carried an interest rate of 13.5%, payable semi-annually. The government had agreed to make interest and principal payments on a monthly basis. The issue was backed by a letter of comfort from the government. KSFC, however, could raise only INR 1.6 billion as against the requirement of INR 2.30 billion. As a result, KSFC agreed to make good the shortfall by contributing the balance INR 700 million (the excess borrowing of the corporation which it had not deployed elsewhere). In 2000–2001, KSFC decided to securitize the receivables due from bondholders and the Karnataka government. Between the proposals from two companies, KSFC short listed SBI Capital Markets, a leading investment bank. SBI Caps had proposed to issue PTC with a tenor of one and a half years at an indicative coupon of 12.5%–12.75%. After discussing with SBI Caps, KSFC decided to set up a separate trust called Karnataka State Finance Corporation Asset Management Trust and assigned its receivables of INR 700 million. The PTCs would represent the investor's proportional beneficial interest in the receivables from the government. The investor's in the certificates are exposed to the performance of the government. Consequently, a rating is normally required. Since the government was already rated A+ by CRISIL (a credit rating agency in India), no new rating was obtained.

The investors in PTCs are exposed to risks other than the non-performance of the underlying asset. So some form of credit enhancement is required to make the issue attractive. In the case of KSFCAMT PTCs, a senior, A-class PTCs, and a junior B-class PTCs were created. The B-class PTCs are subordinated in terms of interest and principal payment to A-class PTCs. KSFCAMT issued Rs 50 million worth B-class PTCs to KSFC.

The government makes payments monthly whereas the PTCs are serviced semi-annually. So the trust should reinvest the proceeds in short-term deposits.

ADDRESSING INFORMATION ASYMMETRY

Mandatory Convertibles

Mandatory convertibles are equity-linked securities that pay a higher dividend (compared to the company's common stock) for a certain number of years and then get converted into common shares on a specified date. These securities have limited capital appreciation potential. In other words, the issuer puts a cap on the appreciation by specifying the conversion terms.

Morgan Stanley's PERCS and PEPS, Merrill Lynch's PRIDES, Salomon Brothers' DECS and Goldman Sachs' ACES are examples of mandatory convertibles.* They unlike ordinary convertibles, are often issued by established large issuers. But the purpose is similar. They help large, high leveraged companies that are seeking equity capital, but want to avoid unnecessary dilution (Arzac 1997).

Avon Products Inc was one of the earliest to issue PERCS (Tiemann 1989, Emery and Finnerty 1995). In 1988, Avon announced a dividend reduction and simultaneously offered to exchange one share of a new $ 2.00 PERCS for each of to 18 million of Avon's shares that would pay dividends at the former dividend rate on the common stock. The new preferred would pay cumulative quarterly dividends of 50 cents accrued from 1 September 1988 to 1 September 1991†. The preferred shares would be mandatorily redeemed on the expiry date‡. The holders would receive one common share for every PERCS share if the price of the stock was less than $ 31.50 or $ 31.50 worth of common stock per PERCS share if the common stock was above that price. As with any preferred stock, the dividend is cumulative but the company cannot pay dividends to shareholders if the preferred dividend is in arrears. Citicorp, Times Mirror and several other companies have issued PERCS in the recent years.

From the shareholders perspective there may be no real difference between alternate dividend plans but drastic reductions in dividends can have a dramatic

---

* PERCS is the acronym for Preferred Equity Redemption Cumulative Stock; PEPS is Preferred Equity Participation Securities; DECS is Debt Exchangeable for Common Stock; PRIDES is Preferred Redeemable Increased Dividend Securities; ACES is Automatically Convertible Enhanced Securities.

† Avon was paying $ 1.0 on common when it announced the PERCS issue.

‡ The company also retained the option of redeeming the issue at any time before the expiry date according to a declining schedule. An issuer is likely to call the PERCS if the share price is above the call price. Since the issue is callable, there is a possibility that the investor may not receive even a single dividend payment. To offset any potential dividend loss, the call prices usually follow a declining schedule. That is, the nearest call price will be the highest, the second siightly lower and so on. The difference between the call price and the purchase price (i.e. capital gain) determines the return to PERCS holders. The call price schedule is designed in such a way that the return to the investor is the same regardless of whether the issue is called or not.

impact on the stock price and firm value. Avon products wanted to both cut the dividend and reassure the investors that the growth prospect for the company is indeed bright. The company exchanged PERCS for common and reduced the dividend on the common by 50%.

A PERCS is like a covered call write*. The covered call writing is being long, underlying instrument (say stock) and being short a call on that instrument. The maximum profit potential is equal to the strike price of the option minus the price of the underlying instrument plus the call price. The short call limits the profit potential of the underlying asset but it buffers the long position from the losses by the amount of the premium received. The holders of PERCS enjoy higher dividends for a certain number of years (three, in the case of Avon) and in return give up a call option.
That is

$$P_p = P + PV\,[D_p - D_s] - \text{Call}$$

where P_p is the price of PERCS, D_p and D_s are dividend payments on the PERCS and common stock respectively, P is the current market price of the share and Call is the value of the call option on the company's stock expiring at the PERCS maturity.

To value the excess dividend stream (i.e. find the present value of the excess dividend stream), one should come up with a suitable discount rate. If we assume that the stream is risk free, we may use the treasury rate. But the stream is unlikely to be risk free. The rate paid by the company on the subordinated notes with approximately the same duration as PERCS dividend might be used to discount the dividend stream.

The value of the call option can be calculated by the Black–Scholes formula based on the following parameters:

1. Strike price equal to cap price
2. Current stock price
3. Time to expiration
4. Risk free rate of interest
5. Volatility

The option value can be calculated using historical or implied volatility. The exercise may be replicated for a range of stock prices and volatilities.

Recently, Anthem Electronics issued a mandatory convertible. The details of the issue are given as follows:

1. Size of the issue : $ 200 million
2. Deal launch date : 3 October 2001
3. Book runner : Goldman Sachs
4. Maturity : 3 years

* A standard derivatives text would discuss options and option strategies in greater detail.

5.	Dividend rate	: 6%–6.5%
6.	Premium	: 18%–22%
7.	Hard call protection	: 3 years
8.	Common stock price	: $ 33–$ 37
9.	Common dividend yield	: 0
10.	Approx. stock market	: $ 1 billion capitalization

Participating Equity Preferred Shares (PEPS) are convertible securities designed to provide investors with high current income and equity participation. These securities mandatorily convert into shares or mature in 3–5 years. The issue price is set equal to the price of the stock into which it converts and conversion premiums range from 18 to 23%. The current yield on the security is usually 5%–7% more than the dividend yield on the underlying common stock. The maximum number of shares PEPS holders will typically receive is one. The characteristics of a PEPS are described as follows:

1. The conversion price of the PEPS is lower than the conversion price of a normal convertible. Consequently, PEPS has more equity sensitivity than an ordinary convertible.
2. A PEPS has a lower bond floor than an ordinary convertible but a higher coupon.
3. PEPS is usually issued by mid-large cap companies aimed at yield-oriented investors.
4. By design, the PEPS units offer low downside protection.
5. They mandatorily convert into stock or mature in 3–5 years.
6. These are suitable for investors who have a bullish view on the common stock and in need of common stock.
7. Since they have higher equity content than ordinary convertibles, the rating agencies consider them 'equity like'.
8. The issuer gets a tax shield on the coupon.
9. The issue price of the PEPS equals the prevailing stock price.
10. The maturity is usually 3–5 years.

The conversion premium in the case of PEPS, unlike ordinary convertibles, is not fixed because the conversion ratio (the number of shares investors receive by converting) is not fixed. It depends on the underlying stock price upon maturity.

A typical pay-off from a PEPS is shown in Figure 3.3.

The PEPS price is on the *y*-axis. A typical design provides 1.0 share if the stock price at maturity is below the issue price, a fraction of a share equal to the ratio of the issue price to the price at maturity if the stock price is in between the issue price and the conversion price; and a minimum number of

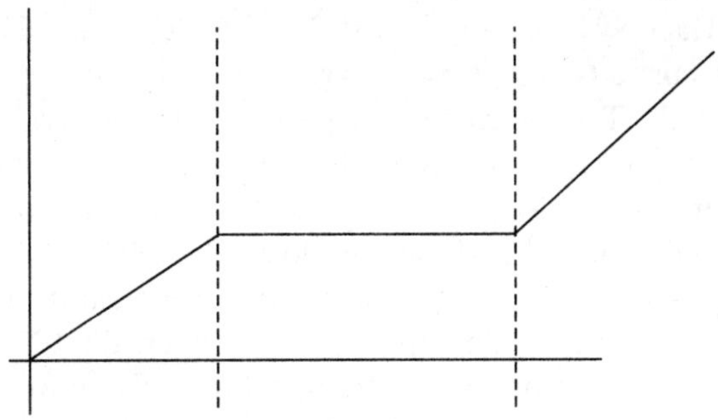

Figure 3.3 Pay-off from a PEPS.

shares (say 0.8) if the price at maturity is above the conversion price. Assume that the issue price is Rs 20 and the conversion price is Rs 25. If the ending stock price is Rs 40, an investor would get 0.8 shares and his investment is worth 0.8 * 40 = Rs 32.

A PEPS, by design, has a much higher coupon yield than the dividend yield on the underlying common stock (yield advantage). So this instrument is for those investors who need high current income and have a favourable view on the underlying common stock. Likewise the issuer finds the instrument attractive because the conversion ratio declines as the price increases. In other words, the issuer shares the upside with the investors. To that extent the instrument aligns the interests of both the issuers and the investors. The flip side is that the issuer has to pay a higher coupon. The yield advantage is typically 5%–7%. A PEPS is a combination of the following:

- The underlying common stock
- Plus (out-of-the money call struck on the stock at the conversion price) * conversion ratio
- Minus at-the-money call struck on the stock at issue price
- Present value of incremental income over the common dividend.

Typical terms of a PEPS issue

1. Issue price : $ 30
2. Underlying stock price : $ 30
3. Conversion premium : 20%
4. Min. conversion ratio : 0.83
5. Max. conversion ratio : 1.0
6. PEPS yield : 8%
7. Common yield : 3%
8. Term to maturity : 4 years

Electronic Data Systems has issued 7.625% PEPS due 17 August 2004. The instrument converts into 0.843 shares of EDS below 59.31, or 0.6996 shares above 71.47. The instrument provides quarterly dividend of $ 0.150. The initial conversion is $ 71.47. In 2001 about $ 708.63 million worth of PEPS issues were outstanding. In 1985, Merrill Lynch introduced a complex security christened Liquid Yield Option Notes (LYON)*. A LYON is a zero coupon, callable, convertible and puttable bond. The instrument is issued at a discount from the par value. The investor can convert the LYON into a fixed number of shares (conversion ratio). The instrument also provides the investor an option to put the bond at predetermined strike prices on pre-specified dates. Finally, the issuer has the option to call the bond at fixed exercise prices. Merrill Lynch has developed a model to value LYONs on the basis of the following:

1. Interest rate of intermediate-term bond
2. Stock price
3. Stock price volatility
4. Dividend yield
5. LYON maturity
6. Conversion ratio
7. Face value
8. Call prices
9. Put prices

ALZA is an emerging pharmaceutical company with leading drug delivery technologies. The company had issued $ 1090 million (face value), 0.0% LYONs in 2000. The security is due on 28 July 2020. The initial conversion price was set at $ 78.60 (31% premium). ALZA was acquired by Johnson & Johnson (J&J) in June, 2001. Consequently, the security converts into 13.7465 shares of J&J. Since the instrument is a zero coupon note, the first coupon will be paid on 28 July 2020. The coupon accrues at 3% (semi-annual). That is, the original yield to maturity is 3%. The security has no soft call provision and is freely callable starting 28 july 2003 at an initial price of 60.277% of par ascending to 100% of par over 17 years. The security is puttable back to J&J starting on 28 July 2003 at 60.277% of par, ascending to 81.185% of par on 28 July 2013.

In 1993, Salomon Brothers issued a equity-linked debt issue called **Equity-Linked Securities** (ELKS) whose returns are tied to the performance of Digital Equipment Corporation's common stock. ELKS are fixed-income,

---

* Coxe, T. Anne, Convertible Structures: Evolution Continues, in Izzy Nelken, (ed.), *Handbook of Hybrid Instruments*, Wiley, New York, 2001.
McConnell, John and Eduardo Schwartz, LYON Taming, *Journal of Finance*, July, 1986.

intermediate term, equity-linked debt securities. Interest on each ELK is payable quarterly. Unlike ordinary debt, the principal payable upon maturity is not fixed in the case of ELKS but is based on the price of DEC common stock. The principal amount payable at maturity will equal the lesser of the following:

1. 135% of the issue price
2. The average closing price of the DEC common stock for the 10 trading days immediately prior to maturity

Since the pay-off of an ELK is based on the average stock price, it is an average-price Asian option.

In 1986 Salomon Brothers issued a new instrument christened SPIN (S&P 500 Indexed Note). A SPIN is a four year, 2% coupon bond which at maturity pays its holder the following:

1. The principal amount of $ 1000 per bond and accrued interest plus.
2. The excess (if any) of the S&P index value over the initial (exercise) value of the index times some predetermined multiplier.

So a SPIN is a combination of a bond and a call option on the S&P index. The call option had the following features:

(a) Exercise price = $ 270.38
(b) Multiplier (the number of call options that the investor receives for every $ 1000 bond principal held) = 3.6985
(c) Option is European type

$$\text{SPIN} = \text{Bond} + (\text{Call option} * \text{Multiplier})$$

The bond component can be valued using a bond valuation model adjusted for dividends. The discount rate to be used is the yield on comparable bonds with similar coupon and maturity. The option component can be valued using the Black–Scholes model adjusted for dividends.

Some companies have issued a variant of converts called **exchangeable bonds** which give the investor an option to convert the bond into stock of *another* company. The issuer deposits sufficient number of convert firm's shares in an escrow account to satisfy the conversion requirement. Exchangeable bonds enable a company to divest a block of stock in another company. Recently AT&T was considering a bond exchangeable into Cablevision*. The details of the issue are given as follows:

1. Deal launch date: 8 October 2001
2. Size: $ 850 million

---

* This is a mandatory convertible.

3. Coupon: 6.5%–7.0%
4. Premium: 18%–22%
5. Maturity: 3 years
6. Convertible par amount: $ 50
7. Hard call protection: 3 years
8. Common stock price: $ 38.96

Exchangeable bonds come with a repurchase guarantee. If the convert firm's stock does not appreciate sufficiently, the investors continue to hold the bond (i.e. investors are entitled for interest and principal payments) and the issuer is left with the stock. In January 2000, Hutchison Whampoa of Hong Kong issued a $ 2.5 billion, three year, bond exchangeable into 536 million Vodafone shares to reduce its holding to 1.7% in steps*. The bond was issued at a premium of £ 3.10 apparently to make a bullish statement that the shares of Vodafone will perform. However, the price of Vodafone share did fall upon announcement making the bond more expensive.

SWORD Financing

Biotech firms depend on innovation for obtaining the competitive edge necessary to survive. Innovation is risky because of uncertainty about commercial viability and regulatory approval of new products. Usually, these companies will not have adequate internal resources because of which external finance is the only alternative. Often these companies suffer from adverse selection problem due to which external financing is expensive.

In a SWORD offering†, a bio-technology company creates an affiliate that raises money by selling units consisting of its own stock and warrants on the original or parent company's stock. That is, each SWORD unit contains one share of callable common stock and one warrant to purchase one share of the parent's common stock. The affiliate then hands over the proceeds to the parent company as payment for research expenses. In return, the affiliate enjoys exclusive rights to the drugs and technologies developed through the research it funds. The bio-tech company holds call options on the affiliate's stock. If the research is successful, the parent buys the sponsor equity at the price set by the repurchase option price, thus acquiring the technology rights. If the research is not successful, the company does not buy the sponsoring entity. A SWORD structure is given in Figure 3.4.

---

* "Hutch did it Again", *Euromoney*, February 2001.

† SWORD is the acronym for Stock with Warrants for financing Off-balance Sheet Research and Development expenditures.

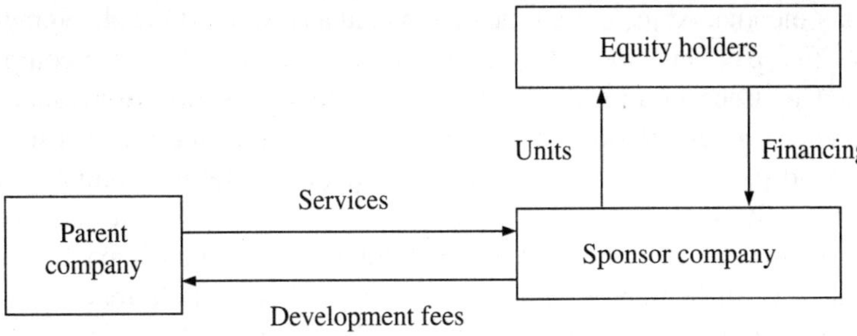

Figure 3.4 A SWORD structure.

A SWORD structure involves contracts between the parties involved just like project financing. The technology license agreement grants the sponsor the right to use the technology associated with the product development. The services agreement binds the parent to provide management and administrative services to the sponsor throughout the development process. The development contract stipulates that the parent carry out the product development at its existing facilities.

Puttable Stock

In a puttable stock, the investors buy packages composed of a share of common stock and a right to buy more stock if the stock price of the issuing firm falls below a certain level. The issuer is obligated to give additional shares if the market price falls below the guaranteed price at the end of a specified period of time, say, two years. From the investors' perspective, the puttable stock behaves like a convertible: they share in the upside but the downside is limited. Puttable stocks are considered equity by regulators in the USA. The puttable stock was first issued by Arley Merchandise Corporation with the assistance of Drexel Burnham Lambert. The Arley units were offered at \$ 8 with an accompanying right to put the stock back at \$ 8 after two years. Since the investor can exercise the option only upon expiration, it is a European-type option.

Puttable stocks, like converts, address information asymmetry and agency issues. If a company's management feels that it cannot get the right price because of information asymmetry, they may sell a puttable stock instead of ordinary stock. An example will clarify the point. Assume that a company's management expects \$ 8 for the stock but the investors are willing to pay only \$ 6, they may issue a puttable stock at \$ 8 with a right to put the stock back at \$ 8.

Taxes and Other Stimuli to Innovation

Companies, for obvious reasons, strive to lower the tax burden. One way to achieve it is to design securities that are debt like so that the payment is made from pre-tax income. At the same time they would also want to avoid commitment to pre-specified payments as in the case of bonds. In other words, the companies would want to issue equity-like instruments without the tax disadvantage.

Preference shares, as opposed to ordinary shares, entitle the investors for fixed dividend payments. The preference dividend paid by the company is not tax deductible. It is paid out of after-tax profits. Often, the preferred stock is compared with debt as both preference dividends and interest payments are fixed in nature. Since interest is tax deductible, whereas preference dividend is not, the preference shares are less popular than straight debt. The managers tend to forget that there is an important distinction between interest payments on bonds and dividend payments on preference shares. While suspension of preference dividend might be unpleasant, the default on a legal contract such as bonds can drive a company to insolvency. The management will be more comfortable with preferred dividends than it will be with the same amount of interest. Some favour preferred stock because rating agencies and analysts may view preferred stock as 'equity like'. But this benefit is at best illusory.

The different tax rates on capital gains, dividend and interest income leads to different tax clienteles. In the USA, for example, 70% of the dividends received by the corporations are tax exempt. So the corporations will be better off receiving dividends of preferred stock rather than interest on debt or capital gains associated with common stock.

Dividend payments are not tax deductible whereas interest payments are. The tax advantage of debt depends on its tax status. This advantage will be more important for a profitable firm than for a non–profitable firm. Empirical studies of preferred stock issuers and investors find that many preferred stock issuing firms have a lower effective rate than industry average and corporations purchasing preferreds have a significantly higher tax rates than the industry average. The same studies find that the percentage of preferred stock in the capital structure decreases as the profitability and tax rate increase.

Due to the tax advantage of preferred dividends vis-à-vis interest on bonds, we would expect the yields on preferred stock to be lower than those on bonds. But tax is not the only consideration. There are many differences between preferred stocks and bonds. For example, there is a difference in the timing of cash flows. Preferred stocks may pay dividends quarterly whereas interest on bonds is paid semi-annually or annually[*].

In 1993 Goldman Sachs introduced a type of preferred stock called Monthly Income Preferred Stock (MIPS)[†]. The periodic payments (dividends)

[*] Estimation of credit risk premium for preferred stock is some what complex and beyond the scope of the book. Interested readers may refer to Fons (1994) and Crabbe (1996).

[†] Irvine, Paul and James Rosenfield, Raising Capital Using Monthly Income preferred Stock: Market Reaction and Implications for Capital Structure Theory, *Financial Management*, Summer, 2000.

Khanna, Arun and John McConnell, "MIPS, QUIPS and TOPrS: Old Wine in New Bottle, *Journal of Applied Corporate Finance*, **11**, (1, Spring), 1998.

made on these securities are tax deductible unlike conventional preferred stock. Because of the tax deductibility these securities have the advantages of debt with no disadvantage—bankruptcy cost, because, in the case of preferred stock, the issuer cannot be forced into bankruptcy when the issuer fails to make a payment. The rating agencies consider these securities preferred stock. To issue MIPS, a company creates a special purpose vehicle, which in turn issues MIPS to investors.

The subsidiary then lends the proceeds to the parent. The parent's interest payments to the subsidiary are tax deductible and the subsidiary's interest income is not taxable because the subsidiary is a tax-free entity. The subsidiary uses the interest payments made by the parent to pay the dividends to the preferred stockholders. The parent company has the option of deferring interest payments if the situation warrants subject to a maximum of, say, five years. The interest payments are cumulative.

Newell Rubbermaid, for instance, has issued 5.25% QUIPS (Quarterly Income Preferred Stock) due 1 December 2027. The instrument has a face value of $ 50 and converts into 0.9865 shares. The instrument pays a quarterly dividend of $ 0.210 USX has issued 8.75% Cumulative Monthly Income Preferred Shares (CMIPS) and 6.75% convertible quarterly income preferred shares through a wholly owned subsidiary, USX Capital Trust.

The dividend payment on conventional preferred stock is fixed. A class of preference shares, called *adjustable rate preferred stock*, allow for quarterly resetting of dividends. The dividend is reset to reflect changes in money market yields. Another class of preferred stock, called *auction rate preferred stock*, allows for more frequent resetting of dividends.

A convertible preferred stock also has features similar to a convertible bond. However, a convertible preferred stock is subordinated to debt of the issuing company. It typically offers a coupon of 6–7%. A convertible preferred typically pays a cash coupon on a quarterly basis and is also perpetual or with a long maturity. The rating agencies like Standard & Poor's assign equity content based on the instrument's features such as the extent of subordination, interest deferral feature, tenor, etc. (on a scale of 0% – 100%). A convertible preferred stock can either be structured as a perpetual preferred stock or a 30-year stock issued via a Delaware Business Trust. Continental Airlines, for instance, has issued 6.00% trust convertible preferred with a face value of $ 50. The instrument converts into 0.8333 shares of Continental. The initial conversion price was $ 60. The security is due on 15 November 2030.

Unbundled Stock Units

In December 1988 American Express, Dow Chemical, Pfizer and Sara Lee announced plans to offer 'Unbundled Stock Units' (USUs). Holders of shares in these companies could surrender their shares in exchange for USUs. In exchange for the shares, the shareholders would get three certificates representing ownership of USUs . The units could be unbundled and traded separately. For each USU, the three different claims were: an Equity Appreciation Certificate (EAC), an Incremental Dividend Preferred (IDP) share, a Priority Income Claim (PIC). The PIC was entitled to quarterly dividends equal to the current dividend on the common. This dividend was to be continued even if the dividend on the common was increased or decreased. The IDP was entitled to dividend equal to any amount by which the common dividend was raised above the current amount. If the dividend on the common was cut, the IDP received no dividends. The EAC received no dividends. The trust was to be dissolved after 30 years. At that time the PIC entitled to a balloon specified in the contract. The IDP holders were paid a nominal sum. The EAC holders would receive excess of the stock price above the PIC and IDP guarantees. The cash flows for the three claims are given as follows:

PIC: For 30 years, the PIC would receive quarterly interest payments equal in amount to the current common dividend. It would also get a balloon payment at the end of 30 years. The interest on PIC would be tax deductible for the company.

IDP: For 30 years, the IDP was entitled to quarterly dividend payments equal to the excess of common dividend over the current dividend. After 30 years, the IDP would receive a small residual payment.

EAC: No payment for 30 years. After 30 years EAC would receive the amount by which the stock price exceeded the payments to the PIC and IDP shares.

For the sake of illustration let us use the American Express data*. Before the announcement of the issue, American Express shares were trading at $ 26.875 and had an annual dividend of 84 cents per year (or 21 cents per quarter). The balloon payment was $ 75. The IDP terminal payment was $ 2 at the end of thirty years.

Other information:

Annual interest rate = 9.8% compounded semi-annually

Annual log standard deviation of stock returns = 33%

The PIC is entitled to quarterly payments of 21 cents for 30 years and a final payment of $ 75. Assuming no default, discount these at a *quarterly* rate. We cannot use 9.8% since it is a *annual* rate compounded *semi-annually*.

$$\text{Quarterly interest rate} = (1 + 0.049)^{1/2} - 1 = 2.42\%$$

$$\text{PIC value} = \frac{75}{(1.0242)^{120}} + \sum_{i=1}^{120} \frac{0.21}{1.0242^{i}}$$

$$= \$\ 12.435$$

* This example is based on an unpublished manuscript by Professor Jonathan Ingersoll of Yale University.

The EAC is entitled to everything that remains after the PIC and IDP are paid their promised $ 75 and $ 2. That is, the EAC is a 30 year European call option on American Express Stock with a strike price of 75 + 2 = 77.

The option can be valued by the Black–Scholes formula. Strike price, $X = 77$, $S = 26.875$, $T = 30$ years, $\sigma = 33\%$, $r = 9.57\%$ and dividend yield $= y = 0.21/26.875 = 0.7814\%$, $n = 30 * 4 = 120$ periods. This is equal to 8.145.

$$\text{IDP value} = \frac{2}{1.0242^{120}} = 0.113$$

The dividend payment to the IDP can be valued as a call option.

$$\text{Each payment} = \text{Max}\ (yS - 0.21,\ 0).$$

Each dividend can be like an option on y shares with a strike price of 21 cents. Alternatively, the pay-off is

$$y.\ \text{Max}(S - 26\ 7/8,\ 0)$$

$$= \$\ 9.743$$

$$\text{IDP value} = 9.743 + 0.113 = 9.856$$

$$\text{The total value of the USU} = 12.435 + 9.856 + 8.145$$

As can be seen, the USU is worth more than the share. An obvious benefit to the corporation is the tax deductibility of interest payments. The 21 cents in dividends would be replaced by 21 cents in interest payments. The tax benefit for the issuer can be valued as a quarterly stream.

$$\text{Tax savings} = T * 0.21 * \text{PVIFA}_{r,\,120}$$

MANAGING ISSUER'S EXPOSURE

The financial environment is a lot more volatile today than it was a decade back. The volatility in interest rates, exchange rates and commodity prices give rise to an increased risk exposure. In this chapter, currency and interest rate swaps used to manage currency and interest rate exposure are discussed. Chapter 6, devoted to risk management, develops a more formal framework for analysing a company's risk exposure and implementing a risk management strategy.

A swap is an agreement to a future exchange of one stream of cash flows for another. Two common types of swaps are: *currency swaps* in which one currency is exchanged for another at pre-specified terms on one or more pre specified future dates, and *interest rate swaps* in which one type of interest rate (e.g. fixed rate) is exchanged for another (e.g. floating rate). Swaps are commonly used by companies and financial institutions to hedge risk or to speculate to make a profit.

A swap is a privately negotiated agreement between two parties in which both the parties are obligated to exchange specified cash flows at periodic intervals for a fixed period of time. A party that intends to swap need not search for a counter party with matching needs. To make our life simple there are swap dealers who take the other side of the transaction. Swap dealers make a profit by charging a fee or by the difference in a bid-ask spread.

Currency Swap

A **currency swap** is an agreement between two parties to exchange a given amount of one currency for another and to repay these currencies with interest in the future. To illustrate, consider a US company that has borrowed SFr 200 million at 6% but intends to transform this liability into dollars. At the same time, another Swiss company wishes to convert a $ 100 million debt bearing 8% interest into Swiss franc liability. Both liabilities have a four year maturity. Since the hedging needs of these companies are matching, a mutually beneficial swap can be arranged in which the US company pays 8% interest on dollars to the counterparty for four years and the $ 100 million principal at maturity; and the counterparty pays 6% interest on SFr for four years plus SFr 200 million at maturity.

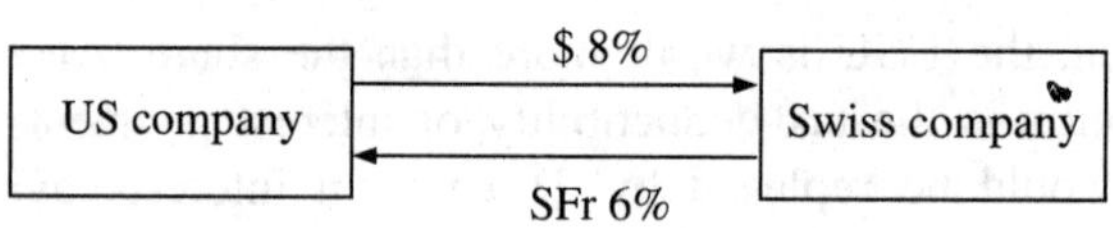

In practice, parties are matched by a swap dealer (a commercial bank, say). Major swap dealers quote bid and offer quotes in all the major currencies for different maturities. The bid and offer rates are the fixed rates in that currency that a bank is willing to pay to a client in exchange for receiving six month LIBOR or to receive from a client in exchange for paying 6 m LIBOR. A hypothetical schedule is tabulated here:

				Maturity (in%)
	3 years		5 years	
	Pay	Receive	Pay	Receive
Dollar	8.79	8.97	9.42	9.58
Pound	11.49	11.70	11.45	11.66
Deutsch Mark	5.80	6.10	6.45	6.75
Yen	7.12	7.28	7.02	7.17

Note: All quotes are annual rates against LIBOR.

The price schedule is prepared from the dealer's perspective. Thus, the dealer is willing to pay Sterling at a fixed annual rate of 11.49% in exchange for 6 million LIBOR and to receive Sterling at an annual rate of 11.7% in exchange for paying 6 million dollar LIBOR.* The spread between the bid and offer rates is the bank's profit. By relating two quotes to LIBOR, swap rates can be quoted between any two currencies. For instance, the dealer would be willing to pay USD for three years at an annual rate of 8.79% in exchange for receiving DM for three years at 6.1%, and to receive dollars at 8.97% in exchange for paying DM at 5.80%.

Currency swaps are not executed in isolation. They are used in conjunction with actual debt issues. Sometimes companies may find foreign capital cheaper. At the same time they would want to avoid exchange rate risk. Currency swaps enable companies to raise capital in one (cheaper) currency and convert it into the desired currency.

Interest Rate Swaps

An interest rate swap is a transaction in which an asset or a liability with a floating rate of interest can be converted into a fixed rate (or vice versa) within the same currency. As the currency and amount remains the same, the principal is not exchanged. While the fixed rate of interest is set for the life of the contract, the floating rate is reset at the beginning of each interval but paid in arrears. LIBOR is often the reference rate.

An Illustration

A firm can issue a dollar denominated fixed rate debt at 10.75% or it can issue a floating rate debt at LIBOR + 25 bp.†

Another firm can issue a fixed rate debt of the same maturity at 11.7% or a floating rate debt at LIBOR + 40 bps.

Firm A prefers floating rate debt while firm B prefers fixed rate debt. Their position is summarized here in a tabulated form.

	Fixed	Floating
A	10.75	LIBOR + 25 bp
B	11.70	LIBOR + 40 bp

A dealer arranges an interest rate swap between the two parties. Firm A pays a floating rate of LIBOR + 15 bp to the dealer in exchange for a fixed

* LIBOR is quoted in all the major currencies.

† bp stands for basis points. 100 basis points equal 1%. Interest rate less than 1% is quoted in basis points rather than in decimal form.

rate of 11%. Firm B pays a fixed rate of 11.1% to the dealer in exchange for a floating rate of LIBOR + 10 bp. The transaction is shown in Figure 3.5.

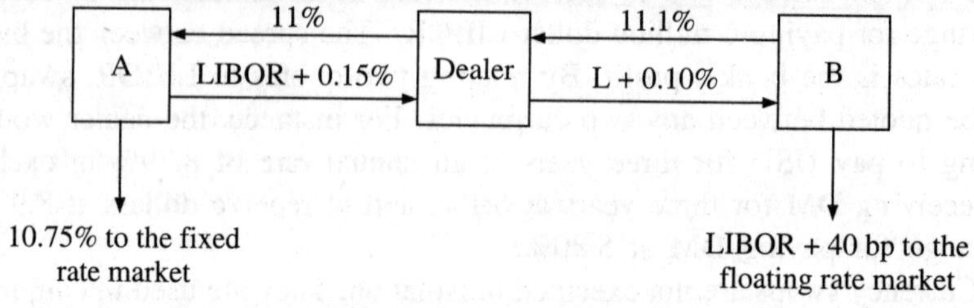

Figure 3.5 Transaction between two firm.

Firm A pays 10.75% to the fixed rate market and LIBOR + 15 bp to the dealer; receives 11% from the dealer. So its net position is LIBOR – 10 bp. Firm B pays 11.1% to the dealer and L + 40 bp to the floating rate market. It receives L + 10 bp. So its net position is 11.40% approximately.* In effect, A has issued debt at LIBOR – 10 bp and B at 11.40%. If A had issued floating rate directly, it would pay L + 25 bp. Due to the swap there is a gain of 35 bp. Likewise, B would have paid a fixed rate of 11.70%. Due to the swap, the firm is able to reduce it to 11.40%. The intermediary gains 10 bp on the fixed rate leg and 5 bp on the floating rate leg.

As with currency swaps, dealers make a market in 6 m LIBOR. The dealer quotes a bid rate which is the rate of interest the dealer will pay for receiving 6 m Libor and an offer rate, which is the fixed rate of interest the dealer is willing to accept as payment in exchange for paying 6 m LIBOR. A hypothetical swap quote (for dollar) is tabulated here:

Years	Bid	Offer
3	8.79	8.97
5	9.21	9.36
7	9.48	9.63

Thus, the dealer is willing to pay 9.48% in exchange for receiving 6 m LIBOR for 7 years and to receive 9.63% in exchange for paying 6 m LIBOR.

Interest rate swaps are used to insure against loss in value of assets and increase in the value of liabilities due to unanticipated changes in interest rates. Apart from reducing the risk, the interest rate swaps can also reduce the all-in-cost of debt. In the previous example, both the parties reduced their cost of borrowing by 30 bp–35 bp.

* The fixed rate and floating rate cannot be added or subtracted directly because of different day count conventions. Fixed rate market assumes a 365 day year whereas floating rate market assumes 360 day year.

The swap terminology and swap terms are in Table 3.2.

Table 3.2 Swap Terminology and Swap Terms

Swap terminology	
Notional	: The underlying assets (e.g. currency) is called notional
Value date	: Date on which swap commences
Maturity date	: Termination date
Tenor	: Period of swap
Swap coupon	: Fixed payment
Interest rate swap terms	
Notional amount	: $ 5–$ 500 million
Maturity	: 1–12 years
Floating rate indices	: LIBOR, T-Bill rate, Commercial paper composite, Prime rate
Floating rate reset	: Daily, weekly, monthly, quarterly or semi-annually
Settlement	: Monthly, quarterly, semi-annually or annually

CONCLUDING REMARKS

The objective of financing strategy is to support a long-term business strategy. The choice of funding sources and amounts depends on *how* the company intends to grow. All companies have generic choices such as acquisitions, putting up green field projects, outsourcing inputs and so on. Each option has a different implication for the size, timing and sequence of funding needs. The starting point for the analysis is the corporate strategy. Once the company has shortlisted the potential strategies, the alternate strategies should be evaluated under various competitive conditions.

A company derives its value from two sources: assets-in-place and future growth opportunities. The DCF methodology captures the first. Projects often have option-like characteristics. For instance, an investment in market research or R&D typically leads to new products and markets. A company should design the financing programs after taking into account the multi-stage nature of investments. Otherwise it may find itself out of cash when the option is ripe.

Many entrepreneurs believe that once the business plan is in place, chances are that the money is available. Raising capital could be a nerve-wracking exercise, especially an IPO with tens of meetings with investment bankers, legal advisors, underwriters and a whole lot of them. Understanding the process of raising capital reduces the time and money involved considerably.

The steps involved in designing a security are given as follows:

1. Determine the nature of a firm's cash flows:
   (a) Short term or long term;
   (b) Denomination of currency; and
   (c) Sensitivity of cash flows to inflation and other economic conditions.
2. Match the nature of cash flows and the features of the security.
3. Factor in the views of rating agencies and analysts.
4. Examine the benefits and costs of the security (taxes, distress costs, marketing and legal fees, etc.).
5. Factor in the information asymmetry in conveying information to markets.

REFERENCES

1. Arzac, Enrique, PERCS, DECS and Other Mandatory Convertibles, *Journal of Applied Corporate Finance*, Spring, 1997.
2. Black F., E. Derman and W. Toy, A One-Factor Model of Interest Rates and its Application to Treasury Bond Options, *Financial Analysts Journal*, Jan–Feb, 1990.
3. Brennan M.J. and Eduardo Schwartz, Convertible Bonds: Valuation and Optimal Strategies for Calls and Conversion, *Journal of Finance*, December, 1977.
4. Courtadon, G. and J. Merrick, The Option Pricing Model and the Valuation of Corporate Securities, *Midland Corporate Finance Journal*, Autumn, 1983.
5. Crabbe, Leland E., Estimating the Credit-Risk Yield Premium for Preferred Stock, *Financial Analysts Journal*, Sep/Oct, 1996.
6. Emery, Douglas and John Finnerty, Using a PERCS-For-Common Exchange Offer to Reduce the Costs of a Dividend Cut, *Journal of Applied Corporate Finance*, **7**, (4 Winter), 1995.
7. Finnerty, John D., Financial Engineering in Corporate Finance: An Overview, *Financial Management*, Summer, 1988.
8. Finnerty, John D., An Overview of Corporate Securities Innovation, *Journal of Applied Corporate Finance*, **4**, 1992.
9. Fons, Jerome S., Using Default Rates to Model the Term Structure of Credit Spreads, *Financial Analysts Journal*, Sep/Oct. 1994.
10. Heath, David, Robert Jarrow and Andrew Morton, Bond Pricing and the Term Structure of Interest Rates: A Discrete Time Approximation, *Journal of Financial and Quantitative Analysis*, **25**, 1990.

11. Hillion, Pierre and Theo Vermaelen, Death Spiral Convertibles, *Working Paper*, INSEAD, May, 2001.
12. Smith, Clifford W., Investment Banking and the Capital Acquisition Process, *Journal of Financial Economics*, **15**, 1986.
13. Tiemann, Jonathan, Avon Products Inc., *Harvard Business School Case No. 289-049*, 1989.

SUGGESTED FURTHER READING

Alderson, Michael J. and Donald Fraser, Financial Innovations and Excesses Revisited: The Case of Auction Rate Preferred Stock, *Financial Management*, Summer, 1993.

——, K. Brown and S. Lummer, Duction Auction Rate Preferred Stock, *Financial Management*, Summer, 1987.

Barber, Brad M., Exchangeable Debt, *Financial Management*, Summer, 1993.

Black F. and M. Scholes, From theory to a New Financial Product, *Journal of Finance*, May, 1974.

Brennan M.J. and Eduardo Schwartz, The Case for Convertibles, *Journal of Applied Corporate Finance*, **1**, (2, Spring), 1988.

Brigham E., An Analysis of Convertible Debentures: Theory and Some Empirical Evidence, *Journal of Finance*, **21**, 1966.

Carow, Kenneth, Gayle Erwin and John McConnell, A Survey of Corporate Financing Innovations, *Journal of Applied Corporate Finance*, **12**, (1, Summer), 1999.

Chen, Andrew and John Kensinger, Puttable Stock: A New Innovation in Equity Financing, *Financial Management*, Summer, 1988.

Chen, Andrew, John Kensinger and Hansong Pu, An Analysis of PERCS, *The Journal of Financial Engineering*, **3**(2, June), 1994.

Chen, Andrew, John Kensinger, Hansong Pu and K.C. Chen, An Anatomy of ELKS, *Journal of Financial Engineering*, **4**(4, December), 1995.

Damodaran, Aswath, Financing Innovations and Capital Structure Choices, *Working Paper*, Stern School of Business.

Deacon, Mark and Andrew Derry, Inflation-Indexed Securities, Prentice-Hall, Europe, 1998.

De Angelo, Harry and R. Masulis, Optimal Capital Structure under Corporate and Personal Taxation, *Journal of Financial Economics*, March, 1980.

Fabozzi, Frank, Andrew Kalotay and George Williams, Valuation of Bonds with Embedded Options, *The Handbook of Fixed Income Securities*, 5th (ed.), Chicago Irwin professional Publishing, 1997.

Francis, Jack, William Toy and Gregg Whittaker, (eds), *Handbook of Equity Derivatives*, Wiley, New York, 2000.

Ganshaw, Trevor and Derek Dillon, Convertible Securities: A Toolbox of Flexible Financial Instruments for Corporate Issuers, *Journal of Applied Corporate Finance*, **13**, (1, Spring), 2000.

Giddy, Ian H., Asset Securitization in Asia, *Unpublished Manuscript*, New York University, 2000.

Graham, John and Campbell R. Harvey, The theory and Practice of Corporate Finance: Evidence from the Field, *Journal of Financial Economics*, **61**, 2001.

Ho Thomas and Sang Bin Lee, Term Structure Movements and Pricing Interest Rate Contingent Claims, *Journal of Finance*, **41**, 1986.

Houston A. and C. Houston, Financing with Preferred Stock, *Financial Management*, Autumn, 1990.

Ingersoll J., An Examination of Convertible Call Policies on Convertible Securities, *Journal of Finance*, **32**, 1977.

A Contingent—Claims Valuation of Convertible Securities, *Journal of Financial Economics*, **4**, 1977.

Iyer, Anand S., Guide to PEPS, Morgan Stanley Dean Witter, *Global Convertible Bond Research*, December, 1998.

Jen, Frank C., Dosoung Choi and Seong–Hyo Lee, Some New Evidence on Why Companies Use Convertible Bonds, *Journal of Applied Corporate Finance*, **10**, Spring, 1997.

Yong-Cheol, Kim and R.M. Stulz, Is there a Global Market for Convertible Bonds?, *Journal of Business*, **65**, 1992.

Mason, Scott, Robert Merton, Andre Perold and Peter Tufano, *Cases in Financial Engineering: Applied Studies of Financial Innovation*, Prentice-Hall, Engdwool Chiff, NZ, 1995.

Miller M.H., Financial Innovation: The Last Twenty Years and the Next, *Journal of Financial and Quantitative Analysis*, December, 1986.

Narayanan M.P. and Lim S., On the Call Provision in Corporate Zero–Coupon Bonds, *Journal of Financial and Quantitative Analysis*, **24**, 1989.

Nyborg K.G., The Use and Pricing of Convertible Bonds, *Applied Mathematical Finance*, **3**, 1996.

Philips, George, *Convertible Bond Markets*, MacMillan, London, 1997.

Ramaswamy, Krishna and S. Sundaresan, The Valuation of Floating Rate Securities, *Journal of Financial Economics*, December, 1986.

Ravid, Abraham, Itzhak Venezia, Shlomith Zuta and Aharon Ofer, When are Preferred Shares Preferred? Theory and Empirical Evidence, *Working Paper, No 01-2*, Marshall School of Business, February, 2001.

Smith, Donald, The Pricing of Bull and Bear Floating Rate Notes: An Application of Financial Engineering, *Financial Management*, Winter, 1988.

Solt, Michael, SWORD Financing of Innovation in the Biotechnology Industry, *Financial Management*, Summer, 1993.

Stanhouse, Bryan and Duane Stock, How Changes in Bond Call features affect coupon rates, *Journal of Applied Corporate Finance*, **12**, (1, Spring), 1999.

Stein J., Convertible Bonds as Back Door Equity Financing, *Journal of Financial Economics*, **32**, 1992.

Tsetsekos, George P., Evaluating a SWORD Repurchase Offer: The Case of Tocor II, *Drexel University Case study*, February, 2000.

EXERCISES

1. A company has the following capital structure:

($)

	Amount	% of total capital
Long term debt @ 14%	700,000	35
Preferred stock @ 10%	300,000	15
Equity	1,000,000	50

The company earned $ 240,000 in earnings before interest and tax last year. Calculate before-tax and after-tax return on capital and return on equity. Suppose the company were to retire preferred stock by issuing bonds, how would after-tax ROE change?

2. A company needs $ 1 million of new long-term financing. The firm is considering the issue of shares or convertibles. The current market price of the stock is $ 20. The new issue could be sold for $ 19. An alternative would be to issue 11%, $ 1000 face value convertible at a conversion price of $ 25 per share. The company currently has 200,000 shares outstanding. The current profit after tax is $ 400,000. Calculate EPS for the two alternatives before and after conversion assuming that earnings remain same.

3. Calculate the conversion price of a $ 1000 face value bond convertible into 50 shares.

4. Calculate the conversion ratio if the bond can be converted to shares at $ 20 per share.

5. Calculate the conversion premium for the same bond if the conversion ratio is 12.5 and the current market price is $ 75.

6. The value of a convertible is the sum of the values of the straight bond component and the conversion option (equity component). The value of the straight bond component can be calculated by discounting the coupon (of the convert) at the prevailing yield on comparable straight bonds. An 8%, $ 100 face value convertible has a tenor of 20 years. If the yield on comparable straight bonds is 9%, calculate the value of the bond component of the convertible.

7. The theoretical value of a warrant is usually written as

$$V = (P - E)N$$

where

V = theoretical value
P = market price of share
E = exercise price of the share
N = No. of shares obtainable with warrant

Calculate the value of the following warrants:

	E	*P*	*N*
A	60	64	1
B	20	26	3

8. A PERCS is like a covered call write, buying the underlying shares and selling call option on the same stock. Consider a stock ABC. There is a PERCS on ABC with a redemption price of $ 39 in three years. There is also a three year listed call option on ABC stock with a strike price of $ 39. The following data is available:

Stock price	= $ 35
Price of PERCS	= $ 35
Call option premium	= $ 4.50
Dividends on the common	= $ 1

Estimate the profit/loss for a covered call strategy of buying 100 shares and selling 1 call over a range of ABC price in three years (say, $ 25 – $ 60). Verify that the profit/loss on PERCS is exactly equivalent to covered call writing.

9. A company had issued PERCS three years ago. The instrument is trading at $ 44 and the underlying stock is trading at $ 42. The instrument pays quarterly dividend of $ 0.5 whereas the underlying stock does not. The instrument has two more years to mature. Calculate the value of the call option embedded in the PERCS assuming that the interest rate on subordinated debt of approximately the same duration as the PERCS is 6%.

10. In 1991, the Republic of Austria offered $ 100 million principal amount of stock index growth notes (SIGNs) in the United States*. The SIGNs mature in 5.5 years and do not make any interest payments prior to maturity. The single interest payment payable at maturity is equal to the greater of zero and

$$10\left\{\frac{P_m - 336.69}{33.69}\right\}$$

where P_m denotes the average closing value of the S&P 500 for the 30 business days immediately preceding the second business day prior to the maturity date. The initial offering price was $ 10 per SIGN. If the value of the index is below 336.69 on the maturity date, an investor receives $ 10. If the value exceeds 336.69, the investor gets $ 10 plus $ 10 * percentage appreciation in the index above 336.69. When the issue was announced, the value of S&P 500 was 336.07.

Republic of Austria has issued the US dollar denominated zero coupon bonds maturing in 1995. The yield on this bond is 8.05% p.a. semi-annually compounded. The dividend yield on the index is 3.3%. The continuously compounded treasury yield is 7.60%. The volatility implied by S&P 500 call option of relevant maturity is 17.98%. Estimate the value of SIGNs. What other factors would you consider in pricing the instrument.

11. On 1 September, 1986 Salomon Brothers issued Standard & Poor's 500 indexed note (SPIN) to the public at par for a total of $ 100,000,000†. The SPIN is a four-year 2% (payable 1% every six months) coupon bond, which at maturity pays its holder:

(a) the principal amount of $ 1000 per bond and accrued interest plus.

(b) the excess, if any, of the S&P 500 index value over the initial (exercise) value of the index times some determined multiplier.

The exercise price of the call option and the multiplier were fixed at 270.38 and 3.6985. The multiplier represents the number of call options on the S&P 500 index that the investor receives for every $ 1000 in bond principal held. The option is European type.

SPIN = Bond + (Call option * Multiplier)

* This is based on John Finnerty, Interpreting SIGNs, *Financial Management*, Summer, 1993.

† Chen K.C., and Stephen Sears, *Pricing the SPIN*, *Financial Management*, Summer, 1990.

Yield on comparable bonds = 8% p.a.
S&P 500 price volatility = 18.4% p.a.
X = 270.38
r = risk-free rate = 6.5%

S = current value of the S&P 500 index, adjusted for the present value of the expected dividends over the remaining life of the option.
Dividend on S&P 500 index = $ 8.28

Estimated average annual growth in dividends = 5.4%

Current value of S&P index = 250

Estimate the value of SPIN. Use the Black–Scholes dividend adjusted model to calculate the value of call option.

12. Compare PERCS and PEPS on the following parameters:

- Issue price
- Current yield advantage
- Conversion feature
- Call protection
- Maturity

13. Assume that your current balance sheet reads like this:

FY2005 ($, m)	
Debt	900
Equity	750
Total	1650

The company had issued $ 350 million worth convertibles two years back and are due next year. You are contemplating on issuing equity or bonds amounting to $ 500 million. The next year's retained earnings are expected to be $ 250 million. Estimate the impact of issuing stock or bonds on the debt ratio if:

(a) There is no debt overhang

(b) There is debt overhang

CHAPTER

4

Initial Public Offerings*

LEARNING OBJECTIVES

After reading this chapter, you should be able to:

- Describe the going public process.
- Highlight some reasons why companies go public.
- Compare and contrast fixed price offers and book building.
- Summarize empirical findings on initial public offerings.
- Discuss pricing of initial public offerings.

INTRODUCTION

As companies grow their funding needs also grow. So it seems obvious that companies eventually go public to satisfy their requirement to bridge their funding needs. The fact that many large companies in the world are unlisted suggests that going public is a choice.

Global equity and equity-related underwriting reached $ 694.8 billion in 2006 compared to $ 526.6 billion in 2005. Much of the annual volume was bolstered by larger global Initial Public Offerings (IPOs) in Europe and Asia. The volume of IPOs reached $ 257.1 billion in the first quarter of 2006. Table 4.1 gives the global scorecard. As can be seen, Asia Pacific and Europe contribute substantially to the global IPO activity.

* This chapter is contributed by Petko Kalev.

Table 4.1 The Global Scorecard of IPO Volume from 1 January 2006 to 31 March 2006

	Proceeds ($, m)	No. of issues
United States	44,542.1	195
Asia Pacific		
Except Australia	73,787.3	365
Australia	3424.2	56
Europe, Middle		
East and Africa	102,954.9	440
Japan	18,404.7	199
Latin America	9962.3	32

Source: Thomson Financial

The companies finance part of their investment from retained earnings and sell new equity or debt to make up any shortfall. The firms sell new securities in a number of ways. They can raise money by placing their securities with a small group of sophisticated investors or sell them to the public (including existing shareholders). The former is called **private placement** and the latter **public issue**. Public issues can be made in a variety of ways. At the one end of the spectrum, securities may be sold to the highest bidder and at the other end, securities may be sold at a fixed price. Generally, first time issues, called **Initial Public Offerings** are fixed price offers. In a fixed price sale, the company advertises the number of shares on sale and the price. The investors then decide how many shares they wish to apply for. If the investors consider the price attractive, they may apply for more shares than on offer in which case the issue will be oversubscribed. The company then has to decide on an allotment rule, such as proportionate allotment. In some countries, IPOs take the form of tender offers. Investors are invited to submit a sealed bid stating how many shares they wish to buy and at what price. The company then determines the price at which the total issue would be sold and all the successful bidders receive shares at that price.

Instead of offering securities to the general public, a company may restrict the offering to existing shareholders who are then free to resell the securities to other investors. These are known as **rights issues**. Suppose a company has issued 8 million shares at $ 20 each. If the company intends to raise $ 80 million, it can offer its shareholders the right to buy two new shares for each share they currently hold at a price of $ 5. In other words, it is a 2:1 rights issue.

In many countries, the law requires the company to offer shares to existing shareholders before offering them to the general public. For instance, Section 81 of the Companies Act in India provides that when a company wants to raise further capital from the public, it has to first offer the same shares to the existing shareholders before issuing them to other parties. This is based on the principle that the current owners should be given the option to decide whether they want to include new shareholders into the company or not. The company will first specify the size of the issue and the rights ratio. The ratio indicates the number of shares that a shareholder can apply for every share already held by him or her in the company. For example, a rights issue in the ratio of 1:4 means that for every four shares already held by the shareholder in the company, he can apply to buy one new share at the rights price.

The share price before the issue is called **cum-rights price** and the price after the issue is called **ex-rights price**.

Let us assume that the company is an all-equity financed.

Current value of equity = No. of shares outstanding * cum-rights price.

= 80 * 20 = $ 160 million

The company issues 16 million shares at $ 5 to raise $ 80 million.

The total number of shares outstanding = 8 + 16 = 24 million.

Ex-rights price = [value of the firm/No. of shares]

= $ [(160 + 80)/24] = $ 10.

Price of right = Ex-rights price – Rights price

= $ (10 – 5) = $ 5

To illustrate the effect of the rights issue on the wealth position of a shareholder, consider a shareholder who currently holds 10 shares. His investment is worth $ 200. At the time of the rights issue he is entitled to receive 20 new shares for $ 5 each. After the issue, his investment is worth

(10 * 10) + (20 * 5) = $ 200

Thus, the shareholder is in the same position.

Let us suppose the company sells twice as many shares at half the price, i.e. 32 million shares at $ 2.50. The shareholder is entitled to receive 40 new shares. The amount raised is the same. The ex-rights price will be $ 6 each.

Value of right = $ (6 – 2.50) = $ 3.50

Value of shares without rights = $ (10 * 6) = $ 60

Value of shares with rights = $ (40 * 3.50) = $ 140

Total value = $ (60 + 140) = $ 200

The investor is in the same position. The message is that the shareholder does not benefit from the discount (to face value) given to him. Nor is he affected from the fall in price after the issue as long as there are no information effects on the stock price.

Companies raise capital by privately placing securities with institutional investors or selling securities to the investing public. Private placements of securities with institutional investors like insurance companies is ideally suited for companies poorly suited for raising capital in public markets. An issue of securities by an existing company is termed as a *seasoned equity issue* and an issue by a new company or an existing company for the first time is termed as an *Initial Public Offering* IPO. This chapter will focus mainly on equity IPOs. The IPO activity is partly dependent on the performance of the stock market. When the return from the market (index) is high, we would expect investors to be more confident of investing in stocks.

FINANCIAL MARKETS

A **financial market** is where financial assets are traded. **Financial assets** are marketable financial claims issued by the government and companies. Financial markets enable effective allocation of real capital among competing users. They perform four important economic functions. *First*, they enable individuals to choose more effectively between current and future consumption. Borrowing enables individuals to consume more whereas lending enables them to postpone consumption. The economic units that have a surplus (investors) invest in those that have a deficit (borrowers). This provides capital to companies in excess of those generated out of business income. *Second*, the interaction between buyers and sellers in a financial market determines the price of the asset, say stocks, or alternatively, the return demanded by investors to invest in the company. Firms can raise further capital if the return on their investments exceeds the return demanded by the investors. *Third*, financial markets provide liquidity to investors. That is, the owner of the financial asset can sell off the asset in the marketplace to realize the cash whenever required. The degree of liquidity may vary from asset to asset and market to market. For instance, shares of blue chip companies are highly liquid. Contrast this with stocks of upstart companies listed on over-the-counter exchange. *Fourth*, financial markets can discipline underperforming companies. The prevailing stock price of a company reflects the opinion of all the market participants regarding the outlook for the company under current management. If another company believes that the company is underperforming, then this company can buy the securities of the underperforming company and put the assets of the company to better use. Without a stock market it would have been extremely difficult to value the performance of the company.

Financial markets are classified as *capital market* and *money market*. Capital market provides resources for long-term investment purposes whereas money market provides resources for short-term purposes like working capital investment. Commercial Paper, Certificate of deposits, T-Bills issued by Government are some of the instruments in the money market. Debentures, stocks and preferred stocks are some of the instruments in the capital market.

The capital market serves the function of channelizing resources from the savers of capital to the users of the capital. The capital market consists of primary market and secondary market. The primary market creates long-term instruments through which companies raise capital. The secondary market provides liquidity to these instruments.

Financial markets around the world can be broadly classified as pre-emerging, emerging, established and mature. Countries such as Vietnam and Russia would be considered pre-emerging whereas India, Korea and Thailand would be considered emerging markets. Similarly, Singapore and the Hong Kong are established markets and the USA and the UK are mature markets. The definition of emerging market itself is not very clear. If age is the basis of differentiation, then India would be considered mature whereas if sophistication is the basis, then Japan would not be considered developed because of its open outcry system. The most widely accepted definition of an *emerging market* is that market which has begun a process of change, and is growing in size and sophistication. Exhibit 4.1 presents the characteristics of some of the emerging and developed markets.

EXHIBIT 4.1

Characteristics of Emerging and Developed Markets

Country	MktCap ($, m Sep 1995)	Standard deviation (%)	Characteristics	No. of listed companies
Emerging markets				
Argentina	18,783	91.7	Volatile and risky	175
Brazil	106,821	63.1	Lack of investor protection	565
Colombia	9079	31.3	Weak disclosure norms	80
India	66,772	29.2	More regulated	9871
Indonesia	26,995	30.7		155
Mexico	65,585	46.2		195
Philippines	32,829	36.8		170
Developed markets				
Australia	137,352	26.3	More stable	1030
Canada	193,156	19.3	Stringent disclosure norms	1119
Germany	344,087	12.6	Issue costs are high	933
Japan	2,050,510	25.0		2470
Switzerland	285,171	19.0		180
UK	842,965	21.2		7651
USA	3,540,304	14.8		1945

Source: Erb Harvey and Vis-kanta 1996

Why Do Companies Go Public?

It seems obvious that companies eventually grow big over a period of time and, consequently, the need for capital increases because of which they go public. The fact that many large companies in the world are unlisted suggests that going public is a choice, which a company may or may not exercise. So why do some companies go public? In other words, what are the benefits and costs of going public? What sort of companies go public?

Moral hazard: Due to information asymmetry between a company's managers and investors it is likely that the managers possess more information about the earnings prospects of the company. This asymmetry is an obstacle for young companies without a track record in going public. Indeed regulators in some (may be many) countries prevent companies without a certain number of years of operating history from going public. Due to the adverse selection problem we would expect bigger companies to go public.

Investment opportunity set: One of the commonly cited reasons for going public is to get access to an alternate source of capital (compared to bank debt or venture capital). So we would expect companies with high investment requirements to go public. Getting a listing on a stock exchange opens up a large source of capital. Subsequent to a public issue, a company may return to the market for additional capital through secondary offerings of shares or bonds or convertibles. Listed companies can often bargain better terms and amount of finance from banks. This is another advantage of going public.

Increase employee commitment and recruiting power: By instituting a stock purchase plan for the employee, the companies may concentrate ownership in the hands of employees which gives them an additional reason to deliver goods. Such plans tend to elicit a stronger employee commitment to productivity and quality.

Facilitate M&A activity: Because public companies may be able to raise additional cash through a secondary offering, they are generally better positioned to finance cash acquisitions. Alternatively, public companies may also be able to finance acquisitions with their own stock. For acquisitions financed by an exchange of stock, the public companies can offer a valuation determined by the market, avoiding the complications of calculating the value of a private company.

Issue costs: Public issue of securities involves underwriting and other issue expenses. The issue expenses can be broken down into fixed and variable components. The fixed costs are as high as \$ 250,000 and the variable costs are about 7% of issue expenses in the USA. Apart from underwriting fees, and registrar's fees a company will have to pay an upfront listing fees and an on-going annual fees to renew the listing every year. The principals must consider the ongoing expenses of producing information for shareholders and regulatory entities, and continuing fees to lawyers and accountants as the company grows. Companies may have to appoint Chartered Accountants for various audits and certifications. Although not always required, a company may also need a public relations firm to help promote the offering. All these entail cash outlay. Table 4.2 provides sample costs associated with a $ 25 million and $ 50 million offering on The NASDAQ stock market. The academic estimate of going public in America is presented in Exhibit 4.2. Further, there are economies of scale in issuing securities (Exhibit 4.3). The issue cost of raising less than $ 10 million is 16.9% of issue proceeds whereas that for more than $ 500 million is 5.7%.

Table 4.2 Sample Costs Associated with a $ 25 Million and $ 50 Million Offering on the NASDAQ Stock Market

Offering value	**$ 25 m**	**$ 50 m**
Total shares outstanding	5,880,000	5,880,000
Item	**Estimated fee**	**Estimated fee**
Underwriting discounts and commissions	1,750,000	3,500,000
Item 13 from registration statement		
SEC fees	9914	19,828
NASD	3375	6250
Printing and engraving	100,000	100,000
Accounting fees	160,000	160,000
Legal expenses	200,000	200,000
Miscellaneous	34,200	34,200
NASDAQ annual fees	11,960	11,960
Transfer agent and registrar's fees	5000	5000
Total	2,353,174	4,115,963

Source: NASDAQ

EXHIBIT 4.2

Costs of Going Public (in %, of Equity IPOs 1990–1994)*

Proceeds ($, m)	**Av. direct & indirect costs (%)**	**No. of IPOs**
2–9.99	25.16	337
10–19.99	18.15	389
20–39.99	18.18	533
40–59.99	17.95	215
60–79.99	16.35	79
80–99.99	14.14	51
100–199	12.78	106
200–499	11.10	47
>500	10.36	10
Total	18.69 %	1767

*Direct and indirect costs include underwriter compensation, selling concession, other issuing expenses plus the initial underpricing.

EXHIBIT 4.3

Issue Costs in Capital Raising

Issue cost as a % of proceeds	Issues less than $ 10 m	Issues greater than 100 m
Debt issues		
Investment grade	1.20%	0.60%
Sub investment grade	7.4	2.9
Convertible	8.8	2.1
Equity issues		
Seasoned equity	13.3	3.2
Initial public offerings	16.9	5.7

Source: Lee, Lockheed, Ritter, and Zhao 1996.

The actual cost to a company will, however, work out lesser than the above percentages because of the tax benefits. Issue expenses, in many countries, are treated as deferred revenue expenditure and are deductible over a period of 3–5 years. Therefore tax savings are available for the immediately following 3–5 years from the date of issue. The presence of (high) issue expenses suggests that only those companies that can afford to bear them would go public.

Information disclosure: A public issue of securities brings fiduciary responsibilities to a company. The company's managers, as agents of shareholders, have an ongoing responsibility to provide timely information to the investors. This results in a loss of confidentiality. So we would expect companies that are R&D intensive and, hence, information sensitive, not to go public (in general).

Sharing corporate control: By selling stock to shareholders, the original owners of a public company are, in essence, relinquishing exclusive control of the company's future. Once public, most companies need shareholder approval to take certain corporate actions such as increasing the number of shares outstanding or creating a new class of common stock. Shareholder approval is also required to institute stock option plans, mergers, etc. Even when an explicit approval is not required, companies must keep shareholders' interest in mind. Exhibits 4.4, 4.5 and 4.6 present the level of IPO activity since 1975, a small list of IPOs and secondary public offerings in the USA and funding raised by industry segment.

EXHIBIT 4.4

IPO Activity in the USA

Year	Number of offerings				Net no. of offerings initially listed on			
	Gross	*Excluded**	*Net*	*PERM*	*NASDAQ*	*AMEX*	*NYSE*	*non-NASDAQ OTC*
1975	14	0	14	12	12	0	0	2
1976	33	0	33	28	30	0	0	3
1977	35	3	32	19	27	0	0	5
1978	50	2	48	31	46	0	0	2
1979	81	3	78	53	75	0	0	3
1980	238	4	234	129	221	0	0	13
1981	450	12	438	300	427	1	0	10
1982	224	25	199	93	140	1	0	58
1983	912	47	865	589	728	7	13	117
1984	572	37	535	272	394	8	11	122
Totals	2,609	133	2,476	1,526	2,100	17	24	335

* Offering included are primarily small offerings that did not use an underwriters. Managed subscription offerings are also included, as are bond offering with equity kickers.

Source: Jay Ritter, University of Florida

EXHIBIT 4.5

Recent IPOs

Company	Price ($)	Shares	Date priced	Exchange
Accredited Home Lenders	8.0	9,650,000	2/14/2003	NASDAQ
Infinity Property & Casualty	16.0	12,378,000	2/12/2003	NASDAQ
Bancshares of Florida	10.0	900,000	2/11/2003	NASDAQ
Constar Foreign Holdings	12.0	10,500,000	2/3/2003	NASDAQ
CPI Aerostructures	4	8,000,000	2/13/2003	AMEX
CRAY Inc	6.20	7,500,000	2/13/2003	NASDAQ
Timken Co.	14.90	11,000,000	2/13/2003	NASDAQ
FTI Consulting	40.00	2,333,534	2/7/2003	NYSE
Cinergy Corp.	31.10	5,700,000	2/4/2003	NYSE

Source: NASDAQ

EXHIBIT 4.6

Funding Raised by Industry Segment between 06/09/2007 and 12/08/2007

Industry	Amount ($, m)	No. of IPOs
Banking/Finance	13,450	28
Services	10,176	56
Energy	6,820	40
Technology	6,665	60
Healthcare	4,960	41
Manufacturing	4,118	14
Real Estate	1,622	10
Other	1,377	4
Consumer products	520.9	6
Internet	331	6

Source: IPO Monitor

Fixed Price Offers Versus Book Building

Conventional wisdom suggests that issuers and investment bankers would do well to assess market demand conditions before setting the terms of an IPO. Yet very few such efforts are made. In the UK, for instance, fixed price offerings advertise the number of shares and offer price 14 days before the acceptance date. Such practices exist in many countries. The public issue process in many countries suffers from numerous shortcomings like inordinate delay between pricing of the issue and the date of opening of the issue. The issue price may become attractive or unattractive depending on the stock price movement in the interim period. If the market declines after the price is set, the issue becomes overpriced. So the issuers tend to underprice the issue. To overcome these shortcomings, many countries have allowed book building in line with practices in the USA. In essence, book building involves little more than polling institutional investors before pricing the offering in an attempt to gauge the market demand. This demand information is then used to determine the size, price and allocation of the offering.

In book building, a syndicate of investment banks brings an issuer's equity to the market. One of the investment banks acts as the arranger with the rest of the members acting as underwriters.

The arranger gives notice of a possible price range. The underwriters sell equity on a best efforts basis. Orders for equity over the stated price range are collected by underwriters and returned to the arranger. Thus, the book building assesses not only the price but also the volume at each price level. The arranger has the final responsibility of setting the actual price at which the equity will be issued and its allocation to investors. The price, thus, reflects the market demand. The issue has two components—*placement portion* and *public portion*. The placement portion is targeted at institutional investors like mutual funds. The book runner drafts the preliminary prospectus and files the prospectus with the concerned authority for approval.

The preliminary prospectus does not contain the issue price. On obtaining the authority's approval, the book runner circulates the preliminary prospectus with intermediaries like merchant banks and brokers inviting them to join the syndicate. The revised version of the prospectus indicates the price range. The intermediaries in turn circulate the prospectus among their clients and place one order for the total quantity on behalf of all the clients. The book runner 'builds the book', records information like the name of the intermediary, the number and price at which the buyer is willing to buy, etc. The book is kept open till the issue gets enough orders. The book runner then, in consultation with the issuer, prices the issue, decides on the amount of underwriting and allocation of securities. The final prospectus is filed with the concerned authority. The issuer advertises the prospectus announcement in the newspaper the next day. The issue opens (typically) 10 days after the announcement and is kept open for three days. Syndicate members send their completed application. Allotment is made partly on a firm basis and partly on the basis of public subscription. If the public portion is undersubscribed, the syndicate members will receive the allotment in the public portion also. Likewise, if the issue is oversubscribed, the syndicate member gets a refund. Securities are allotted and listed on stock exchanges for trading purposes.

Because of better price discovery, the book building results in lower underpricing Loughran, Ritter and Rydqvist (1994). Often critics of book building point out that investment banks make disproportionately large allocations in hot issues to their favoured clients and the market is rigged against the average investor*.

UNDERWRITING

In the case of private placement, the company will have to negotiate with a small group of potential investors. But in the case of public issue, the company will have to employ intermediaries to ensure subscription. The underwriters have several roles to play. They bring credibility to the issue by attaching their name to the issue. Because they have to be in business, they would be concerned about the quality of the issue they handle. They also buy securities from the issuer at a discount and resell to other investors at a later stage, thereby, assuming risk. Underwriters have access to a network of retail investors to whom they can sell the issue. They also assist the issuer in pricing as they have valid market knowledge. The registrar collects application from the collecting banks, scrutinizes the application forms, classifies them, assists in the finalization of the basis for allotment, dispatches allotment letters and certificates, and refunds unsuccessful applicants.

There are two types of underwriting contracts: **firm commitment** and **best efforts**. In a firm commitment contract, the underwriter guarantees the sale of securities at an agreed upon price. If the issue fails the underwriter has the obligation to purchase the securities and keep them in inventory (and sell them later at an available price). Obviously, this is in the interest of the issuer. In a best efforts contract, as the name suggests, the underwriter does not have an obligation to take up the issue if it devolves. Since the risk faced by the underwriter is less in a best efforts contract, the underwriting commission is also less. Often issues are underwritten by a group of underwriters when the issue size is large to limit the risk of failure. The lead underwriter identifies a group of underwriters (investment banks) to sell the issue. The underwriting compensation is shared on the basis of underwriting commitment and

* Benveniste and Wilhelm 1997 prove that it is not so.

responsibility. Exhibits 4.7 and 4.8 give the list of top underwriters in the USA and world.

EXHIBIT 4.7

Top Underwriters in the USA*

When a firm goes public, the underwriting section lists all of the investment banking firms that are part of the underwriting syndicate, along with the number of shares that each underwrites. More prestigious underwriters are listed higher in the underwriting section, in brackets, with the underwriters in brackets underwriting more shares. If an underwriter always appears in the highest bracket, it is assigned the top ranking of 9.1 on a scale of 0.1–9.1.

Firm	1992–2000
ABN Amro	8.1
Bank of America Securities	8.1
Banc Boston Robertson	
Stephens	8.1
Bear Sterns & Co	8.1
CIBC Markets	8.1
Credit Suisse First Boston	9.1
Chase H&Q	8.1
DLJ	9.1
Deutsche Banc Alex Brown	9.1
Goldman Sachs	9.1
J P Morgan	9.1
Lehman Brothers	9.1
Merrill Lynch	9.1
Morgan Stanley	9.1
Paine Webber	8.1

Source: Jay Ritter, University of Florida

Before taking the company public, top company executives must spend substantial time in preparing to go public and, ultimately, in being public. Selection of an IPO team deserves careful consideration: the company must be confident of sharing information with all the team members. Before going public a company must establish an investor relations programme and set aside resources for the same. Because the public issue process involves substantial investment in time and efforts, a company may appoint one or more executives to co-ordinate.

* The 1980–2004 rankings of all underwriters are available on Professor Jay Ritter's home page. See http://bear.cba.ufl.edu/ritter/ipodata.htm (as on 8 February 2007).

EXHIBIT 4.8A

Top Leading Underwriters of IPOs around the World for the Fourth Quarter of 2004

Global IPOs	Credit Suisse
USA	Merrill Lynch & Co
Europe, Middle East and Africa	UBS
Asia except Japan and Australia	N.A.
Japan	Daiwa Securities

Source: Thomson Financial

EXHIBIT 4.8B

Top Lead Underwriters (Global IPOs) 1/1/2006–3/31/2006

Book runner	Proceeds ($, m)	Rank
UBS	23,036.8	1
Morgan Stanley	22,639.0	2
Goldman Sachs	21,409.5	3
Credit Suisse	18,644.5	4
Merrill Lynch	17,943.1	5
J P Morgan	13,889.4	6
Citigroup	12,550.6	7
Deutsche	11,822.0	8
China International	8,039.9	9
ABN Amro	7,446.2	10

Source: Thomson Financial

When an issue is undersubscribed, the underwriters have to accept devolvement. Typically, a certain number of shares in the general pool (shares that were not routed through any underwriter) are credited to each underwriter (proportional to underwriting commitment), and then the net shortfall is established. While choosing a lead manager (investment banker) consideration may be given to the firm's IPO experience, industry knowledge, and distribution and research capabilities. Investment banks differ in their size, expertise and capabilities: some are global (e.g. Goldman Sachs), full-service firms, some are boutiques with industry-sector or product specialty (e.g. Hambrecht and Quist), etc. The investment banker must have sufficient knowledge of the company's industry, its market, business cycles, products and competitors and be creative enough to propose effective financial solutions. The investment bank must be capable of placing the stock with a desired mix of individual and institutional investors, target a particular region of country if necessary, etc. Once listed the lead manager should have the research capabilities to produce timely reports and keep the attention of institutional and individual investors.

PROSPECTUS AND THE IPO TIMELINE

In the United States, SEC (Securities and Exchange Commission) clearance is required to sell securities. The Securities Act of 1933 requires all companies to prepare a prospectus for distribution of securities to investors. The contents of the prospectus and supplemental financial information are governed by the SEC regulations. The prospectus is an important document. The company and its management team are liable for information provided in the prospectus and for omission of any material information. The company's investment banker drafts the prospectus after conducting due diligence investigation of the firm in consultation with the accountant and the legal counsel. The prospectus gives the details of the company's business and management, names of principal shareholders and their level of ownership, audited financial statements, underwriting agreement, information on the use of proceeds, dividend policy and capitalization. A discussion of management's perception of all risk factors and competitive position is also included. The company has to file the draft prospectus with the concerned authority through a merchant banker who sends the prospectus along with the due diligence certificates and other compliances to the authority for approval. On receiving the same, the authority scrutinizes it and may suggest changes within a certain number of days of receipt of prospectus. A company can come out with a public issue any time within a stipulated number of days from the date of the letter from the authority. Once the registration statement is approved by the authority, the marketing of the offering begins. See Figure 4.1.

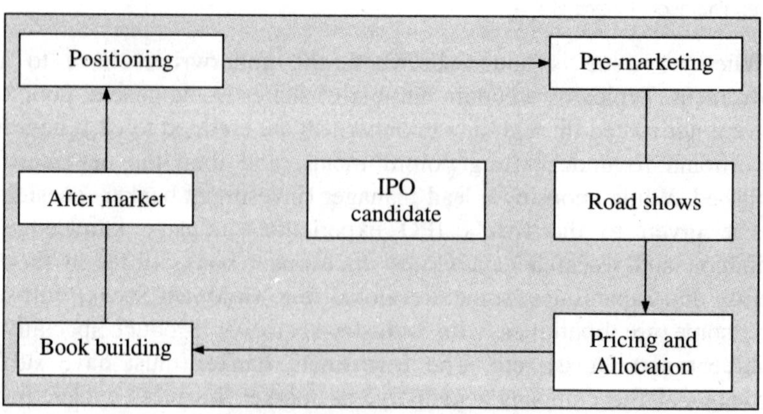

Figure 4.1 The IPO process.

A typical 'road show' lasts 3–4 weeks. A detailed timeline diagram of the IPO process is given in Exhibit 4.9. Once the stock is listed, the underwriter has the obligation to stabilize the price, provide analyst recommendations and make a market in the stock.

EXHIBIT 4.9

IPO Timeline in the USA

Time	Company	Investment bank	SEC
1–6 months before	Select the IPO team; execute letter of intent*	Assess market; Make presentation to board	Confer
1–3 months before	Select printer and transfer agent Begin due diligence	Continue due diligence	Review preliminary registration statement
1–4 weeks before	Executives present the road show	Orchestrate road show	
1–10 days before	Issue press release	Continue due diligence	
1 day before	Price the offering; Execute underwriting agreement		Declare offering effective
5 days after	Provide certificates; Collect proceeds	Assist in closing	

Source: NASDAQ

PRICING OF IPOS

In determining the IPO price, the factors that will be considered are the prevailing market and general economic condition, the history of and prospects for the company and industry, an assessment of the company's management and its operating results, the market prices of securities, and certain financial and operating information as they relate to the market valuations of companies engaged in activities similar to those of the company. There are two approaches for valuing the equity of a company undertaking the IPO–DCF approach and peer comparison approach. The **DCF approach** involves forecasting of cash flows to equity and estimation of the appropriate discount rate to discount cash flows. The value of equity thus arrived is divided by the number of shares outstanding to arrive at the intrinsic value.

* The letter of intent is among the first documents to be signed before the investment banker undertakes any work. The letter protects the underwriter against any uncovered expenses in the event the event is withdrawn due to lack of investor demand or some such thing.

Valuation is both an art and a science. The issuer can come up with a price range and assess the likely market reaction to each of the prices. The final price is set in consultation with the lead manager.

The peer comparison approach requires identification of a set of comparable companies; obtaining for the latter their average P/E and P/BV ratios and the application of these multiples to the earnings of the issuer to estimate the price. Sometimes industry-specific ratios such as market value per cable subscriber, market value per barrel of proved reserves and so on. In the telecommunication industry, for instance, the primary determinant of a company's value is the population of the franchisee territory rather than financial variables (Kim and Ritter 1999, Amir and Lev 1996). The obvious difficulty in this methodology is that it is hard to find peer companies due to differences in product life cycle, size, capital structure, etc. Further, estimation of future revenues and earnings based on short history of the firm's existence is difficult. Some examine the pricing of recent comparable issues in pricing the next issue. The difficulty in this approach is that *P/E* multiples fluctuate rapidly between quarters or days rendering this approach useless. The final pricing typically takes place the day the company is likely to get the clearance.

THE EMPIRICAL EVIDENCE

The cost of issuing securities includes the cost of underwriting and administrative expenses involved in the public issue process. In addition to these, there is a hidden cost of selling securities below their intrinsic values. A number of studies have recorded wide spread underpricing of IPOs. If an investor can make quick money upon listing of the issue, the issue is said to be underpriced. The return on a stock from the day of offer to the day of listing is

$$R = \left[\left(\frac{P_1}{P_0}\right) - 1\right] * 100$$

where

P_1 = price of stock on listing day P_0 = offer price

To remove the effect of the market, market adjusted return could be calculated by subtracting the market return.

Market adjusted return = Raw return – Market return

$$\text{Market return} = \left[\left(\frac{\text{Market index on listing}}{\text{Market index on offer}}\right) - 1\right] * 100$$

Table 4.3 gives the summary of estimates of the underpricing of new securities at issuance in the USA.

Table 4.3 Summary of Estimates of the Underpricing of New Securities at Issuance in the USA

Type of offering	Study	Sample period	Sample size	Estimated underpricing
IPO	Ibbotson (1974)	1960–69	120	11.4 %
IPO	Ritter (1984)	1960–82	5162	18.8
		1977–82	1028	26.5
		1980–81	325	48.4
IPO	Ritter (1985)	1977–1982		
• Firm commitments			664	14.80
• Best efforts			364	47.80

Source: Smith 1986

Exhibit 4.10 presents the level of underpricing in the USA. The amount of money left on the table is defined as the offer price to closing market price on the first-day of trading, multiplied by the number of shares offered. The IPOs considered for the purpose of calculation have a original file price range of at least $ 8.0.

EXHIBIT 4.10

Performance of IPOs in the USA

Year	No. of IPOs	Av. first-day return (%)	Aggregate amount left on the table ($, b)
1990	89	9.46	0.30
1991	250	11.37	1.39
1992	338	9.87	1.65
1993	437	11.64	3.12
1994	319	8.56	1.37
1995	366	20.38	4.16
1996	572	391	6.45
1997	391	13.80	4.22
1998	267	21.76	4.95
1999	446	70.89	35.20
2000	333	57.29	26.29
2001	78	14.15	2.97
2002	67	8.90	1.13
2003	62	12.10	1.01

Source: Professor Jay Ritter, University of Florida

Exhibit 4.11 lists the average initial returns in countries around the world. Studies in America have shown that although there is short run underpricing, there is considerable *overpricing* in the long run. Over the five year period following the IPO, new issues produce significantly lower returns than similar public companies. Between 1970 and 1990 an average new issue in the USA produced annual returns of just 5% while investing an equal amount at the same time in a non-issuing firm would have produced an annual return of 12% (Loughran and Ritter 1995). Other studies have found that firms going public exhibit a substantial decline in post-issue operating performance. Over a six-year period extending from the year prior to the IPO until five years after the offering, the performance of the IPO firms declines significantly relative to their pre-IPO levels (Jain and Kini 1994). Exhibit 4.12 presents returns on IPOs in the long run in the USA. This pattern is not specific to America. Numerous studies replicated around the world confirm these findings (See, for instance, Levis 1993). Why are so many issues underpriced? Many plausible reasons have been suggested. The underwriter, because of his superior experience in marketing IPOs and knowledge of the market can often coax an issuer to set a price low enough to sell the issue.

EXHIBIT 4.11

Average Initial Returns around the World

Country	Sample size	Time period	Average initial return (%)
Australia	381	1976–1995	12.1%
Brazil	62	1979–1990	78.5
China	432	1990–2000	256.9
Denmark	117	1984–1998	5.4
France	448	1983–1998	9.5
Germany	407	1978–1999	27.7
Hong Kong	334	1980–1996	15.9
India	98	1992–1993	35.3
Korea	477	1980–1996	74.3
New Zealand	143	1979–1999	23.0
Philippines	104	1987–1997	22.7
Switzerland	42	1983–1989	35.8

Source: Loughran, Ritter and Rydqvist 1994

EXHIBIT 4.12

Returns on IPOs in the USA during the Five Years After Issuing, 1990–98 (%)

	First	Second	Third	Fourth	Fifth	Geo. Mean
IPO firms	14.9	12.0	11.5	24.2	9.9	14.4
Size matched	14.8	16.6	13.8	23.1	13.9	16.4
Difference	0.1	–4.6	–2.3	1.1	–4.0	–2.0
Percentage returns on IPOs from 1970–2003 during the first five years after issuing						
IPO firms	6.7	5.3	10.3	18.7	13.2	10.7
Size matched	12.2	14.7	14.7	17.3	15.1	14.8
Difference	–5.5	–9.4	–4.4	–1.4	–1.9	–4.1

Source: Jay Ritter, University of Florida

This is obviously in the interest of the underwriter. But an underwriter's ability to set unduly low prices is limited by his desire to protect his reputation. Another explanation is based on information asymmetry between different groups of investors. If the underwriters have no superior skills in accurately pricing all issues, we would expect some issues to be overpriced and some issues to be under priced. If the informed investors were able to identify the overpriced issues, we would expect them to avoid such issues and invest only in under priced issues. The uninformed group realizes the incentive faced by the informed group and demands a discount on *all* issues. Another plausible explanation for short run underpricing and long run overpricing is that analysts tracking IPOs are overly optimistic about the earnings potential of these companies and investors pay attention to analyst forecasts. A study by Rajan and Servaes 1997 suggests that analyst following is positively related to IPO underpricing and that analysts are overoptimistic about the growth performance and earnings of IPOs. Usually the terms underpricing and undervaluation are used interchangeably. But are they? **Undervaluation** refers to the difference between the price and fair value. In other words, price and value are not the same. As discussed in the section on pricing, IPOs are priced on the basis of multiples of comparables and the DCF approach. If IPOs were priced too high compared to the valuations of comparable companies, we would expect prices of IPOs to revert to their intrinsic value in the long run. In other words, is the long run underperformance of IPOs due to over valuation at the time of offering? The answer appears to be yes (Purnanandam and Swaminathan 2002). One study finds that in a sample of more than 2000 relatively large capitalization IPOs from 1980–1997, the median IPO firm is over valued by about 50% relative to its industry peers. Studies have found that an IPO, on average, leaves $ 9.1 million on table. Yet issuers and shareholders of the issuing company rarely complain. Why? The reason is that the shareholders receive the bad news—that the issue was under priced, and the good news—that their wealth is much higher than they had anticipated simultaneously!* Prospect theory hypothesizes that issuers care more about changes in wealth than about levels of wealth. Issuers may, therefore, obtain greater utility from expected gains in wealth generated by a future increase in the value of the shares and the stock options they retain than from leaving money on the table.

HOT AND COLD MARKETS

Like mergers, IPOs come in waves. There are certain periods in which IPOs produce high initial returns (called 'hot' markets) followed by 'cold' markets. Academic studies of IPOs show that there are pronounced cycles in the number of new issues per month and also in the average initial return per month. Exhibit 4.13 shows the monthly IPO volume and return in percentage between 1960 and 2000. For example, the 15-month period starting in January 1980 and extending through March 1981 the average initial return on IPOs was 48.4%. The average return for the rest of 1977–82 was 16.3% (Ritter 1984). There have been many hot and cold periods during the last 40 years. The exhibit suggests that the periods of high initial returns are followed by high IPO volume. This is contrary to what we would expect. If the issuers were concerned about the proceeds from the issue, we would expect them to issue during periods immediately following low underpricing, i.e. low returns. In other words, low returns should be followed by high volume. In particular, we are interested in two interesting puzzles:

- Why do we see hot and cold markets?
- Why are high returns followed by high volume?

If the risk complexion of firms conducting IPOs were different in different periods, we would experience high returns in those periods in which many high-risk companies issued equity and low returns in those periods in which many low-risk firms issued equity. To test the same, academic studies have taken suitable proxies for risk and investigated the relationship between risk and return. The findings are broadly consistent with these expectations.

At first glance the fact that more companies go public following the periods of high return looks puzzling. If issuers learn during the registration process, which they may at least partially incorporate into pricing, they may raise more money than they had previously thought (Lowry and Schwert 2002).

* Loughran and Ritter present a prospect theory model to explain this phenomenon. See Loughran and Ritter 2002.

EXHIBIT 4.13

IPO Market Cycles 1960–2002

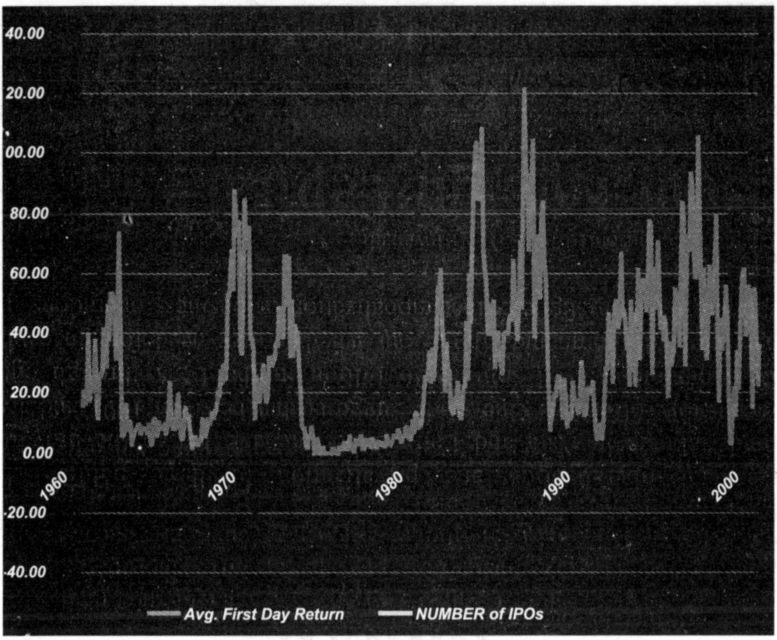

CONCLUDING REMARKS

For every seller there has to be a buyer. Since, in any given year, tens or hundreds of issues are made, investors should have a yardstick to measure the worth of an IPO. One may rank the issue on several criteria, say, on a scale of four (with four being the best). Some of the potential criteria for ranking include:

1. Business model (company's products and services, future potential)
2. Financial strength
3. Reputation of underwriters
4. Management and its experience in the business
5. Superiority of the issuing company's technology over its competition
6. Shareholding base (are the original shareholders successful venture capitalists or institutional shareholders?)
7. Intended use of proceeds
8. State of competition
9. Trading comparables
10. Major customers and their position

One may calculate an aggregate score for the company by summing up scores on each component and decide to purchase or not.

APPENDIX A: LISTING FEE COMPARISON—THE MAJOR US STOCK MARKETS

Year	Corporate event	Shares outstanding	NASDAQ ($)	NYSE	Amex
First year	initial entry fee	12.5 m	84,875	110,850	42,500
	Annual fee	12.5m	17,755	24,260	12,500
Second year	annual fee	12.5m	17,755	24260	12500
	Declare 2:1 stock split		17,500	43750	17500
Third year	annual fee	25m	22,795	32340	14500
	Acquisition facilitated By 5 m share issuance		17,500	17500	17500
Fourth year	annual fee	30m	26,625	32340	14500
Fifth year	annual fee	30m	26,625	32340	14500
Total fees after five years			231,430	317,640	146,000

Source: NASDAQ

REFERENCES

1. Amir, E. and Lev, B., Value Relevance of Non-Financial Information: The Case of Wireless Communication, *Journal of Accounting and Economics*, **22,** 1996.
2. Benveniste, Lawrence and William Wilhelm, Initial Public Offerings: Going by the book, *Journal of Applied Corporate Finance*, **10:** 1(Spring), 1997.
3. Erb, Claude B., Campbell Harvey and Tadas Viskanta, Expected Returns and Volatility in 135 Countries, *The Journal of Portfolio Management*, Spring, 1996.
4. Jain, Bharat A. and Omesh Kini, The Post-Issue Operating Performance of IPO Firms, *Journal of Finance*, **49**, 1994.
5. Kim, M. and Jay Ritter, Valuing IPOs, *Journal of Financial Economics*, **53**, 1999.
6. Lee, I., S. Lockheed, J Ritter, and Q. Zhao, The Costs of Raising Capital, *The Journal of Financial Research*, **19**, 1996.
7. Levis, Mario, The Long-Run Performance of Initial Public Offerings: The U.K Experience 1980–88, *Financial Management*, **22**, Spring, 1993.
8. Loughran, Tim, Jay Ritter and Kristian Rydqvist, Initial Public Offerings: International Insights, *Pacific Basin Journal*, **2**, (June), 1994.

9. Loughran Tim and Jay Ritter, Why Don't Issuers Get Upset About Leaving Money on the Table in IPOs?, *Review of Financial Studies*, **15**, 2, (March), 2002.

10. Lowry, Michelle and William Schwert, IPO Market Cycles: Bubbles or Sequential Learning?, *Journal of Finance*, **57**, 2002.

11. Purnandam, Amiyatosh K., and Bhaskaran Swaminathan, Are IPOs Underpriced?, *Working Paper*, John Graduate School of Management, Cornell University, May, 2002.

12. Rajan, Raghuram and Henri Servaes, Analyst Following of Initial Public Offerings, *Journal of Finance*, **52**, 1997.

13. Ritter, Jay R., The Hot Issue Market of 1980, *Journal of Business*, **57**:2, 1984.

14. Smith, Clifford, Investment Banking and the Capital Acquisition Process, *Journal of Financial Economics*, 1986.

SUGGESTED FURTHER READING

Aggarwal, Reena and Sandeep Dahiya, Capital Formation and the Internet, *Journal of Applied Corporate Finance*, **13**, 1 (Spring), 2000.

Benveniste, Lawrence and Paul Spindt, How Investment Bankers Determine Offer price and Allocation of initial Public Offerings, *Journal of Financial Economics*, **24**, 1989.

Benveniste, Lawrence and William Wilhelm, A Comparative Analysis of IPO Proceeds Under Alternative Regulatory Environments, *Journal of Financial Economics*, **28**, 1990.

Brealy, Richard and Stewart Myers, *Principles of Corporate Finance*, 5th Ed., McGraw Hill, New York, 1981.

Cornelli, Francesca, and David Goldreich, Book Building and Strategic Allocation, *Journal of Finance*, **LVI:** 6 (December), 2001.

Divecha, Arjun B, Jaime Drach and Dan Stefek, Emerging Markets: A Quantitative Perspective, *Journal of Portfolio Management*, Fall, 1992.

Ellis, Katrina, Roni Michaely and Maureen O'Hara, A Guide to Initial Public Offering Process, *Working Paper*, Johnson Graduate School of Management, Cornell University, January, 1999.

Garfinkle, Norton, Burton Malkiel and Costin Bontas, Effect of Underpricing and Lock-up Provisions in IPOs, *Journal of Portfolio Management*, Spring, 2002.

Ibbotson, R.G., J. Sindelar and J.R. Ritter, The Market's Problems with the Pricing of Initial Public Offerings, *Journal of Applied Corporate Finance*, **7**, 1994.

Ibbotson, R.G. and J.R. Ritter, Initial Public Offerings, in Robert Jarrow, Vojislav Makismivic and William Ziemba, (eds.), *Handbooks of*

Operations Research and Management Science: Finance, North-Holland, Amsterdam, 1995.

Lerner, Josh, Venture Capitalists and the Decision to go Public, *Journal of Financial Economics*, **35**, 1994.

Loughran, Tim and Jay Ritter, The New Issues Puzzle, *Journal of Finance*, **50**, 1995.

Narasimhan, M.S., L.V. Ramana and G. Raghavendran, Initial Public Offerings in India: A Study of their Performance, *Working Paper*, Number 2, IFMR.

Pagano, Marco, Fabio Panetta and Luigi Zingales, Why do Companies Go Public? An Empirical Analysis, *The Journal of Finance*, **LIII:**, 1 (February), 1998.

Ritter, Jay, The Long Run Performance of Initial Public Offerings, *Journal of Finance*, **46**, 1991.

Ritter, J.R., Initial Public Offerings, *Contemporary Finance Digest*, **2:** 1 (Spring), 1998.

Beatty, Randolph B., and Jay R. Ritter, "Investment Banking, Reputation, and the Underpricing of Initial Public Offerings, *Journal of Financial Economics*, **15**, 1986.

Rock, Kevin, Why New Issues Are Underpriced, *Journal of Financial Economics*, **15**, 1986.

Welch, Ivo and Jay Ritter, A Review of IPO Activity, Pricing and Allocations, *Yale ICF Working Paper No.* 02-01, February, 2002.

EXERCISES

1. IPOs are priced on the basis of the DCF methodology and multiples. The following data is available for a company that is about to go public.

Post-IPO book equity = \$ 30 million
Net-Income in the year of going public = \$ 5 million
Post-IPO book value of debt = \$ 6 million

Financial data for comparable companies is given in a tabular representation here:

	Company A	Company B	Company C	Company D
Net income	180 m	80 m	60 m	40 m
B.V of equity	900 m	700 m	375 m	200 m
Long-term debt	0	200 m	150 m	60
Total assets	1.2 b	1.0 b	550 m	300 m
Stock price	90	40	36	35
No. of shares	38 m	40 m	25 m	24 m

Calculate the value of equity using M/B and P/E multiples.

2. In 2001 the management of Heritage Foods (a fictitious company) was considering an IPO. The company had witnessed high growth in the past three years. To sustain the high growth, the company needed frequent injections of capital. The company had depleted its borrowing capacity. So the company decided to go public. Exhibit 1 presents the most recent income statement and balance sheet data.

EXHIBIT 1

Recent Financials

Income Statement ($ '000)

	2000	2001
Sales	19,120	46,923
COGS	13,310	29,541
Gross profit	5810	17,382
Operating Exp.	4437	12,270
EBIT	1373	5112
Interest	817	1819
PBT	556	3293
Tax		278
PAT	556	3015

Balance Sheet ($ '000)

Total assets	27,752	34,305
Working capital	6394	6879
Debt	13,534	16,065
Preferred stock	1257	1145
Equity	(258)	2598

Other data:

No. of shares outstanding	3,445,000	4,980,000
Capital expenditure	411	834

The forecast of key financial variables is given as follows.

	2002	03	04	05	06	07 and beyond
Revenue growth (%)	50	40	30	20	15	10
Pretax operating margin (%)	11	12	13	14	15	16
Working capital/ Revenues (%)	13	13	13	13	13	13
Capex/Revenues (%)			4			
Tax rate = 35%						

The company expects to maintain its long-term debt at $ 6 million and book equity at $ 26 million in the post-IPO phase. Assume that cash flows grow at 6% p.a. in perpetuity after the forecast period.

The unlevered beta for comparable companies is 1.0, R_f = 6%, market risk premium = 7.5%. In the post-IPO phase, the cost of debt for the company is expected to be 9%.

(a) Forecast free cash flow. Estimate the value of the firm and equity.

(b) How and where would you factor in issue costs?

(c) What are the implications of short run underpricing for the issuer and investor?

3. Max RE Capital LTD is a Bermuda-based reinsurance provider of life, annuity, disability, property and casualty insurance. Max RE LTD is the principal operating company and Max RE Capital LTD is a subsidiary. Reinsurance is insurance that is purchased by direct insurers or insurance companies to reduce the risk they assume in underwriting insurance. The reinsurer, Max RE Capital LTD, for example, agrees to indemnify an insurance company for all or a portion of their risks under their insurance policies. Max RE Capital LTD generates revenue by underwriting insurance and investing its own assets for capital returns. The company went public in 2001 at an offer price of $ 17.50. The details of the IPO are given as follows.

MAX RE CAPITAL LTD			NASDAQ: MXRE
Company		**Offering**	
Location	ASCOT HOUSE 28 QUEEN STREET HAMILTON BERMUDA HM11	Filing	S-1/A 07/24/01
Phone	(441)296-8800	Pricing	TBA
Website	http://www.maxre.bm	Share Type	Common Stock
Industry	FIRE, MARINE & CASUALTY INSURANCE	Price Range	$16.50 - $18.50
SIC Code	6331	Shares Offered	14,285,000
2000 Revenue	$451,322,000	Total Shares	50,359,461
2000 Net Income	$8,699,000	Percent Floated	28.36%
Projected Market Cap	$881,290,567	Est. Amount Raised	$249,987,500
Lead Underwriter		**Co Managers**	
Morgan Stanley & Co. Incorporated Salomon Smith Barney Inc		Goldman, Sachs & Co. Banc of America Securities LLC Dresdner Kleinwort Wasserstein Securities LLC	

Source: IPOguys.com

Net tangible book value per common share before offering: $ 14.75

Initial public offering price per common share: $ 17.5

The relevant information for comparable companies is presented in Exhibit 2. Compare the multiples of Max RE with its competitors. Is it overvalued? Why? Collect data on the subsequent stock price performance of Max RE. Does it fit into the general finding that IPOs are underpriced in the short run and overpriced in the long run?

EXHIBIT 2

Trading Comparables

Trading Comparables

Price & Volume	
Recent Share Price	69,200.00
52 Week High	74,600.00
52 Week Low	53,500.00
Volume Traded	0.5
Growth & Value	
Sales Growth %	41.73
3 yr. Aver. Sales Growth %	49.09
Price To Book Value	8.14
Price to Earnings Ratio	51.6
Rev. Per Share	65450

Price & Volume	
Recent Share Price	83.25
52 Week High	103.75
52 Week Low	72.7
Volume Traded	5,124.20
Growth & Value	
Sales Growth %	9.35
3 yr. Aver. Sales Growth %	13.48
Price To Book Value	4.65
Price to Earnings Ratio	33.43
Rev. Per Share	80.5

Price & Volume	
Recent Share Price	15.85
52 Week High	18.18
52 Week Low	15.45
Volume Traded	106.3
Growth & Value	
Sales Growth %	31.16
3 yr. Aver. Sales Growth %	60.85
Price To Book Value	0
Price to Earnings Ratio	0.01
Rev. Per Share	NA

4. Summarize the empirical finding on IPO pricing, allocation and activity.

CHAPTER

5

Raising Foreign Capital*

LEARNING OBJECTIVES

After reading this chapter, you should be able to:

- Explain the rationale for globalizing funding sources.
- Describe the process of issuing depository receipts.
- Introduce the listing norms of global stock exchanges.
- Discuss pricing of depository receipts, estimation of cost of equity in emerging markets.

INTRODUCTION

Spurred by the boom in global demand for their products, companies are scaling up operations. Often companies increase their scale by either setting up a green field project or acquiring another company. Tata Steel, a major steel company in India, acquired Corus Steel of the UK to form the fifth largest steel company in the world. Funding such acquisitions often involves issuance of securities abroad. This chapter provides an overview of the process of raising foreign capital.

Financial liberalization and privatization of large public sector undertakings in Asia and Latin America have led to the growth of depository offerings. One study suggests that between 1991 and 1996, non-US companies raised some $ 36 billion in the USA through equity offerings. How do companies figure out whether they need foreign capital? Conventional wisdom suggests that globalization of business operations must

* This chapter is contributed by S.R. Vishwanath.

be accompanied by globalization of sources of funding. The objective of raising foreign capital is to reduce the cost of capital and increase the shareholder value. The cost of capital may reduce because of sharing of risk among more number of investors who are globally diversified with lower expectations of returns. The flip side is that due to increasing correlation between financial markets, i.e. their tendency to move together, the benefits of international diversification are reducing. The net impact of these two opposite effects is not known (Stulz 1995).

Exhibit 5.1 lists some of the depository offerings in the recent years. Exhibit 5.2 presents the statistics on American Depository Receipts (ADR) trading data as of 2007.

EXHIBIT 5.1

Depository Receipt Issues from Emerging Market Companies

Company	Year	Amount raised ($, m)	Type of DR	Stock exchange
BPL Cellular	1997	100	ADR	NASDAQ
CTC Chile	1990	100	ADR	NYSE
VSNL	1997	448	GDR	LSE
MTNL	1997	360	GDR	LSE
PT Indosat (Indonesia)	1994	873	ADR	NYSE
Telemex (Mexico)	1991	2200	ADR	NYSE
CANTV (Venezuela)	1996	1200	ADR	NYSE

Source: Private Sector, April 1998

Depository receipts represent shares of a company held in a depository in the issuing company's country. The receipts are quoted in the host country currency and treated similar to the host country shares for the purpose of clearing, settlement, transferring and registration purposes. The depository receipts are held in the custody of the custodian bank in the home country till the investor cancels or redeems the receipt with the depository bank. The share is denominated in dollars. A Global Depository Receipt (GDR) may be issued for one or more underlying shares held with the domestic custodian bank. For instance, Reliance Industries, a large conglomerate in India, issued two shares per GDR whereas Southern Petrochemical Industries Corporation

EXHIBIT 5.2

ADR Trading Data as of 8 February, 2007

Share volume ('000)	6,082,895
Value of trading ($, M)	197,527
Issues up	309
Issues down	150
Issues unchanged	23

Source: J P Morgan

issued five shares per (GDR)*. The company issues the shares to an intermediary, called the **depository**, in whose name the shares are registered. The depository subsequently issues shares to the investors. But the physical possession of the shares will be with the custodian. The GDRs can be denominated in any freely convertible currency. But the shares underlying GDRs and the shares issued upon conversion in the case of Foreign Currency Convertible Bonds (FCCBs) are denominated only in home currency. A GDR does not entitle the holder to any voting rights. A non-resident holder may either transfer the receipt or ask for redemption. The overseas depository bank will request the domestic custodian bank to get the underlying shares released in the home country stock market to realize cash. Although GDR is denominated in foreign currency, the dividend outflow is in the currency of the home country. So the issuer does not assume foreign exchange risk. The depository converts the local currency into foreign currency and pays the investor after deducting a withholding tax.

Global depository receipts are traded on major international stock exchanges such as London Stock Exchange and in the over-the-counter market in the USA. Issuers of GDRs need not comply with the US Generally Accepted Accounting Principles (GAAP) or the disclosure requirements of the SEC of the USA. But the issuing company should meet the listing requirements of the concerned exchange.

American depository receipts began trading in the late 1920s to offer American investors a way to invest in foreign securities and to provide non-US companies entry into the US markets. ADR (listed on American Stock

* American Depository Receipts can also be issued for one or more underlying shares. Embotelladora Andina of Chile, for instance, has issued six shares for every depository receipt whereas Astra and Scania of Sweden have issued one receipt for every share. The number of shares underlying a receipt is determined by the market price of receipts of comparable companies. Issuers can fix the price by changing the number of shares/receipt. This is necessary because investors get confused when the prices of receipts from companies in similar businesses are in different trading range because of differences in the number of shares/receipt.

Exchanges), as opposed to GDRs, requires the issuer to comply with the US GAAP and the SEC disclosure requirements. Although ADRs provide higher visibility, they require higher standards of disclosure. The non-US companies listing shares on a US stock market must register with the SEC, the chief regulatory authority for stock markets in the USA. This involves filling a form F-20 registration statement—a comprehensive report of the company's business activities and financial results. For companies offering securities for sale, the SEC typically requires a form F–1 initially, followed by a form 20–F, due each year within six months of the company's fiscal year end. Issuers of ADRs are required to recast their financial statements according to the US GAAP. ADRs are bought mainly by institutional investors such as CIGNA, Delaware Management and Capital Guardian, and have better liquidity than the underlying shares.

Issuers can choose from five types of ADR facilities: unsponsored, three levels of sponsored ADRs and Rule 144 A (private) ADR facility. There are three levels of sponsored ADR programmes depending on whether the issuer is seeking a listing or raising new capital in the US. They differ mainly in the degree of reporting requirements. Exhibit 5.3 presents a schematic representation of the types of depository programmes and Exhibit 5.4 lists the salient features of the four types of DR programmes.

EXHIBIT 5.3

Types of ADR Programmes

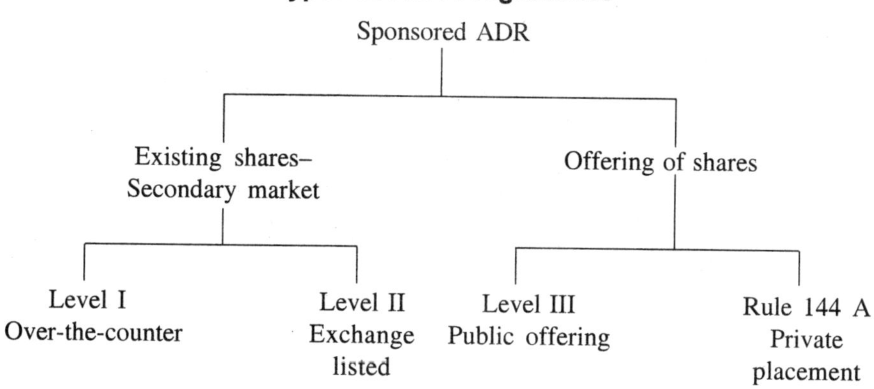

A depository may establish an unsponsored facility without participation by the issuer of the deposited securities. An unsponsored depository programme is not initiated by the issuer but by a bank in response to investor demand. A broker acts as a market maker for the issue and works in conjunction with a US bank (depository). The depository and the issuer submit an application to the SEC seeking exemption from reporting requirements. Upon receipt of approval from the SEC, the depository files the limited disclosure registration statement. Unsponsored depository programs are exempt

EXHIBIT 5.4

Types of DR Programmes

	Level 1 (Unlisted)	Level II (Listing)	Level III (the US Listing and public offering)	Rule 144 A (US Private Placement)
Objective	Develop/ broaden US investor base	Raise equity in US	Raise equity in US	Raise equity in US among QIBs
Disclosure	Home market	US GAAP	US GAAP	Home market (US GAAP optional)
US reporting requirements	Exempt	Form 20-F	Form 20-F	None
SEC registration	Form F-6	Form F-6	Form F-6 and Form F-1	None
Trading	OTC	NYSE, Amex NASDAQ	NYSE, Amex NASDAQ	PORTAL
Estimated timing mandate to launch	5–9 weeks	14 weeks	14 weeks	7 weeks

Source: J P Morgan

from compliance with SEC's reporting requirements and are traded in the OTC market. The issuer has little control over unsponsored ADR programme. The three levels of sponsored programme provide the issuer with greater control because of the depository agreement with the bank.

The process of issuing depository receipts involves the following steps:

1. Obtain the approval of the Board of Directors of the company and shareholders.
2. Appointment of a financial advisor such as an international investment bank to manage the process. The lead manager coordinates the issue and advices the company on the appropriate structure for the issue. The lead manager will also:
   (a) Represent the company to institutional investors;
   (b) Assist in the preparation of prospectus;
   (c) Appoint and liaise with legal advisors; and
   (d) Evolve a marketing strategy for the issue.
3. Obtain the approval of the concerned ministry.
4. Appointment of listing agent to liaise between the exchange and the company. The listing agent is responsible for:

(a) Advising on all aspects of listing rules;
(b) Reviewing the prospectus;
(c) Getting the prospectus approved from the listing authority; and
(d) Compliance with listing requirements.

5. Appointment of a depository bank such as J P Morgan or Citibank in the host country. The depository bank acts as a representative of the shareholders in collecting dividends and maintains a register of DR owners.
6. Appointment of a custodian bank in the home country to physically carry the underlying shares.
7. Preparation of prospectus. The prospectus provides potential investors with information on the company and its securities. The following information, among other things, is to be included in the prospectus:
   (a) Date and country of incorporation.
   (b) Description of the company's principal activities.
   (c) Summary of contracts relating to the issue such as the deposit agreement and custodian agreement.
   (d) Description of the issuer's share capital.
   (e) Profit and loss account, balance sheet and cash flow statements for the past three years.
   (f) Statement of accounting principles being used and any material departure from International Accounting Standard.
   (g) Auditor's Report with the name and address of the auditor.
   (h) Any material change in the financial position of the company since the end of the last financial year.
   (i) Analysis of sales by geographic area and category of activity.
   (j) Names, addresses, function and remuneration of directors.
8. Appointment of legal advisors to the issue. The legal advisor will ensure that the information provided in the prospectus is correct and accurate, oversee the legal aspects of the underwriting agreement, deposit agreement and other contracts entered into between the company and the lead manager and depository receipt holders.
9. Appointment of accountants who ensure that the financial information provided in the prospectus is correct. The accountants also play an important role in the due diligence process.
10. Setting the number of shares representing each receipt.

The issuing company determines the number of shares to be sold and delivers the shares to the custodian bank. It registers the shares in the name of the depository bank who determines the number of depository receipts to be sold and issues them to the underwriters.

A timetable such as the one given in Exhibit 5.5 might be prepared.

EXHIBIT 5.5

Depository Issue Time Table

12–24 weeks before listing	Appoint advisors Prepare detailed time table
8–12 weeks before listing	Prepare Draft prospectus Prepare first draft of other documents Initial review of pricing Submit draft documents to the listing authority Review PR presentations Analyst's presentation
2–8 weeks before listing	Due diligence on prospectus PR meetings and road shows Submit all documents to listing authority Print Preliminary Prospectus
1 week before listing	All documents approved by the listing authority Pricing and allocation meeting Register prospectus Formal application for listing Pay listing charges Sign subscription agreement Print final prospectus
Admission week	Submit documents to exchange Listing granted Trading begins

Source: London Stock Exchange

Depository receipts are marketed through the book building route. The lead manager builds the order book by forming a syndicate of institutional investors. The actual pricing of the ADR is done on the basis of intrinsic worth of the company and the bids received. Many issues are priced mainly through an analysis of comparable companies' price/earnings and price/book value multiples.

MECHANICS OF ADR ISSUANCE AND CANCELLATION

A broker-dealer can purchase existing ADRs in America or purchase underlying shares in an issuer's home market, and have new ADRs created or issued by the depository bank. To create new ADRs, underlying shares are deposited with the depository's custodian bank in the issuer's home market. The depository then issues ADRs representing those shares. The process for cancelling ADRs is similar to the issuance process, but the steps are reversed.

The steps involved in buying ADRs are as follows:

- The US investor instructs a broker to purchase ADRs.
- The broker either purchases existing ADRs from the market or buys ordinary shares in the local market.
- To create new ADRs, the ordinary shares must be deposited with the local custodian of the ADR depository bank.
- Upon receipt of local shares at its custodian, the depository bank issues ADRs and delivers them through DTCC to the original US broker.

The steps involved in selling ADRs are given as follows:

- The US investor instructs a broker to sell ADRs.
- The broker either sells the ADRs in the US market, or sells the ordinary shares in the local market.
- If the ordinary shares are sold in the local market, the broker must deliver the ADRs to J P Morgan for cancellation.
- Upon receipt of the ADRs, the depository cancels them and instructs its custodian to deliver the local shares to the purchasing party.

BENEFITS OF INITIATING AN ADR PROGRAMME

Non-US companies can issue ADRs to the US investors to enhance investor base, facilitate introduction of stock option plans to overseas employees, acquisition of overseas companies. Table 5.1 gives a list of benefits to issuers and investors.

Table 5.1 List of Benefits to Issures and Investors

Issuers	Investors
Broaden and diversify a company's US investor base	Easy to purchase and hold a non-US issuer's security
Enhance a company's visibility, Status and profile in the US	Trading and settlement in dollars
Establish/increase the US liquidity	Facilitate diversification into securities of foreign issuers
Develop and/or increase research coverage in the US	Provide the US style disclosure and accounting
New source of equity	Provide dividend payments in the US dollars
Source of acquisition currency	
Facilitate initiation of stock option plan for overseas employees	Eliminate global custody safekeeping charges

Source: J P Morgan

PRICING DEPOSITORY ISSUES

The issue price depends on the market price of the company's stock in the domestic market, and future earnings and cash flows.

It is now a standard practice to estimate the value of a company's equity by discounting free cash flow to firm by Weighted Average Cost of Capital (WACC), and deducting value of debt on the books of the company or discounting equity cash flows by cost of equity.

Free cash flow = EBIT – Cash taxes + Depreciation – Capital expenditure – Δ Working Capital.

Equity cash flow = Free cash flow – Debt service + New borrowings

The capital asset pricing model suggests that:

$$\text{Cost of equity} = R_f + \beta[E(R_m) - R_f]$$

The capital asset pricing model is appropriate if the portfolio returns can be completely characterized by the mean and standard deviation. A large number of studies have shown that emerging market returns are non-normal and, hence cannot be described by mean and variance[*]. If you examine the case of Mexico (Exhibit 5.6) you will see that there are many small returns and a large number of negative returns. If the Mexican returns were generated from a normal distribution, we would not expect so many negative returns of that magnitude. Thailand is similar to Mexico with some extreme negative observations. The same is true of many other countries. Emerging market returns are not only higher than the returns from the developed markets, but also far more volatile due to economic shocks, military coups and such other factors. In addition, the mean and variance of returns change over time.

In many emerging countries, the stock markets lack depth. Typically, a handful of companies account for more than half the market capitalization. So the stock market index would be a poor proxy for market portfolio which is supposed to represent the portfolio of all risky assets held by the marginal investor.

A recent study of the emerging market returns suggests that there is no relation between expected returns and beta measured with respect to the world market portfolio.[†] Further, according to CAPM, expected return is a function

---

* 1. Erb, Claude B., Campbell Harvey and Tadas Viskanta, Expected Returns and Volatility in 135 countries, *The Journal of Portfolio Management*, Spring, 1996.

2. _______, Risk in Emerging Markets, *The Financial Survey*, July–August, 1998.

3. _______, Political Risk, Economic Risk and Financial Risk, *Financial Analysts Journal*, Nov/December, 1996.

4. Beaker, Geert and Campbell Harvey, Emerging Equity Market Volatility, *Working Paper*, Duke University.

† Campbell, Harvey R., Predictable Risk and Returns in Emerging Markets, *Review of Financial Studies*, 8, 1995. He found that the regression of average returns on average betas produces an R^2 of zero.

of beta, the latter is measured by analysing the way the equity returns covary with a benchmark return. In many countries beta cannot be estimated because the equity market does not exist!

One can estimate the beta of the company, if there is a stock market, by regressing stock returns against an international index such as the Morgan Stanley Capital International (MSCI) emerging market index.

The risk premium for a company in a non-US country could be expressed as:*

Risk premium = Base premium for a mature market + Country premium

Cost of equity = R_f + β (base premium for mature market like the US) + Country premium.

EXHIBIT 5.6

Returns from Mexico

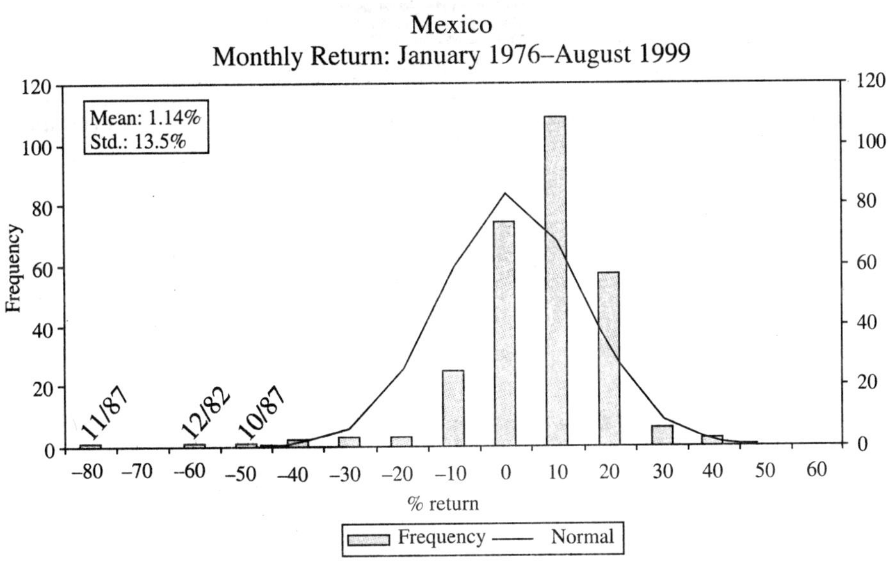

where $R_f = T$ – Bond rate, a proxy for risk-free rate, base premium is the geometric average premium (i.e., $R_m - R_f$) earned by stocks over bonds over a long period of time, 6.1% in the case of the USA. The country premium is added on the assumption that the country risk cannot be diversified due to cross market correlation. Put differently, a major portion of the country risk is systematic. The equity risk premium of a country is a function of country default risk and the volatility of equity market relative to the country bond market.

* See Damodaran, Aswath, Estimating Risk Premiums, *Working Paper*, Stern School of Business, Undated.

Other approaches for estimating the cost of equity in emerging markets are discussed in Appendix A of this chapter.

Country equity risk premium = Country default spread $*$ $[\sigma_{equity}/\sigma_{country\ bond}]$

The country risk can be measured by the credit rating given by international credit rating agencies like Standard & Poor's and Moody's*. These agencies publish default spread over T-bond rate and spread over corporate bonds with similar rating in the USA. Exhibit 5.7 presents the Moody's country ratings and the default spread (at the time of writing). Either the Corporate spread or the Country spread could be used as a default risk premium. The default risk premium should be translated into equity risk premium.

Country equity risk premium = Country default spread $*$ $[\sigma_{equity}/\sigma_{country\ bond}]$

where σ_{equity} is the standard deviation of returns on the country's stock market index and $\sigma_{country\ bond}$ is the standard deviation of country bond prices.

The cost of equity can be used to discount FCF to equity investors to value the company's equity.

EXHIBIT 5.7

Country Ratings and Default Spread

Country	Long-term bond rating*	Country risk premium
Argentina	Ba3	4%
Australia	Aa2	0.65%
Austria	Aaa	0.00
Belgium	Aaa	0.00
Brazil	B2	5.5%
Canada	Aa2	0.65%
Chile	Baa1	1.2%
China	A3	0.95%
India	Ba2	3%
Indonesia	B3	6.5%
Japan	Aa1	0.60%
Pakistan	Caa1	7.5%
Sweden	Aa2	0.65%
Switzerland	Aaa	0.00

Source: Aswath Damodaran, Estimating Risk Premiums, *Unpublished Working Paper*, Stern School of Business, Undated

* Spread between interest on foreign currency country bond and that on the US corporates with similar rating.

COMPARISON BETWEEN AMERICAN DRS AND GLOBAL DRS

There is no legal or technical difference between ADRs and GDRs. As pointed out earlier there are three levels of ADRs. They are listed on NYSE whereas

* See www.moodys.com.

GDRs are listed on London Stock Exchange or Luxembourg Stock Exchange. The disclosure requirements in the case of ADRs are more and foreign companies seeking listing in the US must reconcile their accounts with the US GAAP. This is a major deterrent for foreign companies seeking a level 3 listing on an exchange like NYSE. While GDRs do not provide voting rights, ADRs do. ADR holders vote through the depository. Some companies from Latin America and Europe have issued shares with differential voting rights (Pinegar and Ravichandran 2001). The shareholders of B class shares of Saga Petroleum, a Norwegian company, have no voting rights but holders of A shares have full voting rights. Mexican companies have issued L shares, which provide limited rights to elect the number of directors and such other matters. Two Swedish firms—Astra and Scania—have issued two classes of shares, A and B. A class shares have one vote each and B shares carry 1/10 vote each.

In 1998 Daimler Chrysler AG issued a single Global Registered Share (GRS) certificate that trades on stock exchanges around the world. The GRS is quoted and traded in dollars in the USA (NYSE) and in deutschmarks/euros on the Deutsche Bourse and in a host of other markets (21 in all) (Karloyi 2000). A GRS is the share of a company unlike a depository receipt which is issued against shares. To facilitate the issue and trading of shares, registrars and transfer agents are appointed in all the countries. A comparison between ADRs and Global Shares is given in Table 5.2.

Table 5.2 Comparison between ADRs and Global Shares

Criteria	ADRs	Global shares
Definition	Negotiable claim created by a depository bank; $ denominated	Ordinary shares that trade and transfer freely across national borders and quotes as the US security and as a local security in home market • Local currency denomination • Local trade/settlement rules • Same share certificate
Advantages	$ denominated Clears and settles in the US Dividends in the USD Depository maintains records	$ quoted/traded Clears and settles in the USA Dividends in the USD No additional intermediaries Fully fungible All shareholders have equal status
Disadvantages	Additional intermediary	Requires co-ordination among multiple clearance and settlement facilities
	Not fungible	Substantial establishment costs

S&P ADR Index

The S&P ADR index is based on the non-US stocks comprising the S&P Global 1200 which is comprised of the S&P 500 for the US, and the five non-US indices: S&P Europe 350, S&P/TOPIX 150 (Japan), S&P/ TSX 60 (Canada), S&P Asia Pacific 100 and S&P Latin America 40. The S&P ADR index is made up of those companies from the S&P Global 1200 that offer either level II or level III ADRs; global shares, or ordinary shares in the case of Canadian equities. As additional S&P Global 1200 companies list eligible securities on the US exchanges, these securities will be added to the index. The methodology of the S&P ADR index follows that of other S&P's equity indices. The index is market cap weighted with all pricing and valuation taken from the US exchange with the primary listing. The S&P ADR index is a US dollar denominated version of the S&P Global 1200 ex US Index. It covers 25 foreign markets, but all in one currency. ADR prices typically move in line with the actual foreign shares.

The portfolio characteristics of the index are given as follows (also see Table 5.3):

No. of companies:	267
Adj. market cap:	3724.13
Av. company size:	13.95

Table 5.3 Country Weights and Number of ADRs

	Country weights	No. of ADRs
Great Britain	30.63%	51
Japan	1010%	22
Canada	9.18%	51
France	7.94%	17
Argentina	0.05%	3

THE ROLE OF ADRS AS ACQUISITION CURRENCY

As the non-US corporations seek to compete globally and in the US, the ADR is increasingly becoming an acquisition currency to execute cross border transactions. Deutsche Telekom's bid for Voice Stream Wireless and Vivendi's proposal for Seagram are two prominent examples of such transactions. Here a list of foreign purchases of the US and Canadian entities using ADRs as the acquisition currency is given.

Date	Target	Buyer	Value ($, b)
Jan 99	Air Touch	Vodafone	60.3
Aug 98	Amoco	British Petroleum	54.3
May 98	Chrysler	Daimler Benz	40.5
July 00	Voice Stream	Deutshe Telekom	50.7
Jun 00	Seagram	Vivendi	34.0
Apr 99	Arco	B P Amoco	26.8
Dec 98	Pacificorp	Scottish Power	12.6

Source: J P Morgan

The use of equity as a percentage of the acquisition currency for all the US public company takeovers has steadily risen from 7% in 1988 to 57% in 2000.

Sarbanes-Oxley Act and its Effect on Non-US Issuer Listings and ADR Programmes

The Sarbanes-Oxley Act of 2002, which institutes a broad set of new rules regarding the corporate governance of publicly traded corporations listed in the US was signed into law on 30 July 2002. The scope of the Act generally extends to all public corporations, including those ADR issuers which have their securities listed on exchanges.

The recent US corporate and accounting scandals (e.g. Enron) has resulted in the initiation of new corporate governance standards to restore investor confidence and make corporations more efficient. The Act makes it more difficult for foreign issuers to list in the USA.

Both NYSE and NASDAQ have proposed a new set of rules and listing standards to institute the mandates stemming from Sarbanes–Oxley, and to strengthen their issuers' corporate governance and disclosure standards.

The summary of the Act is as follows:

1. The CEO and CFO must certify in writing that the issuer's periodic reports filed with the SEC do not contain any material misstatements or omissions; that the financial statements and other financial information in the report fairly present the issuer's financial condition and results of operation; and that certain internal accounting controls and disclosure controls, and procedures have been established and followed.
2. The management must submit an internal control report which evaluates the effectiveness of the company's internal controls followed in the compilation of the financial report.
3. Only independent directors can serve on the audit committee.
4. Issuers are generally prohibited from extending personal loans or credit in any form to any executive officer or director.

5. Disclose the identity of all the financial experts serving on audit committees.
6. Disclose the code of ethics.
7. Disclose off-balance sheet transactions.
8. Disclose proforma or non-GAAP financial information.

Foreign Currency Convertible Bonds

The foreign currency convertible bond is an unsecured debt instrument carrying a fixed rate of interest and an option of conversion into fixed number of shares or GDRs of the issuing company. Typical maturities of FCCBs are in the range of five years with a conversion premium of 10% .The issuer specifies the exchange rate at which the bond will be converted. But in the case of FCCBs, the interest payments and redemption of non-convertible portion will be made in foreign currency. The investor has the option to get the bond converted to shares or retain it as a bond. Interest payments on bonds until the conversion option is exercised is subject to tax deduction at source, say, 10% and the dividends received upon conversion into shares are also subject to tax, say, 10%.

International companies can also source long-term debt from the US in three forms: (i) publicly traded, SEC registered bonds; (ii) Private placements and (iii) Rule 144A private placements (Johnson and Funkhouser 1997). A yankee bond is an underwritten, dollar denominated, publicly issued bond. These offerings should adhere to the disclosure norms of Securities Exchange Commission. Yankee bond offerings range in size from $ 100 million–$ 1 billion. The issuer will have to hire one or more lead managers and two or more co-managers to market the issue. The lead manager is responsible for successful marketing of the issue. In addition, the lead and co-managers provide post-issue trading, research and market support. In return, the lead and co-managers charge a management fee and an underwriting fee.

A private placement of debt, unlike a bond offering, is sold to a group of authorized investors like banks and insurance companies, and does not require SEC registration. Private placements can be arranged for any amount with one or no credit rating. But most issues are restricted to $ 25 million–$ 250 million. Since the issue is sold to a small group of investors the issue expense is much lower than public offerings. Private placements are arranged by the lead agent on a best–efforts basis. The placement memorandum tends to be similar to that required by SEC.

The Rule 144A market was established to facilitate a secondary market for privately placed securities. The rule permits resale of privately placed securities to qualified institutional buyers. In an underwritten 144A issue, an investment bank purchases securities from the issuer and resells them to other investors at a later date. These transactions need not comply with the SEC disclosure requirements. Some of the former Rule 144 restrictions governing resale of privately placed securities have been lifted under 144 A provided the sale is made to Qualified Institutional Buyers (QIB). A QIB is defined as an institution which owns and invests at least $ 100 million in securities of an unaffiliated entity.*

A MINI CASE

In 1998–99 Infosys Technologies, an international software company with offices in North America, Europe, India and Japan, issued 1,800,000 American Depository Shares (ADS) representing 900,000 equity shares. Each ADS offered represented one half of one equity share. That is, two ADS equalled one equity share. The offer size was $ 50.18 million†. Infosys provides a wide range of IT services to some of the top Fortune 500 companies. Industry sources estimated a strong growth in demand for IT services from $ 177 billion in 1998 to $ 291 billion in 2001. Since Infosys has operations spread all over the globe and had set itself high growth targets, an international listing would enhance its image in the eyes of the customers and open up new sources of capital. The financial statements of Infosys are displayed in Exhibit 5.7.

Companies from emerging markets are often constrained by the small size of capital markets in their home countries. The size of the capital markets in countries such as Chile and Mexico, for example, is a small fraction of the size of the US capital market.

Apart from providing access to one of the largest pools of capital in the world, a US listing can help companies in one or more of the following ways:

- Depending on the industry, the US investors may be more familiar with and value a company or product more than investors in the company's country of origin, resulting in better valuation for the company's stock.
- Listing in the US gives a company a chance to broaden its US shareholder base, and may complement an already existing listing in the company's home country.
- Larger institutional investor/analyst following.
- Increased visibility. Listing on a US market is a good way to raise a non-US company's profile—both in the US and in its home country.
- Enable the US employees to invest in the parent company. A US listing can help support a company's incentive programme for its US employees by providing a liquid market in the USA for its shares. This may also help the company in attracting more qualified employees.

---

* There is also a net worth requirement. There are about 4000 + QIBs as on date.

† The details of the issue are (were) available at www.edgarpro.com

American depository receipts are priced by DCF calculation or by attaching sales/book value multiples derived from comparable companies. The DCF methodology involves estimation of cash flows to equity and cost of equity. Exhibit 5.8 gives the forecast of cash flows to equity for Infosys*.

EXHIBIT 5.8

Forecast of Free Cash Flow for Infosys ($, m)

	1999	2000	2001	2002	2003	2004
Revenues	1505.00	2314.57	3559.62	5474.41	8419.20	12948.06
Operating profits	278.61	438.25	689.36	1084.35	1705.65	2682.95
Net income	250.75	394.42	620.42	975.91	1535.08	2414.65
Depreciation	6.80	9.66	13.72	19.48	27.67	39.31
Inc. W.C.	3.92	5.59	7.96	11.34	16.15	23.00
Capex	11.20	15.90	22.60	32.1	45.5	64.7
FCFF*	242.43	382.59	603.60	951.99	1501.06	2366.27

* Infosys does not have debt. So free cash flow to firm and free cash flow to equity are the same. The terminal value can be estimated as a stable perpetuity or a growing perpetuity @, say, 5%.

Cost of Capital for International Firms

The cost of equity estimate depends on the company's beta, which could be estimated using the home country index or some global index. The choice depends on the investment opportunity set facing the company's investors. If the investors are assumed to be internationally diversified, the returns on a global portfolio would be a better benchmark for assessing the cost of equity. As long as there are benefits from international diversification, a portion of what seems to be systematic risk in a domestic context may be a diversifiable country risk at a global level. If markets are completely integrated there would be no benefit from international diversification. Although the tendency of markets to move together has increased in the recent years, the correlation is still less than one. So there is still risk-reducing opportunities.

The impact of globalization of capital markets has important implications for the cost of capital for international companies. An estimate of cost of capital based on local CAPM is based on the assumption that each market is segmented from the rest of the world. Using a global CAPM would give more realistic estimates of expected returns for international firms.

*Diederich, Noelle, et al., Infosys Technologies Ltd., *Case Study*, Fuqua School of Business, 1996. Also see William Coughlin and Walter Kuemmerle, Infosys: Financing an Indian Software Start Up, *HBS Case study No. 9-800-103*, April 20, 2001.

Market Reaction to Depository Issues

Announcement of new security issues convey information to market, which gets manifested through stock price changes. A number of academic studies have documented stock market reaction to corporate decisions to list abroad.* The results are mixed. Some have documented positive reaction and some negative. These studies have documented the abnormal returns for a sample of listing firms upon announcement of the decision to cross list and upon actual listing. If there is indeed a reasonable reduction in the cost of capital by financial globalization, we would expect the equity of a company seeking cross listing to increase in value substantially because the stock would be valued at a (lower) global cost of capital rather than the cost of capital of a segmented market (Stulz 1999). Academic studies do not support this hypothesis although, on average, stock markets react positively to cross listing.

Estimating Cost of Equity for Infosys

To estimate the cost of equity for Infosys one could use any of the Indian stock market indices (e.g. Bombay Stock Exchange Sensitive Index or Crisil 400 Indian Software Index) or some international index such as MSCI emerging markets data processing and Reproduction index or MSCI International Software Index.

Plugging a risk-free rate of 13.6%, a market premium of 10% and a beta estimate of 1.48 for Infosys in the *local* CAPM yields a cost of equity of 28.4%. Remember that the forecast of free cash flows is in *dollars*. Using a *rupee* discount rate to discount the cash flows denominated in *dollars* would be inappropriate.

The discount rate can be calculated in home currency and then translated to host currency. The conversion of home currency discount rate to host country discount rate involves the application of interest rate parity condition. Interest rate parity stipulates that the expected rate of change in the spot exchange rate equals the ratio of the prevailing interest rates in the two currencies.

$$(1 + \Delta s) = \frac{(1 + r_1)}{(1 + r_2)}$$

* Alexander G., C. Eun and S. Janakiraman, International Listings and Stock Returns: Some Empirical Evidence, *Journal of Financial and Quantitative Analysis*, **23**, (1988).
Miller, Darius, The Market Reaction to International Cross Listings: Evidence from Depository Receipts, *Journal of Financial Economics*, 51, 1999.
Foerster, Stephen R., and Andrew Karloyi, The Effects of Market Segmentation and Investor Recognition on Asset Prices: Evidence from Foreign Stock Listing in the US, *Journal of Finance*, June, 1999.

where Δs = expected change in spot rate. r_1 and r_2 are yields on comparable government bonds denominated in the currencies in question.

The WACC in one currency can be converted into another by multiplying by the expected annual change in the exchange rate. While changes in the exchange rates may correspond with the changes in the differential in national inflation rates in the long run, there are sharp deviations from this parity relationship for shorter intervals. The inflation rate in many emerging markets is much higher than that in stable economies. So discounting foreign cash flows with interest rate in that country would be inappropriate. Likewise, managers in low interest rate economies like Japan should not use the Yen rate. This will inflate the NPV of the investment. Back to Infosys. Let us sum up the issue: Is the cost of equity for Infosys in dollars the same as that in rupee? Or for that matter is the cost of equity for any company the same in any two currencies? The answer is no. One must come up with a dollar discount rate. The global CAPM expressed in dollars states that (O'Brien, 1999):

$$E(R_{\$}) = R_{f\$} + \beta_{g\$}\ \text{[Global risk premium in dollar]}$$

where $\beta_{g\$}$ = global beta in the US dollars measured by regressing monthly data for Infosys and, say, MSCI Emerging Markets Data processing and Reproduction Index.

$R_{f\$}$ = risk-free rate in dollars

Global risk premium = [Return on the global portfolio in the US dollar – Dollar risk-free rate]

= 3 to 5.4% (say 4%)*

The dollar rate might be used to discount dollar FCFs to estimate the value of equity. Dividing this value by the number of shares outstanding and the number of shares on offer would yield price per share. Since each depository share represents one half of a share, the price should be divided by 2.

CONCLUDING REMARKS

Cross listing is usually beneficial—especially for companies from emerging markets, which are constrained by illiquid, local capital markets. Some studies have shown that there is a substantial price decline in some issues in the post-listing period. The large price declines, in some cases, have resulted in what

---

* What cost of equity in Rupee is consistent with the dollar rate obtained from Global CAPM above? How do you translate the WACC in one currency into WACC in another currency? The answer to these questions is beyond the scope of this book. Interested readers may refer to Tom O'Brien's article mentioned above. Also see Schramm , Ronald M., and Henry Wang, Measuring the Cost of Capital in an International Framework , *Journal of Applied Corporate Finance*, **12**, (3, Fall), 1999.

is known as 'flowback', which refers to a situation in which investors surrender the DRs to the depository bank who, in turn, cancels them and instruct the custodian bank to sell the underlying shares in the home market and repatriate the proceeds. The increase in supply of shares in the market exerts pressure on the stock price in the home market*.

Prior to merger, Daimler Benz ordinary shares traded in Frankfurt and its ADRs on the NYSE; Chrysler stock traded on the NYSE and in Frankfurt. During the months leading up to the merger announcement, there was an increase in the New York (Frankfurt) trading activity for Daimler (Chrysler). Within six months, Daimler Chrysler's new global share programme experienced significant flow back to Frankfurt (Karloyi, 2000).

Many depository receipt offerings have failed due to unrealistic pricing, crowding of too many issues from similar companies, improper forecasting of investor demand and unreliable regulatory framework in the country of the issuer. Videsh Sanchar Nigam Limited (VSNL), a public sector telecom giant from India had to shelve its $ 1 billion Euro Issue because it could not realize the issue price of INR 1400–1600. The investors were willing to pay only INR 1100–1200. To make matters worse, MTNL, a competitor announced another billion dollar issue around the same time. The investors probably benchmarked the VSNL issue against the MTNL issue and decided to invest in MTNL. More recently, Chunghwa, Taiwan's biggest telephone company, had to hold its 118 billion 10-for-1 ADR issue due to disagreement on pricing between the government and the underwriters Goldman Sachs, Merrill Lynch and UBS Warburg‡. Meanwhile, another Taiwan telecom company, Far EasTone was also planning to launch an ADR issue. With stock prices falling and several other telecom companies coming to the market, the issue price seemed unrealistic.

Cross listing in an overseas market creates an alternate trading venue (for international investors) for a company's stock. When the linkages between the two markets are strong we would expect rapid dissemination of information due to an increase in the number of traders, a reduction in spreads and an improvement in the overall quality of the market. But when market linkages are weak there might be a diversion of order flow overseas, a reduction in liquidity and an increase in volatility in the domestic market† (Demowitz, Glen and Madhavan 1998).

---

* See G. Andrew Karloyi, Sourcing Equity Internationally through Depository Offerings: Two Exceptions that Prove the Rule, *Journal of Applied Corporate Finance*, **10** (4, Winter), 1998. GDRs are usually partially fungible. Fungibility refers to the extent to which GDRs are interchangeable. An investor can cancel the GDR and convert it into shares without any lock in period after a cooling period (of, say, 45 days). But the company cannot reconvert the released shares into GDRs for sale to international investors.

† Chunghwa ADR hangs fire on pricing, *Euromoney*, March 2001.

So cross listing makes sense if benefits exceed costs.

EXHIBIT 5.9

Financial Performance of Infosys Technologies (INR m)

	1995	1996	1997	1998
Revenue	577.00	934.10	1438.10	2603.70
EBDIT	198.60	339.50	500.60	886.10
PAT	133.20	210.10	336.80	603.60
Dividends	23.10	36.30	39.90	70.30
Capital investment	252.30	155.50	273.10	344.10
Working capital	324.70	411.70	542.00	972.30
ROE (%)	29.71	29.53	34.96	42.24
ROCE (%)	31.79	33.12	40.16	46.09

Source: Infosys Annual Reports

APPENDIX A: ESTIMATING COST OF EQUITY IN EMERGING MARKETS

In the recent years a great deal of research has been done on asset pricing in emerging markets. This note explains three studies.

Godfrey–Espinosa Approach*

The Godfrey–Espinosa model for estimating the cost of equity in emerging markets suggests that:

$$K_i = R_{f,\text{us}} + \text{Credit spread}_i + 0.6\ [\sigma_i/\sigma_m][\text{Risk premium}_{\text{us}}]$$

where

$R_{f,\text{us}}$ = risk-free rate in the USA = 6%

σ_i = annualized equity market volatility of the country in question

σ_m = annualized equity market volatility of the USA

Credit spread = difference in yields on the public debt of two countries denominated in common currency

The credit spread and other inputs for estimating the cost of equity in some countries in 1996 are tabulated here:

---

* Godfrey, S., and R. Espinosa, A Practical Approach to Calculating Cost of Equity for Investments in Emerging Markets, *Journal of Applied Corporate Finance*, **9** (3, Fall), 1996.

Country	Credit spread	Annualized volatility	Adjusted beta	Cost of equity
Argentina	4%	54.74%	3.39	28.7
Brazil	4.1%	53.75%	3.33	28.4
Mexico	3.8%	36.56%	2.26	22.3
Philippines	2.0%	32.05%	1.99	18.9
India	1.6%	29.95%	1.86	17.8
Indonesia	1.0 %	27.19%	1.68	16.3

Source: Godfrey and Espinosa 1996.

Goldman Sachs Model*

The Goldman Sachs model is specified as

$$R = R_{us} + \text{Premium}$$

where R_{us} = risk-free rate in the USA.
It calculates premium in two following steps:

- The country risk spread, R_s, the spread over treasuries for sovereign, dollar denominated emerging market bonds of similar maturity.
- A leveraged measure of the US equity risk premium (E_u) defined as the equity risk premium in the US adjusted by the ratio of daily volatility (S_b) over the volatility of the US market (S_u).

$$\text{Premium} = R_s + (S_b/S_u)E_u$$

So the cost of equity $R = R_{us} + [R_s + (S_b/S_u)E_u]$

The components of the risk premium are not independent leading to a problem of double counting. To obtain a realistic discount rate, the equity risk premium is adjusted by subtracting the correlation of dollar returns between the stock market and sovereign bond as follows:

$$\text{Adjusted premium} = [R_s + (S_b/S_u)E_u][1 - \text{corr}\ (S, B)]$$

$$\text{Cost of equity} = R_{us} + [R_s + (S_b/S_u)E_u]\ [1 - \text{corr}\ (S, B)]$$

International Cost of Capital and Risk Calculator (ICCRC)†

The Erb–Harvey–Viskanta (E–H–V) model, unlike the other models that calculate expected equity returns using stock market or economic data, focuses

* Mariscal, Jorge, and Kent Hargis, A Long Term Perspective on Short Term Risk, *Goldman Sachs Research*, Oct., 1999.

† Campbell Harvey, The International Cost of Capital and Risk Calculator, Unpublished Manuscript. Erb, Claude B., Campbell Harvey and Tadas Viskanta, Expected Returns and Volatility in 135 countries, *The Journal of Portfolio Management*, Spring, 1996.

on country credit ratings. The result of credit risk ratings of 75–100 bankers conducted bi-annually by Institutional Investor is the basis for their model*. Since the country ratings take into account macroeconomic factors such as political and expropriation risk, exchange rate volatility, sensitivity to global economic shocks, E–H–V take country risk ratings as proxy for fundamental risk, and try to model equity data and associated credit ratings for some 135 countries.

That is,

$$R_j = a_0 + a_1 \text{ Log (CCR}_j) + \varepsilon_j$$

where

R = semi-annual return in the US dollars for the country

Log (CCR) = natural logarithm of the country credit rating

ε_j = regression residual

The log of the credit rating is used to capture non-linear relationship between CCR and expected return. Further, the E–H–V study indicates that the country credit ratings also pick up country risk and that the higher rating (lower risk) leads to lower expected returns.

Their study established the following regression model:

$$\text{Country hurdle rate} = \text{Risk-free rate} + 0.944 - 0.177 \text{ Log (CCR)}$$

The risk ratings and expected returns for some countries are presented in a tabular form as follows:

Country	**Credit rating (Sep 1995)**	**Expected return (%)**
Australia	71.2	18.1
Belgium	79.2	15.9
Brazil	34.9	33.0
China	57.0	22.8
Germany	90.9	13.0
Hong Kong	67.0	19.4
India	46.1	27.2
Indonesia	52.4	24.5

The problem with this approach is twofold: *first*, this methodology yields a countrywide cost of equity and cannot be applied at the company level. *Second*, the numerical value of the ratings is highly subjective.

* These bankers rate each country on a scale of 0–100, with 100 representing the lowest risk of default.

APPENDIX B: CONTENTS OF OFFER DOCUMENT

Global Depository Receipts

1. Details of the company and the group to which it belongs, details of shareholding, description of board members.
2. Market price information for five years with quarterly high and low.
3. Dividends paid per share and the total amount of dividends in the last five years.
4. Description of GDRs covering:
   (a) Transferability
   (b) Payment of dividends, bonus and shares
   (c) Voting rights
   (d) Conversion into shares
5. Country information covering economic indicators, economic policies, foreign investment policy, imports and exports, inflation, exchange rates, etc.
6. Taxation of the income arising out of holding the instrument.
7. Financial statements of the company for four years along with the auditors report.

Foreign Currency Convertible Bonds

1. Summary information about the issue.
2. Capitalization structure of the company.
3. Financial information for the previous five years.
4. Details regarding the business of the company.
5. Terms and conditions of the bond.
   (a) Details of the trustee, registrar and transfer agent
   (b) Denomination
   (c) Transfer of the instrument
   (d) Method of (and amount) interest and principal payments
   (e) Conversion
   (f) Redemption, purchase and cancellation
   (g) Taxation
   (h) Meeting of bond holders
   (i) Governing law and jurisdiction
6. Details of the company's stock price, dividends and principal shareholders.
7. Description of shares into which the bonds would be converted.

APPENDIX C: LISTING REQUIREMENTS OF LONDON STOCK EXCHANGE

International companies can list three types of securities on London Stock Exchange: shares, depository receipts and bonds (including eurobonds, euro denominated bonds, convertible bonds, euro convertible bonds and medium term notes). In the following sections is a brief summary of listing requirements of LSE.

Depository Receipts

1. To qualify for listing, a company must have three years of trading record.
2. The market value of depository receipts should be at least around \$ 1.15 million and 25% of the depository receipts should be held by persons unconnected with the company.
3. The depository should hold shares on trust for the DR holders.
4. The company and its depository should be duly incorporated in their home country.
5. The issuing company should appoint a qualified listing agent to co-ordinate between the company and the exchange.
6. All depository receipts must be freely transferable.
7. The UK listing authority requires the following documents to be lodged:
   (a) Draft prospectus
   (b) Declaration by an authorized officer of the listing agent confirming that the listing requirements have been met
   (c) An application signed by a duly authorized officer of the company
   (d) Copy of certification of incorporation
8. The issuer should pay listing fees.
9. Once listed, the issuing company should abide by the continuing obligations set out by the exchange.

Bonds

International companies list different debt securities on London Stock Exchange. These include the following:

1. Eurobonds,
2. Euro-denominated eurobonds,
3. Convertible bonds,

4. Euro convertible bonds, and
5. Medium-term notes.

The listing requirements for eurobonds including euro denominated securities are as follows:

1. Two-year trading and financial record. The listing company should be able to present independently audited accounts covering the past two years. The financial information included in the listing document need not be prepared in accordance with the international accounting standards and need not be consolidated.
2. The issuer must prepare a listing document complying with the UKLA's listing rules.
3. The market capitalization of the class of securities to be listed must be at least $ 330,000.
4. The securities must be freely transferable.

The issuers of convertible bonds should satisfy a three-year trading record. The securities into which these bonds are convertible should be listed on London Stock Exchange or any regulated, recognized open market. Other listing requirements for bonds—both convertible and non-convertible—are similar to those of DRs.

The listing document in the case of non-convertible eurobonds includes the following:

(a) A corporate responsibility statement.
(b) A brief description of the group to which the company belongs.
(c) Information on any significant legal or arbitration proceedings pending or threatened.
(d) Names and functions of the directors.
(e) A capitalization table.
(f) A statement that the annual accounts have been audited.
(g) Information on any material change in the financial or trading position since the end of the last financial period for which either audited accounts or interim financial statements have been published.
(h) A statement of recent developments.

In addition to these requirements, issuers of convertible bonds and equity warrants must also include the following:

- Profit and loss account, balance sheets and cash flow statements for the last three years.
- Information on the shares into which the bonds are convertible.
- Additional information on the issuer's activities.
- Information on the issuer's directors.
- Information on the issuer's prospects.

APPENDIX D: LISTING REQUIREMENTS OF NEW YORK STOCK EXCHANGE

The standards for listing shares on NYSE for the non-US corporations are given in a tabular form as follows:

Round lot holders (Nos. of holders of a unit of trading—generally 100 shares)	5000 worldwide
Public shares	2.5 million worldwide
Public market value	$ 100 million worldwide

Minimum Quantitative Standards: Financial Criteria

Earnings

Pre-tax income	
Aggregate for the last three years ... together with	$ 100 million
Minimum in each of the two most recent years	$ 125 million

Operating cash flow

For companies with market capitalization (worldwide) Not less than $ 500 million and revenues (in most recent 12 months) of $ 200 million	
Aggregate cash flow for last three years ... together with	$ 100 million
Minimum in each of the two most recent years	$ 25 million

Global market capitalization

Market capitalization	$ 1 billion (worldwide)
and	
Revenue (most recent fiscal year)	$ 100 million

Listing Standards for ADRs

Registration under Securities Exchange Act of 1934	Full registration required Form 20-F or schedule 8A initially and 20-F thereafter
Quantitative min standards	
No. of shareholders	5000 worldwide (round lot holders)
Publicly held shares	2.5 million worldwide
Average monthly trading volume	N.A.
Average market value of publicly held shares	$ 100 million worldwide

Net tangible assets	\$ 100 million
Pre-tax income	\$ 100 million aggregate for last three years with \$ 25 million minimum in any one year
Fees	\$ 100,000 minimum
Annual fees	\$ 16,170–\$ 500,000 max

APPENDIX E: LISTING REQUIREMENTS OF NASDAQ NATIONAL MARKET

A company must meet all the requirements under at least one of the three listing standards for initial listing and meet at least one continued listing standard to maintain its listing on the National Market.

Requirements	Initial listing			Continued listing	
	Std. 1	*Std.2*	*Std.3*	*Std 1.*	*Std.2*
Net tangible assets ($, m)	6	18	N/A	4	N/A
Market cap Total assets Total revenues			75 m or 75 m and 75m		50 m or 50 m and 50 m
Pre-tax income (in latest fiscal or 2 of last three fiscal years)	1m		N/AN/A	N/A	N/A
Public float (shares)	1.1 m	1.1 m	1.1 m	750,000	1.1m
Operating history	N/A	2 yrs	N/A	N/A	N/A
Market value of public float	8 m	18 m	20 m	5m	15m
Min Bid price	5	5	5	5	5
Round lot holders	400	400	400	400	400
Market makers	3	3	4	2	4

Following is a list of NASDAQ IPOs in 1999:

Issuer	Country	Offer price ($)	Global offering value ($)	Offer date	Lead manager
I-Cable Comm.Ltd	China	27.0	522,450,000	11/18/99	Merrill Lynch
Ectel Ltd	Israel	12.0	42,000,000	10/26/99	Chase H&Q
El Sitio Inc	Argentina	16.0	150,880,000	12/9/99	C S First Boston Lehman brothers
Satyam Infoway	India	18.0	86,423,000	10/18/99	Merrill Lynch
Korea Thrunet Co	Korea	18.0	209,070,000	11/16/99	Lehman Brothers
Chartered Semi conductor	Singapore	20.0	517,500,000	10/29/99	Salomon Smith Barney & CSFB

The list of IPOs in 2007 is as follows

Date	Symbol	Company name	Price ($)	(Mil.) ($)
02/15	OPXT	Opnext Inc.	15.00	150.0
02/15	QRR	Quadra Realty Trust Inc.	15.00	250.1
02/15	GAC	Geneva Acquisition Corp.	6.00	60.0
02/15	SLRY	Salary.com Inc.	10.50	44.1
02/14	TIL	Trans-India Acquisition Corporation	8.00	92.0
02/13	COINU	Converted Organics Inc.	5.50	9.9
02/09	OPTR	Optimer Pharmaceuticals Inc.	7.00	49.0
02/09	FIG	Fortress Investment Group Holdings LL	18.50	634.3
02/09	PRTS	U.S. Auto Parts Network Inc.	10.00	80.0
02/09	CHIP	VeriChip Corp.	6.50	20.1

REFERENCES

1. Stulz, Rene, Globalization of Capital Markets and the Cost of Capital: The Case of Nestle, *Journal of Applied Corporate Finance*, **8** (3), 1995.
2. Pinegar, Michael and R. Ravichandran, The Idiosyncratic Nature of Sibling ADRs Issued by Mexican Firms: A Clinical Study, *Unpublished Working Paper*, Northern Arizona University, May, 2001.
3. Karloyi, G. Andrew, Daimler Chrysler AG, The First Truly Global Share, *Working Paper*, Ohio State University, 2000.

4. Johnson, Greg and Thomas Funkhouser, Yankee Bonds and Cross Border Private Placements, *Journal of Applied Corporate Finance*, **10** (3, Fall), 1997.

5. Stulz, Rene, Globalisation, Corporate Finance, and the Cost of Capital *Journal of Applied Corporate Finance*, **12** (3, Fall), 1999.

6. O'Brien, Thomas, The Global CAPM and a Firm's Cost of Capital in Different Currencies, *Journal of Applied Corporate Finance*, **12** (3, Fall), 1999.

7. Domowitz, Ian, Jack Glen and Ananth Madhavan, International Cross Listing and Order Flow Migration: Evidence from an Emerging Market, *The Journal of Finance*, **LIII**, (6, December), 1998.

EXERCISES

1. The rule 144A market was established to provide a secondary market for privately placed securities. Explain.

2. The primary difference between the three levels of depository issues lies in reporting requirements and ability to raise capital. Explain.

3. A Eurobond is generally marketed to investors in Europe. Elaborate.

4. The principal difference between a GDR and an ADR lies in their voting rights. Discuss.

5. The principal assumption behind adjusting discount rates for projects in emerging markets is that emerging market risk is non-diversifiable. Discuss.

6. The country risk premium can be determined by calculating the spread between the Eurodollar yield of the country in question and the US treasury bonds. Explain.

7. The situation in which shares underlying depository receipts get redeemed and flood the home market is known as ____________.

8. In 1997, a US multinational requested a 'bulge bracket' investment bank to value two of its divisions in Argentina and Brazil. Will Smith, an analyst with the bank was asked to forecast free cash flow and estimate suitable discount rates for each of these divisions. Exhibit 1 presents the forecast of free cash flow for the two divisions.

EXHIBIT 1

Forecast of Free Cash Flow (in $ '000)

	1998	1999	2000	2001	2002
Argentina	6930	7117	7331	7617	7990
Brazil	10920	11215	11551	12002	12591

Cash flows are expected to grow at 6% p.a. after 2002 in perpetuity. The cash flows from local currency were translated into the US dollar using the estimated exchange rate for each period. The only task remaining is the estimation of discount rate. Smith discovered that the businesses in Latin America had no pure play proxies. Most of the competitors were subsidiaries of large, diversified companies. So the determination of beta for each country operation was difficult. In addition, the efficiency of the local stock markets was questionable and so was the estimate of risk premium.

The analyst obtained the dollar borrowing rate, tax rates and target capital structure information from relevant sources. These are displayed in Exhibit 2.

EXHIBIT 2

Subsidiary	Borrowing rate (%)	Tax rate (%)	Target D/V (%)
Argentina	8	35	20
Brazil	12	35	20

To calculate the cost of equity, the analyst can choose between two approaches under the CAPM method. The first approach involves usage of local CAPM parameters. The second approach involves estimation of parameters (and cost of equity) for the US which would then be adjusted for individual country risk to yield estimates for these subsidiaries. Other relevant data are given as follows:

Foreign Currency Debt Rating

	Moody's	S&P
Argentina	B1	BB–
Brazil	B1	B+

The US treasuries are yielding:

	YTM%
1 year T-Bill	5.92
10 year	6.80
30 year	7.0

Median beta and capital structure information for the comparable US industries are given as follows:

	1	2	3	4
Unlevered median beta*	0.86	0.79	0.74	0.76
Mean D/V ratio (market value)	0.2	0.18	0.17	0.19

Refer to other data given in the chapter. Estimate an appropriate discount rate for (and the value of) each division.

* Beta when leverage is zero. The relationship between levered and unlevered beta is as follows:

$$\beta_L = \beta_U\ [\ 1 + (1 - T)D/E]$$

CHAPTER

6

Corporate Risk Management*

LEARNING OBJECTIVES

After reading this chapter, you should be able to:

- Provide a rationale for risk management.
- Explain a methodology for measuring risk exposure.
- Highlight the results of academic surveys of risk management practices.

INTRODUCTION

Due to increased volatility in asset prices, companies are increasingly turning to derivative instruments to manage risk. But is risk management something good? This chapter provides an overview of all the issues in risk management.

Financial markets are more volatile today than they were a couple of decades back. Consequently, firms are exposed to a more risky environment. To deal with the same, managers have access to a wide range of risk management tools such as swaps, options and futures. A survey by the Wharton School found that 50% of the firms contacted use derivatives.[†] The same survey also found that of the firms using derivatives, foreign exchange risk is the risk most commonly managed with derivatives (see Exhibit 6.1).

---

[*] This chapter is contributed by Ravishanker Mateti.

[†] Bodnar, Gordon M., Gregory Hayt, and Richard Marston, 1998 Wharton Survey of Financial Risk Management by US Non-Financial Firms, *Financial Management*, **27**, 4, (Winter), 1998.

EXHIBIT 6.1

Risk Management Approach across Risk Classes
Percentage of Derivative Users Active in that Class

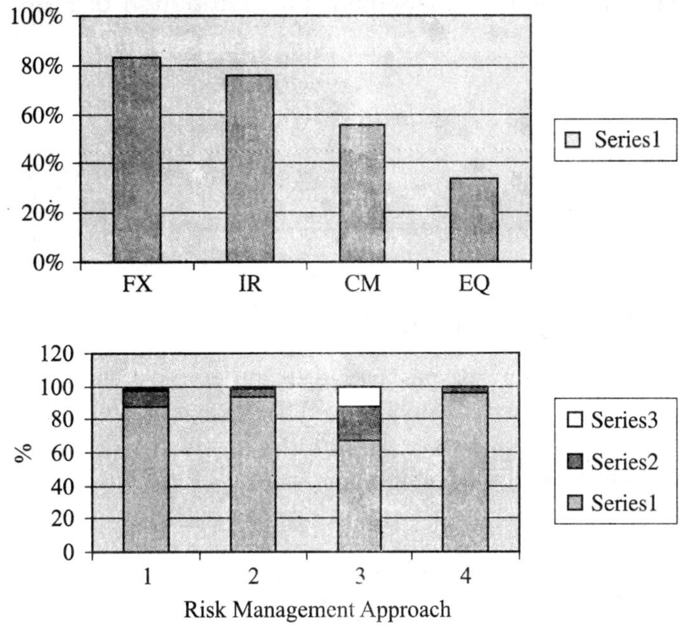

Note:
Series 1— Centralized;
Series 2— Decentralized with centralized co ordination;
Series 3— Decentralized

The exhibit presents risk management approach for different risk classes such as foreign exchange risk, interest rate risk, commodity price risk, and equity price risk. Firms use derivatives with many objectives like reducing funding cost, hedging contractual commitments and anticipated transactions, and reducing fluctuations in the market value of the firm. In this chapter we intend to present the rationale for risk management.

Is Risk Management *Good*?

Economic models of investors' behaviour assume that investors are risk-averse in the sense that they prefer higher returns for a given level of risk or lower risk for a given level of return. Hedging reduces the volatility of a firm's earnings, which in turn reduces the volatility of cash flow available to investors (see Exhibit 6.2). Consequently, investors' may demand a lower risk premium due to the reduction in volatility. The lower risk premium for a given level of cash flow translates into a higher firm value. In other words, stock prices of firms that hedge exceed stock prices of firms that do not, all else equal. Risk management is, therefore, good.

EXHIBIT 6.2

Impact of Risk Management on Distribution of Firm Value

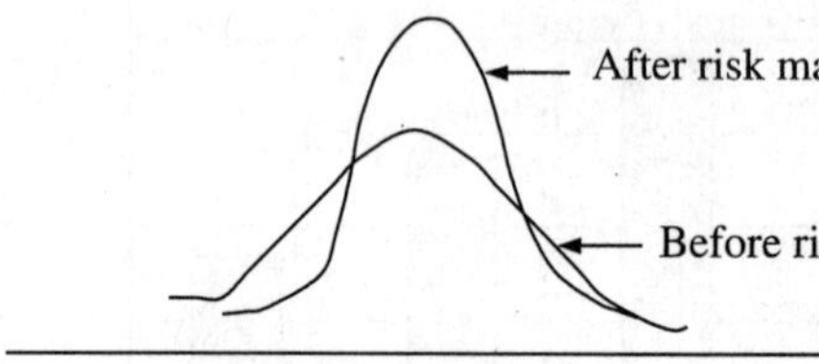

Is Risk Management *Bad*?

A firm generates returns commensurate with the risk it takes. If a firm avoids or transfers risks, it loses returns as well. If risk reduction is the motive, firms' may simply avoid taking risky projects. There would be no need for hedging. In other words, risk reduction results in loss of returns. Consequently, risk management is bad.

Is Risk Management *Irrelevant*?

The theory of capital structure starts with the Modigliani and Miller theorem that debt policy does not matter. The market value balance sheet of a company is given in Table 6.1.

Table 6.1 Market Value Balance Sheet of a Company

Assets	Liabilities
Assets-in place	Equity
Present value of future growth opportunities	Debt
Firm value V	V

Franco Modigliani and Merton Miller were among the first to analyse the capital structure decision rigorously. They analysed the effect of a change in the firm's capital structure on the market value of the firm, first in a hypothetical world with no corporate taxes and then in a world with corporate taxes. They proved that the value of the firm, V, is independent of the debt policy of the firm. That is, V is constant regardless of the mix of D and E as long as the left-hand side of the balance sheet is held constant. Their theorem is based on certain following assumptions:

- Investment opportunities of the firm remain fixed. Corporate real investment and operating decisions are not affected by capital structure.
- The business risk of a firm can be measured by the standard deviation of earnings, and firms can be grouped into distinct business risk classes.
- Investors have homogeneous expectations about future corporate earnings and the volatility of these earnings.

Modigliani and Miller argue that the market value of the firm is determined by the magnitude and riskiness of cash flows generated by the firm's assets. The firm's capital structure merely indicates how this stream of cash flows is divided between shareholders and bond holders. Stated in a different fashion, it is the magnitude and risk of cash flow stream and not its partitioning between shareholders and bond holders that determines the market value of the firm. Whether you cut a pizza into six or eight slices will not *increase* the size of the pizza. The same is true of companies also. In other words, companies can make money by good *investment* decisions and not by good *financing* decisions.

Since the company has already decided on what projects it should undertake and all investors agree upon the expected cash flows and the appropriate discount rate to discount these cash flows, the firm must sell for the PV of project cash flows whether it is 50% debt financed or all-equity financed. See Figure 6.1.

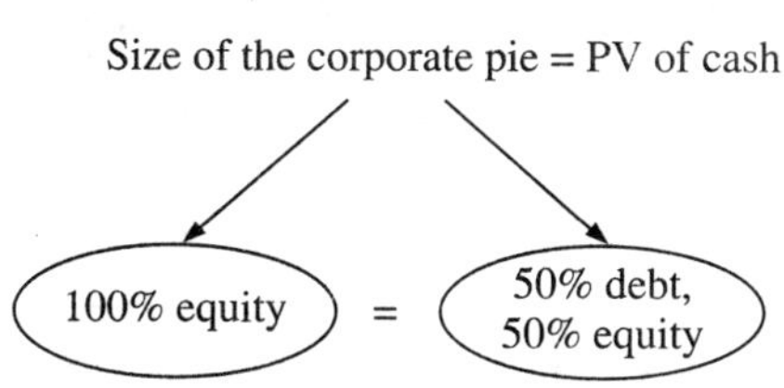

Figure 6.1 Two firms differing in capital structure.

Consider two firms that are similar in all respects except for their capital structure. One firm is all-equity financed and the other has 50% debt carrying an interest of 12%. In a world without taxes, the decision to borrow will not affect firm value. Let us suppose, the optimal capital structure for a company is 70% equity (30% debt) that maximizes firm value, say PV. But managers resort to sub-optimal capital structure due to which the firm value is only 0.9 PV. If this happens, investors can buy the firm for 0.9 PV, repackage securities to attain the optimal capital structure, sell the company for PV. The difference of 0.1 PV is the riskless profit. Under competitive conditions it is not possible to make riskless profit as demonstrated in Figure 6.1.

Likewise, assume that there are two firms that are identical in all respects except their risk management practice. Suppose the share price of the firm that does not manage risk is P_A and that of another firm that manages risk is P_B. Let P_A be less than P_B. An investor who notices the difference might purchase the shares of the first firm, make changes in the risk management policy and cash out.

The main assumption behind 'hedging irrelevance' proposition is that investors can hedge whatever risk they wish to shed depending on their risk taking appetite at their level and that the firm is not uniquely positioned to execute a risk management programme at the company's level. Assume that a US company is exposed to foreign exchange risk, French Francs to be precise. The company exports to France and the invoice is denominated in Ffr. The company is hurt by a depreciation of the Ffr. Either the company or the investor could get into a forward or a futures contract to shed the foreign exchange risk. A risk-averse investor could sell Ffr forward. Consider another investor who imports from France. The investor suffers a loss if Ffr appreciates. This investor would be hurt by the firm's risk management programme. In sum, hedging is neither good nor bad.

A related argument is that since investors can hold a diversified portfolio of assets, they are not concerned with firm specific risk. If they hold the stock of oil firm in their portfolio that suffers if oil prices fall, they can offset the impact by holding the stock of another firm that benefits from decline in oil price. Since investors can diversify such firm-specific risk, the company need not hedge oil price risk at the company level.

WHY MIGHT RISK MANAGEMENT MATTER?

Despite the three different views of hedging, risk management might matter. The hedging irrelevance proposition, like MM propositions of capital structure, is based on certain restrictive assumptions like no taxes, transaction costs, information asymmetry, agency conflicts, bankruptcy costs and so on. We can relax each of these assumptions to figure out why risk management may add value.

Taxes

Risk management can create value by reducing the tax burden. A progressive tax structure provides an incentive to smooth earnings and risk management enables such smoothing. Assume that tax rates increase as income increases. Suppose the tax rate for \$ 10 million or less in profit is 20% and above \$ 10 million, the marginal tax rate is 30%. If a firm earns \$ 10 million in two years, its tax bill is \$ 4 million. Consider another firm that earns the same \$ 20 million in two years but with a difference: \$ 0 in the first year and \$ 20 million in the second year. The tax bill for this firm is \$ 5 million, \$ 1 million more.

Further, paying taxes later than sooner reduces the present value of taxes. Firms pay taxes when income is high. They do not pay taxes when income is low. Likewise, shifting a dollar of income from when the income is high to when the income is low results in tax savings.

Risk management can also create value by increasing debt capacity. Bond holders care about total risk (and not systematic risk) because the firm's ability to service debt depends on total risk. Risk management can reduce total risk by reducing the volatility of cash flows. This results in an expansion of debt capacity. The increased debt ratio leads to higher tax shields.

Agency Conflicts

Agency cost arises whenever there is a cooperative effort even when there is no agency relationship. Agency cost can arise due to conflict of interests between shareholders and managers, shareholders and bond holders. Bond holders suffer opportunity wealth loss due to a firm's investment, financing and dividend decisions. If the firm sells bonds, and the bonds are priced assuming that no additional debt will be issued, the bond holders' claims get diluted if the firm issues additional debt of the same or higher priority. Due to claim dilution, bond holders suffer capital loss.

A company suffering losses may be tempted to take on business gambles, the gains from which largely go to shareholders, whereas if they fail shareholders have little to lose and it is the lenders who suffer. It is a heads-I-win, tails-you-lose situation. Smart bond holders recognize the incentive faced by shareholders and make estimates of the behaviour of shareholders. The price that bond holders pay for the issue will be lower to reflect the possibility of subsequent wealth transfers to stockholders. Bond holders try to protect themselves with restrictive loan covenants. The loan covenants may lead to reduced efficiency and lower firm value. Through risk management a firm might commit not to increase certain types of risks that decrease bond holder wealth and, therefore, reduce the cost of debt.

Financial Distress

The costs of bankruptcy are of two kinds, *direct* and *indirect*. Direct costs include lawyers' and accountants' fees, other professional fees and the value of managerial time spent on administering bankruptcy. Indirect costs include lost sales (and, hence, lost profits), the possibility that the firm may not be able to obtain additional credit or to issue securities except under strict terms. A firm may lose sales rapidly if the firm is a manufacturer of long lived products that require continuous servicing or replacement parts as customers may use their *perception* of the financial condition of the company to make their purchase decisions. For instance, the value of a computer is not only determined by its hardware but also by the manufacturer's continued provision of hardware and software support. An obsolete software or hardware is worthless. So a customer may settle for an inferior alternative with a lower probability of bankruptcy based on the perception that this firm is risky.

Software firms may refuse to support computer firms that have high probability of bankruptcy because these companies are unlikely to be around for long thereby accelerating distress. Likewise, airlines depend on frequent flier plans to attract business travellers. No amount of advertising may bring credibility to the claim made by those companies. Similarly, retailing companies may not obtain goods or credit from wholesalers. Since these firms do not get credit, their competitiveness will be lost. The indirect cost of bankruptcy can arise from the bankruptcy process itself. The bankruptcy trustee, as an agent of the court, may not run the firm in a value maximizing way as he has no incentive to do so. The firm incurs an opportunity loss due to the sub-optimal decision-making of the agent. Another possible indirect cost of bankruptcy is the higher compensation that the managers of a highly levered firm will receive because of the higher probability of unemployment they may face.

Since financial distress is costly, firms may use risk management to decrease the probability of financial distress. Risk management in this case adds value if the benefits arising out of protecting market share and sales exceed the cost of implementing risk management.

Information Asymmetry

Value is created when companies make investments that increase cash flows. A company may fund its projects internally if it has retained earnings or raise capital from public capital markets by selling debt or equity. External finance is usually costly than internal finance due to information asymmetry between managers and investors. For instance, studies have shown that the stock market reacts negatively to equity issues because of which firms prefer to sell securities that are less information sensitive (e.g. debt). If, on the other hand, a firm were to sell debt it might end up highly leveraged. Leverage, in this case, might interfere in the company's product market strategy in the sense that the firm might not get additional funds in future because of its highly levered position to support its strategy. One study finds that firms cut down on investment when cash flow declines rather than raise capital from capital markets[*]. Information asymmetry is severe for hi-tech R&D intensive firms. A firm may reduce variability in cash flow by risk management. By managing risk, a firm would be able to predict with more certainty its future cash flows and set a realistic level of investments[†].

[*] Fazzari, Steven R., Glenn Hubbard and Bruce Petersen, Financing Constraints and Corporate investments, *Brookings Paper on Economic Activity*, No. 1, 1988.

[†] This argument was presented by Kenneth, Froot, David S. Scharfstein and Jeremy Stein, Risk Management: Coordinating Corporate Investment and Financing Policies, *Journal of Finance*, December, 1983. A less technical version is: Kenneth, Froot, David S. Scharfstein and Jeremy Stein, "A Framework for Risk management", *Harvard Business Review*, Nov-Dec, 1994.

A related benefit is that smoothening of earnings makes it easier for investors to judge managerial effectiveness. The company's management can measure the performance of its managers more accurately and provide incentives for better performance.

Underinvestment

Managers acting on behalf of shareholders will ignore positive NPV projects when shareholders have no chance of receiving any proceeds when debt falls due. Because bond holders receive all the proceeds when their payment falls due, managers reject projects (even riskless projects) thereby reducing the firm value. This reduces the value of bond holders and, hence, the price bond holders would be willing to pay *today*. Underinvestment occurs due to volatility in the value of the firm coupled with a high debt-equity ratio. Through risk management, firms may control volatility in the value of the firm and, hence, underinvestment. The results of empirical studies of derivative usage are consistent with the notion that firms use derivatives to avoid costly underinvestment problem*.

MEASURING RISK

Financial institutions hold portfolios of assets that may include stocks, bonds, currencies and derivatives. These institutions need to quantify the amount of loss the portfolio may incur in the course of a day, week, month or year. Banks need to assess potential loss in order to set aside enough capital to cover them. *Value at Risk* (VaR) is an estimate of the largest loss that a portfolio is likely to suffer during all but exceptional periods. VaR is the maximum loss that an institution can be confident of losing a certain fraction of time over a particular time period. For example, a bank may estimate that, on average, in 98 trading days out of 100, the loss on the portfolio will not exceed $ 1 million over a one-day horizon. VaR can be used to assess the potential loss on a portfolio of assets generally.

Firms worry about the absolute level of cash flow because it affects the firm's ability to service debt, invest and grow. To measure risk a non-financial firm has to forecast the distribution of cash flows. The firm can set a threshold below which the firm will experience financial distress and use the cumulative distribution of cash flows to find out the probability of a cash flow below this level. The cash flow shortfall corresponding to the probability level chosen by the firm is called *cash flow at risk* at that probability level. A *cash flow at risk* of $ 200 million at the 5% means that there is a probability of 5% that the firm's cash flow will be lower than its expected cash flow by at least $ 200 million.

* Gay, Gerald, and Jouahn Nam, The Underinvestment Problem and Corporate Derivatives Use, *Financial Management*, Winter, 1998.

If there is a probability that the level of cash flow will be less than the threshold, the company should take actions to reduce the risk of cash flow and ensure that it earns the cash flow corresponding to the threshold level 95% of the time. Cash flow at risk is analogous to VaR commonly used by financial firms. Measuring VaR requires enumerating every asset, quantifying the risk exposures of these assets and aggregating them across the entire portfolio of assets. Likewise, measuring CaR involves identification of all risks to a firm's cash flows. Implementing CaR the way VaR is measured is likely to be difficult or erroneous because non-financial firms are exposed to non-financial risks (apart from financial risks like FX risk) that are difficult to identify or measure. One solution is to look at historic, quarterly cash flow data for, say, five years. But this yields few data points. Including comparable companies' data increases the number of observations*. With sufficiently high number of observations, it becomes possible to estimate 5% tail probabilities with some confidence. One may choose comparables on the basis of market capitalization, industry risk, profitability and stock price volatility.

As pointed out earlier risk management adds value by reducing the variability of cash flows. In order to quantify the benefits of risk management one needs the probability distribution of cash flows. Measuring CaR tells us how valuable risk management is.

To get a measure of the sensitivity of the value of a firm to changes in the financial prices, a statistical regression equation that reveals the sensitivity of the firm's stock price movements to changes in the general market may be estimated (Smithson and Smith 1994). In other words, the model regresses the rate of return on the firm's equity against a number of variables like exchange rate, interest rate, and commodity price exposures. The correlation coefficients are used to estimate the sensitivity of the firm's value to changes in each of the variables. For instance, the regression might be:

$$R_t = \alpha + b_1(\Delta 3mL/3mL) + b_2\,(\Delta 10YT/YT) + b_3(\Delta P_{oil}/P_{oil})$$

where $3mL$ = 3 month Libor, 10YT = 10 year treasury rate and P_{oil} is the price of oil. One may also include relevant exchange rates into the regression.

SURVEY RESULTS

Academic surveys of risk management practices have sought to find out what type of risk firms hedge and how; whether the usage of derivatives is determined by firm size and industry; the objective of derivatives use; and reporting and control policy followed. The Wharton survey mentioned earlier

* Stein J., Stephen Usher, Daniel LaGattuta, and Jeff Youngen, A Comparables Approach to Measuring Cash flow-at-Risk for Non-Financial Firms, National Economic Research Associates, *Working Paper No. 39*, August, 2000.

has been replicated in New Zealand, Sweden and Germany (Berkman, Bradbury and Magan, 1997; Alkeback and Hagelin 1999; and Bodnar and Gebhardt 1999). The result of the survey conducted in New Zealand is presented in Exhibit 6.3. It shows that in New Zealand, 100% of the firms with market value of equity greater than $ 250 million use derivatives, compared to 65% in the USA. Of the firms with market value of equity less than $ 50 million, 36% of New Zealand firms use derivatives, compared to 12% of the US firms. The same pattern holds for firms with market value in the range of $ 50–$ 250 million, with 70% of New Zealand firms using derivatives compared to 30% of the US firms. Large firms hedge more than small firms probably because of scale economies in hedging that is unavailable to small firms. The same survey shows that both the US and New Zealand firms use derivatives to hedge contractual commitments and anticipated transactions within 12 months.

EXHIBIT 6.3

Use of Derivatives by Firm Size in New Zealand

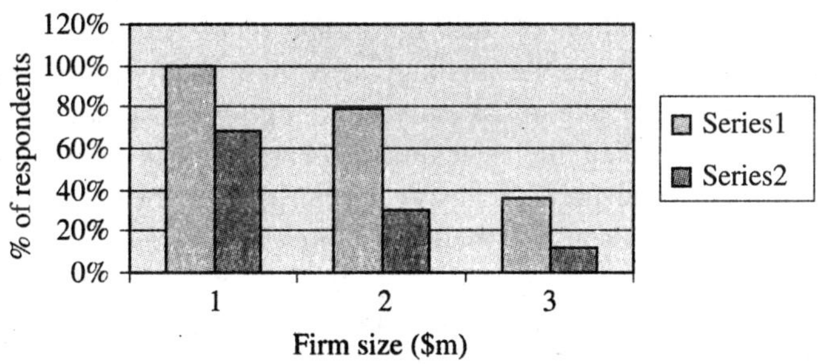

Note:

Series 1—NZ firms with market values of $ 250, $ 50–$ 250 and < $ 50 million, respectively.

Series 2—The US firms with market values of $ 250, $ 50–$ 250 and < $ 50 million, respectively.

The Hedging Process

Having understood the rationale for and the practice of risk management, we move on to the design of risk management programme. An effective hedging programme is not necessarily the one that eliminates all the risk. Indeed, as academic surveys suggest companies do take a view on the movement of interest, exchange rate and commodity prices before deciding how much (and if at all) to hedge. Implementing a risk management programme involves the following steps:

1. **Identification of risks:** The first step in the process is to identify risks the company is willing to bear and the ones it wishes to hedge.

Risks can be classified as operating and financial. **Operating risk** refers to the risks associated with manufacturing and marketing (for non-financial firms). **Financial risk** arises from exposure to interest rate, exchange rate, commodity and stock price. Non-financial firms that do not have unique knowledge of forecasting market movements would do well to hedge these (financial) risks. For example, a computer manufacturer like Dell is rewarded for bearing technological risk and developing new products whereas bearing FX risk is not. The actual decision on whether to hedge or not depends on the costs and benefits of hedging. Implementing a hedging programme involves cash outlay. Hedging makes sense if benefits exceed costs.

2. **Deciding whether to hedge or not:** The objective of hedging is to reduce risk, not speculate. At times managers may have a view on the direction of asset prices that they may incorporate in their hedging decision. In doing so they implicitly assume that not hedging is optimal at times. Hedging 100% of risk exposure at all times completely eliminates risk. But this might not be the optimal strategy. In general, the decision to hedge or not also depends on the risk-taking ability of managers and their incentives. In those companies where the management has high equity ownership, managers will have an incentive to hedge because not reducing risk would jeopardize their wealth. Executives with stock options, in contrast, would prefer to leave certain risk exposures open because stock options reward managers for taking bets and increasing volatility. Reduction in volatility makes options worthless. A study by Peter Tufano of the risk management practices of gold mining firms confirms these expectations*.
3. **Choosing a hedging vehicle:** Managers have access to a number of derivative instruments to hedge risk. Interest rate risk, for example, could be hedged using interest rate swaps, interest rate futures, caps, and collars. The choice of the instrument depends on the all-in-cost of the instrument, accounting treatment and its impact on financial statements. Assume that you borrow at floating rate and use a floating-to-fixed rate swap to hedge the interest rate risk. The fixed rate the company obtains by engaging in a swap should be compared with the rate the company would get if it were to borrow directly in the fixed rate market.
4. **Evaluating hedging performance:** The effectiveness of the hedge is to be ascertained by comparing the outcome of the transaction

---

* Peter Tufano, Who Manages Risk? An Empirical Examination of the Risk Management Practices of the Gold Mining Industry, *Journal of Finance*, September, 1996.

with what was anticipated. The fixed rate swap, for example, is a substitute for a fixed rate bond. Assume that interest rates fall after getting into the swap. It is incorrect to say that the swap did not work. This would have been the outcome if the firm had issued a bond instead. The right comparison is between the fixed rate swap and the fixed rate bond.

5. **Establishing an information system:** A well-designed hedging programme requires an information system that documents the following:
   - Which risks are to be hedged?
   - Who is authorized to hedge?
   - Who should receive updates of the transactions?

This is of paramount importance for financial firms. The information system must combine data from different trading units and estimate the aggregate risk for the firm.

Merck is a $ 6.6 billion, international pharmaceutical company that operates in over 100 countries. The potential loss in dollar value of net revenues earned overseas represents the company's most significant economic and financial exposure. Currency hedging at Merck involves the following five steps*:

1. Review of the likelihood of adverse exchange movements.
2. Quantification of the potential impact of adverse exchange movements over the period of the plan.
3. Critical examination of the reasons for hedging.
4. Selection of which instruments to use and how to execute the hedge.
5. Simulation of alternative strategies to choose the most cost-effective hedging strategy to accommodate their risk tolerance profile.

APPROACHES FOR RISK MANAGEMENT

As pointed out earlier, risks can be classified as operating and financial. Firms may reduce risk by operational risk management, design of capital structure, and using financial instruments such as derivatives†.

Reducing operating leverage increases a firm's operating flexibility. Microsoft, for example, is exposed to technological risk and sudden demand shocks. By using a greater number of temporary employees, Microsoft essentially converts fixed cost (salary) into a variable expense. To the extent

* Lewent, J.C., and A.J. Kearney, Identifying, Measuring and Hedging Currency Risk at Merck, *Journal of Applied Corporate Finance*, **2** (4): 19–28, 1990.

† Lisa Meulbroek, " Integrated Risk Management for the Firm: A Senior Manager's Guide", Harvard Business School Working Paper No. 02-046, 2002.

that these temporary employees are as skilled and loyal as permanent employees, Microsoft retains the ability to respond quickly to demand shocks. Likewise, Disney's decision to locate its theme park at Orlando, Florida was partly motivated by weather risk it faces. Bad weather reduces the number of visitors to its park. Locating the theme park in a sunny location reduced the exposure.

Like operating leverage, a reduction in financial leverage also reduces the impact of risks. More specifically, a low debt ratio reduces the chance that the firm becomes financially distressed.

The third alternative is to use derivative instruments such as options, futures, and swaps to manage risks. For example, Disney could buy insurance against bad weather. It is far easier to implement a derivative transaction than to make operational changes. The actual choice depends on the relative costs and benefits of the alternatives. Firms may also issue debt instruments whose payments are denominated in some asset other than cash. For example, a company exposed to gold price risk may issue gold denominated debt.

CONCLUDING REMARKS

The goal of risk management is to eliminate *lower-tail outcomes*. While there are benefits from risk management, there are also costs. More specifically risk management can exacerbate agency problems by allowing managers to bypass the discipline of capital markets. The cash flow hedging rationale advanced by Froot, Scharfstein and Stein (1993) is based on the assumption that all hedging is in the interest of shareholders. It does not account for usage of risk management by managers to protect pet projects that enhance their welfare due to private benefits but reduce shareholder value. In other words, while cash flow hedging might take away the need to resort to expensive financing it may do so by eliminating the discipline capital markets would impose on firms that attempt to fund poor projects[*].

In most firms the management of different types of risk rests with different people. For example, the insurance team may negotiate insurance contract for insuring plant and equipment. Likewise, another team may hedge foreign exchange risk. Although these people are addressing different types of risk, their goal remains the same—reduction of risk. In other words, an integrated approach to risk management might reduce the cost of risk management by hedging *net* exposures[†]. A fire that destroys a factory also eliminates the chance that the company will have to pay for product liability. If the company were to separately hedge these risks, the cost would go up due to covering unwanted exposures.

---

[*] Peter Tufano, Agency Costs of Corporate Risk Management, *Financial Management*, **27**(1, Spring), 1988.

[†] Lisa Meulbroek, A Better Way to Manage Risk, *Harvard Business Review*, February, 2001.

Honeywell, for example, has developed an innovative insurance contract with the assistance of American International group that covers not only traditionally insurable risks like property and product liability, but also several exchange rates. Bundling the company's risk has enabled the company to cut its overall costs by more than 15%.

REFERENCES

1. Alkeback, P. and Niclas Hagelin, Derivative Usage by Non-financial Firms in Sweden with an International Comparison, *Journal of International Financial Management and Accounting* **10:** 2, 1999.
2. Berkman, H., M. Bradbury and S. Magan, An International Comparison of Derivatives Use, Winter, 1997.
3. Bodnar, G., and G. Gebhardt, Derivatives Usage in Risk Management by US and German Non-financial Firms: A Comparative Survey, *Journal of International Financial Management and Accounting* **10:** 3, 1999.
4. Froot, K.A., D.S., Scharfstein and J. Stein, Risk Management: Coordinating Corporate Investment and Financing Policies, *Journal of Finance*, **5**, 1993.
5. Smithson, C. and C. Smith, Strategic Risk Management, in Donald Chew, (ed.), *The New Corporate Finance: Where Theory meets Practice*, McGraw Hill, 1994.

SUGGESTED FURTHER READING

Beaver, W. and G. Parker (ed.), *Risk Management: Problems and Solutions*, McGraw-Hill, 1995.

Bernstein, P., The New Religion of Risk Management, *Harvard Business Review*, March-April, 1996.

Bodnar, G., G. Hayt and R. Marston, 1998 Wharton Survey of Financial Risk Management by US Non-Financial Firms, *Financial Management*, Winter, 1998.

Chacko, G., P. Tufano and G. Verter, Cephalon Inc.: Taking Risk Management Theory Seriously, *NBER Working Paper* 7748, June, 2000.

Culp, C., Structured Debt and Corporate Risk Management, *Journal of Applied Corporate Finance*, Fall, 1994.

———, The Revolution in Corporate Risk Management: A decade of Innovations in Process and Products, *Journal of Applied Corporate Finance*, Winter, 2002.

Froot, K.A., D.S. Scharfstein and J. Stein, A Framework for Risk Management, *Harvard Business Review*, Sep/Oct, 1994.

Geczy, C., B. Minton and C. Schrand, Why Firms Use Currency Derivatives, *Journal of Finance*, September, 1997.

———, Choices Among Alternative Risk Management Strategies Evidence from the Natural Gas Industry, Working Paper, *Wharton School and Ohio State University*, November, 1999.

Gibson, M.S., Information Systems for Risk Management, *International Finance Discussion Papers No.* 585, July, 1997.

Giddy, I., The Corporate Hedging Process, *Unpublished Manuscript*, Stern School of Business, Undated.

Howton, S. and S. Perfect, Currency and Interest Rate Derivatives Use in US Firms, *Financial Management*, Winter, 1998.

Lewent, J.C. and A.J. Kearney, Identifying, Measuring and Hedging Currency Risk at Merck, *Journal of Applied Corporate Finance*, **2**(4): 19–28, 1990.

Meulbroek, L., A Better Way to Manage Risk, *Harvard Business Review*, February, 2001.

———, L., Integrated Risk Management for the Firm: A Senior Manager's Guide, *Working Paper*, Harvard Business School, Boston MA, 2002.

Petersen, M. and R. Thiagarajan, Risk Measurement and Hedging, *Working Paper*, Kellogg Graduate School of Management, April, 1997.

Schrand, C. and H. Unal, Hedging and Coordinated Risk Management: Evidence from Thrift Conversions, *Journal of Finance*, **53,** 1998.

Shapiro, A. and S. Titman, An Integrated Approach to Corporate Risk Management, *Midland Corporate Finance Journal*, Summer, 1985.

Smith, C. and R. Stulz, The Determinants of Firm's Hedging Policies, *Journal of Financial and Quantitative Analysis*, **20**, 1985.

Smith, C., C. Smithson and S. Wilford, Managing Financial Risk, in Joel Stern and Donald Chew, (eds.), *The Revolution in Corporate Finance*, 2nd Ed., Basil Blackwell, 1992.

Stein J., S. Usher, D. Lagattuta and J. Youngen, A Comparables Approach to Measuring Cash Flow-at-Risk for Non-Financial Firms, *NERA Working Paper* No. 39, August, 2000.

Stulz, R., Optimal Hedging Policies, *Journal of Financial and Quantitative Analysis*, **19**, 1984.

Stulz, R., Rethinking Risk Management, *Journal of Applied Corporate Finance*, **9**, 1996.

———, Why Risk Management is not Rocket Science, *Financial Times*, June, 2000.

Stulz, R., and Rohan Williamson, Identifying and Quantifying Exposures, *Working Paper*, Fisher College of Business, Ohio State University, August, 1996.

Tufano, Peter, Who Manages Risk? An Empirical Examination of Risk Management in the Gold Mining Industry, *Journal of Finance*, **51**, 1996.

———, Why Manage Risk, *Harvard Business Study Case No.* 9-294-107, March, 1994.

———, The Determinants of Stock Price Exposure: Financial Engineering and the Gold Mining Industry, *Journal of Finance*, June, 1998.

———, Agency Costs of Risk Management, *Financial Management*, **27**, 1998.

PART IV

PROJECT FINANCE

CHAPTER

7

Project Financing*

LEARNING OBJECTIVES

After reading this chapter, you should be able to:

- Introduce a financial innovation called project finance.
- Describe how project finance achieves several important benefits like risk sharing.
- Introduce sources of funding.
- Provide an overview of the project finance market.
- Highlight the role of bilateral and multilateral agencies in project finance.
- Highlight valuation issues in high leverage settings.

INTRODUCTION

Due to increased demand for infrastructure, countries around the world have liberalized investment in infrastructure-related projects. Project finance, a method of lending in which the lender has no recourse to the sponsor, is becoming increasingly popular to fund such investments. This chapter provides an overview of the features, issues, benefits and costs of project finance.

Global project financing, borrowing increased 20.2% to reach $ 140.3 billion in 2005 (see Exhibit 7.1 for global project finance scorecard). **Project finance** is a method of financing an economically viable project on the basis of the cash flows it is expected to generate. The project

* This chapter is contributed by S.R. Vishwanath.

is a separate legal entity and its cash flows are segregated from the sponsoring organization. The sponsor may be the main user of the project's output, contractor or supplier, a consortium or a government. The revenue generated from the project should be adequate to cover all the operating expenses, debt-servicing burden and provide an adequate return to the equity investors. This enables the sponsors to shift the operating risk and debt-servicing burden to the project entity while retaining some benefits from the project. Project finance is usually restricted to large scale, capital intensive projects and often involves a high proportion of debt finance provided by a group of lenders. Toll roads, tunnels, bridges, ports and power projects are general candidates for project financing.

EXHIBIT 7.1

Global Project Finance Scorecard

Region	**1/1/2005–12/31/2005** *Proceeds* ($, m)	*No. of Issues*
Global	140,302.8	513
Americas	20,979.2	92
Europe, Middle East and Africa	94,370.4	303
Asia-Pacific	24,953.2	118

Project finance is not dependent on the credit support of the sponsors of the project but on the expected cash flows and/or the collateral value of project assets. Typically lenders have no recourse to the sponsor in the case of a project failure. As a result, lenders should have a high degree of confidence in the performance of the project. Accordingly, extensive feasibility studies are necessary so that cash flow projections are accurate. As one project is not like the other, project finance package should be custom built and careful financial engineering is required to allocate risks and rewards among the participants. Project financing is ideal when the project's output has a strong demand and parties are willing to enter into long-term contracts. A typical project structure is shown in Exhibit 7.2.

The sponsors might be the company or a consortium of companies such as suppliers, contractors, purchasers or users of the project's output. The borrowing entity may or may not be the project company. The structure of financing and of the operations of the project will be determined by a range of considerations including tax, exchange controls and the enforceability of claims in the host country. In a project there could be several borrowers each raising funds separately to cover its individual participation in the venture.

The construction, operation and maintenance contractors are responsible for timely completion and effective maintenance, respectively. The project sponsor undertakes bidding, financing and implementing. The complexity of

EXHIBIT 7.2

Project Structure

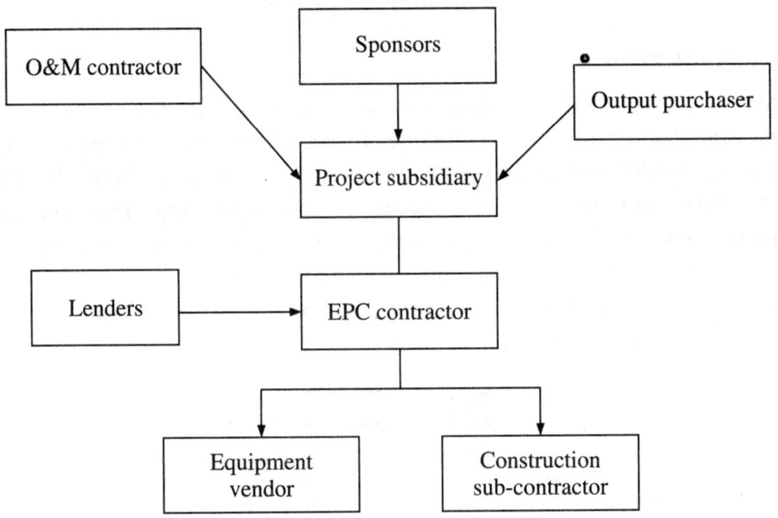

the documentation necessitates the retention of a law firm, at least in the case of large-scale international projects.

In many cases, the host government does not participate directly in the project finance as the borrower or as the owner of the project company. Host governments may, however, take an equity stake through an agency or be the output purchaser.

Table 7.1 gives some of the prominent project finance transactions.

Table 7.1 Prominent Project Finance Transactions

Project name	Sector	Country
Hub Project	Power	Pakistan
PetroZuata	Oil & Gas	Venezuela
Mozal	Aluminium	Mozambique
Hopewell	Power	Philippines
Mass Transit System	Infrastructure	Thailand

WHY USE PROJECT FINANCING?

Project financing provides certain advantages vis-à-vis conventional financing. Some of these advantages are as follows:

- Sharing of risk
- Reduced agency cost of debt

- Reduced agency cost of free cash flow
- Expansion of sponsor's debt capacity
- Reduction in costs of information asymmetry

Sharing of Risk

The risks associated with a project may be so great that it may not be possible for one organization to bear them alone. Project financing involves sharing of risk among project participants who are equipped to handle them efficiently. Project risks can be broadly classified as—**operating** and **financial**. Technology risk, performance risk, completion risk are some of the operating risks whereas interest rate risk and currency risk are financial risks. The different phases of a project and the risks associated with each of the phases of a project and their sharing are shown in Exhibit 7.3.

EXHIBIT 7.3

Risk Sharing Among Project Participants

Project phase/risk	Participant
Developmental phase	
• Technology risk	Sponsors
• Credit risk	Banks, developers, sponsors
• Bid risk	Sponsors, financial advisors
Construction phase	
• Completion risk	Contractors, sponsors, suppliers
• Cost overrun risk	Sponsors, sub-contractors
• Performance risk	Sponsors
• Political risk	Sponsors
Operating phase	
• Performance risk	O&M contractor
• Cost overrun risk	Sponsors
• Liability risk	Government, insurance companies
• Offtake risk	Sponsors, consumers

Source: Biedelman, et al. (1990)

The terms shown in Exhibit 7.3 are explained in Appendix A. The risk of death or injury on the operating facility is called **liability risk**. The risk that a sponsor may not meet the quality standards or deadlines is called **sponsors performance risk**. The risk that the project revenue may not meet projections because of changes in the market price is called **offtake risk**. The size of the project itself can be a source of risk if the outcome is strongly correlated with returns from other businesses of the group so that losses coincide. Once the risks are identified, suitable mechanism should be evolved to cover each of them. For instance, sponsors may be asked to subscribe to equity to cover technology risk during the developmental phase. A major source of risk in a project is the completion risk which refers to the actual costs of constructing the project may exceed the estimated costs, the completion date may be subject to unexpectedly long delays, the facility may be incapable of producing the output in the right quantity and quality as originally planned. Project-level risks are usually mitigated through contractual agreements. Sponsors minimize revenue exposure to changing market conditions through sales or revenue contracts. The *sales agreement* insulates the sponsor from fluctuations in prices of the project's output. The *supply agreement* obligates the supplier to deliver inputs in the right quantity at the contracted price. Although the uncertainty in quantity and price is removed, the contract, in essence, presents an opportunity cost to the company should the prices decline. The *concession agreement* with the local authority provides the project company the right (and obligation) to build, own and eventually transfer the project to the public sector. Risks can vary according to the nature of the project. For instance, market demand and interconnectivity charges are sources of risk in the case of telecommunication projects whereas low asset coverage and low toll collections are the risk factors in the case of road projects.

Agency Cost of Debt

An agency relationship is a contract under which one or more persons (the principal(s)) engage another person (the agent) to perform some service on their behalf, which involves delegating some decision-making authority to the agent. If both are utility maximizers, then there is a good reason to believe that the agent will maximize *his* utility. So the principal may have to incur monitoring costs to check his behaviour and limit divergence. The principal may suffer reduction in welfare due to divergence of interest. **Agency cost** is the sum of monitoring costs and residual loss. It arises whenever there is a co-operative effort even when there is no agency relationship. Agency cost can arise due to conflict of interests between shareholders and managers, shareholders and bond holders. Bond holders suffer opportunity wealth loss due to a firm's investment, financing and dividend decisions. If the firm sells bonds, and the bonds are priced assuming that no additional debt will be issued, the bond holders' claims get diluted if the firm issues additional debt of the same or higher priority. Due to claim dilution, bond holders suffer capital loss. There is another form of agency cost. A company suffering losses may be tempted to take on business gambles, the gains from which largely go to shareholders, whereas if they fail the shareholders have little to lose and it is the lenders who suffer. It is a heads I win, tails you lose situation.

Smart bond holders recognize the incentive faced by the shareholders and make estimates of the behaviour of the shareholders. The price which the bond holders pay for the issue will be lower to reflect the possibility of subsequent wealth transfers to the stockholders. The bond holders try to protect themselves with restrictive loan covenants. The loan covenants may lead to reduced efficiency and lower firm value. Since the nature and boundaries of the project in the case of project finance are clear, lenders are less exposed to agency cost. This may result in lower interest cost and higher firm value.

Petrozuata, a $ 2.4 billion oil field development project in Venezuela, is a joint venture between Conoco, a subsidiary of Du Pont, and Maraven, a subsidiary of Petroleos de Venezuela S A (PDVSA)*. The project was set up to develop the Orinoco belt, the largest known heavy oil field in the world. The sharing of risk in this project is shown in Exhibit 7.4.

EXHIBIT 7.4

Risk Sharing in the Petrozuata Project

Stage and type of risk	Description	Who bears the risk
Pre-completion		
Resource risk	Inputs are not available	Sponsors (suppliers)
Technological risk	Technology does not yield the required output	Sponsors (contractor)
Force Majeure	Acts of God	Third party insurers
Completion risk	Combination of technology and timing risk	Sponsors (contractor)
Operating risks		
Supply or input risk		
Throughput risk	Non-availability of raw material	Sponsors (suppliers)
Market risk (quantity)	Output quantities are too low	Sponsors
Market risk (price)	Insufficient demand Output prices decline	Conoco (off taker) Sponsors (creditors)
Sovereign risks		
Exchange rates	Changes in exchange rates	Sponsors Venezuelan Government
Currency convertibility	Inability to convert and repatriate	Sponsors Venezuelan Government
Inflation	Nominal contracts become vulnerable to price changes	Sponsors Venezuelan Government
Political and legal risks		
Expropriation	Govt. seizes assets or cash flow	Sponsors Venezuelan Government

* Esty, Benjamin, Petrozuata: A Case Study of the Effective Use of Project Finance, *Journal of Project Finance*, Fall, 1999.

Free Cash Flow Problem

Free cash flow is the residual cash flow available to managers after meeting the normal investment and debt-servicing needs. The managers have the discretion over the use of free cash flow in the sense that they can return it to the shareholders or reinvest in some other business. Left to their own device, the managers may pursue negative NPV projects for the sake of growth leaving the shareholders in lurch. Project financing can give the investors control over free cash flow. Since the project has a finite life, the free cash flow is typically redistributed to the shareholders who in turn decide where to invest their money (agreements prevent the siphoning of project cash flows through dividends or other channels). Moreover, heavy debt financing in the case of project finance enforces financial discipline on the managers.

Expansion of Sponsors' Debt Capacity

As pointed out earlier, a project finance is not dependent on the credit support of the sponsors of the project but on the strength of the contractual arrangement between parties and expected cash flows. This means that the sponsor who does not have a high credit rating can also lever up on the basis of the project-related contracts—more specifically, the one with the output purchaser. This enables the sponsor to avail the benefit of debt— the tax shield and, hence, higher firm value. The projects undertaken by project companies generally have low bankruptcy costs, as their assets are largely tangible assets that are not affected by the bankruptcy process (Brealy, Cooper and Habib 1996). For instance, a change in ownership in the case of a power project or toll road is not likely to affect its efficiency. Further, if the bankruptcy costs of the sponsor are higher than that for the project company, it is beneficial to isolate the debt in the project company.

Inside Information

Information asymmetry occurs when the management of a company has valuable information about the earning prospects that investors do not have, may be because the managers are unwilling to disclose information due to strategic reasons or the information is too technical and complex to be communicated.

Project financing reduces the cost of information asymmetry particularly in the case of large-scale, high-risk projects as project finance involves a small group of investors.

Other Advantages

Project financing can provide clearer information to investors' as the project is separately identifiable. Consequently, the effect of the project's failure on the share price of the parent company may be less. The performance of the project's managers can be assessed more accurately in the case of a stand-alone project. More importantly, managerial incentives can be tied to the performance of the project.

TYPES OF CONTRACTS

Long-term agreements relating to purchase and sale are a characteristic of project finance. Some of the widely used types of contracts are as follows:

- Take-or-pay contract
- Take-if-offered contract
- Hell-or-high water contract
- Throughput agreement
- Put-or-pay contracts

In a **take-or-pay contract** the purchaser is obligated to pay for the output regardless of whether the purchaser takes delivery or not. But the purchaser has the option to take delivery. Also the purchaser is not obligated to pay if the project is unable to deliver the output. Payments under take-or-pay contracts may be set to cover all the fixed costs or may cover only a part of the project's capacity.

Las Raffan is an LNG project in Qatar owned by Qatar General Petroleum Corporation and Mobil Oil. The project was able to get an investment grade rating (though the project is based in a country with BBB rating) and successfully issued bonds in the US because the company had a long-term (25 year) purchase agreement with Korea Gas Corporation to buy natural gas.

A **take-if-offered contract is similar** to the take-or-pay contract except that the purchaser has the obligation to take the delivery.

In a **hell-or-high water contract**, as the name suggests, the purchaser has the obligation to pay for the output regardless of whether the output is delivered or not. Obviously, such a contract is in the interest of the lenders as they get more protection.

Many oil pipeline loans involve a throughput agreement. In a **throughput agreement** if other companies do not make sufficient use of the pipeline, the owners themselves should ship enough oil through it to provide the pipeline company with the cash it needs to service the loan.

Put-or-pay contracts provide for a secure supply of project raw materials. If the supplier is unable to provide the inputs, it agrees to indemnify the project company for excess cost incurred in securing the inputs from the third parties, or, if the third party supply is unavailable, for revenue losses due to the project's inability to comply with the off-take agreements.

FINANCIAL AGREEMENTS

Although project finance, in its pure form, involves lending with no recourse, we do not see it in reality. Lenders look for financial agreements and guarantees for comfort. A financial guarantee could take the form of a letter of credit or a guarantee from a financially sound third party such as a bank. Some of the ways in which a sponsor can provide guarantee are as follows:

- **Cash deficiency agreement:** Under this agreement, the project's owners agree to provide the operating company with enough funds to maintain a certain level of working capital.
- **Capital subscription agreement:** Under the capital subscription agreement, one or more creditworthy parties are required to purchase securities for cash when the project company experiences cash shortfall.
- **Claw back agreement:** Under the claw back agreement, the sponsors are required to return cash benefits back to the project when there is a shortfall. The amount depends on the dividends and other benefits received by the sponsors (from the project).

The claw back agreements, also called **cash traps**, ensure that the lenders continue to receive timely payments. For example, no dividend distributions would be allowed if the project was not able to maintain the DSCR (Debt Service Coverage Ratio). If the non-compliance persists, the project may be considered in default and the lenders may seize all cash flow to prepay the debt.

The concession agreement between sponsors, Special purpose vehicle (SPV) and the local authority gives the SPV the right to recover the project costs, and Operation and maintenance (O&M) costs through the levy of fees over the concession period (say 30 years). The base fee rate set in the concession agreement is indexed to the consumer price index to protect the revenue potential from being eroded by inflation.

The shareholders agreement specifies the inter se rights and obligations of the shareholders. It includes the understanding between shareholders in relation to their shareholding, management of the company, constitution of the board, reorganization of the company, dividends, capital expenditure, material amendment to the project document, etc.

Public-Private Sector Partnerships

It has been found that there is a high degree of correlation between an increase in a country's GDP and an increase in its infrastructure. In other words, infrastructure development is crucial for growth. Till recently, much of the financing of infrastructure development in many countries came from government sources, multilateral institutions and export financing agencies.

Quite often, governments in emerging markets lack the financial capacity or credit worthiness to support the volume of infrastructure projects required to develop their economies.

In the case of large infrastructure projects, it is becoming inevitable for public and private sectors to come together and jointly apply their skills and strengths to develop the project more quickly and efficiently. The joint venture between Railtrack and British Rail in the UK to set up a high speed rail project is an example of such a partnership. Such partnerships try to involve the private sector in the process of designing, building, financing and operating public utilities. The Government defines the services required, makes arrangements, which enables the private sector to be the service provider and ensures that public services will be delivered at a specified quality at competitive prices. A number of public-private financing structures exist. Some of the schemes which can achieve the objectives are as follows:

- Build-Operate-Transfer (BOT) model
- Build-Transfer-Operate (BTO) model
- Buy-Build-Operate (BBO) model

In a **BOT model**, a private entity gets the mandate to finance, build and operate the project (which is otherwise a public sector project) for a specified period of time (say 25 years) at the end of which the ownership reverts to the local government. Typically, the sponsoring organization makes an equity investment of 20% to 30% of the project cost and the rest is raised from international banks, multilateral agencies and domestic financial institutions. The host Government generally gives a concession to carry out the construction and operation of the project and credit support for project borrowings. The license agreement clearly spells out the commercial and financial terms. The BOT concept has been used in transportation (e.g. roads), energy (power projects), sewage, and water treatment plants and hospitals.

In a **BTO model**, the private entity transfers the facility to the Government soon after the project clears the completion test and leases it back for a specified period of time. The project company runs the facility and collects revenues during the lease term. At the end of the lease term, the title passes on to the Government (or the public sector entity).

In a **BBO Model**, a private entity buys an existing facility, modernizes it, and operates it as a for–profit, public use facility. The BBO model is ideal in many developing countries where existing facilities require modernization/expansion. Roads and bridges are candidates for this model. Exhibit 7.5 presents the list of top 10 infrastructure projects for the period 1984–1995. Exhibit 7.6 gives the details of top sponsors of infrastructure deals in 2005.

EXHIBIT 7.5

Top 10 Private Infrastructure Investment Projects, 1984–1995

Location	Project	Contract	Cost ($, m)
France/UK	Channel Tunnel	BOT, 55 years	19,000
Taiwan	Taipei Mass Rapid Transit System	BOT	17,000
Japan	Kansai International Airport	BOT	15,000
Argentina	Buenos Aires Water And Sewer Services	BOT, 30 years	4000
Thailand	Telecom Asia Comm. Network	BTO, 25 years	4000
China	Dayar Bay Nuclear Power Plant, Phase 1	BOO	3700
Malaysia	North-South Toll Expressway	BOT, 30 years	3400
Mexico	Petacalco Coal-fired Power Plant	BOT	3000
Thailand	Bangkok Elevated Road and Train System	BOT, 30 years	2981

Source: World Bank

A typical project goes through the following phases:

- Planning
- Implementation
- Construction
- Operation
- Transfer

During the planning phase, the Government identifies the need for a service and the quality and quantity of service required. Upon identification of the project, the Government invites bids from qualified service providers. The most cost-efficient bid is awarded the contract. Once the contract is awarded, the contractor begins detailed engineering, design and construction work, usually under a fixed price contract. Upon completion, the project is tested for its suitability. If the project clears the hurdle, the private sector participant gets to run the project for a specified period of time after which it reverts to the public sector entity (or Government). Exhibit 7.7 presents the different phases in a BOT scheme.

EXHIBIT 7.6

Top Sponsors of Project Finance

Top 10 Sponsors by Investment and Region, 1990–2005 (US$ million)

Sponsor	Total investment	East Asia Pacific	Europe and Central Asia	Latin America and the Caribbean	Middle East and North Africa	South Asia	Sub-Saharan Africa
Telefonica SA	66,877	0	11,242	53,932	1,704	0	0
Telecom Italia	37,421	0	3,845	33,576	0	0	0
Carso Group	31,360	0	0	31,360	0	0	0
SUEZ	28,743	8,257	1,808	14,360	4,154	0	164
France Telecom	26,506	1,009	18,976	1,285	3,370	0	1,867
America Movil	25,712	0	0	25,712	0	0	0
AES Corporation	19,153	1,998	2,165	13,274	415	6	332
Portugal Telecom	18,690	0	0	16,688	1,704	0	299
Deutsche Telekom	17,909	1,185	16,642	0	0	0	82
Singapore Telecom	15,765	10,078	0	0	0	57	0

Source: World Bank

Funding Sources

Although the financing package for a project is tailor made, the basic form of funding remains the same, namely, equity and debt. Project debt is either of the non-recourse or limited recourse type. Commercial banks remain the most important source of project financing. Some banks have set up subsidiaries to serve the growing need of infrastructure. Bank loans can be either secured or unsecured. They may involve a single bank or a syndicate of banks. These loans are either fixed rate or floating rate, and have tenors ranging from 5 to10 years. The loan agreement between the lender and the borrower is the primary document that covers the following details:

1. The amount to be borrowed
2. Term of the loan and the repayment schedule
3. Commitment fees for unused amounts
4. Interest rate
5. Representation and warranties of the borrower which includes the use of proceeds, title to assets, contingent liabilities and so on
6. Financial covenants

In addition to the contractual arrangements between the parties, the Government may provide supplemental counter guarantee to comfort the lenders. Traditionally, the multilateral agencies like Asian Development Bank (ADB) and International Finance Corporation (IFC), Washington have been active in funding infrastructure projects. For instance, IFC has financed CESC's 250 mw coal fired power station in Budge and GVK Industries' 235 MW gas-based combined cycle power station in Andhra Pradesh, India (see Exhibit 7.7).

EXHIBIT 7.7

Phases of a BOT Scheme

	Phase	Activities
A.	Identification and definition	Preliminary feasibility study and tendering
B.	Selection	Bid evaluation and project award
C.	Development of the project	Form project company, negotiate contracts and agreements
D.	Financing	Equity contribution from promoters, Financial closure
E.	Actual construction	
F.	Completion	Testing and acceptance
G.	Operation	Operation and maintenance
H.	Transfer of assets to the Government	

The Asian Development Bank is a multinational development finance institution dedicated to fostering economic growth and co-operation in the Asia–Pacific region, and contributing to the economic development of its developing member countries. The bank was established in 1966 with its head quarters in Manila, Philippines. The bank is an infrastructure-oriented institution. It has financed the Bangkok Expressway in Thailand, Hopewell power project in Philippines, Port Qasim in Pakistan, Guangzhou power project in Peoples Republic of China among others. It provides both loan and equity capital. Infrastructure funds like Global Power Investments of GE capital, Asian Infrastructure Fund have come up to provide equity to infrastructure projects. Exhibit 7.8 gives the details of some infrastructure investment funds, Exhibit 7.9 lists out some mutual funds that invest in listed securities of infrastructure firms*. The Asian Infrastructure fund has been set up with equity contributions from IFC, ADB, Peregrine Investment Holdings, Frank Russell Company and Soros Fund Management. Export credit agencies finance imported equipment from reputed international suppliers such as GE, ABB, Siemens among others.

* This data is from Andrea Anayiotos, Infrastructure Investment Funds, *Private Sector*, July, 1994.

EXHIBIT 7.8

Infrastructure Funds

Fund	Core investors	Investment target
AIG Asian infrastructure fund	American International Group	Region: Asia-Pacific Sector: Power, Telecom Transport Size: $ 1–2 billion
Asea Brown Boveri funding	Asea Brown Boveri	Region: North America Sector: Power, transport Size: $ 0.5–$ 1 billion
Alliance SeanEast Fund L.P.	Equitable life Assurance AIG, IFC, EBRD	Region: CIS, Baltic States, Eastern Europe Sector: Power, telecom Size: $ 22 million
Central European Telec Investments L.P	IFC	Region: Poland and Hungary Sector: Telecom Size: $ 42 million

EXHIBIT 7.9

Infrastructure Mutual Funds

Fund	Size ($, m)
Super Asia Infrastructure fund	16
Nomura Asian Infrastructure fund	40
Emerging markets infrastructure fund	223
Emerging Markets Telecom fund	125
Gabelli Global Telecommunications fund	120
GT Global Telecommunications fund	2100

The AIG Asian Infrastructure Fund (Asia I) is a $ 1.08 billion fund established in 1994 to invest in infrastructure and related industries in Asia. Asia 1's investments are structured primarily as direct private placements of shares and equity-related securities in infrastructure projects and companies. As of 1 September, 2002, Asia 1's outstanding commitments totalled approximately $ 619.9 million in 15 projects, of which approximately $ 611 million has been disbursed. Exhibit 7.10 presents Asia 1's outstanding commitments by country and by sector.

EXHIBIT 7.10

Outstanding Disbursements of Asia 1 as on 30 July, 2002 ($, m)

Country	Power and water	Telecom	Transportation	Total
China			39.4	39.4
India		152.9		152.9
Indonesia		50.5		50.5
Korea		0.3		0.3
Malaysia	25.2			25.2
Philippines		100.6	75.3	175.9
Taiwan			69.6	69.6
Thailand			22.7	22.7
Regional	74.8			74.8
Total	100.0	304.2	207.1	611.3

AIG Asian Infrastructure Fund 2 is a $ 1.67 billion fund, which had its first closing and commenced its investment activities in November 1997. As of 26 November, 2002, Asia 2 has committed over 60% of its resources in 17 projects. Exhibit 7.11 presents Asia 2's outstanding commitments by country and by sector.

EXHIBIT 7.11

Outstanding Commitments of Asia 2 Fund ($, m)

Country	Telecom	Power	Transport water	Cement	Basic industries
China	10.00		181.10		113.10
India	100.00			100.00	30.0
Korea	176.00				35.5
Regional	150.00	81.60		84.96	
Total	436.00	81.60	181.10	184.96	178.60

The syndicated credit market is an important source of project finance. Transactions with loan amount of $ 750 million–$ 1 billion are not uncommon. A syndicated credit is one in which two or more banks contract with a borrower to provide credit on common terms and conditions governed by a common document. Syndicated loans are floating rate loans—the interest being reset after one, two, three or six months. The interest rate reset period is chosen by the borrower. One member of the group of banks (syndicate) is appointed to act as the agent for the syndicate. The agent bank coordinates all negotiations, payments and administration between the parties. A syndicated credit is usually of medium-term maturity, i.e. 3–10 years although transactions with maturities ranging from 6 months to 25 years could be arranged. Dual currency loan, term loans, stand by letter of credit are some of the instruments in the syndicated credit market. Bank loans have a number of disadvantages such as short maturity, floating interest rate and restrictive loan covenants. Exhibit 7.12 presents the list of top arrangers of global project finance loans.

EXHIBIT 7.12

Top Arrangers of Global Project Finance Loans in 2005

Arranger	Amount ($, m)
Royal Bank of Scotland	8891.0
BNP Paribas	7647.6
Societe Generale	7214.3
Calyon	6902.3
Mizuho Financial Group	5530.1
Caja Madrid	3838.5
Mitsubishi UFJ Financial	3633.3
WestLB	3620.3
Dexia SA	3545.9
RBC Capital Markets	3512.9

Insurance companies such as AIG provide both equity and debt to infrastructure projects. They can also provide both subordinated and senior debt, and can provide credit enhancement that make a non-investment grade transaction an investment grade transaction. Some of the insurance companies manage emerging market funds that contribute equity to projects in emerging markets.

Sometimes *equity kickers*, such as convertible debentures and stock warrants are also issued to allow investors to share in the upside potential of the project while limiting the downside risk.

Though small, the public bond market is also an important source of finance. Project bonds, unlike bank loans, have longer maturity; carry fixed interest rate and less restrictive covenants. In the recent years, a number of projects such as Ras Laffan (Qatar), Petrozuata (Venezuela), Quezon (Philippines) and Enron's Sutton Bridge Project (the UK) have floated bond offerings in international capital markets. The Sutton Bridge project, sponsored by Enron, is an integrated electricity and natural gas company. Through a finance subsidiary, the project raised $ 150 million in the US dollar denominated bonds and 195 million in Sterling denominated bonds in the US and the UK simultaneously.* The sterling bonds were priced at 135 basis points over gilts and the dollar bonds were priced at 120 bp over treasuries. The bonds cover different credit periods—the *construction period* and the *operating period.* Over the 25 year-term of the Sutton Bridge bonds, the underlying credit changes as the project moves from one phase to another. The sterling denominated bonds carry a coupon of 8.625% and the dollar denominated bonds carry a coupon of 7.97%. Both the bonds are due in 2002.

Typically, power projects enter into fuel supply and power purchase agreements which lock up the prices of input and output. While this insulates the producer from fluctuations in prices, it also precludes flexibility in the sense that the producer cannot realize better input and output prices if, for example, the input price falls after getting into a contract. One of the interesting aspects of the Sutton Bridge project is that it has no such agreements. The project, instead, has a tolling agreement with Enron Capital under which the project is supposed to make the generating capacity available to Enron Capital which in turn supplies natural gas. Enron Capital bears the price risk associated with purchasing natural gas.

Leasing is often a viable alternative in power project financing. It can be arranged to fund equipment, real estate and industrial facilities. Power plants are good candidates for leasing because of their long useful life, predictable salvage values, and well-known operating characteristics.

Export credit agencies like the US Exim Bank offer funding if the borrower buys equipment or technology or services from a source in the ECA's country. Loans are offered in the form of a buyer credit. Since the ECAs are expected to promote export from their respective countries, the interest on these loans is generally low—1–1.25% above LIBOR. These loans carry a maturity of 7–12 years with a moratorium of two years. ECA credits can be either in the form of direct loan or as a guarantee to another lending institution.

Credit Rating Constraints

Issuing project bonds is a viable alternative only if the issue gets an investment grade rating. Companies in emerging markets are often constrained by their sovereign rating even though the project's economics are robust†. A sovereign's rating on its foreign currency obligations has been regarded as the ceiling on ratings for all issuers domiciled in the country. The assumption is that a sovereign default will force all the domestic issuers to default.

* Vernon, Erid, and Louis Martarano, Enron's Sutton Bridge IPP: A New Generation of Projects Taps the International Capital Markets, *Journal of Project Finance*, Winter, 1997.

† See Esty, Benjamin and Mathew Mateo Millet, Petrolera Zuata, Petrozuata C.A., *Harvard Business School Case No.* 9-299-012, December, 1998.

For the purpose of rating project finance transactions, rating agencies like Standard & Poor's (S & P) and Moody's review the technical and construction risks, financial projections, political risk and currency market volatility. S&P bases its evaluation on the following:

1. Engineering and design, choice of technology, operating history of similar projects and experience with other rated projects.
2. Independent engineer's report on the technical feasibility of the project.
3. Political and legal support to the project.
4. Controls for management of construction funds.
5. Achievability of construction schedule and budget.
6. Creditworthiness of the EPC contractor to honour contingent liabilities.
7. Construction contractor's experience and reputation.
8. Testing and commissioning procedure.
9. O&M expertise, planning, budgeting and staffing details.
10. Quality of cash flows, financial and sensitivity analyses.

The rating assigned is the opinion of the rating agency on the project company's ability to service all obligations associated with the rated securities.

Standard & Poor's has also developed the criteria to rate project developers. A *project developer* is an entity that invests in infrastructure projects. The rating measures the credit risk associated with such project developers. The rating is an opinion of the developer's ability to meet its financial obligations. The S&P methodology employs four steps to measure the credit risk of project developers as follows:

- Determining the weighted average quality of the cash flow generated by a portfolio of investments;
- Analyzing the diversification characteristics of the pool of investments for concentration and correlation risks;
- Examining management's strategy and ownership structure of the investments and the project developer; and
- Conducting in-depth financial and sensitivity analysis.

Since the project developer's ability to service debt obligations depends on the quality and predictability of cash flows, the first step in the process is to assess the quality of the cash flows. S&P follows the scoring pattern for cash flows as shown in Table 7.2.

Table 7.2 Scoring Pattern for Cash Flows of S&P

Residual cash flow rating	Quality score
Highly predictable	1, 2
Somewhat predictable	3, 4
Somewhat certain	5, 6, 7
Highly certain	8, 9, 10

Standard and Poor's has defined *highly predictable*, for example, as follows:

(a) High predictability of cash flow, such as a regulated pipeline with 100% of the capacity under long-term contracts with counter parties rated in the A category.

(b) No restrictive covenants in the indenture that limits cash distributions.

The rating of some project developers (at the time of writing) is presented in Exhibit 7.13.

EXHIBIT 7.13

Rating of Project Developers

Issuer	Credit rating
AES China Generating Co.	BB-
Calpine Corp.	BB+
Cogentrix Energy	BB+
Edison Mission Energy	BBB-
Hopewell Holdings	BB-
Kenetech Corp.	D

THE ROLE OF BILATERAL AND MULTILATERAL ORGANIZATIONS

The World Bank group provides a variety of support to infrastructure projects in developed and developing countries. The group consists of International Bank for Reconstruction and Development (IBRD), International Development Association, International Finance Corporation and Multilateral Investment Guarantee Agency. IBRD provides loans to middle-income countries whereas IDA supports poorer developing countries. IBRD lends at rates slightly higher than those available to AAA borrowers. IBRD can either lend to the project entity directly or to the host government which in turn can lend to the project as shown in Exhibit 7.14.

EXHIBIT 7.14

IBRD Loan to a Project Company

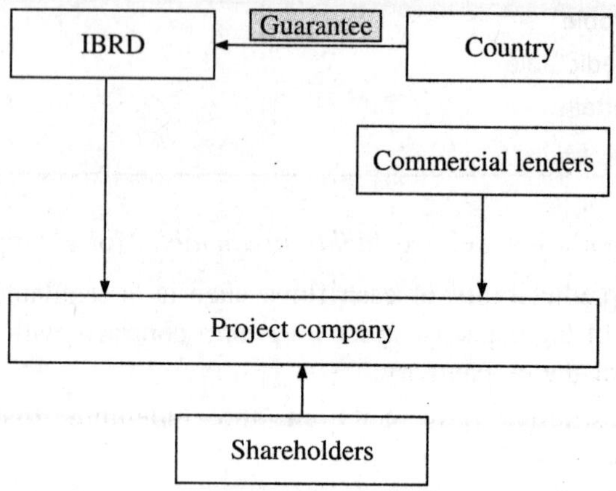

Within the World Bank Group, IFC and MIGA are active in supporting private sector projects. IFC supports through equity and debt financing, the syndicated B-loan programme, security and underwriting (see Esty and Qureshi 2000)*. MIGA provides political risk insurance primarily for equity. Other multilateral agencies like Asian Development Bank, European Development Bank and European Bank for Reconstruction and Development also provide guarantees. Bilateral agencies like Export Import Bank often provide guarantee in association with the World Bank.

The IFC support is shown in Figure 7.1:

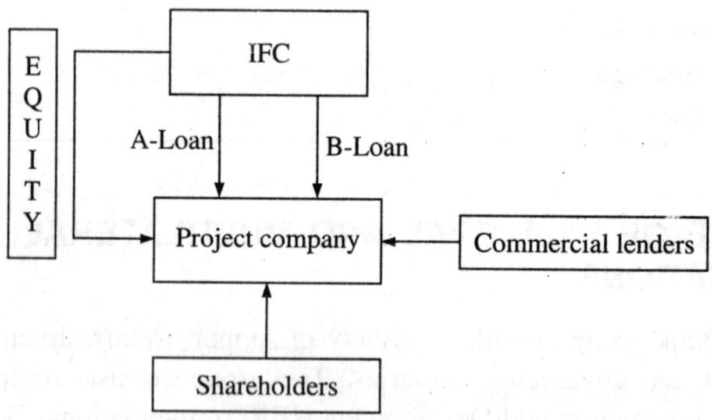

Figure 7.1 IFC support system.

---

* Benoit, Philippe, The World Bank Group's Financial Instruments for Infrastructure, *Private Sector*, January, 1997.

Benoit, Philippe, Mitigating Project Risks—World Bank Support for Government Guarantees, *Private Sector*, May, 1996.

Political Risk in Emerging Markets

Investments in emerging markets are invariably exposed to political risk which includes civil war and unrest, inconvertibility of currency, expropriation of profits, breach of contracts undertaken by Government, etc.

Obviously, investors are concerned about host country interference which results in higher project cost. The possibility of cost overruns necessitates complex insurance to cover political risk. One solution is to get a guarantee from the host Government covering project payments. But this solution may not be acceptable to host Governments and multilateral institutions. Moreover, there is a limit to the extent of guarantees a Government can provide. The international insurance agencies like American International group have expertise in writing coverage for completion risk, operating risk, political risk and off-take risk. They also cover clean up expenses (environmental liability), bodily injury to workers and property damage for off-and on-site exposures. This is particularly important because the public interest in environmental issues is on the rise and activist groups are too active when it comes to projects that involve international investors.

There are many professional political risk measurement services which measure country risk. Some of the popular ones are as follows:

- Economist intelligence unit
- Institutional investor
- *Euromoney*
- Political risk services: International Country Risk Guide (ICRG)

Each of the rating providers combines a range of qualitative and quantitative information into a risk measure. For instance, *Economist* bases its analysis on an index of 100 points with 33 assigned to economic factors, 50 to political factors and 17 to societal factors. *Economist* includes the following factors:

Political factors

- Authoritarianism
- Longevity of regime
- War
- Illegitimacy

Economic factors

- Inflation
- GDP per capita
- Food production per capita
- Capital flight
- Foreign debt as a percent of GDP

Societal factors

- Fundamentalism
- Corruption
- Ethnic tension

The *Institutional Investor* country risk ratings are based on a survey of 75–100 international bankers who are asked to grade each country on a scale of 0–100 (100 represents maximum creditworthiness). The ratings are published twice a year in March and September. The March 2000 rankings of some countries is given as follows:*

Mar '00	Sep '99	Country	Credit ranking
1	1	Switzerland	93.8
2	2	Germany	92.9
5		United States	92.9
3	5	France	91.7
7	6	UK	91.1
37	40	China	56.6
48	47	Mexico	49.8
57	57	India	45.3
70	71	Brazil	38.5
89	88	Iran	29.2
134	144	North Korea	6.8
135	145	Afghanistan	5.7

Source: Institutional Investor

Euromoney provides country risk score on the basis of nine categories. They are as follows:

1. Political risk (25% weighting, 0 to 10)
2. Economic performance (25% weight)
3. Debt indicators (10%)
4. Debt in default or rescheduled (10%)
5. Access to bank finance (10%)
6. Access to short-term finance (5%)
7. Access to capital markets (5%)
8. Discount on forfeiting (5%)

* More recent ratings are available on *Institutional Investor* website http://www.iimagazine.com/

Euromoney rankings of some countries are given in Table 7.3*.

Table 7.3 Euromoney Rankings of Some Countries

Sep'99	Country	Total score
1	Luxembourg	98.68
2	Switzerland	97.79
3	United States	94.51
18	Australia	88.10
50	China	55.09
59	India	51.80
78	Venezuela	41.33
116	Guyana	32.50
117	Algeria	32.32

Source: Euromoney, September, 1999

ICRG considers 5 financial, 13 political and 6 economic factors to calculate the risk indices in each of these categories and a composite risk score. A higher score indicates lesser risk. The political risk measure is given twice the weight of economic and financial risk. The composite score is a combination of individual indices score.

Organizations like Overseas Private Investment Corp (OPIC), Japan Exim Bank, US Exim Bank and COFACE (France) provide Political Risk Insurance (PRI). The PRI coverage includes insurance for sovereign risks such as expropriation and inconvertibility of currency, remittance of dividends on equity investments, interest and principal payments on bank loans. The OPIC has been set up by the US government to facilitate the participation of the US investment in the economic development of emerging countries.

World Bank Guarantee Programme

The guarantee programme of the World Bank tries to address the need to offer political risk mitigation products to enable the implementation of infrastructure projects in developing countries. The Bank can either lend to a project or provide a guarantee.

The Bank offers three types of guarantees. **Partial credit guarantees** cover debt service defaults on a specified portion of a loan or a bond. **Partial risk guarantees** cover debt service defaults on a loan to a private sector project caused by a Government's failure to meet its contractual obligations related to a private project. They are *partial* in that they cover the minimum number of risks and the smallest amount of debt consistent with successful

* *Euromoney* scores are available on *Euromoney* website http://www.euromoney.com/

implementation of the project. **Policy-based guarantees** (PBGs) cover a portion of debt service on a borrowing by an eligible member country from private foreign creditors. The Bank has recently approved to test a new product—policy-based guarantees*. PBG's help crisis stricken countries to re-enter international markets. They are a class of partial credit guarantees that cover defaults on long-maturity interest or principal payments. The partial risk guarantees are likely to be useful to infrastructure projects located in countries that are about to attract international investors. The presence of a World Bank guarantee helps accelerate investment. The partial credit guarantee is likely to be needed where the failure to refinance as well as the pricing of loans and guarantees can be determined on the basis of the Bank's knowledge of the financing marketplace.

Exhibit 7.15 presents the structure of a partial risk guarantee.

EXHIBIT 7.15

IBRD Partial Risk Guarantee

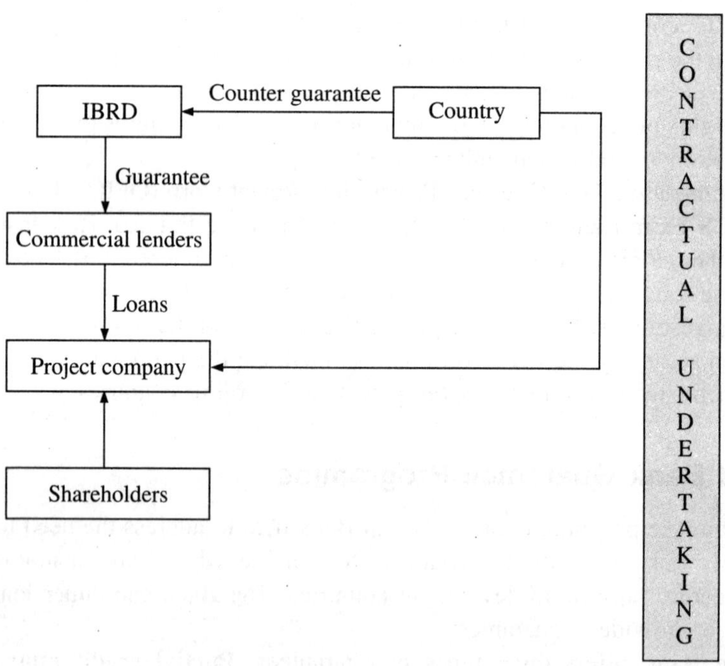

International Finance Corporation is the largest multilateral source of debt and equity financing for private sector projects in developing countries. As of 1998, IFC had funded 1138 companies in 111 countries. Exhibit 7.16 gives the maximum and average amount disbursed by IFC for a project for the

* World Bank turns to Guarantees, *Euromoney*, September 1999. Also see, Bidding for Private Concessions: The use of world bank guarantees, *RMC Discussion Paper Series 120*, World Bank.

period 1989-98. IFC has financed about 233 projects, of which 67 are in Asia, 61 are in Latin America and Caribbean, 43 in Europe, 26 in Sub-Saharan Africa and 36 are in Central Asia, Middle East and North Africa. The total investment by IFC as of 30 June, 1997 is shown in Exhibit 7.16. Exhibit 7.17 presents the statistics on the IFC investment by region as of 2006. IFC offers a syndicated loan programme (known as B-loan programme) along with some 280 commercial banks and financial institutions. IFC invests through debt, equity and quasi-equity (subordinated loans and convertible loans). IFC loans have a tenor of 8 years or more and interest rates range from 0.5% to 4% above LIBOR. IFC also lends from its own resources (A-loan) apart from providing equity and quasi-equity.

EXHIBIT 7.16

IFC Project Finance (As of 30 June, 2006, $, m)

	2006	2005
Committed loans and equity	20,318	18,108
Loans	16,407	14,781
Equity	3912	3327
Off balance sheet exposure on risk management and guarantee products	1309	1146
Total committed portfolio for IFC's own account	21,627	19,253

EXHIBIT 7.17

IFC Investment by Region, as of 2006

Region	Amount ($, m)
Latin America and the Caribbean	8627
South Asia	2384
Europe and Central Asia	6300
East Asia and the Pacific	1225
Middle East and North Africa	1871
Sub-Saharan Africa	2201

Source: IFC

AN ILLUSTRATION

International Finance Corporation has invested $ 115 million in Minera Loma de Niquel (MLdN) for exploration of nickel deposit in Caracas, Venezuela. MLdN will mine and smelt lateritic nickel ore to produce an annual average

16,000 metric tons of nickel, principally for export, over the estimated 27 year life of the deposit. Construction of the mine, smelter and associated infrastructure were expected to be completed by early 2000. The project will be supported by long-term contracts for electricity and natural gas supply and for ferro nickel offtake. Upon completion of financing, MLdN will be owned indirectly 81.5% of Minorco S A of Luxembourg. Venezuela's Corporacion Caracas and Canada's Jordex Resources each hold 7.5%. IFC will invest $ 74.5 million of its own funds: $ 65 million in loan (IFC A-Loan) and will acquire 3.5% of MLdN's equity. A further $ 50 million will be funded by banks participating in an IFC syndicated B-Loan, jointly managed by IFC and Dresdner Bank Luxembourg SA, which is also underwriting the transaction. Additional debt financing of $ 100 million will be supplied by KfW with maturities equivalent to IFC's loans.

The IFC financing is tailored to projected MLdN cash flows. The IFC A- and B-loans have maturities of 13 and 10 years respectively, reflecting the long deposit life. The repayment schedule is flexibly structured to accommodate lower amortization payments, under certain circumstances, in years of lower average nickel prices, considering the historical volatility of nickel prices. IFC has also helped raise $ 329 million to finance investment in the rehabilitation and expansion of Buenos Aires Water and Sewerage Services in Argentina, a $ 185 million digital cellular network in Hungary, a $ 1.3 billion aluminium smelter project, MOZAL, in Mozambique among other projects. MIGA guarantees cover risks of expropriation or breach of contract by host Government, war and civil disturbance in developing member countries. MIGA guarantees are long term in nature (up to 15–20 years) and non-cancellable. MIGA's coverage for equity and equity-related investments is in addition to the World Bank guarantee products outlined previously (see Figure 7.2).

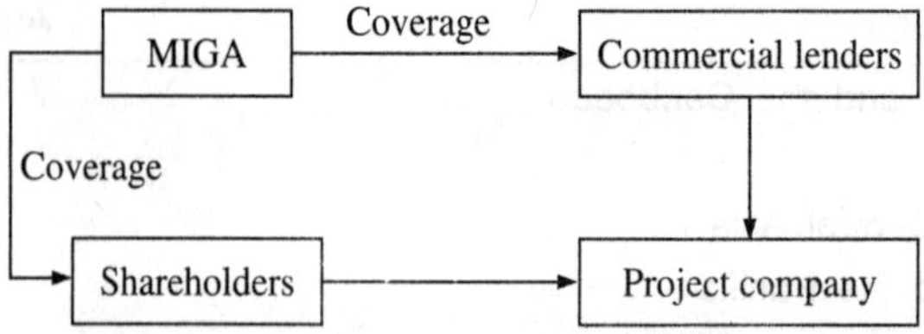

Figure 7.2 MIGA's coverage for equity and equity-related investment.

In sum,

- IBRD provides loans and guarantees
- IFC provides A- and B-loans, equity and quasi-equity
- MIGA provides political risk insurance
- IDA lends to poorer countries

All four organizations may work together in a project.

BENEFITS OF GUARANTEES

The World Bank guarantees benefit for both the borrowers and the sovereign governments. Some of them are as follows:

- By covering risks that the market cannot assume, guarantees facilitate access to financing that would not otherwise be available to certain projects.
- Guarantees can extend the maturity of the loan beyond loan period that would not be possible without a guarantee.
- Partial risk guarantees reduce host governments' exposure to a project.
- Credit guarantees enable borrowers to select the currency, interest rate basis (fixed or floating) and maturity to best match the project's requirements.
- The presence of Bank guarantee obviates the need for a country premium usually charged by lenders.

For providing the guarantee, the Bank charges a standby fee, a guarantee fee, and a front-end fee. In addition, the Bank may also charge an initiation fee, and a processing fee for a particular project. Charges differ from one guarantee structure to the other. The fee is usually charged in advance of each interest period and non-payment of fees results in the lapse of the guarantee. The 1292 MW Hub Power Project in Pakistan was the first private sector project to receive a World Bank guarantee*. The Bank's guarantee protects the commercial lenders from sovereign risks associated with the project. The project achieved financial closure in 1995. A special purpose project company, Hub Power Company, has been set up to own and operate the power station. The project costs $1.8 billion, of which 80% is debt mobilized on a project finance basis. The financing structure is shown in Figure 7.3. The security structure is shown in Exhibit 7.18.

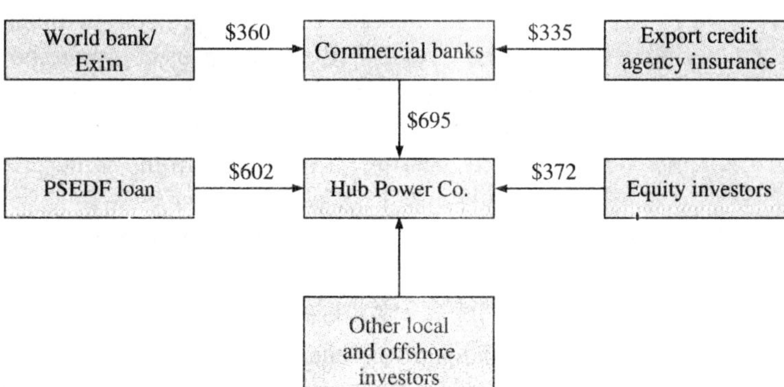

Figure 7.3 Financing structure of Hub Power Company.

* World Bank Project Finance and Guarantees, June 1995. Also see Michael Gerrard, Financing Pakistan's Hub Power Project, *RMC Discussion Paper Series 118*, World Bank, 1997.

EXHIBIT 7.18

Security Structure of Hub Power Project

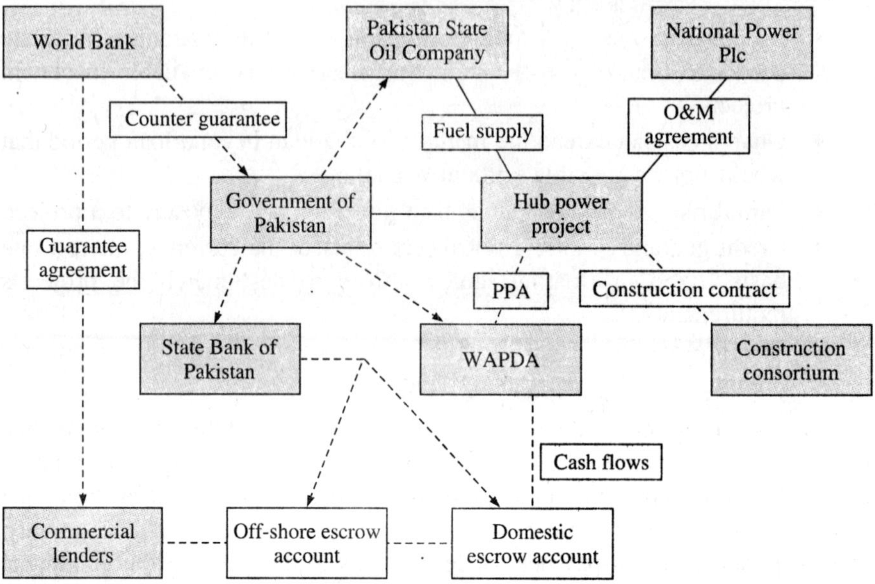

PROJECT FEASIBILITY STUDIES

Because of the non-recourse feature, extensive project feasibility studies are conducted. Elaborate projections are made for each of the cost and revenue items for the life of the project, and profitability measures like NPV and IRR are calculated. Accounting measures such as return on investment and return on equity (ROE) are quite popular in infrastructure projects. For instance, a 16% return on equity is allowed in the case of power projects in India. ROE is a single period measure. The actual IRR of the project might be much lower. ROE is a function of timing of equity investment and timing of returns in the case of multi-period projects. It might not be meaningful to calculate ROE as it is an accounting-based measure. It suffers from the same pitfalls as ROI.

The DCF methodology requires the estimation of Equity cash flows or Total cash flows.

$$\text{Free cash flow} = \text{EBIT} - \text{Cash taxes} + \text{Depreciation} - \text{Capital expenditure} - \Delta\ \text{Working capital.}$$

$$\text{Equity cash flow} = \text{Free cash flow} - \text{Debt service} + \text{New borrowings}$$

Typically, the lenders expect the sponsor to maintain a Debt Service Reserve Account equal to six months of interest and principal payment. This amount should be deducted to arrive at equity cash flows.

If the NPV of the project is positive, the project can be accepted. This approach assumes two things:

1. The capital structure remains the same throughout the life of the project and, therefore, a single discount rate (WACC) can be used for all the cash flows.
2. The discount rate can be estimated using book value weights instead of market value weights as the latter is typically not available.

Both the assumptions are questionable (See Esty 1999). In most project finance situations, the leverage rises from 0% to 60-80% and then falls back to 0. Therefore, using a single discount rate (WACC) is inappropriate. A project can be evaluated either from the equity investors' perspective or from the perspective of all the investors. The cost of equity, which is the discount rate in the former approach, is a function of systematic risk which depends on leverage*. Calculating the project's cost of equity using the maximum leverage or average leverage gives erroneous answers. So it is necessary to calculate a different discount rate for each year based on leverage in existence in that year.

The equity beta

$$\beta_E = \beta_A\left(\frac{V}{E}\right)$$

where β_A = asset beta, V and E are values of firm and equity, respectively.

The asset beta can be estimated using regression analysis and a set of comparable, publicly traded companies. To illustrate, if asset beta is 0.8, V and E are 100 and 35.

$$\text{Equity beta} = 0.8\left(\frac{100}{35}\right) = 2.28$$

If risk-free rate is 12%, market premium is 10%, cost of equity = 12 + 2.28 (10) = 34.8%.

Beta and the cost of equity can be estimated for each year by using actual leverage. Quite often, the capital structure is measured using book value. According to modern finance theory, investors demand returns based on market values and not book values. The two values rarely coincide. Unfortunately, measuring market value of equity is difficult. The market value of equity is the present value of equity cash flows but the discount rate used to discount ECFs itself is supposed to be based on market value of equity. That is, there is a circularity problem. We can get over this problem by using the Quasi-Market Valuation.† Further, DCF is unsuitable for projects characterized by varying degrees of risk resolution (Mandron 2000). For example, in the

* Cost of equity also goes into the WACC under the latter approach.

† For more on QMV, see Esty article cited earlier.

case of oil exploration projects or pharmaceutical R&D projects, the exploration/research phase differs from development and production phases in terms of risk.

CONCLUDING REMARKS

Project financing is likely to be successful if there is no significant correlation between the cost and the revenue of the project with those of the parent company. The participants should have a sound understanding of the cost and time required to complete the project, pattern of cash flows and the risks involved. As project finance involves complex contractual arrangements and documentation between the participants, the advantages of risk pooling and sharing of expertise should be high enough to warrant the setting up of a separate project company. The characteristics of viable project financing are as follows:

- The sponsor should be credit worthy and financially sound to build and operate the project over the project life.
- Supply contracts and off-take agreements must be in place.
- The product must have an established market.
- The sponsor should have the technical expertise to operate the project.
- Government approval must be in place.
- The project's assets should be adequately insured.

The differences between corporate finance and project finance are outlined in Table 7.4:

Table 7.4 Differences Between Corporate Finance and Project Finance

Corporate finance	Project finance
Lend to existing entity	Lend to new entity
Full recourse (access to corporate assets as security for loans)	Limited recourse (access to assets of the project or transaction)
Lend against the balance sheet of the company	Lend against the income stream

In the financial structuring of projects, the World Bank guarantees can complement loans from IFC and IBRD and insurance from MIGA. Guaranteed debt is often arranged at lower cost and longer maturities than would otherwise be possible.

APPENDIX A: TAXONOMY OF RISKS

Completion risk refers to the risk that the project might not be completed due to, say, unexpected delay in construction schedule or shortage of critical inputs. A higher than expected input costs or lower than anticipated output price might reduce the profitability of the project.

The risk that the proposed technology will become obsolete or less efficient is called **technological risk**. This is particularly important for hi-tech industries where the technology is rapidly evolving.

The risk that the raw material or other factors of production may become unavailable during the life of the project is called **raw material supply risk**. This is especially important where natural resources are critical inputs.

The risk that the demand for the project's product will not be sufficient to meet all the expenses and provide a satisfactory return to equity investors is called **economic risk**.

When floating rate debt is used to finance a project, there is a risk that rising interest rates could jeopardize the viability of the project and the ability to service debt. This is referred to as **financial risk**.

Currency risk arises when the project's revenues stream or its costs are denominated in different currencies or in more than one currency. Changes in the foreign exchange rate will affect the profitability of the project.

In some international projects there is a possibility that political leaders in the host country may interfere in the execution of the project and in extreme cases, the cost overrun will be so high that the project may no longer be viable. This is referred to as **political risk**. The case of Enron Corporation in India serves as a good example*.

REFERENCES

1. Biedelman, Carl R., Donna Fletcher and David Veshosky, On Allocating Risk: The Essence of Project Finance, *Sloan Management Review*, Spring, 1990.
2. Brealy, Richard R., Ian A. Cooper and Michael A. Habib, Using Project Finance to Fund Infrastructure Investments, *Journal of Applied Corporate Finance*, Fall, 1996.
3. Esty, Benjamin, Suzie Harris and Kathy Krueger, An Overview of the Project Finance Market, *Harvard Business School Case Study No. 200-028*, December, 1999.

* See Rangan, Kasturi and Krishna Palepu, Enron Development Corporation: The Dabhol Power Project in Maharashtra, India, *Harvard Business School Case No. 9-596-099*, July, 1998.

4. Esty, Benjamin and Fuaad Qureshi, Financing the Mozal Project, *Harvard Business School Case No. 9-200-005*, February, 2000.
5. Esty, Benjamin and Mathew Mateo Millet, Petrdera Zuata, Petrozuata C.A., *Harvard Business School Case No.* 9-299-012, December, 1998.
6. Mandron, Alix, Improved Techniques for Valuing Large Scale Projects: A follow Up, *Journal of Project Finance*, Spring, 2000.

SUGGESTED FURTHER READING

Benoit, Philippe, The World Bank Group's Financial Instruments for Infrastructure, *World Bank Research Paper No. 101*, January, 1997.

———, Mitigating Project risks—World bank Support for government Guarantees, *Public Policy Journal*, Note no. 79, May, 1996.

Brennan, Michael J and Eduardo Schwartz, Evaluating Natural Resource Investments, *Journal of Business*, **58**: (2), 1985.

Diamonte, Robin, John Liew and Ross Stevens, Political Risk in Emerging and Developed Markets, *Financial Analysts Journal*, May–June, 1996.

Esty, Benjamin C., Improved Techniques for Valuing Large–Scale Projects, *The Journal of Project Finance*, Spring, 1999.

Esty, Benjamin, and Michael Kane, Chase's Strategy for Syndicating the Hong Kong Disneyland Loan, *HBS Case No. 9-201-072*, March, 2001.

Finnerty, John D., *Project Financing : Asset Based Financial Engineering*, Wiley, New York, 1996.

Henderson, Wallace, Case Studies of Project Finance in Latin America, *The Journal of project Finance*, Winter, 1999.

Hoffman, Scott L, The Law and Business of International Project Finance, *Kluwer Law International*, London, UK, 1998.

International Finance Corporation, Project Finance in Developing Countries, *Lessons of Experience Number 7*, Internation Finance Corporation, Washington DC, 1999.

Jensen, Michael C., Agency Costs of Free Cashflow: Corporate Finance and Takeovers, *American Economic Review*, **76**, May, 1986.

Kensinger, John and John Martin, Project Finance: Raising Money the Old Fashioned Way, *Journal of Applied Corporate Finance*, Fall, 1988.

Lake, Thomas and Henry Davis, Termo Emcali, *The Journal of Project Finance*, Winter, 1999.

Luehrman, Timothy, Texas High-speed Rail Corporation, *Harvard Business School Case No.* 9-293-072, July, 2003.

Mao, James C.T., Project Financing: Funding the future, *Financial Executive*, April, 1982.

Nevitt P., *Project Financing*, Euromoney Publications, London, 1989.

Percopo, Bob and Peter Haller, Insurance Solutions for Project Finance, *The Journal of Project Finance*, Summer,1999.

Qureshi, Fuaad A. and Benjamin Esty, Financing the Mozal Project, *Harvard Business School Case Study No. 200-005*, February, 2000.

Rhodes, Tony, (ed.), *Syndicated Lending: Practice and Documentation*, Euromoney Publications PLC, London, 1996.

Shah, Salman and Anjan V. Thakor, Optimal Capital Structure and Project Financing, *Journal of Economic Theory*, **42**, June, 1987.

Wang, Shou Qing, Robert Tiong, S.K. Ting and D. Ashley, Risk Management Framework for BOT Power Projects in China, *The Journal of Project Finance*, Winter, 1999.

So, Jae and Ben Shin, The Private Infrastructure Industry–A Global Market of $ 60 Billion a Year, *Private Sector*, October, 1995.

Standard & Poor's Infrastructure Finance, 1999.

Wells, Louis T. and Eric S. Gleason, Is Foreign Infrastructure Investment Still Risky?, *Harvard Business Review*, Sep–Oct, 1995.

West, Gerald, Political Risk Investment Insurance: A Renaissance, *The Journal of Project Finance*, Summer, 1999.

Wynant, Larry, Essential Elements of Project Financing, *Harvard Business Review*, May–June, 1980.

EXERCISES

1. The equity cash flows and leverage for a project are presented as follows*:

* This is based on Benjamin Esty, Improved Techniques for Valuing Large-Scale Projects, *Journal of Project Finance*, Spring, 1999.

($ '000)

Year	ECF	Equity	Debt
0	(300,000)	300,000	0
1	(170,000)	470,000	700,000
2	(254,349)	724,349	1,300,000
3	171,446	724,349	1,275,000
4	175,490	724,349	1,250,000
5	167,058	724,349	1,225,000
6	159,901	724,249	1,175,000
7	153,143	724,349	1,125,000
8	147,661	724,349	1,050,000
9	155,080	724,349	975,000
10	150,023	724,349	900,000
11	146,243	724,349	800,000
12	142,864	724,349	700,000
13	140,761	724,349	575,000
14	139,060	724,349	450,000
15	138,636	724,349	300,000
16	144,114	724,349	150,000
17	212,953	724,349	0
18	278,987	724,349	0
19	281,798	724,349	0
20	284,638	724,349	0
21	287,506	724,349	0
22	290,403	724,349	0
23	293,330	724,349	0
24	296,286	724,349	0
25	299,275	724,349	0

Asset beta = 0.6, Risk-free rate = 8%, Market risk premium = 7.4%.

Calculate NPV using a constant discount rate assuming a funding mix of 64% debt and 36% equity. Recalculate NPV by using multiple discount rates. Compare the results.

2. State whether true or false unless otherwise mentioned.

(a) Project finance is a method of lending in which the lender has no recourse to the sponsor.

(b) In a take or pay contract, the purchaser is obligated to pay for the output regardless of whether the purchaser takes delivery or not.

(c) In a take-if-offered contract, the purchaser is obligated to pay for the output regardless of whether the purchaser takes delivery or not.

(d) Under a claw back agreement, the sponsors are required to return cash benefits back to the project when there is a shortfall.

(e) In a BTO model a private entity transfers the facility to the government soon after the project clears the completion test and leases it back for a specified period of time.

(f) IBRD and IDA are together known as the World Bank.

(g) IFC has A and B loan programs. The difference between the two lies in the amount of money lent.

(h) Partial risk guarantees cover debt service defaults on a specified portion of a loan or a bond.

(i) Multilateral Investment Guarantee Agency (MIGA) writes coverage for equity and equity-related investments.

(j) COFACE and OPIC provide political risk insurance.

(k) It is usually correct to resort to high leverage for a project when the agency cost of debt is high and agency cost of equity is low.

(l) One way to mitigate the free cash flow problem is to force managers to borrow.

(m) Project finance is ideal when the returns from the project and that of the sponsor are not significantly correlated, ceteris paribus.

(n) A 144A offering is a bank loan.

(o) Asset return increases when leverage is increased.

(p) ICRG Provides country risk scores. A higher score indicates higher risk.

(q) Partial credit guarantees cover debt service defaults on a loan to a private sector project caused by a government's failure to meet its contractual obligations related to private project.

(r) The Institutional Investor's ranking of a country's creditworthiness is based on a survey of international bankers.

3. The ———— project was the first private sector project to receive a World Bank guarantee.

4. The asset beta and E/V ratio for a project are 0.8 and 35% respectively. Estimate equity beta.

5. The risk that the demand for the project's product will not be sufficient to meet all expenses and provide a satisfactory return to equity investors is called ———————— risk.

PART V

STRUCTURING INCENTIVES

CHAPTER

8

Performance Measurement and Incentive Compensation*

LEARNING OBJECTIVES

After reading this chapter, you should be able to:

- Highlight the controversy surrounding CEO pay.
- Discuss the merits and demerits of alternate measures of performance.
- Introduce a relatively new performance metric called EVA.
- Discuss stock options.

INTRODUCTION

The rise in executive pay in the USA and elsewhere has generated substantial controversy on the efficacy of such plans. Many well-known companies have come under the scrutiny of investing public and regulatory authorities. This chapter provides an overview of the issues in executive compensation, the design of stock option plans and the EVA compensation.

Few topics in finance have attracted as much scholarly attention as top management compensation. One reason for the interest in the subject is the spectacular rise in CEO compensation and the executive stock option explosion. Exhibit 8.1 compares CEO pay in 1990 and 2000 in the USA. The change in compensation is unbelievably high in some industries. For example,

* This chapter is contributed by S.R. Vishwanath.

compare the compensation of Jack Welch in 1990 with that in 2000. His compensation was 26 times more in 2000 compared to 1990!

EXHIBIT 8.1

CEO Compensation in 1990 and 2000 in the USA

Industry	**1990** *Largest company*	*CEO comp. ($)*	**2000** *Largest company*	*CEO comp. ($)*
Financial services	Citicorp. John Reid	1,201,242 Sanford Weill	Citigroup	150,688,160
Conglomerates	GE John Welch	4,828,873 John Welch	GE	125,340,263
Beverages	Pepsi Wayne Calloway	5,218,206 Doug Daft	Coca Cola	109,410,444
Brokerage	Merrill Lynch William Schreyer	2,046,500 Philip Purcell	Morgan Stanley	34,204,391
Retailing	Sears Roebuck Edward Brennan	1,867,877 Lee Scott	Wal-Mart	16,683,532
Telecom	AT&T Robert Allen	3,410,971 Michael Armstrong	AT&T	21,792,791
Energy	EXXON Lawrence Rawl	5,473,704 Lee Raymond	Exxon Mobil	33,207,948
Computer Hardware	IBM John Akers	7,662,209 Louis Gertner	IBM	37,708,807
Automotive	General Motors Robert Stemple	2,618,380	General Motors Richard Wagoner	10,155,667

Source: Fortune 25 June, 2001.

The second reason for the rise in interest is that some studies have found that there is *no* correlation between pay and performance. Further, more than 120 companies in the USA, including well-known companies such as Analog Devices, Apple Computer, Aspen Technology, and Bed Bath and Beyond have come under scrutiny for past stock option grants.

This chapter addresses the following issues:

- What measures of performance are typically used in companies?
- How should CEO pay be correlated with a measure of performance?
- Are CEOs paid too much for what they do?
- What are the characteristics of a good measure of performance?

Most executive pay packets contain four components—*a base salary, an annual bonus, stock options* and long-term incentive plans. The base salary is usually determined on the basis of the company's size, profitability, the executive's experience, education and past performance. Consideration is also given to compensation practices in comparable companies both within the industry group and outside. The annual bonus depends on the actual performance on one or more measures such as return on investment, net income, cash flow, EPS or EVA. Exhibit 8.2 presents the measures used in annual incentive plans in 177 large corporations in the USA. As can be seen from the exhibit, of the companies that use a single measure of performance, a large number of them consider earnings or EBIT in determining the incentives*. Likewise, in firms with more than one measure of performance, attention is given to earnings, EBIT and sales.

EXHIBIT 8.2

Performance Measures Used in Annual Incentive Plans in 177 Large US Corporations†

		Industrials n = **125**		**Finance and** n = **21**		**Utilities** n = **31**	
Firms with a single performance measure			50		11	7	
	Performance measures (Number of firms)	Earnings	32	Earnings	8	Earnings	6
		EBIT	7	EBIT	2	EVA	1
		EVA	5	Discretionary	1		
		Discretionary	2				
		Indiv. performance	2				
		Other financial	2				
Firms with two or more performance measures							

Source: Kevin Murphy 1999

The executive does not get the bonus unless he meets a threshold. Further, the executive cannot earn unlimited amounts in bonus. That is, the bonus is capped. Exhibit 8.3 presents the level and composition of CEO pay in countries around the world. It depicts the average CEO pay for a company with annual sales of at least $ 500 million. As can be seen from the exhibit, the use of stock options is more common in the USA than in other countries. Indeed stock options are non–existent in many countries such as Argentina, Belgium and Germany.

* Earnings are defined in a variety of ways such as net income, pre-tax income, return on equity, return on assets and return on capital employed.

† The table is incomplete.

EXHIBIT 8.3

Level of CEO Pay Around the World in 2001

Argentina	879,000
Canada	787,000
Germany	455,000
Hong Kong	736,500
Japan	508,000
Mexico	866,000
Spain	430,000
UK	668,500
US	2,900,000

Source: Towers Perrin

MEASURES OF PERFORMANCE

Since the objective of a firm is to maximize the shareholders wealth, a performance measure should have high correlation with changes in the shareholders wealth. Managers are commonly appraised on measures such as return on assets, earnings per share and return on equity that does not capture value. They focus on cash flows while evaluating capital investments; but when it comes to performance measurement, accounting measures take over. If a company changes its accounting method from FIFO to LIFO during a period of high inflation, cash flow increases but earnings fall. Similarly, when a company acquires another company, there may be special write-offs like amortization of good will that are non-cash in nature. The earnings per share fall but cash flow is unaltered. Moreover, these measures can be easily manipulated due to 'denominator management': One can increase the value of these ratios by simply cutting down whatever that appears in the denominator.

Profit itself is not an appropriate measure of performance because it does not capture either the amount of capital used to generate those earnings or the required rate of return on capital. A good performance measure is one that incorporates all three.

The purpose of value analysis is twofold. *First*, evaluate the performance of current strategy. *Second*, evaluate the potential strategies for each of the business units. For instance, a company may have the following options for a business unit: modernize the plant, hold, harvest, or sell out. Even if the unit is currently losing money, it might make sense to invest in the unit if the spread between ROE and cost of equity is expected to become positive in the foreseeable future implying that executives will have to take a long-term view of business prospects before a strategic decision is made.

Value creation should be the guiding factor in executive decision-making. But how do you measure value? This is important for two reasons. *First*, managers need to know how their performance will be evaluated and *second*, how to work towards that goal.

Shareholder value analysis is the process of analysing how business decisions affect the company's economic value (i.e. NPV of cash flows discounted at WACC). One of the measures of shareholder value is the Total Shareholder Return (TSR). It is the rate (IRR) that equates the purchase price (cash outflow) and dividends, and sales proceeds (cash inflows) at the end of the holding period.

If the holding period is one year, then

$$\text{TSR} = \text{Div} + (P_1 - P_0)/P_0$$

The TSR of the company may be compared with that of the peer group to evaluate performance. More importantly, executives may be encouraged to be in the top 10% of the peer group year after year. The Boston Consulting Group examines the performance of large, quoted companies from around the world and ranks them on the basis of TSR. Exhibit 8.4 gives the list of top 10 companies on the basis of average annual TSR for 2000–2004.*

EXHIBIT 8.4

The Global Top Ten 2000–2004

Ranking	Company	TSR (%)
1	Hyundai Motors	69.7
2	Harman Intl	55.7
3	NOK	55.3
4	Dr Horton	52.9
5	Vale Do Rio Doce	48.5
6	Esprit Holdings	44.5
7	Petsmart	44.1
8	Varian Medical	42.1
9	Enterprise Inns	41.0
10	St. Jude Medical	40.5

Source: Boston Consulting Group

Exhibit 8.5 presents the list of best and worst performing CEOs in the USA in 2006 on the basis of TSR. Note that the best performing CEOs are invariably not the highly paid. Conversely, the highest paid CEOs rarely figure in the list of top performers.

* More recent rankings are available on the BCG website www.bcg.com.

EXHIBIT 8.5

List of Top and Worst Performing CEOs in 2006

CEO	Company	Annualized return (% during tenure)	Relative to S&P (%)
Top Performing CEOs			
John Bucksbaum	General Growth Prop	28	127
Brett Harvey	Consol Energy	32	130
Michael McCallister	Humana	35	135
Richard Kinder	Kinder Morgan	26	124
Robert Kole	New Century Financial	24	117
Mark Pigott	Paccar	23	114
Aubrey McClendon	Chesapeake	28	116
Joseph Ficalora	New York Community	28	116
Joseph Tomkinson	Impac Mortgage	22	119
John Martin	Gilead Sciences	33	122
Worst Performing CEOs			
Steven Appleton	Micron Technology	5	94
Scott McNealy	Sun Microsystems	16	104
Paul Curlander	Lexmark International	6	102
Alain Belda	Alcoa	1	100
Lawrence Montgomery	Kohl's	6	104

Source: Forbes

Another measure of value is the Cash Flow Return On Investment (CFROI). It is similar to the IRR of a project. It compares the cumulative cash invested in a business with the cash the business producing while recognizing the importance of asset ages, asset lives and inflation. HOLT Value Associates measures CFROI in two steps: *First*, the inflation adjusted cash flow available to all capital owners is compared with the inflation adjusted gross investment made by the capital owners, *second*, HOLT then translates the ratio of gross cash flow to gross investment into an IRR.

Under the *residual income* method, an explicit cost of capital is specified for the investment centre and is applied on the investment base to arrive at the capital charge. To illustrate, if the invested capital is \$ 100,000 and EBIT is \$ 40,000, the residual income at a capital cost of 15% would be:

$$\text{Residual income} = \text{EBIT} - (\text{Cost of capital} * \text{Invested capital})$$
$$= 40000 - (0.15 * 100000)$$
$$= \$\,25000$$

The Sensitivity of CEO Pay to Performance

The rise in the usage of stock options and management compensation has attracted lot of attention in the media. The critics complain that executive compensation is excessive and that stock-based compensation does not motivate employees to outperform competitors. Academic studies of the link between pay and performance have sought to address the following issues:

- What elements of compensation lead to superior corporate performance? For example, do those executives who get fixed salaries do as well or better than those who get a variable pay?
- How should CEO pay be correlated with performance?
- How has direct stock ownership of CEOs changed over time?
- How sensitive is pay for performance?

As mentioned earlier, CEO pay packets contain salary, bonus, stock option and long-term incentive plans. To test the association between pay and performance, it is necessary that they be defined correctly. Academic studies have broadly tested for correlation between pay (as measured by salary and bonus) and changes in the market value of the firm. One of the most widely quoted studies on executive compensation is by Jensen and Murphy (1990a, b). They use a least squares regression to calculate the relation between the dollar change in salary and bonus and in the shareholder wealth for all companies with at least seven years of pay-change data from 1975 to 1988. They use last year's performance (shareholder wealth) in addition to the current year's performance. The regression result for one CEO is given as follows:

(Change in salary and bonus) = $ 32,300 + 0.000,986 (Change in this year's shareholder wealth) – 0.000,219 (Change in last year's shareholder wealth).

The total expected change in salary and bonus is the sum of the two coefficients— +98.6 cents and –21.9 cents (equal to 77 cents) per $ 1000 change in value. They estimate regressions for all CEOs and find that for the median CEO in the 250 largest companies, a $ 1000 change in corporate value corresponds to just 6.7 cents in salary and bonus over two years. CEOs also hold stock options. Jensen and Murphy also estimate the changes in the market value and the value of stock option holding. If we account for all monetary benefits—cash, bonus, stock options, shares owned, a $ 1000 change in corporate value corresponds to a change in CEO compensation of $ 2.59.

The common view of CEO compensation is that there is essentially no correlation between firm performance and CEO pay. This 'zero correlation' belief is based on the widely cited result that CEO wealth rises by only $ 3.25 for every $ 1,000 increase in firm value (Jensen and Murphy 1990a, b) and the findings that the elasticity of CEO salary and bonus with respect to firm market value is only 0.1. Using a new 15-year panel data set of CEOs in the large US firms, Hall and Leibman (1998) report a variety of pay-to-performance measures using a broad measure of CEO compensation that includes changes in the value of CEO holdings of stock and stock options. They find that CEO compensation is highly responsive to firm performance. For example, for only a moderate change in firm performance, the compensation of the median CEO in their sample increases by almost 50%, which represents about $ 1.5 million. They estimate that the elasticity of CEO compensation with respect to firm value is 3.3 (at the median) for 1994. This value is 20 to 30 times larger than previous elasticity estimates that ignore the effects of changes in the value of stock and stock option holdings. They also find that both the level of CEO compensation and the sensitivity of CEO compensation to firm performance have grown dramatically over the past 15 years. In their sample, the compensation of the mean (median) CEO increased by 207% (146%) from 1980 to 1994. The large increase in stock option awards and in the value of stock holdings has approximately doubled pay-to-performance sensitivities over this period.

Some studies have looked at the correlation between accounting measures of performance and pay. A recent study of the 161 US domiciled companies suggests the following:

- As the amount of compensation pegged to corporate financial performance rises as a percent of overall compensation, the company's return on equity rises in direct proportion above the industry average.
- Paying a higher percentage of compensation in cash salaries does not lead to superior corporate performance.
- There is a direct positive correlation between the amount of unexercised stock options a CEO holds and the corporate performance of his or her firm relative to an industry peer group.
- Increasing the percentage of incentive-based rewards increases the relative returns at all levels of compensation.

Executive Stock Options

A couple of decades ago executives receiving compensation in cash and stock options were virtually non-existent. It is now common for senior executives to get substantial proportion of their compensation in the form of stock options. Michael Eisner of Disney, for example, exercised 22 million options in 1998 alone netting more than $ 500 million. Steven Jobs of Apple Computers received options worth $ 872 million in 2000 (see Exhibit 8.6). While many executives have made a fortune by exercising stock options, it is not clear whether the stock options are good for companies. The objective of incentive compensation is to make managers behave like owners. They should identify themselves with the fortunes of the company. A potential source of conflict between managers and shareholders lies in their risk tolerance. The shareholders would want the managers to take riskier projects because of larger upside potential whereas the managers would want to limit downside because their career would be jeopardized in the case of a failure. Another source of conflict lies in the time horizon of investments. If managers were rewarded on the basis of current profits, they would have little incentive to invest in long-term projects even if it is desirable. The objective of the compensation plan is to reduce such conflicts.

Awarding stock options is one way to achieve this. Options limit the downside while at the same time allowing participation in the upside because stock options are sensitive to the volatility of the stock price*. The higher the volatility, the more valuable is the option. But higher volatility makes pay-off riskier. The value of the option depreciates when the stock price falls as quickly as it appreciates when the stock price rises. Executive stock options are call options which give the holder the right but not the obligation to purchase a company's shares at a specified exercise price. These are mostly at-the-money-options, i.e. the exercise price matches the stock price at the time of grant. The options usually come with certain restrictions: they cannot be sold to a third party and they must be exercised before a stipulated period of time (say 10 years). Many of them also have a vesting period (say 3–5 years) before which the executive cannot exercise the option. A time-line diagram of events is given in Figure 8.1. The executive gets shares once the options are exercised. The executive may sell the stock thereafter.

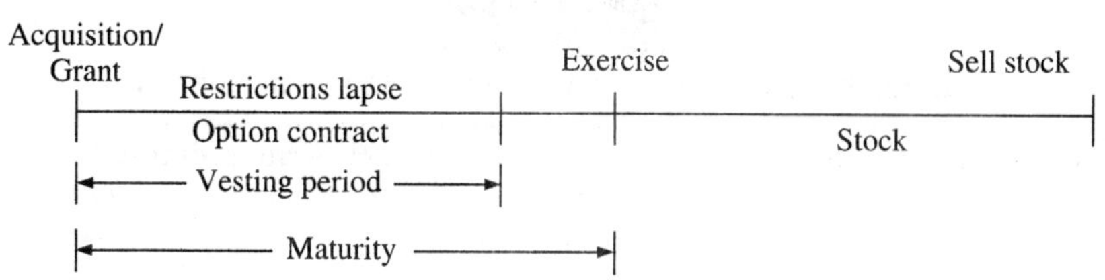

Figure 8.1 A time-line diagram of events.

TYPES OF EMPLOYEE STOCK OPTION PLANS

While it is common for many companies in the USA to issue stock options, apparently not many of them pay attention to the details of the plan. There are three types of stock option plans: Fixed Value Plan, Fixed Number Plan and Mega grant plan (Hall 2000).

Under the fixed value scheme, an executive gets the options worth a specified amount (as determined by the Black–Scholes formula) every year for a certain number of years. For example, an executive might get $ 1 million worth of options every year for 3 years. If the stock price rises, the executive gets *lesser number* of options every year. Likewise if the stock price falls he gets more number of options. But the value of the options itself remains constant at $ 1 million. In other words, the executive is saddled with more number of options when the company does not do well and the link between pay and performance is weak in the sense that the value of the options does not change with changes in stock price.

* It is a misconception that stock options have *no* downside risk. If the stock price falls below the exercise price, the option has no value. Indeed options can get worthless more easily than the underlying stock. The practice of repricing stock options when the stock price falls can, however, blunt the impact.

Under the fixed number plan, an executive gets a fixed number of options every year for a certain number of years. If the stock price rises after the executive gets the options, the value of his holding increases because call options increase in value when the underlying stock price increases. Likewise, the value of the holding decreases if the stock price falls. In sum, the link between pay and performance is better in the case of fixed number plan.

A mega grant plan is a one-time lump sum distribution unlike the other two plans that extend over many years. Under the mega grant plan, an executive gets options worth the present value of a multi year plan. In the above example, the executive would get options worth the present value of $ 3 million (say, $ 2.5 million) .The value of the holding is highly sensitive to changes in stock price. In other words, the sensitivity of pay-to-performance is the maximum in the case of mega grant plans. Disney, for example has instituted mega grant plan for its CEO, Michael Eisner.

EXHIBIT 8.6

Highest Paid US CEOs and Largest Options Grants

Year	Highest paid US CEOs *Company/ CEO*	*Amount ($, m)*	Largest options grants *Company/ CEO*	*Amount ($, m)*
1990	Time Warner Steven Ross	75	Time Warner Steven Ross	215
1991	Coca-Cola Roberto Goizueta	61	US Surgical Leon Hirsch	170
1992	Bear Sterns Alan Greenberg	16	Merck Roy Vagelos	35
1993	Eastman Kodak George Fisher	29	Eastman Kodak George Fisher	67
1994	Allied Signal Lawrence Bossidy	34	Allied Signal Lawrence Bossidy	63
1995	GreenTreeFinancial Lawrence Coss	66	GAP Millard Drexler	79
1996	Walt Disney Michael Eisner	194	Walt Disney Michael Eisner	506
1997	Cendant Henry Silverman	194	Cendant Henry Silverman	570
1998	Dell Computer Michael Dell	94	Dell Computer Michael Dell	272
1999	Computer Associates Charles Wang	507	Quest Comm. Joseph Nacchio	257
2000	Apple Computer Steven Jobs	381	Apple Computer Steven Jobs	872

Source: Fortune, 25 June, 2001

Highest Paid US CEOs in 2006

Rank	Name	Company	Total Compensation ($, m)
1	Richard D Fairbank	Capital One Financial	249.42
2	Terry Semel	Yahoo	230.55
3	Henry Silverman	Cendant	139.96
4	Bruce Karatz	K B Home	135.53
5	Richard Fuld Jr	Lehman Bros Holdings	122.67
6	Ray Irani	Occidental Petroleum	80.73
7	Lawrence Ellison	Oracle	75.33
8	John Thompson	Symantec	71.84
9	Edwin Crawford	Caremark RX	69.66
10	Angelo Mozilo	Countrywide Financial	68.95

Source: Forbes

Stock options are usually priced at-the-money at the time of the grant. If the stock price falls below the exercise price after the option is granted, the option becomes worthless. Such options are termed 'underwater options'. The employers of such companies face a dilemma: should they do nothing or reprice the option? Shareholder activists maintain that since shareholders do not have the luxury of repricing their shares when the price falls, why should employees have the privilege? Proponents of repricing contend that it is necessary to reprice options to retain talented employees. One recent study sought to analyse the characteristics of firms that reprice their executive stock options (Chidambaram and Prabhala 2003). They found that that repricings are economically significant compensation events. The study found that repricers are rapidly growing firms that experience a deep, sudden shock to growth and profitability. Repricers are typically smaller, younger; more concentrated in technology, trade or service industry sectors, and have smaller Boards of Directors relative to firms that did not reprice ESOs despite similar return shocks. Repricers have abnormally high CEO turnover rates, and do not show low institutional ownership or more diffuse ownership of their equity. Over 40% of the companies that reprice do not include the CEO in the list of executives repriced. Collectively the study's evidence provides little support for the view that repricing primarily reflects managerial entrenchment or ineffective governance in firms.

The concern that out-of-the-money stock options are not an effective way to motivate managers has led Boards of Directors to consider measures such as lowering the exercise price of underwater options, or issuing new option grants, to restore the incentive the managers have to increase shareholder value. But is such a measure needed: do out-of-the-money options lose their power to align incentives? Jin and Meulbroek (2001) address this question by estimating how the incentive-alignment power of options changed over the course of the year 2000, a year that for many firms marked the derailment of the long-running bull stock market. Examining the sensitivity in the value of the manager's stock option to the changes in the firm's stock price (one metric for incentive-alignment power), they found that in general the ability of the options to align incentives remained remarkably intact. This resilience in incentive-alignment power stems from the long maturity of executive stock options, the relatively high stock price volatility of firms that experienced stock price declines, and to a lesser extent, the increase in volatility levels that accompanied weakening stock prices. They conclude that even a steep decline in stock price can leave incentive levels intact, so restoring incentive alignment is seldom a good justification for resetting the stock price or issuing new option grants.

A wide range of strategies is available to the managers of such companies. A brief list is provided in Exhibit 8.7.

EXHIBIT 8.7

Possible Underwater Option Strategies

Strategy	When it is appropriate	Advantages	Disadvantages
Do nothing	Price drop is 20%–30% Only a portion of options are underwater	Does not use additional shares	Could lead to employee turnover
Provide additional options • No effect on existing options	Stock price drop is more (25%–50%) When the company has shares available for options	Provides additional incentives if price rises	Depletes shares
Reprice options	Stock price drop is >50% Retention issues are severe	Resolves retention issues	Criticism from shareholders Employees will have to restart

Indexed options: A disadvantage of stock options is that they reward *all* the managers whether they perform or not when the market rises. An executive who gets the option during a bull run can make money by just showing up. That is, the executive gets paid for *any* performance. This is the drawback of fixed exercise price option contracts. Shareholders expect managers to deliver superior returns. Consequently, the executive should be rewarded for relative performance. Stated in another fashion, the executive should be rewarded for returns equal to or better than those earned by the company's peer group or by market indexes. The exercise price could be tied to some benchmark index (say, a stock market index or an index of peer companies) to rectify the drawback of fixed price contracts. The strike price rises and falls along with the benchmark index*. For example, if the index rises by 15%, the exercise price also increases by 15%. The executive cannot exercise the option unless the stock price has risen by 15% or more†. One advantage of indexing is that the executive is not penalized when the market declines since the exercise price is reset. He is rewarded as long as he outperforms the index. Since the executive is exposed to higher risk(s), he is to be given a higher number of options than normal options. The number of options should be set in such a way that the executive gets the same value under both the schemes. As a thumb rule one may award two indexed options for every conventional option held. In the case of 'out performance stock options', the stock price is indexed to the performance of Standard & Poor's 500 stock index. The option holder benefits when the firm's stock appreciated faster than the S&P 500 index. By design, outperformance option provides no reward for modest stock price performance relative to the index. Further, the number of shares increases as the firm performs better than the index.

Valuation of Employee Stock Options

Stock options are non-tradable and are to be forfeited if the executive leaves the company before vesting. The exercise price is usually set at the fair market value on the grant date. Some stock options are offered at a discount or premium. Setting the exercise at a premium partly addresses the problem of free lunch. But it does not solve the problem of rewarding executives for sub-par performance, however.

The Black–Scholes option valuation formula modified to incorporate continuous dividend payments is given by

$$\text{Option value} = Pe^{-\ln(1 + d)T}\, N(z) - Xe^{-\ln(1 + r)T}\, N(z - \sigma\sqrt{T})$$

where:

P = stock price
X = strike price
T = expiration term (years)

---

* Alfred Rappaport, New Thinking on How to Link Executive Pay with Performance, *Harvard Business Review*, March-April, 1999.

† Meulbroek (2001), however, proves that an option with a variable stock price linked to an index is *not* an effective way to implement a relative performance compensation system.

d = annualized dividend yield
σ = Annual stock price volatility
r = risk free interest rate

$$z = \frac{\ln(P/x) + (\ln(1+r) - \ln(1+d) + \sigma^2/2)T}{\sigma\sqrt{T}}$$

N ( ) = cumulative normal distribution function

The annualized yield on a treasury security maturing on the option's expiry date is taken as the risk-free rate. Dividend yields are measured as the annualized yield over the past one, two or three years. The stock options are not the same as stock. The stock option holders get price appreciation alone and not dividends. Consequently, an increase in dividend rate has a negative impact on option values*. Likewise an increase in volatility has a positive impact because the probability of ending in-the-money is more.

Either historical or implied volatility could be used in valuation†. For those companies that do not have exchange traded options, one may use historical volatility of the company's stock. Volatility itself could be measured over three or six months. Since executive stock options have longer maturity than exchange-traded options, it might be improper to use short-term implied volatility derived from option values. In sum, in many cases, historical volatility is a better measure than implied volatility.

Since stock options are non-tradeable, their values are somewhat lower than standard options traded on exchanges. Since managers are undiversified, they are exposed to the total volatility of the firm whereas an investor is exposed to the systematic component of risk. The value of stock option, therefore, is less than its market value‡.

The Black–Scholes value overestimates the executive value of the stock option. Consideration should be given to the risk aversion of the executive, the possibility of early exercise, tax status of the option compensation and the possibilities of leaving the organization before vesting to arrive at the value of option compensation.

ACCOUNTING FOR STOCK OPTIONS

The Accounting Principles Board (APB) created accounting standards for

* If dividends have a negative impact on stock options, we would expect companies in which executives hold substantial stock options to pay-out less. That is, reduce the dividend rate. Academic findings are consistent with the expectation.

† Implied volatility is derived from exchange-traded options on the same company's stock. Given all the parameters of the Black–Scholes formula and the option price, one can estimate the volatility by trial and error.

‡ The exact derivation of the wedge between the two values is beyond the scope of this book. One study suggests that executives place 30%–50% lower value than market value.

stock options and other stock-based plans in APB opinion 25 issued in 1972. The standard distinguishes between fixed and variable options plans. As mentioned earlier, the exercise price and the number of shares to be awarded are fixed in the case of fixed option plans. Under the variable plans, either the exercise price or the number of underlying shares is unknown at the grant date. The unknown variable is set subsequently when specified performance goals are achieved.

The standard prescribes that the fixed plans be recorded using the intrinsic value method. Under the intrinsic value method, an expense for the cost of executive stock options is recorded only if the option's exercise price is less than its fair value at grant date. For options that satisfy this requirement, the spread between the stock price and the exercise price is recorded as compensation expense. For options with an exercise price equal to the stock price at the date of grant, no expense is recorded[*].

In 1993, the Financial Accounting Standards Board, the US accounting standards setting body, issued a draft requiring companies to use the fair value method of reporting both fixed and variable option plans. Under the fair value method, option pricing models like Black–Scholes are used to estimate the fair value of the option and the fair value is recorded as a compensation expense[†]. In the case of indexed options, the difference between the stock price and the exercise price must be reported each year as an expense.

The EVA Financial Management System

Economic Value Added (EVA)[‡] is an accounting-based measure of operating performance. The period could be a month, quarter, half year or a year. The entity whose performance is being measured could be a division or the firm itself. The EVA is the difference between the accounting earnings—with suitable adjustments for interest and some accounting methods—and the cost of capital used to generate these earnings.

Expressed as a formula,

$$\text{EVA} = \text{NOPAT} - (\text{WACC} * \text{Net assets})$$

where

$$\text{NOPAT} = \text{net operating profit after tax} = \text{EBIT}(1 - \text{T})$$

Net assets = adjusted book value of net capital at the beginning of the period

$$\text{WACC} = \text{weighted average cost of capital} = D/V\,(1 - \text{T})K_d + (E/V) * K_e$$

[*] The treatment for variable plans is somewhat complex.

[†] In 1995 the Board withdrew its earlier ruling. Currently firms can follow either the intrinsic value method or the fair value method.

[‡] EVA is the registered trademark of Stern Stewart and Co.

where

D = market value of firm's debt.

E = market value of equity = number of shares * current market price.

Convertible debt/preferred securities must be converted if in-the-money and options must be included if in-the-money

$V = D + E$

T = marginal tax rate

K_d = marginal cost of borrowing long term after adjusting for offering discount and issuance cost.

K_e = cost of equity estimated by capital asset pricing model.

The EVA has certain following characteristics:

- It provides greater accountability for investor capital as it measures the required return on all investments.
- It is custom made to a company's specific circumstances making only those accounting adjustments that are necessary.
- It is easy to communicate.
- It aligns managerial and shareholders' interests by tying management compensation to improvements in EVA.

Economic value added differs from residual income method in several ways. *First*, it does not take balance sheet numbers directly since a balance sheet is prepared on historical cost basis. Accounting adjustments are made to produce a balance sheet that reflects economic values of assets in place and to remove the effect of managers' focus on current earnings. Stern Stewart and Co. considers about 250 accounting adjustments in moving to EVA. In defining and refining its EVA measure, Stern Stewart & Co. has identified over 120 shortcomings in conventional accounting.

Another reliable measure of management's long run success in adding value is Market Value Added (MVA). The aim of the management is to maximize the amount by which the company's market value exceeds the capital supplied by the firm's investors. MVA is the difference between the company's current market value, as determined the market price of its securities, and its economic book value.

$$\text{MVA} = \text{Market capitalization} - \text{Invested capital}$$

where

Market capitalization = market value of debt and equity.

Invested capital = book value of debt and equity including equity equivalent (reserves like R & D expenses)

Thus, if a company's market value of debt and equity is \$ 100 million and the adjusted book value of capital is \$ 50 million, the MVA is \$ 50 million. A negative MVA implies that the company will generate returns below its cost of capital whereas a positive MVA implies the opposite. If MVA is a better indicator of performance, why calculate EVA? MVA has a limitation. The MVA cannot be calculated for privately held firms and non-profit organizations, as they are not listed on the stock exchange. Studies is America have shown that there is a high degree of correlation between the EVA growth and the MVA. Since the EVA is correlated with the MVA, increase in the EVA results in higher MVA. At the company level, the MVA is simply the present value of the future EVAs. The list of top high-growth value adders in the North America, Europe and Asia is presented in Exhibit 8.8*. Stern Stewart ranked companies on the basis of revenue growth as well as on MVA and then on the ratio of MVA to revenue growth. To produce a composite ranking they add the revenue growth score and the MVA/revenue scores. The lower the combined number, the higher is the company's position in the list of high-growth value adders.

EXHIBIT 8.8

Top High-growth Value Adders in North America, Europe, Asia, Africa and Australia

Rank	North America Company	Europe Company	Asia Company	South Africa and Australia
1	GE	Nestle	Toyota	BHP Billiton
2	Wal-Mart	Total	NTT	Telstra
3	Altria group	Glaxosmithkline	Samsung	News Corporation
4	Home Depot	Eni	Sony	Woolworths
5	Microsoft	BP	Honda	Rio Tinto
6	Exxon Mobil	Royal Dutch Shell	Canon	SAB Miller
7	IBM	Nokia	Mitsubishi	Coles Myer
8	Johnson & Johnson	France Telecom	Hitachi	Brambles Group
9	Pfizer	Deutsche Telekom	Hitachi	Wesfarmers
10	Dell	Telefonica	NEC	Amcor

Source: Bennett Stewart III 2004

Evidence on EVA Companies

There is evidence that Stern Stewart's EVA clients substantially outperform the peers†. The latest findings show that the amount of outperformance varies in step with the degree to which the companies use EVA, and Stern Stewart's special incentive-plan architecture, as the basis for compensation. The study analysed the total returns to shareholders for up to five years after the companies began to implement EVA with Stern Stewart's assistance. On

* More recent rankings are available from Stern Stewart & Co. See www.sternstewart.com

† This section is based on the findings of Stern Stewart & Co. See www.sternstewart.com

average, investments in the shares of these companies produced 49% more wealth after five years than equal investments in shares of competitors with similar market capitalizations. Companies that used the full Stern Stewart compensation architecture did even better. Investment in their shares produced 84% more wealth over five years than equal investments in their competitors. Overall, the Stern Stewart clients created some $ 116 billion more in market value than they would have if they had performed the same as their competitors. The study includes 66 publicly owned US clients for which at least 24 months of stock-performance data were available.

The starting date for each comparison is the month that a company began to implement the EVA. The performance comparisons were made against the competitors in the same four-digit SIC codes as the EVA companies. The competitors used in the study, which they call comparators, were the 10 closest in market capitalization to the EVA company at the starting date. In a handful of cases, fewer than 10 comparators were available. Using companies in the same industries and with similar market capitalizations eliminates as much 'systematic' risk as possible, so that the comparisons reflect specific company performance to the greatest extent possible.

Does EVA Really Work?

A financial performance measure must be highly correlated with the changes in shareholder wealth where the latter is defined as the abnormal return (also called *alpha*) earned by the shareholders in any given period. That is,

Abnormal return = Actual return – Expected return (as measured by CAPM)

A firm derives its value from two sources: *assets in place* and *future growth opportunities*. Balance sheets prepared by accountants capture the value of assets in place. Stern Stewart & Co. considers a number of accounting adjustments to produce an 'economic balance sheet' that reflects the value of assets in place more accurately than the balance sheet prepared by accountants. But it still does not produce a market value balance sheet that would capture the value of future growth opportunities.

Further, the EVA is calculated by deducting a capital charge on the *economic book value* of the assets using WACC based on market *value weights* (from NOPAT). Apparently, there is a problem. Bacidore et al. (1997b) propose that a variant of EVA, called **refined EVA**, REVA, be used in which the capital charge is applied on the *market* value of the firm. They conclude that:

- Both the EVA and the REVA are positively correlated with abnormal returns.
- The market rewards the unexpected increases in the EVA. So rewarding managers for the total EVA results in rewarding managers for inferior performance.

- The REVA contains information not captured in the EVA that is relevant for predicting abnormal returns.
- The REVA could be used to compensate senior executives and the EVA could be used to compensate those at the lower levels.

But unfortunately, according to finance theory, no single measure of operating performance is supposed to be correlated with abnormal stock returns. An operating decision can add substantial value in the period in which it is made even if it reduces that period's operating performance and there is no reason to expect an appropriate measure of one period's operating performance to be significantly correlated with the same period's abnormal stock returns (Ferguson and Leistikow 1998).

Leveraged Equity Purchase Plans

One of the measures of managerial performance is the appreciation in the stock price or stock returns derived from the stock prices. Tying executive compensation to stock prices requires the managers to take on too much risk. More over, stock prices are affected by extraneous factors not controllable by the executives. The EVA does not suffer from this drawback. It is a useful tool for executive compensation. Indeed, the EVA is more a compensation tool than a financial management tool. The executives can be paid for the performance of the entire company or of their own division. In a group incentive scheme, a plant or business unit sets financial or operational performance target. If the unit hits the target, everybody gets a payout. The payout increases if the unit beats the target. Typically, executives get several times the incentive opportunity for rank and file employees.

The EVA compensation system has two components—cash bonus plan and leveraged stock option plan (Stern et al. 1995)*. The cash bonus plan rewards improvements in EVA rather than absolute EVA in order to reward the value addition due to managerial efforts as in the case of a business turnaround. The EVA bonus does not have a ceiling. Executives can earn unlimited amounts depending on their performance. A part of the annual bonus award is held in a bonus bank and distributed only if there is a continuous improvement in the EVA. Usually, two-thirds of the bonus is carried forward. The EVA targets are set by a predetermined formula and not by annual negotiation. The EVA compensation encourages performers to stay on and pursue their business plans aggressively and forces the underperformers to leave.

Under the leveraged stock option plan, the managers are given the option to buy shares (unlimited) at a discount to the prevailing market price. But the managers are not allowed to exercise their option immediately. The option is held in a bank. The exercise price of the option increases at a rate that reflects the cost of capital for the company. To illustrate, the strike price increases at

* The leveraged equity purchase plan is not to be confused with stock options.

15% if the cost of capital is 15% during the planning period. Managers win only if the stock price rises at a faster rate than strike price. They use a part of their cash bonus awards to make leveraged purchase of stock.

A leveraged equity purchase plan has the following three features (Stewart 1990):

1. Most of the purchase price for the shares is financed through a loan from the company that is secured solely by a pledge of the stock.
2. The rest of the purchase price (say, 10%) comes from the managers' personal wealth.
3. The loan from the company accrues interest at a rate equal to the company's cost of capital.

Calculation of the incentive compensation under the EVA system involves the following four steps:

1. Establish a bonus target equal to a certain percentage of base pay (say, 35%). The executive earns the target bonus if the bonus unit is valued at $ 1.0.
2. Establish a baseline EVA level. The EVA for the following year changes by a specified percentage of the difference between the actual EVA achieved and the baseline EVA for the prior year. This makes the system self-adjusting.
3. A base unit value is established for each ensuing year. It indicates the target bonus amount an executive can earn by hitting the baseline EVA. To illustrate, if the base unit value is $ 0.8 in a year, simply repeating the EVA baseline performance will produce only 80% of the target bonus.
4. Establish a bonus sensitivity factor (say, $ 1,500,000) that is added to or subtracted from the base unit value to create a total unit value.

CONCLUDING REMARKS

While the stock price or returns generated from the stock accurately usually measures the performance of senior managers, it is inappropriate for measuring the performance of business unit managers because the link between their actions and stock price is not clear. Instead, they should be rewarded for enhancing the value of the business unit. Since the value of a company is the sum of its constituent businesses, enhancing the value of each business unit leads to an overall improvement in value. The value of each business unit can be estimated separately (using the DCF methodology) and managers could be rewarded for shareholder value added. Each business has some leading indicators of value. For Home Depot, for example, new store growth is a leading indicator of value*. An improvement in value drivers like sales growth or profit margin could be rewarded.

* Recollect the discussion on value drivers from Chapter 1.

Some companies use non-financial measures such as product quality, customer satisfaction and market share in performance measurement and compensation systems. Academic studies have found that non-financial measures are also significantly associated with future financial measure.

REFERENCES

1. Bacidore J.M., J.A. Boquist, T.T. Milbourn and A.V. Thakor, The Search for the Best Financial Performance Measure, *Financial Analysts Journal*, May–June, 1997b.
2. Chidambaram, N.K. and N.R. Prabhala, Executive Stock Option Repricing, Internal Governance Mechanisms, and Management Turnover, *Journal of Financial Economics*, **69** (1), 2003.
3. Ferguson, R. and D. Leistikow, Search for the Best Financial Performance Measure: Basics Are Better, *Financial Analysts Journal*, January/February, 1998.
4. Hall, B. and J. Leibman, Are CEOs Really Paid Like Bureaucrats?, *Quarterly Journal of Economics*, August, 1998.
5. Hall, B.J., What You Need to Know About Stock Options, *Harvard Business Review*, March–April, 2000.
6. Jensen M.C. and K. Murphy, CEO Incentives—It's Not How Much You Pay, But How, *Harvard Business Review*, May–June, 1990a.
7. ———, Performance Pay and Management Incentives, *Journal of Political Economy*, **98,** (2, April), 1990b.
8. Jin, L. and L. Meulbroek, Do Underwater Executive Stock Options still Align Incentives? The Effect of Stock Price Movements on Managerial Incentive-Alignment, *Harvard Business School Working Paper No. 02-002*, 2001.
9. Meulbroek, L., Designing an Option Plan that Rewards Relative Performance: Indexed Options Revisited, *Harvard Business School Working Paper No. 02-022*, 2001.
10. Murphy, K.J., Executive Compensation, in Ashenfelter, Orley and David Card, *(ed.), Handbook of Labour Economics*, **3:** North Holland, 1999.
11. Stern, J., B. Stewart and D. Chew Jr, The EVA Financial Management System, *Journal of Applied Corporate Finance*, **8**(2, Summer), 1995.
12. Stewart, B.G. III, Remaking the Public Corporation from Within, *Harvard Business Review*, July–August, 1990.

13. ———, Champions of Profitable Growth, *Harvard Business Review*, July-August, 2004.

SUGGESTED FURTHER READING

Abowd, J.M. and D.S. Kaplan, Executive Compensation: Six Questions that Need Answering, *NBER Working Paper No. 7124*, May, 1999.

Akhigbe, A., J. Madura and A. Tucker, Market Controlled Stock Options: A New Approach to Executive compensation, *Journal of Applied Corporate Finance*, **9**(1, Spring), 1996.

Bacidore, Boquist, J.A., T.T. Milbourn and A.V. Thakor EVA and Total Quality Management, *Journal of Applied Corporate Finance*, **10**(2 Summer), 1997a.

Baker, G., M.C. Jensen and K. Murphy, Compensation and Incentives: Practice vs Theory, *Journal of Finance*, **XLIII** (3, July), 1988.

Banker, R., G. Potter, and D. Srinivasan, An Empirical Investigation of an Incentive Plan Based on Non-financial Performance Measures, *Working Paper*, University of Pittsburgh, February, 1998.

Biddle, G., R. Bowen and J.S. Wallace, Does EVA Beat Earnings? Evidence on Associations with Stock Returns and Firm Values, *Journal of Accounting and Economics*, **24** (3), December, 1997.

Biddle, G.C., R.M. Bowen, and J.S. Wallace, Evidence on EVA, *Journal of Applied Corporate Finance*, **12** (2, Summer), 1999.

Birchard, B., Mastering the New Metrics, *CFO Magazine*, October, 1994.

———, Making it Count: How Innovative Companies Really Use the New Metrics, *CFO Magazine*, October, 1995.

Brickley J., C. Smith and J.L. Zimmerman, Transfer Pricing and the Control of Internal Transactions, *Journal of Applied Corporate Finance*, **8**(2, Summer), 1995.

Brennan M.J., Executive Compensation in UK, *Journal of Applied Corporate Finance*, **9**(1, Spring), 1996.

Colvin, G., The Great CEO Pay Heist, *Fortune*, 25 June, 2001.

Damodaran, A., Enhancing Value: Back to the Future, *Working Paper*, *Stern* School of Business, New York University, Undated.

Dearden, J., The Case Against ROI Control, *Harvard Business Review*, May–June, 1969.

Delves, D., Underwater Stock Options, *Strategic Finance*, December, 2001.

Ehrbar, A., *EVA: The Real Key to Creating Wealth*, Wiley, New York, 1998.

Ehrenfeld, T., The Case of the Unpopular Pay Plan, *Harvard Business Review*, Jan–Feb., 1992.

Fernandez, P., Shareholder Value Creators and Shareholder Value Destroyers in USA: Year 2000, *Working Paper*, IESE Business School, (4 June), 2001.

Glassman, D., Contracting for Value: EVA and the Economics of Organisations, Journal of Applied Corporate Finance, **10** (2, Summer), 1997.

Glassman, D., Twelve Ways to Strengthen your Incentive Plan, *Journal of Applied Corporate Finance*, **12** (2, Summer), 1999.

Glassman, D., Herman Miller: Growth in the New Economy, *Evaluation*, **3**:(1), February 2001.

Hall, B. and K. Murphy, Optimal Exercise Prices for Executive Stock Options, *American Economic Review*, May, 2000a.

———, Stock Options for Undiversified Executives, *NBER Working Paper No. 8052*, 2000b.

Hull, J. and A. White, How to Value Employee Stock Options, *Working Paper*, Rotman School of Management, University of Toronto, September, 2002.

Hill, N.T. and K. Stevens, Structuring Compensation to Achieve Better Financial Results, *Strategic Finance*, March, 2001.

Jensen, M.C. and W.H. Meckling, Divisional Performance Measurement, in M.C. Jensen, (ed.), *Foundations of Organizational Strategy*, Harvard University Press, Boston, 1998.

Jensen M.C., *Foundations of Organizational Strategy*, Harvard University Press, Boston, 1998.

Jensen M.C. and W.H. Meckling, Specific Knowledge and Divisional Performance Measurement, *Journal of Applied Corporate Finance*, **12**(2, Summer), 1999.

Kaplan, R.S. and D. Norton, Linking the Balanced Scorecard to Strategy, *California Management Review*, **39** (1), 1996.

———, The Balanced Scorecard—Measures that Drive performance, *Harvard Business Review*, Jan-Feb., 1992.

———, Putting the Balanced Scorecard to Work, *Harvard Business Review*, Sep-Oct., 1993.

Kohn, A., Why Incentive Plans Cannot Work, *Harvard Business Review*, Sep-Oct., 1993.

Kulatilaka, N. and A. Marcus, Valuing Employee Stock Options, *Financial Analysts Journal*, Nov-Dec., 1994.

Maisel, L., Performance Measurement Practices: A Long Way from Strategy Management, *Balanced Scorecard Report*, HBS Publishing, May-June, 2001.

McIntyre, E. V., Accounting Choices and EVA, *Business Horizons*, Jan-Feb., 1999.

Mctaggart, James, Peter Kontes and Michael Mankins, The Value Imperative, The Free Press, 1994.

Milbourn, Todd T., The Executive Compensation Puzzle: Theory and Evidence, *IFA Working Paper No 235*, London Business School.

Myers, Randy, Metric Wars, *CFO Magaine*, October, 1996.

———,Measure for Measure, *CFO Magaine*, November, 1997.

O'Byrne, Stephen F., Total Compensation Strategy, *Journal of Applied Corporate Finance*, Summer, 1995.

Peterson, Pamela and D.R. Peterson, Company Performance and Measures of Value Added, The Research Foundation of the Institute of the Institute of Chartered Financial Analysts, 1996.

Rappaport, Alfred, New Thinking on How to Link Executive Pay with Performance, *Harvard Business Review*, March-April, 1999.

Salter, Malcolm, What is Fair Pay for the Executive, *Harvard Business Review*, May-June, 1972.

———,Tailor Incentive Compensation to Strategy, *Harvard Business Review*, March-April, 1973.

Stern, J., B. Stewart and D. Chew, (ed.), Corporate Restructuring and Executive Compensation, *The Institutional Series in Finance*, Ballinger Publishing, Cambridge, 1989.

Stewart, B.G., The Quest for Value, *Harper Business*, 1991.

———, Rethinking Rewards, *Harvard Business Review*, November-December, 1993.

———, EVA: Fact and Fancy, *Journal of Applied Corporate Finance*, **7**(2, Summer), 1994.

Uyemura, D.G., C. Kantor and J. Petit, EVA for Banks: Value Creation, Risk Management, and Profitability Measurement, *Journal of Applied Corporate Finance*, **9**(2, Summer), 1996.

Wallace, J., Adopting Residual–Income Based Compensation Plans: Do You Get What You Pay For?, *Journal of Accounting and Economics*, **24**(3, December), 1997.

Zimmerman, J.L., EVA and Divisional Performance Measurement: Capturing Synergies and Other Issues, *Journal of Applied Corporate Finance*, **10**(2, Summer), 1997.

EXERCISES

1. The following data is available for a company for the period 2000–04.

($ '000)

	2000	2001	2002	2003	2004
NOPAT	235,029	270,140	281,950	296,642	362,744
Beginning Capital	1,430,280	1,981,285	2,551,826	2,901,126	3,465,870
Long-term debt	1,013,967	2,152,208	2,577,134	1,546,824	3,255,236
Av. shares outstanding	46970	49840	51905	52670	52272
Share price	58	66	44	49	45
Tax rate (%)	45	46	34	34	34
T-Bond rate (%)	10.74	8.14	8.76	9.11	8.62
Yield on the company's bond (%)	12.19	10.37	10.55	10.75	10.35
Beta	1.35	1.3	1.15	1.10	1.10

Calculate EVA, cumulative annual EVA, and percentage change in cumulative EVA between 2000 and 2004. If the book value of equity is $ 815,000 in 2000, calculate MVA.

2. A company is in the process of estimating EVA for two of its divisions—beverages and Restaurants. The estimation of EVA requires an estimate of divisional cost of capital. The industry beta and average debt ratio for several industry groups are given as follows:

Industry	Industry Leverage Beta	Cost of equity (%)	Cost of debt (%)	Debt/ Capital (%)	Cost of capital (%)
Aerospace	0.68	8.6	9.1	38.6	7.3
Airlines	0.89	10.8	9.8	70.4	7.4
Beverages	0.89	10	8.1	45.7	9.3
Cars and trucks	1.03	12.4	8.5	46.6	8.7
Computers and peripherals	1.36	12.9	8.6	30.7	12.7
Electronics	1.51	14.1	10.6	39.1	13.5
Oil and gas (integrated)	0.60	7.9	8.6	46.7	6.9
Restaurants	0.80	9.5	10	46.4	8.6

Source: Stern Stewart & Co.

The beverages division has a target debt/value ratio of 40% and the restaurants division has a target debt ratio of 35%. Calculate the cost of equity for the divisions assuming a risk-free rate of 6% and a risk premium of 7.5%.

3. SPX is a global leader in providing vehicle service solutions to dealers and independent service locations, service support to vehicle manufacturers and vehicle components to the worldwide motor vehicle industry. But, even though the product lines are the standard of the industry, they were a billion dollar company losing money. It was a classic turnaround challenge*.

   As part of that turnaround, the SPX board and the company's leadership team adopted EVA (Economic Value Added) because it is the measurement tool that gives the best estimate of the true profitability of a business. EVA is a company's after-tax profit (after correcting for accounting anomalies) less the cost of the operation's total capital—not just the cost of debt, but the cost of equity as well.

   The EVA compensation system the company established with Stern Stewart's expertise rewards people only for continuous, permanent EVA improvement. Nearly 80% of SPX associates are now participants in an EVA incentive plan.

   For the two years ended in December 1997, the operating profit margins more than doubled, the EVA improved by \$ 45.4 million and the company created \$ 744 million in market value for shareholders. This reflects the more than quadrupling of the stock price from \$ 15 to \$ 69 over a two-year period. Given below is the stock price history. The stock price chart gives the impression that it is the implementation of EVA compensation that resulted in an increase in stock price. As a skeptic how would you disprove the merits of EVA? More specifically, what must Stern Stewart do to credibly establish that EVA indeed results in performance improvement?

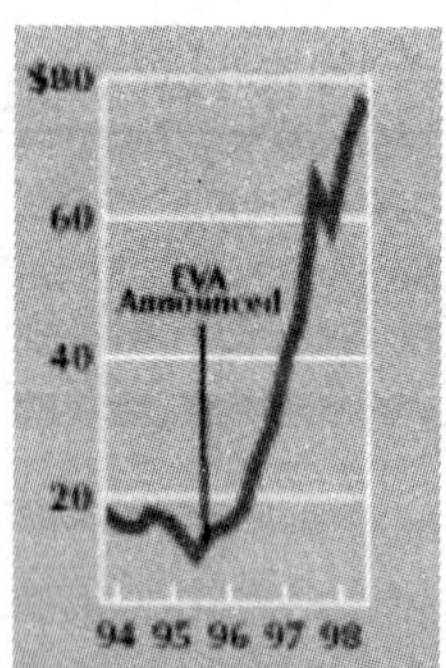

4. Given below is the result of a Boston Consulting Group study on the correlation between % change in EVA and shareholder value in 1994–95.

---

* Based on a story that appears on the Stern Stewart website www.sternstewart.com.

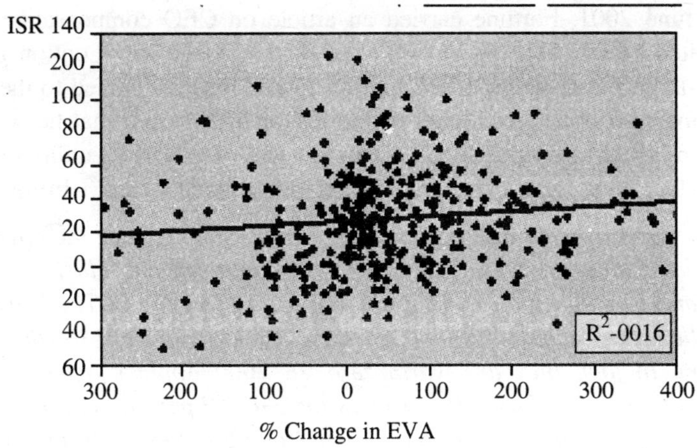

Source: Boston consulting group

What can you infer from this study? Does it weaken the claim made above?

5. George Baker, a second-year MBA student at a major Business School in the US has been offered jobs by two companies. Like most MBAs, Baker considers compensation the most important aspect of a job. The details of the pay packets offered by the two companies are given as follows:

	Company X	Company Y
Base salary	$ 150,000	$ 90,000
Signing bonus	0	0
Annual bonus as % of base salary	30	10
Annual option	0	200 options (or 2000 shares)

The current stock price of company Y	= $ 19
Exercise price	= $ 19
Years to maturity	= 5 years
Dividend yield on stock	= 0
90 day annualized volatility of the stock	= 40 %
180 day annualized volatility	= 35 %
Risk-free rate	= 6%

Which company offers a better compensation package? Conduct your analysis assuming a five-year time horizon.

6. In June 2001, Fortune carried an article on CEO compensation in the United States*. The magazine claimed that Steve Jobs' option grant is the largest ever-worth $ 872 million. Steve Jobs responded to the article in the next issue (in a letter to the Editor of Fortune) that he would be happy to sell the options to Fortune for half of the $ 872 million because "in fact, they are worth zero since they are underwater"†. In his words:

> *I was surprised and flattered to have my photo grace the cover of your June 25 issue. The cover also contained one glaring error, and I am writing to you in the hope of correcting it. The headline below my photo says that my Apple stock options are worth $ 872 m. In fact, they are worth zero. In 2000 Apple granted me an option to purchase 20 m shares for $ 43.59 per share. Since then the stock has declined and is now trading around $ 24 per share. So Apple's current stock price will have to almost double before my option are worth a nickel. Of course, your excellent staff must know how stock options work, so I assume it "bent" the truth in this case to help sell magazines. If I'm in error, and you really do think my penniless stock options are worth $ 872 m, I will be pleased to offer you the deal of a lifetime and sell them to you for just half that amount. And I also have a bridge you may be interested in buying.*

Do you agree that Steve Jobs' options are worthless? Why or why not?

Following is the Fortune's response:

> *While we should have stated in the story that Jobs' options are currently underwater, they don't expire for 10 years. If Apple stock appreciates for the decade after the grant at the rate it did for the decade before (about 9.2% annually), his 20 m options would give him a gain of $ 1.2 billion. Our $ 872 m figure was the grant's face value: the number of share times the market price on the grant date. That is a common way of expressing the size of such grants and was discussed in the article. While we think his offer to sell us his options for $ 436 m is amusing, and potentially a good deal, FORTUNE isn't sufficiently capitalized at present to take advantage.*

What do you think of this reaction? Assume that Fortune were to buy Steve Jobs' options. How should they estimate the purchase price? More specifically, how would you find out whether $ 436 m is a good deal for the options?

---

* Geoffrey, Colvin, The Great CEO pay heist, Fortune, 25 June, 2001.

† Letter to the Editor, Fortune, 23 July, 2001.

7. Disprove the following statements*:

(a) Employee stock options do not represent a real cost to the company.

(b) The employee cost of stock options cannot be estimated because of lack of liquidity. Consequently, recording the cost of stock options is difficult.

(c) Expensing stock options hurt young businesses.

8. Employee stock options have the following features:

(a) There is usually a vesting period of during which the options cannot be exercised. The vesting period is typically four years.

(b) When employees leave their jobs during the vesting period, they forfeit their options.

(c) When employees leave after the vesting period, they forfeit out-of-the-money options and exercise in-the-money options.

(d) Employees are not permitted to sell options. They must exercise the options and sell the underlying shares in order to realize cash.

(e) When stock options are exercised, new treasury stock is issued resulting in dilution.

How would you account for these factors in pricing employee stock options?

* For answers see Bodie, Zvi, Robert S. Kaplan, and Robert Kaplan, For the Last Time: Stock Options are an expense, *Harvard Business Review*, March, 2003.

CHAPTER

9

EVA and Incentive Compensation*

LEARNING OBJECTIVES

After reading this chapter, you should be able to:

- Reinforce material covered in Chapter 8.
- Discuss incentive compensation under the EVA financial management system.

INTRODUCTION

The rise of controversy surrounding executive pay is forcing companies to take a relook at their compensation practices. Many companies have implemented pay-for-performance incentive plans. Two approaches have become popular—employee stock options and EVA compensation system. This chapter describes the later.

By the turn of the century, the view that incentive compensation should play an important role in driving the performance of organizations had begun to take root in virtually every culture in the world. Major corporations on every continent were adopting, or at least contemplating, the US-type incentive plans that would spur their managers to work harder and smarter. But the awful truth is that most incentive plans, including the ones typically used in the USA, do exactly the opposite of what their designers

*This chapter is contributed by All Ehrbar and adapted from Al Ehrbar, *EVA: The Real Key to Creating Wealth,* Wiley, New York, 1998.

intend. Instead of propelling the managers to greater achievements, they act as powerful breakes on the performance. They cause the managers to be much more conservative than shareholders would prefer, and often encourage them to engage in behaviour that actually destroys wealth rather than create it.

This need not be so. While not simple, it is possible to structure truly effective incentive systems that solidly align the financial interests of managers with those of shareholders that improve motivation and morale, and create an atmosphere in which the managers constantly strive—in good years and bad—to create as much wealth as they can. Effective incentive systems do this by making the managers think and act like owners of the portions of the business they influence most directly. What is more, the proper design of incentives is independent of whether one believes the fundamental goal of the corporation should be to create shareholder wealth or to maximize the well being of all its stakeholders groups. Companies that use resources more effectively and generate higher economic returns will, *ceteris paribas*, have more funds to pay higher wages, create new jobs, develop better products, improve service, or engage in any other desirable activity.

DIMENSIONS OF COMPENSATION SYSTEMS

Compensation systems have three dimensions: *level*, *composition*, and *functional* form. The first two are important, but fairly easy to resolve. The level of compensation determines the quality of workers that a company attracts. Most companies arrive at appropriate compensation levels by trial and error, and by observing what other employers pay in their principal markets. The composition of pay—how much is cash and how much takes the form of equity participation, in kind fringe benefits, retirement savings, lavish offices, or perquisites such as cars and club memberships—depends on a number of cultural and institutional factors, not the least of which is the country's tax treatment of various forms of pay. The composition also figures into incentive plans, particularly when it includes stock options.

It is the third dimension, the functional form of pay that is the principal determinant of how compensation affects behaviour. The functional form encompasses such things as the relative size of fixed versus variable compensation, and the determinants and composition of variable compensation. The functional form determines what people work on and how hard they work on it. It also has an important impact on recruitment and retention of employees, and, therefore, determines the type of people in an organization. If pay is highly variable (such as the low base pay and the rich option packages offered by Silicon Valley startups) the firm will attract risk takers. If the pay is essentially fixed, the firm will tend to attract bureaucrats.

In thinking about the functional form, it is important to keep in mind that *all* compensation systems contain incentives. Even the most bureaucratic system, with no bonus plan at all, has incentives, most notably in the type of behaviour that is rewarded with promotion to a higher pay grade. Equally important, *every* system punishes people for doing things that are good for the organization and pays them to do things that are counterproductive. A prime example is when the total compensation (with or without explicit incentive payments) is based, wholly or in part, on the so-called 'Hay points', which measure the number of people and the amount of resources under a manager's control. Both the Hay points and the bureaucratic system of reward-by-promotion create enormous incentives for any organization to grow, even when that growth returns less than the cost of incremental capital and, thus, destroys shareholder wealth. This incentive to build empires is particularly pernicious and extremely difficult to root out of an organization.

The challenge is to minimize those perverse incentives as much as possible while also providing positive incentives for managers and workers to take actions that help the organization.

OBJECTIVES OF INCENTIVE COMPENSATION

When companies introduce variable incentives to the functional form, they typically have four key objectives:

1. To align the management and the shareholder interests by giving the managers the motivation to choose strategies and make operating decisions that maximize shareholder wealth.
2. To provide sufficient leverage, as measured by the variability of potential rewards, to motivate managers to work long hours, take risks and make unpleasant decisions such as laying off staff or closing a plant.
3. To limit retention risk, or the risk that valued managers will bolt for a better offer, especially during industry downturns and recessions.
4. To keep shareholder costs at a reasonable level.

Balancing the four basic objectives obviously entails difficult tradeoffs, many of them quite difficult. A plan with extremely high leverage, for example, may pack huge incentive power, but leverage also increases the risk that valued employees will leave for a better offer in bad years. High leverage combined with poor alignment can bring unacceptably high costs as the company rewards *achievements* that do not contribute to the shareholder wealth. Alternatively, for a plan to achieve both low retention risk (not much downside) and low shareholder cost (not much upside), it will necessarily have too little leverage to truly motivate.

The two crucial elements in balancing the four objectives are: *first*, the performance measure used to the determine incentive awards and, *second*, the way in which compensation is linked to the measure. Most incentive systems fail because of errors in both the measure and the linkage mechanism. Analysing why conventional plans fail is the easiest way to understand how effective incentive systems should be designed. We begin with failures in linkages and then take up the measure itself.

COMPENSATION SYSTEM IN THE USA

The dominant compensation strategy in the USA (and the model for many companies elsewhere) is what is often called a **competitive pay plan**. Under this type of plan, a company sets its target compensation levels at a given percentile within its industry in order to attract and retain the caliber of executives it wants. It then assembles a compensation package typically containing base pay, a target cash bonus and a stock option grant. If the target bonus and option package comprise 30% or more of the total, which is not uncommon, it appears that the plan contains a large quotient of leverage. Not so. *First*, consider the dynamics of the cash bonus. Target bonuses typically are paid if the executive achieves a budgeted profit plan that is negotiated annually. The Conference Board, a US management group that monitors incentive practices, found in a 1997 survey that managers, on average, get no bonus at all unless they achieve at least 80% of the profit plan. If they do hit 80% of budget, they get half the target bonus. The bonus payment rises in step with profits, reaching 100% of target at 100% of the budgeted profit, and tops out at 150% of the target bonus when the profits hit 120% of budget. The executive gets no incremental bonus if the profit goes above 120% of the budget, and the bonus is zero at anything below 80% of the budget.

Conventional wisdom in the compensation arena is that this type of plan handily balances the objectives of adequate leverage and acceptable shareholder cost. As the Conference Board stated in its report on incentive practices: "This type of plan is often very attractive to shareholders as both a minimum performance level and a maximum payment are established". In fact, the principal effect of the cutoff points (no bonus below the minimum performance level, no additional bonus above the maximum) is to reduce the shareholder returns from what they otherwise would be.

This scheme does have enormous leverage, but only at the single point at which profits reach 80% of plan and the bonus jumps from 0 to 50% of the target level. You can be sure that no manager will ever end a year at 79% of budgeted profit. After that, the plan offers an incentive only along a narrow segment of the spectrum of possible outcomes. Once a manager knows that the year's profit is certain to be less than 80% or more than 120% of budget—which often is clear before the fiscal year is half over—he or she no longer has a monetary incentive to maximize the performance in the current year. The manager gets no extra reward for turning a good year into a great one, and faces no extra penalty for allowing a bad year to become even worse. These cutoffs in conventional bonus plans can be thought of as the *go golfing* points, because once a manager knows that profits will be solidly below or above them, he or she can head for the links secure in the knowledge that slacking off will not affect the bonus.

An incentive does remain beyond the cutoff points, but it is to *minimize* performance at the margin. This is one of the most important ways that typical incentives *pay* people to do very bad things. If the year is a bad one, a manager might as well let it become very bad, since that is likely to result in an easier profit plan next year. The only economic incentive working in the shareholders' interest on the nether side of the go-golfing points is the manager's fear of letting performance become so terrible that it jeopardizes chances for promotion or, at the extreme, survival in the company. If it is a good year, on the other hand, the manager wants to make sure it is not too good, because that could cause the corporate office to raise the bar to an uncomfortably high level in the next budget round. Several years ago, for example, the president of a multi-billion-dollar division of a *FORTUNE* 100 company instructed the business-unit heads reporting to him to suppress profits as much as possible because they were running too far ahead of the 12% growth he had promised to the CEO. He issued the order in April, less than a third of the way into the year and just two weeks before the CEO told shareholders at the annual meeting how hard everyone was working on their behalf.

Some companies eliminate formal bonus caps, but not necessarily in ways that serve shareholders. One major US Corporation offers senior executives employment contracts with a choice of bonus plans—either a guaranteed minimum bonus of $ 100,000 a year or more, or a purely discretionary bonus that is set by the CEO. The message embedded in the choices is clear: Take the guaranteed minimum and that is about all you will ever get, but cast your lot with the big guy and he will reward your show of faith by seeing to it that you always get much, much more than the guaranteed minimum. Company lore has it that no one has ever opted for the guaranteed bonus. If you think these executives worry a lot about how their actions will affect shareholders, guess again.

If anything, the true leverage in competitive pay plans is even less than this analysis suggests. Under a competitive pay strategy, companies recalibrate bonuses and option awards each year so that the total value of the package remains at the same *competitive* level and minimizes both the retention risk and the shareholder cost. This means that a manager starts each year with the same expected compensation (abstracting, that is, from the general upwards trend in pay levels). As a result, very little of the executive's *wealth*, as represented by the present value of expected compensation over the entire course of his or her remaining career with the company, ever is at risk. All the manager really stands to lose—or gain—is a portion of this year's bonus payment. Despite the appearance of significant leverage, the manager really does not have much on the line at all. Other factors, such as the chance of promotion or of landing a better job at another employer, may motivate outstanding endeavours, but competitive pay plans do not.

The ubiquitous practice of negotiating annual performance targets undermines both leverage and alignment with shareholder interests even more. Smart managers quickly learn that the name of the game is to beat the budget, and they behave accordingly. They try to ensure that they get the biggest possible bonus payoff by negotiating the most comfortable budget they can sell to their superiors. To them, the best plan is the most easily achievable, so they negotiate for something less than they believe they can achieve rather than striving for the greatest possible gains. And to top it off, the practice of renegotiating performance targets annually encourages the shortest of short-term thinking.

The bonus negotiations, known euphemistically as the *annual planning process*, become unnecessarily protracted, tying up valuable time and energy as managers try to manage the expectations of their superiors instead of the business itself. The superiors, knowing full-well that the subordinates are trying to sandbag them, waste their time trying to control opportunism. "Our planning process amounts to little more than collective bargaining for executive compensation," says the CFO of a major company with a classic bonus plan. What is more, all this wrangling over the budget goals usually goes on without any explicit consideration of how the resulting plan will affect the shareholder wealth.

At the bottom, the effect of conventional incentive plans is to produce managers who think and act like creditors, not like owners, because their claims on the company are essentially fixed, just like those of a lender. The value of the future stream of salary, bonus and options varies so little from year to year that it looks very much like an interest payment on debt. Since the manager has so little to gain from the greater success and so much to lose if the company or division fails, his or her focus instinctively goes to the risk side of risky opportunities, not to the opportunity side. Throw in the perverse incentives to game the system and sell superiors on easy goals, and one has to conclude that conventional incentive plans are formulas for mediocrity that impede rather than impel performance.

THE PROBLEM WITH STOCK OPTIONS

The corporate governance movement in the USA has made Boards of Directors acutely sensitive to the feeble connection between executive compensation and shareholder value. A research by Harvard Professor Emeritus Michael C. Jensen and others has demonstrated that the cash compensation paid to the top management is largely unaffected by the stock performance; the CEO makes out handsomely regardless of how the shareholders fare. Boards have responded to those findings—and to the rampant political and press criticism of escalating CEO compensation—by supplementing chief executive pay packages with stock options, lots of stock options.

Options are an effective way to achieve alignment between the interests of CEOs and shareholders, but their usefulness (other than as a tax-effective method of compensation) rapidly diminishes as you move down through the executive ranks. To be sure, share ownership or stock options can give employees a greater sense of belonging, a feeling that they are part of a community instead of just a hired hand. But options are not very effective at motivating specific types of behaviour.

For one thing, a middle manager has an exceedingly difficult time seeing the connection between his or her individual performance and the value of the company's stock. While the value of the stock ultimately represents the accumulation of the individual performances of everyone within the organization, the contribution of any one person, even the head of a business unit, usually is an imperceptible part of the whole. Stock ownership is simply too abstract and too remote to have a strong influence on the behaviour. This makes options extremely susceptible to what economists call the free-rider problem—sitting back and letting everyone else take care of the stock price—and emasculates their power as an incentive.

What is more, the types of options granted by most corporations are an unnecessarily expensive way of achieving alignment even for the CEO. With comparatively few exceptions, Boards of Directors bestow options that have a life of ten years and an exercise price that is fixed at the market price on the day they are granted. Since the exercise price is fixed, the option holders profit from *any* increase in the stock price, even one that is too small to provide the shareholders with a minimally acceptable return on their investment. That is, the conventional options begin rewarding managers long before the managers create any wealth for the shareholders. The solution to this disconnect between rewards and performance is to grant options with an exercise price that rises each year in line with the cost of equity capital, an alternative advocated by compensation guru Graef Crystal and others.

ACCOUNTING MEASURES AND INCENTIVE COMPENSATION

The typical incentive plan would still fail to align the interests of managers and shareholders even if the design flaws were corrected. That is because the vast majority links incentive pay to poor measures of performance—indeed, to measures that sometimes bear strikingly little relation to the performance of share prices. Most corporations tie their bonus payments to top corporate officers on achieving targeted levels of earnings, earnings per share, return on equity or return on assets. Bonuses for business-unit managers and others typically are based on the performance of the business unit itself, measured in terms of pre-tax operating profits.

These would seem to be the performance measures that matter. But the relationship between accounting earnings and share prices has broken down. Over the last 25 years or so, the accountants' ruling bodies in most countries have adopted auditing principles that require the expensing of all investments in intangible assets in the current year. This includes research and development, advertising and brand building and start-up costs on new projects. Even goodwill on acquisitions is written off much too quickly. The distortions in accounting earnings have been growing in step with the increasing importance of intangibles in all types of business, with the result that for almost all old economy firms and virtually all new-economy Internet and other high-tech companies, accounting earnings do not drive share value.

Another problem with accounting earnings is that the bottom line—net income after tax—includes interest charges for the cost of debt capital, but equity capital rides free. Charge too little for the use of capital, and the management is sure to use too much of it. The problem of undercharging for capital is exacerbated even further when managers are measured on the basis of operating profits. These measures do not even include interest charges on debt, and often exclude depreciation of capital equipment as well.

The universal practice of undercharging for the use of capital in the performance measure has been a formula—a very successful formula—for over-investment in mature industries. That is because any investment with a positive return, no matter how small, will cause operating earnings to rise. Even after-tax earnings and earnings per share can rise as a result of investments that destroy prodigious amounts of shareholder wealth. Consider a company with a weighted average cost of capital of 10%, an after-tax borrowing cost of 5%, and a 30% debt/equity mix. For an incremental investment to lift accounting earnings, it needs to produce only a 1.5% rate of return (representing the higher interest expense on the 30% of the cost that is funded with 5% debt). But with a 10% cost of capital, an investment with a 1.5% return would destroy 85 cents of every dollar invested.

Measures such as ROE and ROA are even worse than earnings, even though they do take the balance sheet—and, indirectly, the cost of equity capital—into account. To quote Michael Jensen, "If the performance measure is a ratio, it's wrong". Why? Because managers can *improve* any ratio (that is, make it look better) by taking actions that affect the numerator or denominator in ways that actually diminish economic performance and destroy shareholder wealth. The fact that both the numerator (earnings) and the denominators (shareholders equity or assets) in ROE and ROA are distorted by the accounting anomalies simply compounds the problems with them, since there is no reason to expect that a ratio of the two will convey any meaning at all.

ROE suffers from the added shortcoming of being easily manipulated. So long as the return on assets exceeds the after-tax cost of debt, top management can boost ROE at will simply by issuing bonds and repurchasing stock. Paying the heads of business units for increases in ROA actually can create the worst of all worlds. A division head whose ROA is, say, 25%, will turn down proposed investments that promise anything less, even if they will return more than the cost of capital and would add to the shareholder wealth. But the head of a division with an ROA of 5% will try to spend his way out of trouble by accepting just about any investment. He will be better off even if an investment returns less than the cost of capital and destroys shareholder wealth.

CHARACTERISTICS OF A GOOD MEASURE OF PERFORMANCE

The performance measure that all companies ought to use is some form of economic profit or residual income. This is a profit measure that includes an explicit charge for the opportunity cost of all the capital, both debt and equity. Following Jensen, it should be a dollar measure rather than a rate of return. And the measure should correct the anomalies that are baked into conventional accounting. In sum, the performance measure should meet the following five requirements:

1. It has to correlate highly with the changes in share values.
2. It has to be reasonably simple and straightforward, so that non-financial operating. managers can understand it and want to use it in their decisions.
3. It should encourage managers to invest in all projects with a positive net present value and reject all negative NPV proposals.
4. It should encourage the management to disgorge surplus capital to shareholders if the return on marginal investments is less than the cost of capital.
5. It should give the same answer when valuing businesses as the present value of the future free cash flows.

Those are precisely the requirements that Stern Stewart & Co. sought to satisfy in developing its EVA, or economic value added, measure of performance. In the author's view, EVA is the very best performance measure to use in incentive compensation plans, but any similar measure of economic profit will be vastly superior to conventional accounting earnings.

So how can a company link bonuses to EVA (or another economic profit measure) in a way that creates truly effective incentives? The answer is an incentive system that causes managers to think and act like owners of the portions of the business they influence most directly by paying the managers like owners. Stern Stewart's EVA bonus plans effectively give managers an ownership interest in performance improvements by paying bonuses that are a fixed percentage of *all* the changes in EVA. In other words, they provide a continuous incentive across the entire spectrum of performance outcomes. They give the managers the opportunity to earn an *unlimited* upside bonus in exchange for facing genuine downside risk.

The absence of bonus caps is made possible by holding back part of the bonus earned in very good years and making it subject to loss if EVA subsequently falls. This *banking* feature—genuinely having something at risk—is what transforms managers into owners. It also minimizes the opportunities for gaming the system by insuring that the companies pay only for sustained increases in performance, and it stretches out a manager's horizon, obviating the need for a separate long-term incentive plan.

The key elements in the bonus plan are discussed now.

Pay for all increases in EVA: This is the most reliable way to link the size of the bonus to the amount of wealth management creates for the shareholders, and is a pre-condition of making the managers to think and act like owners. The bonus has no threshold and no cap; the managers get an unlimited share of EVA improvement, but bonuses also can be negative.

Use the right EVA: The particular EVA that determines the bonus varies with the manager in question. For the CEO and other top corporate officers, the consolidated EVA of the company is the appropriate measure. Operating managers, on the other hand, should be gauged largely or entirely by the EVA performance of their particular areas of responsibility. As a general rule, companies should try to keep the measures of EVA for bonus purposes focused as tightly as possible on areas where the employees have a clear line of sight and can affect outcomes through their individual actions.

A target bonus: This is a competitive bonus based on peer company compensation practices. For several reasons, however, an EVA target bonus is larger than a conventional target bonus. *First*, most companies put too much of a manager's compensation in the fixed portion of the pay package and too little in the variable portion. In the Conference Board survey, for example, bonuses ranged from an average of 15% of base pay for the lowest-ranking employees in the plans to just 42% of base pay for the core group of top decision-makers. Real incentives require more leverage. *Second*, the EVA target bonuses should be higher because the potential for negative bonuses makes the EVA plans inherently riskier.

A bonus bank: There are several variations as to how the bonus bank works, but the intent is always to filter large bonus swings and to defer the impact until it can be ascertained that they are associated with permanent changes in shareholder wealth. In one version of the banking system, bonuses that are deemed to fall within an acceptable range, say from zero bonus up to two times a target bonus award, are paid out each year. However, negative bonuses and exceptional positive bonuses are deposited in the individual's notional bank account, and then a portion, say one-third, of any net positive bank balance in the account is also paid out each year. The unpaid balance in the bank is carried forward and the same procedure is repeated in subsequent years.

It is difficult to over-emphasize the importance of the bonus bank, which performs a number of vital functions. *First*, it insures that the managers collect bonuses only for sustained improvements in EVA. Bonus banking also is the principal mechanism for lengthening the planning horizons of the managers, since they know that gunning short-term performance will not do them any good if it harms longer-term results. Banking also smoothes out bonus payments, which can be especially helpful in limiting retention risk in highly cyclical industries. In those cases, the managers build up hefty bank balances in good years and draw down on them in the poor years. Finally, the bonus bank acts as a set of golden handcuffs for highly successful managers because any uncollected bank balance is forfeited if a manager resigns.

Performance targets set by formula instead of negotiation: Managers earn their target bonus when the dollar increase in EVA is equal to what we call expected improvement. This is similar to the performance targets in conventional plans, but with several crucial differences. *First*, the annual amount of expected improvement typically is pre-set for periods of five years or so instead of being negotiated annually. *Second*, the base to which expected improvement is added is automatically reset up or down each year in line with actual experience.

For a public company, expected EVA improvement at the corporate level is based heavily, though not entirely, on a calculation of the expected future improvement implicit in the stock price, with an appropriate amortization schedule for metering the dollar amount of total improvement into each year's EVA. Other factors, which obviously become the predominant ones when calculating expected EVA improvement for private companies and for separate business units within a public company, are management forecasts, historical EVA improvement, the historical volatility of performance, and analyses of publicly owned peer companies.

Regardless of technique, the critical element here is to set multi-year improvement targets and stick to them. This is what removes incentive compensation from the annual profit planning process, and is one of the most crucial elements in motivating stellar performance. Planning suddenly progresses much faster, and managers start proposing new ways to improve performance instead of trying to manage down their bosses' expectations. The result is budgets that are driven by aggressive strategy instead of strategy that is driven by timid budgets.

What every company wants is a culture of continuous improvement, responsibility and accountability. Enlightened companies today also want all of their employees to feel involved, be creative and to welcome if not precipitate change. In other words, they want to instill an ownership culture that eliminates the need to constantly control behaviour from above. To achieve that, what every company needs is an incentive system that clearly, objectively, predictably and continuously rewards the managers for creating shareholder wealth and penalizes them for destroying it. That is what the EVA bonus plans do.

CONCLUDING REMARKS

Companies choose to implement EVA for a variety of reasons. Some of them are as follows:

- Setting goals
- Communicating
- Evaluating strategies
- Reviewing capital projects
- Analysing acquisitions
- Evaluating operational initiatives
- Measuring performance
- Paying bonuses

The EVA framework provides an integrated approach to move from Seeing the value to Understanding Value Creation as shown here:

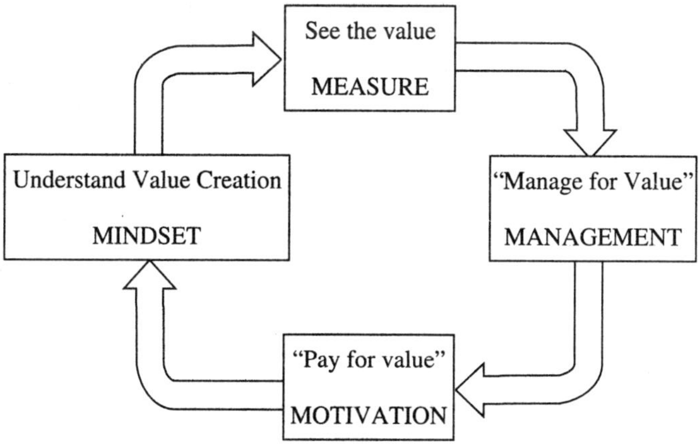

The following steps are involved in implementing the EVA:

Phase 1: Measurement

- Consists of management interviews.
- Defining EVA, EVA centres, making accounting adjustments, estimating the cost of capital.

Phase 2: Management tools

- EVA strategic planning and goal setting.

- Establishing EVA drivers.
- EVA-based capital budgeting.
- EVA reporting.

Phase 3: Incentive compensation

- Review of existing incentive plan.
- EVA-based incentive plan design.

Phase 4: Training and communication

- Develop communication and training material.
- Develop a comprehensive communication and training plan.

The key features and benefits of EVA-based performance linked compensation are as follows:

Features	Benefits
• Bonuses are linked to changes in the EVA not absolute EVA or PBT.	• Reinforces continuous improvement focus. • Greater focus on tax and balance sheet impact.
• Bonuses paid out are costed before the EVA targets are met.	• Cost of scheme is funded through business performance, therefore very shareholder friendly.
• No caps, no floors in pay-off profile.	• Avoids the kinks in pay-off profile that can encourage undesirable behaviour.
• Multi-year targets, de-linked from annual budgets.	• More productive budgeting process, more stretch thinking.
• Bonus bank.	• Encourages longer-term focus. • Smoothens the impact of business cycles. • Helps retain top performers.
• EVA drivers and individual performance factored in bonus distribution to team.	• Mix of team and individual rewards.

PART VI

CREATING VALUE THROUGH CORPORATE RESTRUCTURING

CHAPTER

10

Overview of Corporate Restructuring*

LEARNING OBJECTIVES

After reading this chapter, you should be able to:

- Highlight the forces driving restructuring initiatives.
- Describe the different types of restructuring.

INTRODUCTION

Competition, pressure from shareholder groups, economic forces, and regulation are forcing companies around the world to restructure their operations and create shareholder value. Corporate restructuring has become an important event in the corporate landscape. This chapter provides an overview of the factors driving restructuring initiatives, and the types of restructuring.

One of the most high profile features of modern business is corporate restructuring—mergers and acquisitions, leveraged buyouts, divestitures, spin-offs, equity carve outs, targeted stocks and the like. These techniques of corporate finance often have an impact on the financial markets far beyond the individual companies and sectors they involve. In general, stock prices of participating companies rise in response to announcements of mergers and corporate restructuring. But are such events good for investors beyond the short term?

* This chapter is contributed by Chandrasckhar Krishnamurti.

Corporate restructuring and improved corporate governance are essential parts of economic reform programmes under way in many countries, especially in East Asia. Corporate restructuring involves restructuring the assets and liabilities of corporations including their debt-to-equity ratios in line with their cash-flow needs to promote efficiency and to restore growth. Corporate governance refers to the framework of rules and regulations that enable the stakeholders to exercise appropriate oversight of a company to maximize its value and to obtain a return on their holdings[*]. Both corporate and financial sector restructuring are central to ongoing reform programmes in the East Asian economies such as Indonesia, Korea, Malaysia and Thailand[†].

During the 1990s, East Asian corporations, for example, borrowed heavily and expanded into many low-margin or loss-making businesses and markets. The financial crisis sparked by the fall of the Thai baht in July 1997 made it difficult for these highly leveraged corporations to service their debt, undermining the health of the financial institutions that had extended loans to them. The failure to shed marginal businesses and resolve unsustainable debt has left corporations, banks, and national economies less competitive, less able to respond to real growth opportunities, and vulnerable to future shocks[‡].

Before the crisis hit, many East Asian corporations expanded into sprawling conglomerates making extensive use of debt, because equity markets were undeveloped and, in many cases, owners preferred to retain control of firms with concentrated holdings. There were also structural weaknesses in these countries' banking supervision systems and internal bank management. Much of the debt owed to banks and corporations were unhedged and short term, which led to extreme over indebtedness following the devaluations and high interest rates of 1997 and 1998.

Two factors that made financial crises in East Asia difficult to manage are the large, **short-term internal and external debts** and **openness of many East Asian economies**, both of which constrain their monetary and exchange rate policies.

Corporations, government, and banks have close relationships in many East Asian countries. Many sectors of their economies are dominated by conglomerates controlled by a small group, non-transparent accounting, interlocking ownership between the corporate and financial sectors, and weak minority shareholder rights. It is estimated that the top 10 families in

---

[*] Chapter 13 discusses Corporate Governance in greater detail.

[†] Magdi, Iskander, Gerald Meyerman, Dale Gray and Sean Hagan, Corporate Restructuring and Governance in East Asia, *Finance & Development*, March, 1999.

Mako, William, Corporate Restructuring in East Asia: Promoting Best Practices, *Finance & Development*, March, 2001.

[‡] Stone, Mark, Corporate Debt Restructuring in East Asia: Some Lessons from International Experience, *IMF Paper on Policy Analysis and Assessment 98/13* (Washington), 1998.

East Asia: The Road to Recovery World Bank, (Washington), 1998.

Indonesia in 1997 controlled corporations worth more than half the country's market capitalization. Comparable figures are one-half in Thailand, one-fourth in Korea and Malaysia, but only 2%–3% in Japan (Claessens, Djankov and Lang 1999). Fundamental cultural and institutional changes are required if a new corporate governance structure is to be established with arms-length, transparent relations between corporations, government, and banks. Changing corporate governance, however, is a long-term process.

Since 1980, for example, the US public companies with more than a trillion dollars in assets have filed for Chapter 11 bankruptcy or restructured their debt out of court. Over the same period, More than 500 companies have spun-off businesses with a combined equity capitalization exceeding $ 250 billion. And by some estimates, as many as 20 million employees have been laid off in the US under corporate downsizing programs (see Gilson 1998).

Corporate restructuring is no longer a rare event. It is a common and important event in the professional lives of most managers. In recent years, unprecedented numbers of companies around the world have restructured their assets, operations, liabilities, and other obligations in response to new competitive challenges in their markets or major shifts in their business environment.

As these statistics, suggest restructurings impact millions of investors, employees and the society at large. Further, corporate restructuring has also become global (the case of Daewoo serves as a good example), as heightened competition in international product, capital, and labour markets puts tremendous pressure on companies worldwide to increase their competitiveness and maximize their market value. Companies must battle to defend their markets and their margins against pressures, including new competition, over which they have no control. Some resort to mergers and acquisitions in self-defense, which may well double their trouble while others seek to transform their creaking empires into powerhouses of modern management, at which most fail. Why do these once-mighty management machines find it so desperately difficult to extricate themselves from stagnation (e.g. General Motors)? One reason is complacency. Kodak's loss of market share to Fuji, and its failure to develop powerful new businesses, turned it, perhaps permanently, from leader to follower; sales fell by a quarter over the 1990s. Managers who resist change ignore the changing rules of the game.

Senior managers customarily complain about resistance to change among the lowest ranks. In fact, resistance among middle managers is both stronger and harder to eradicate. But their conservatism is generally outdone by their seniors. Top executives not only lived under the previous dispensation: they created it. If the past decade is any guide to the future, the pace of change will only increase. So it is necessary for the managers to be proactive and be able to identify and respond to the potential restructuring opportunities facing their firms. Understanding 'best practice' in corporate restructuring is the key to achieving competitive advantage, and to creating value for shareholders and the firm's various constituencies.

WHAT IS CORPORATE RESTRUCTURING?

Corporate restructuring is about creating value for stakeholders. For many companies restructuring is a response to deterioration in financial and competitive position. The need for restructuring often arises when the company's market value falls below its intrinsic value due to mistakes in the company's strategy or the inability of the capital market to correctly value the company's stock. The 'value gap' (the difference between current stock price and the potential price that would result from various improvements) can be sometimes as high as 60%.* Companies can reduce the value gap by improving operations, using leverage and selling divisional units to the best owner thereby unlocking the value. Restructuring involves taking necessary steps to bridge the value gap. Spin-offs, for example, are designed to cure undervaluation by capital markets.

Factors Driving Restructuring

The patterns of industrial development through mergers and restructuring, like those of economic activity, are crude and imperfect. However, there do seem to be some common forces driving the restructuring process.

- **Technological changes:** Technology creates new markets, introduces new competitors and is intertwined with regulatory change. Changes in technology make old regulatory boundaries obsolete (e.g. Telecom)†.
- **Regulatory changes:** Many of the most active M&A sectors over the past few years—media and telecommunications, financial services, utilities, health care—have been stimulated by deregulation or other political turmoil. Before deregulation, a number of industries owed their very existence to regulatory boundaries.
- **Conglomerate discount:** One of the disadvantages of a diversified firm is that the more profitable units subsidize the less profitable ones leading to heart burns and managerial defection. The general conclusion of some financial economists is that unrelated diversification does not increase returns although related diversification may help to some extent. A recent study suggests that the average value loss due to diversification is about 13%–15%, largely a product of over investment and cross subsidization.‡ Some corporate restructurings are supposed to cure the conglomerate discount.

---

* Fruhan, William, Corporate Raiders: Head 'em Off at Value Gap', *Harvard Business Review*, July-August, 1988.

† Sadtler, David, Andrew Campbell and Richard Koch, Breakup: When Large Companies are Worth More Dead than Alive, *Capstone*, 1997.

‡ Berger, Philip and Eli Ofek, Diversification's Effect on Firm Value, *Journal of Financial Economics*, 37, 1995.

- **Leadership:** Mergers or restructuring do not occur in a mechanistic fashion. A human element is involved—the top man who leads a company to change.
- **Financial:** According to modern finance theory, companies with lots of investment opportunities can be expected to issue short-term debt to preserve financial flexibility and to protect lenders against greater uncertainty in the company's future.* Further, growth firms ought to use relatively less debt to prevent the underinvestment problem. Conversely, for mature companies whose value comes mostly from assets-in-place, the costs of bankruptcy are likely to be low. Such firms can afford to have high leverage ratios to prevent wastage of free cash flow by the managers. Conventional wisdom suggests that companies should avoid combining high operating leverage (which leads to high business risk) and high financial leverage (which leads to high financial risk). Earnings are boosted in good times because of the presence of fixed costs and debt; but (earnings) get depressed in bad times for the same reason, viz. the presence of interest payments on debt and other fixed costs.

Massey Ferguson, a multinational producer of farm machinery, industrial machinery and diesel engines sought to increase its market share by turning to the developing countries for growth. Massey manufactured its products in the UK and Canada and sold the output to LDCs (Less Developed Countries) in the late 1970s. This strategy worked quite well in the initial years. Compared with competitors, Massey had an aggressive debt policy and an aggressive product market strategy. It was unwise to couple a risky strategy in a cyclical industry with high (short-term) debt†. When short-term interest rates shot up and the demand (and, hence, revenue) dried up for its products for various reasons, Massey was thrown into distress. John Deere, its major competitor, however, had moderate debt ratio because of which it had the financial flexibility to make capital investments. When Massey and another competitor, International Harvester were busy resolving distress, Deere pursued aggressive tactics to lock up market share. In the 1980s, a large number of American firms undertook leveraged recapitalizations and leveraged buyouts to improve shareholder value and operating efficiency. Many firms that undertook management buyouts in the late 1980s encountered distress due to poor structure of the deals (in terms of price) and adverse regulatory and economic developments. Academic studies in the US found that the firms encountering

* The cost of long-term debt will be unacceptably high for growth firms because of uncertainty in their future.

† Customers in less developed countries are more risky compared to customers in developed countries.

distress were more highly leveraged than other firms and exhibited poor post-recap operating performance due to industry wide problems.*

- **The size-simplicity paradox:** In many businesses scale matters, and bigger seems to mean better to most managers. Maybe it is a critical mass, or technology and globalization, or integration, or plain agency problem, but there is a natural imperative towards scale. However, just as some companies keep getting bigger, others (in the same business) shed their skin and become smaller. The imperative towards focus and simplicity is as strong as that for size.

TYPES OF RESTRUCTURING

The urge to merge is ever-present among corporate managers. The urge to demerge or spin-off or sell-off, however, is weaker and less likely to result in action. One major reason for this contrast in attitudes is the agency problem that plagues many companies. Even a modest acquisition or merger adds visibly to the management's power: by the same token, an asset sale, removing a substantial business from the corporation, subtracts from the managerial might. But asset sales and spin-offs are becoming more prominent. In 2000, reports KPMG, over a quarter of British companies in the Footsie 100 engaged in demergers or disposals. Two years before, only four of the 100 companies got involved in demerger/disposal deals of significance (meaning that they were worth at least 5% of the parent's market capitalization).† The urge to demerge can be found in widely disparate sector. BT in telecommunications and Kingfisher in stores have long been publicly exploring the possibilities, while the separation of the Accenture consultancy business from accountants Arthur Andersen was one of the largest ever.

Spin-offs

In a spin-off, one or more divisions of a listed company are detached from the parent and the parent company distributes shares in a controlled subsidiary to its shareholders, pro rata, as dividend. These entities continue to be owned by the original shareholders of the parent company. The spun-off company thereby becomes a stand-alone company and gets listed on a stock exchange. The announcement of spin-offs is usually accompanied by an increase in the value of the original business suggesting that investors view the components as worth more than the whole.

---

* Denis, David J. and Diane K. Denis, Causes of Financial Distress following Leveraged Recapitalizations, *Journal of Financial Economics*, 37, 1995.

† Heller, Robert, Business Corporate Strategy: Demergers and the Risks of Breaking up the Business, *Edward de Bono and Robert Heller's Thinking Managers*, Undated.

Demerger or spin-off is a special form of the disposal which becomes necessary when the management, for whatever reason, does not wish to continue with a viable business. The special aspect of demerging (and of the closely related management buyout or buyin) is that the disposed entity continues as a business on its own, pursuing its own destiny. That is why the abilities of the demerging management may come into question—because the board implicitly concedes that its management cannot win the best possible results from the subsidiary. The shareholder benefits of spin-offs depend on the reaction of the stock market. The classic situation is where the subsidiary is in a highly rated sector and the parent is unfashionable. A spin-off unlocks the hidden value for shareholders who receive some of the demerged equity. ICI's shareholders, for instance, were not receiving full value from its pharmaceuticals.* Spun-off as Zeneca, the demerged pharma company was merged with Astra of Sweden later. The new company is worth 20 times as much as ICI. The lower valuation of the original parent is usually due to unneeded, heavy and often counter-productive command and control it exerts over its subsidiaries. Heavy-handed central managements can get out of proper touch,† not only with the businesses they demerge, but with those left behind.

A well-conceived spin-off results in a highly focused entity. The demerged company ideally operates in a single product or services market, in which all its managers are experienced. In the original state, as managers of a subsidiary, they do not control their own funds, their own investment decisions, their own acquisition strategies—all the ingredients of entrepreneurial success. Instead of thinking and acting like entrepreneurs, they are forced to think and act like bureaucrats. It does not follow, however, that a spin-off automatically improves, let alone maximizes, the performance of the spun-off unit. The bifurcation of Courtaulds between textiles and its other interests created no miracles. Another example is Lucent Technologies. Spun-off from the AT&T telecommunications colossus, Lucent's manufacturing and research business attracted enormous interest. Its market valuation soared, and so did the reputation of its management. But Lucent was actually heading for a disastrous fall. The shares reached $ 140 and then fell to single figures, with investors having to absorb shocks like the $ 6.7 billion of credit extended to customers, and a $ 679 million overstatement of the year's revenues. The very factor that excited the investors—Lucent's position as a telecommunications supplier—worked against the company as telecommunication cooled off. A spin-off stems from the fact that most multi-business companies are worth less than their parts. This does not prove mismanagement, only that the stock

---

* This section is based on Robert Heller, Business Corporate Strategy: Demergers and the Risks of Breaking up the Business, *Edward de Bono and Robert Heller's Thinking Managers*, Undated.

† See, for example, Wruck, Karen and Sherry Pelkey Roper, Sink or Swim? Cytec Industries' Spin-Off, *Harvard Business School Case No. 5-897-053*, 1997.

market discounts conglomerates. Partial or total break-up, therefore, offers the prospect of releasing the value for the shareholders, but at the price of destroying the company. It is not an easy choice.

Asset Sales

A sell off or a divestiture involves the sale of a subsidiary, a division or a product line in exchange for cash or securities or some combination thereof. The buyer can be another company or the firm's management (in which case it is called management buyout) or another management team (in which case it is called a **leveraged buyout**). The cash realized from the sale might be used to retire debt or pay a dividend to shareholders.

Often, the divested divisions would have been acquired under another acquisition programme. If companies were acquired to create value, then how can acquisitions and subsequent divestitures both be rational? The shareholders of the selling company win only if the selling price is greater than the present value of expected cash flows from the division/company. That is, the asset should be worth more to the buyer than to the seller. This is possible if the asset can provide synergies to the buyer not available to the seller. If the buyer can generate higher cash flows from the business or lower the cost of capital, the value of the division increases. Another plausible reason for divestitures is that they enable the selling company to correct the past mistakes. Those assets that no longer fit the company's portfolio may be divested, thereby unlocking the shareholder value.

It is logical to divest those divisions that do not earn the cost of capital. To decide whether the firm should continue with an existing division, liquidate or sell it to someone else, a manager should estimate the value of the division not only to the firm but also to other potential acquirers. There are three measures of value. The *first* is the continuing value which is the present value of the expected cash flows from continuing with the investment through the end of the asset's life. The *second* is the liquidation value which is the cash flow a firm will receive if it terminated the division today. The *third* is the divestiture value which is the price paid by the highest bidder. The decision to continue, liquidate or sell depends on which of the three values is the highest. If the continuing value is the highest, the firm should continue with the division even if the division is not earning the cost of capital. If the divestiture value is the highest, then there is a potential for value creation by selling the division to the highest bidder.

The decision to sell a company/division is as important as buying one. But selling generally lacks the kind of planning that goes into buying. Quite often, the decision and the choice of the buyer is arbitrary resulting in a raw deal for the selling company's shareholders. It is important to understand that selling needs the same set of skills as required for buying. At some point in time the executives of a company may have to take the decision to divest a division. There is nothing wrong in selling a division if it is worth more to someone else. The decision to sell may be prompted by poor growth prospects for a division or consolidation in the industry. That is, divisions with low productivity are more likely to be sold. Given the fact that the need to sell may arise any time it makes sense for executives to be prepared. More specifically, the managers need to know their company's worth. Consideration may be given to strengths and weaknesses in production, marketing, value of synergy to potential buyers, value of brand equity, etc.

Siemens, for example, committed itself to selling assets with $ 10 billion in turnover. Some assets which look like suitable cases for treatment will be underperforming, some undervalued, some simply bad fits. Nokia exited from paper, tyres, metals, electronics (including PCs), cables and TV sets. The bold strategy was to concentrate on a single growth market, mobile phones—which duly rewarded the management with phenomenal success. Strategic considerations are crucial in opting for demerger. Under Jack Welch, for instance, General Electric bought businesses ranging from modest units to record-breakers such as RCA and Honeywell. But Welch has also been a heavy seller, even dropping the small appliances that had long been GE's standard bearers. The appliance sale was bitterly opposed and resented by old-line managers who regarded appliances as the core business of the corporation. The disposal followed naturally from Welch's famous strategic insistence that GE businesses which were not first or second in their markets would be revamped or sold. Strategy is central to any intelligent thinking on disposal, whether by sale or by demerger.

Like other forms of asset sale, buyouts generate tremendous value. But they can be very painful. Cadbury Schweppes sold Premier Brands (including Smash, Marvel and Typhoo) to the management in 1986, when the bundle had just lost £2.4 million: two years later, profits of £11.2 million had made the management into multi-millionaires. Their gain was the Cadbury shareholders' loss—and the experience has been replicated by many buyouts since.

Equity Carve Out

In an **equity carve out**, a public company sells a portion of its stake in a subsidiary to the general public in an initial public offering. The carved out subsidiary becomes an independent company with its own board and management. The parent company continues to provide administrative support. A carve out differs from a spin-off in at least two ways. *First*, a spin-off results in the distribution of subsidiary shares to existing shareholders whereas a carve out is a sale of subsidiary shares to general investing public which brings in new capital. *Second*, in a spin-off the parent company relinquishes control over the subsidiary company whereas a carve out creates a public minority interest. Typically, the parent company continues to hold a substantial portion of the subsidiary company's shares. Maintaining a majority ownership over the subsidiary helps retain control. Indeed, the accounting and tax consolidation of the carved out subsidiary with the parent depends on the extent of retention of ownership. In short, a carve out creates a public market for the subsidiary stock. Thermo Electron, Enron, Genzyme and The Limited have carved out in the recent years.

Targeted Stocks

Targeted stocks, also called tracking stocks, are a class of parent company stock that track the performance of a particular division, line of business, geographic segment or product line. The control of the division in question remains in the hands of the company's management unlike in spin-offs and carve outs in which a new board and management team is created. Further, the assets of the division are not separated from those of the parent company as in a spin-off. The revenues and earnings of the divisions are reported separately and dividends are computed on the basis of the earnings of the targeted division. As with spin-offs, assets and liabilities are allocated to divisions. But the allocation, in the case of targeted stocks, is for financial reporting. The legal titles to the assets and the responsibility for the liabilities will not be affected by allocation. It is important to understand that although the tracking stock tracks the performance of a division, the stock is a legal claim on the company and not on the division. To sum up, in a spin-off there are two (or more) stocks and two (or more) companies whereas in a targeted stock there are two (or more) stocks and one company.

A targeted stock structure is a compromise between the conglomerate structure and a spin-off. USX Corp, Genzyme, K Mart, Ralston Purina and Fletcher Challenge, among other companies, have issued tracking stocks.

Exhibit 10.1 presents the difference between a conglomerate and a targeted stock structure.

EXHIBIT 10.1

Conglomerate Structure Versus Targeted Stock Structure

Common stock structure	Targeted stock structure
Valuation on the basis of performance of all divisions	Valuation on the basis of the unit being tracked
Common voting rights	Differential voting rights
Fixed dividend rights	Differential dividend rights

ESTIMATION OF POTENTIAL FOR VALUE CREATION

As pointed out earlier, the companies can bridge the value gap by improving operations, using leverage, selling divisional units to the best owner and separating out divisions to cure undervaluation. The actual type and sequence of restructuring depends on the particular challenges faced by the company. A company contemplating on restructuring would want to know how the restructuring is likely to affect the enterprise value. Managers involved in the process may estimate the impact of various initiatives by discounting the incremental cash flows generated by the restructuring at a suitable discount rate. More specifically, one may find the sum of present values of the following:

- After-tax savings arising out of lower salaries and wages due to downsizing (net of costs like one time payments made to employees).
- After-tax incremental free cash flows generated by improvements in operating margin and sales growth arising out of refocusing.
- Tax shields due to higher leverage (due to higher interest expense).
- After-tax proceeds from sale of assets.
- Any other savings.

Companies may benchmark the best competitor or industry average to estimate the potential for value creation.

Restructuring is not a free exercise. Companies will have to spend on closing down of plants and so on. So the sum total of (present values of) of costs has to be deducted from the benefits to arrive at net benefits.

When one is dealing with free cash flow to firm, the appropriate discount rate is the weighted average cost of capital; likewise when one is dealing with free cash flow to equity, the appropriate discount rate is the cost of equity (as estimated by CAPM).

As far as the valuation methodology itself is concerned, managers have the choice of using any of the methods such as adjusted present value, capital cash flow valuation etc.

A summary of the different types of restructuring is given Table 10.1.

Table 10.1 Different Types of Restructuring

	Spin-off	Carve out	Tracking stock
Change of ownership	Yes	No	Usually no
Raise capital	No	Yes	Usually no
Stock market reaction	+ve	+ve	+ve
Preserve synergy	No	Yes	Yes
Cure undervaluation	Yes	Yes	Yes
Attract new investors	Yes	Yes	Yes/No
Improved analyst coverage	Yes	Yes	Yes

REFERENCES

1. Classens, S., S. Djankov, H.L. and P. Lang, Who Controls East Asian Corporations?, *Policy Research Working Papers 2054*, World Bank, Washington DC, 1999.

2. Gilson S.C., Course Overview: Creating Value through Corporate Restructuring, *Working Paper*, Harvard Business School, 1998.

SUGGESTED FURTHER READING

Alexander, G.J., G. Benson and J. Kampmeyer, Investigating the Wealth Effects of Announcements of Voluntary Corporate Sell Offs, *Journal of Finance*, **39**, 1984.

Altman, E., Financial Ratios, Discriminant Analysis and the Prediction of Corporate Bankruptcy, *Journal of Finance*, **23**, 1968.

———, Corporate Financial Distress and Bankruptcy, 2nd ed., New York, John Wiley, 1993.

Asquith, P., R. Gertner and D. Scharfstein, Anatomy of Financial Distress: An Examination of Junk-Bond Issuers, *NBER Working Paper No. 3942*, December, 1991.

Anslinger, P., D. Carey, K. Fink and C. Gagnon, Equity Carve—Outs: A New Spin in the Corporate Structure, *The McKinsey Quarterly*, Number 1, 1997.

Baldwin, C., Massey-Ferguson, 1980, *Harvard Business School Case No. 9-282-043*, 1990.

Barclay, M.J. and C. Smith Jr., The Maturity Structure of Corporate Debt, *Journal of Finance*, (**2** June), 1995.

Bhide, A., Reversing Corporate Diversification, in Donald Chew, (ed.), *The New Corporate Finance: Where theory Meets Practice*, McGraw Hill, 1999.

Billett, M.T. and D. Mauer, Diversification and the Value of Internal Capital Markets: The Case of Tracking Stock, *Working Paper*, University of Iowa, October, 1998.

Billett, M.T. and D. Mauer, and A. Vijh, The Market Performance of Tracking stocks, *Working paper*, University of Iowa, February, 2001.

Bowman, E. H., H. Singh, M. Useem and R. Bhadury, When Does Restructuring Improve Economic Performance, *California Management Review*, **41** (2), Winter, 1999.

Chemmanur, T. and I. Paeglis, Why Issue Tracking Stock? Insights from a Comparison with Spin-offs and Carve outs, *Working Paper*, Boston College, June, 2000.

Claessens, Stijn, *Systemic Bank and Corporate Restructuring*, Washington DC: World Bank, 1998.

Markides, C.C., To Diversify or Not to Diversify, *Harvard Business Review*, Nov–Dec., 1997.

Cusatis, P., J. Miles and R. Woolridge, Restructuring through Spin-offs: The Stock Market Evidence, *Journal of Financial Economics*, 1993.

———, Some New Evidence that Spin-offs Create Value, *Journal of Applied Corporate Finance*, **7**(2, Summer), 1994.

DeAngelo, H., L. DeAngelo and K.H. Wruck, Asset Liquidity, Debt Covenants and Managerial Discretion in Financial Distress: The Collapse of L.A Gear, *Journal of Financial Economics*, **64**, 2002.

Donaldson, G., Strategy for Financial Emergencies, *Harvard Business Review*, Nov–Dec., 1969.

———, Corporate Restructuring in the 1980s–and its Import for the 1990s, *Journal of Applied Corporate Finance*, **6**(4, Winter), 1994.

Dranikoff, L., T. Koller and A. Schneider, Divestiture: Strategy's Missing Link, *Harvard Business Review*, May, 2002.

D'Souza J. and J. Jacob, Why Firms Issue Targeted Stock, *Journal of Financial Economics*, **56**, 2000.

Fridson, M. and J. Jonsson, Contingent Claims Analysis, *Journal of Portfolio Management*, Winter, 1997.

Garvin, D.A., Spin-offs and the New Firm Formation Process, *California Management Review*, **XXV**(2), January, 1983.

Gillan, S., J. Kensinger and J. Martin, Value Creation and Corporate Diversification: The Case of Sears, Roebuck & Co., *Journal of Financial Economics*, **55**(1, January), 2000.

Gilson, S., *Creating Value through Corporate Restructuring: Case Studies in Bankruptcies, Buyouts and Breakups*, Wiley, 2001.

Gilson S. and J. Cott, Humana Inc., *Harvard Business School Case No. 9-294-062*, 1994.

Gilson S. and J. Cott, USX Corporation, *Harvard Business School Case No. 9-296-050*, 1996.

Gilson S.C., Valuing Companies in Corporate Restructurings, *Harvard Business School Case No. 9-201-073*, 2000.

Habib, M.A., D.B. Johnsen and N.Y. Naik, Spin-offs and Information, *Journal of Financial Intermediation*, **6**(2).

Healy, P., and K. Palepu, The Challenges of Investor Communication: The Case of CUC International Inc, *Journal of Financial Economics*, **38**, 1995.

Hite, G. and J. Owers, Security Price Reactions Around Corporate Spin-off Announcements, *Journal of Financial Economics*, **12**, 1983.

Hite, G., J. Owers and R. Rogers, The Market For Interfirm Asset Sales: Partial Sell-offs and Total Liquidations, *Journal of Financial Economics*, **18**, 1987.

Jain, P.C., The Effect of Voluntary Sell-off Announcements on Shareholders Wealth, *Journal of Finance*, March, 1985.

Jensen, M., Active Investors, LBOs and the Privatization of Bankruptcy, *Journal of Applied Corporate Finance*, Summer, 1989.

Klein, A., Timing and Substance of Divestiture Announcements: Individual, Simultaneous and Cumulative Effects, *Journal of Finance*, **41**, 1986.

Lang, L., A. Poulsen and R. Stulz, Asset Sales, Firm Performance, and the Agency Costs of Managerial Discretion, *Journal of Financial Economics*, **37**, 1995.

Linn, S.C. and M. Rozeff, The Corporate Sell-off, *Midland Corporate Finance Journal*, Summer, 1984.

Logue, D., J. Seward and J. Walsh, Rearranging Residual Claims: A Case for Targeted Stock, *Financial Management,* Spring, 1996.

Maksimovic, V. and G. Phillips, The Market for Corporate Assets: Who Engages in Mergers and Asset Sales and are There Efficiency Gains, *The Journal of Finance*, **LVI**(6, December), 2001.

Michaely, R. and W.H. Shaw, The Choice of Going Public: Spin-offs vs. Carve outs, *Financial Management*, **24**(3, Autumn), 1995.

Monroe, A., Sale of the Century, *CFO Magazine*, January, 1994.

Nichols III, C. and L. Sharp Pyne, Marriott Corporation, *Harvard Business School Case Study No. 9-394-085*, 26 June, 1997.

Parrino, R., Spin-offs and Wealth Transfers: The Marriott Case, *Journal of Financial Economics*, **43**, 1997.

Schipper K. and A. Smith. Effects of Recontracting on Shareholder Wealth: The Case of Voluntary Spin-offs, *Journal of Financial Economics*, December, 1983.

———, The Corporate Spin-off Phenomenon, *Midland Corporate Finance Journal*, (Summary), 1984.

———, A comparison of Equity Carve Outs and Seasoned Equity Offerings: Share Price Effects and Corporate Restructuring, *Journal of Financial Economics*, June 1986.

Slovin, Myron, Marie Sushka and Steven Ferraro, A Comparison of the Information Conveyed by Equity Carve Outs, Spin-offs and Asset Sell-offs, *Journal of Financial Economics*, **37**, 1995.

Stein, Jeremy, *USX: Targeted Stock Restructuring*, Casenet, Southwestern College Publishing.

Stern, Joel, Bennett Stewart and Donald Chew, (ed.), Corporate Restructuring and Executive Compensation, *The Institutional Investor Series in Finance*, Harper and Row, 1989.

Stone, Mark, Corporate Debt Restructuring in East Asia: Some Lessons from International Experience, *IMF Paper on Policy Analysis and Assessment 98/13* (Washington), 1998.

Vijh, A., Long term Returns from Equity Carve Outs, *Journal of Financial Economics*, **51**, 1999.

Weston, Fred, Divestitures: Mistakes or Learning, in Joel Stern and Donald Chew, (ed.), *The Revolution in Corporate Finance*, Blackwell, 1992.

World Bank, *East Asia: The Road to Recovery*, (Washington), 1998.

Wruck, Karen, and Sherry Pelkey Roper, Sink or Swim? Cytec Industries' Spin-off, *Harvard Business School Case No. 5-897-053*, 1997.

Zuta S., Diversification Discount and Targeted Stock: Theory and Empirical Evidence, *Working Paper*, University of Maryland, 2000.

EXERCISES

1. A company has three business units. The relevant data for these divisions are presented as follows:

	ROE (%)	K_e (%)	Growth (%)	Book equity ($, m)
A	25%	19	8	25
B	20	20	12	5.5
C	10	17	4	20.0

Division C is losing money currently. That is, its ROE is less than the cost of equity. There are four potential strategies for this division.

Modernize by investing in capital equipment. The investment is expected to be $ 5 million, 60% financed with debt. The technology upgradation is expected to result in cost savings and an improvement in ROE (20%).

Stop growing. Under this strategy ROE is expected to stabilize at 17% (equal to the cost of equity).

Slowly **liquidate** assets or redeploy assets in other divisions. Under this strategy ROE is expected to be 15%.

The Economic Value/Book Value of the division under the three strategies is 1.3, 0.8 and 0.9, respectively. Estimate the value created by each strategy. Which strategy would you choose? Why?

2. The performance of three companies is presented in Exhibit 1. Assume that you are a consultant advising the first company in restructuring. What are the restructuring opportunities for this company? Benchmark the second company in estimating the improvements. Estimate the value of various restructuring opportunities assuming that cash flows are perpetual (or alternatively, some finite period, say, five years). Assume that the borrowing rate for the first company is 17%.
3. Discuss the differences between spin-offs, carve outs and targeted stocks. When is targeted stock appropriate?
4. The financial details of a company are given as follows:

	2000	2001	2002
Sales	3.7m	1.8m	3.6m
Net income	1.3m	0.9m	1.5m
Total assets	16m	19.8m	33.3m
Equity	11.8m	15.3m	26.9m

This company has three divisions-healthcare, property development and hotels. The contribution of these divisions towards turnover and profit before tax of the company is given as follows:

($)

	2000	2001	2002
Sales contribution			
A	2.5m	1.3m	2.4m
B	1m	0.3m	0.9m
C	0.2m	0.2m	0.3m
PBT contribution			
A	0.9m	0.7m	1.1m
B	0.3m	0.09m	0.2m
C	0.5m	0.06m	0.059m

EXHIBIT 1

Performance Comparison (for 1999, 2000, and 2001 in $ '0 m Except Ratios)

	A			B			C		
	1998–99	*1999–00*	*2000–01*	*1998–99*	*1999–00*	*2000–01*	*1998–99*	*1999–00*	*2000–01*
Sales	16,002.3	17,257.1	17,320.4	6,885.1	7,015.2	7,845.2	2,627.5	2,714.0	3,596.2
Cost of production	11,564.7	11,821.7	12,368.3	4,733.1	4,179.8	4,375.1	2,647.3	2,595.5	2,716.2
Gross fixed assets	30,771.5	28,307.9	28,129.6	10,032.2	10,668.3	11,258.2	8,615.5	8,635.3	8,649.1
Current ratio	1.07	0.83	0.79	1.05	0.94	0.92	0.11	0.77	0.89
Total interest-bearing debt as a % of total assets	61.1%	57.2%	54.9%	50.6%	43.8%	40.2%	26.8%	29.9%	34.4%
Total short-term interest-bearing debt as a % of total interest-bearing Debt	20.4%	24.2%	25.5%	6.3%	8.4%	8.9%	34.6%	31.4%	28.4%
Net working capital cycle (days)	257	200	162	113	117	95	172	132	136
Avg. Days of Debtors (days)	46	42	39	74	70	62	15	17	17
Avg. Days of Creditors (days)	42	36	43	91	100	104	73	77	76
Inventories (Closing)	6,832	4,606	4,519	1017	945	922	1009	1111	1207
Raw Materials	689	720	650	173	160	179	189	176	192
WIP	0	0	0	25	28	29	398	0	0
Finished Goods	4,782	2,819	2,939	564	527	474	0	494	597
Inventory turnover ratio (times)									
Raw materials turnover	6.43	7.21	7.93	7.04	6.62	6.65	5.96	7.7	8.08
Stores turnover	1.41	1.59	1.73	1.44	1.34	1.55	0.66	0.69	0.66
Semi-finished goods turnover				207.59	155.84	151.99	13.29	13.03	
Finished goods turnover	2.56	3.81	4.53	9.95	9	10.18	7.95	11.11	5.32
Debt equity ratio	3.03	3.12	3.34	1.81	1.33	1.18	0.78	0.63	0.78
Quick ratio	0.18	0.19	0.19	0.44	0.38	0.37	-0.52	0.14	0.16
Interest coverage ratio	0.18	0.04	0.56	1.29	1.64	2.11	-0.25	-0.44	0.18
Debtors turnover	7.9	8.77	9.34	4.94	5.22	5.85	24.29	22.02	21.15
Creditors turnover	8.61	10.13	8.57	4.02	3.66	3.5	5.01	4.74	4.78
Employee cost (Wages)	2,393.9	2,772.4	3,134.8	1065.4	957.1	922.4	255.2	272.5	407.7
Number of employees	NA	NA	NA	NA	NA	NA	NA	NA	NA

The P/E multiples of the company and the (average of) peer group is given as follows:

	2000	2001	2002
Company	9.5	12	10
Healthcare	9	12	9
Property development	10	20	8
Hotels	18	40	22

The P/E multiple of the company more closely follows the healthcare sector than hotels, may be because much of its revenues comes from healthcare. The company feels that spinning off the hotels division would provide a higher price-earnings multiple to the division and, hence, result in a higher valuation for the company.

Assess the financial performance of the company by conducting a Du Pont analysis. Is restructuring necessary? Which division is experiencing the maximum growth? Assume that each division contributes to the net income in the same proportion as PBT. What is the stand-alone value of the hotels division based on peer group multiple? What is the value of the company's equity? Is a spin-off desirable? What are the advantages and disadvantages of a spin-off?

CHAPTER

11

Leveraged Recapitalizations and Leveraged Buyouts*

LEARNING OBJECTIVES

After reading this chapter, you should be able to:

- Introduce high leverage restructurings like LBOs.
- Compare and contrast recapitalizations with buyouts.
- Discuss the rationale for LBOs.
- Discuss the design of an LBO.

INTRODUCTION

A large number of the US corporations took their companies private in the 1980s and 1990s. Such (purchases) going private transactions are often funded with heavy debt. These high leverage transactions generate substantial value due to valuable interest tax shields. They also expose the sponsors to bankruptcy risk. This chapter provides an overview of the two types of high leverage transactions—recapitalizations and buyouts.

The confluence of low default rates, strong earnings, extraordinary liquidity and the resulting unprecedented binge in M&A and Leveraged Buyout (LBO) activity allowed the 2006 US syndicated loan issuance to surge to a new record of $ 1.67 trillion, according to Reuters Loan Pricing Corporation.

* This chapter is contributed by Atul Gupta.

With such a benign global environment, 2006 was an auspicious time for borrowers to transform themselves. And so they began to merge. The loan market facilitated the transformational deals taking place, and 2006 saw $ 421 billion of merger financing. While $ 307 billion of this financing backed corporate mergers, it was the record setting $ 114 billion in loans backing LBOs that captured most of the headlines. 2006 not only saw LBO activity surpassing records set in the late 1980s, it was also the year HCA Inc. finally toppled RJR Nabisco's 18-year reign as the issuer of the largest LBO loan. At more than $ 16 billion, HCA Inc. also was a trailblazer as it included an $ 8.8 billion 'institutional loan'—the largest loan tranche ever to be sold to non-bank or institutional lenders (such as hedge funds, mutual funds and Collateralized Loan Obligations, or CLOs).

Institutional lenders played an unprecedented role in providing the essential funding to finance not only LBO loans, but also the record setting $ 612 billion in leveraged loans—loans backing companies with a rating of less than BBB-/Baa3 and with a loan margin of at least 1.5% over LIBOR. Institutional loan issuance topped $ 366 billion last year—10 times that of 2001—and more than twice the $ 137 billion of the US high yield bond issuance tracked by Reuters.

The objective of this chapter is to answer such questions as when and why do some companies resort to high leverage; what are the benefits and costs of BOs; what are the sources of funding for a typical LBO and what are the valuation issues in a high leverage transaction.

In a market economy, the primary task of corporate management is to maximize shareholder wealth. The owner-manager of a sole proprietorship clearly follows this objective, because the ownership and control functions reside within the same person. The separation of ownership and control that characterizes the corporate form of organization creates incentive conflicts between the firm's shareholders (owners) and those in control (management), and gives rise to a variety of costs that are discussed under the rubric of 'agency-theory' (see, Jensen and Meckling 1976, Myers 1977, and Jensen 1986, 1993). The essence of the agency problem is that conflicts of interest between owners and managers can lead to value leakages and even value destruction, outcomes that run counter to the objective of maximizing shareholder wealth.

Mechanisms designed to reduce the value destroying potential of agency conflicts include the internal governance system embodied in the Board of Directors, equity holdings and incentive-based compensation systems for senior management, and the market for corporate control, which serves as an outside monitor of corporate activities. The Board of Directors has a fiduciary responsibility to the firm's stockholders, and is supposed to provide an oversight of managerial plans and actions. This internal governance system serves as the first line of defence against the possibility of management taking actions designed to enhance personal wealth at the expense of the firm's owners. Managerial equity holdings and incentive compensation systems are designed to align managerial incentives with those of the stockholders; the idea is that value losses from adverse incentives can be reduced if maximizing the shareholder wealth simultaneously maximizes the managerial wealth. In the cases where internal governance is ineffective and compensation systems are not designed to align shareholder interests with those of the management, corporate investment and financing policies can lead to value destruction. In such cases the market for corporate control serves as the third line of defence; firms that follow policies that do not maximize shareholder wealth face the threat of a takeover, and can be bought out and restructured in a manner that enhances the wealth of the firm's owners.

The internal governance system, compensation policy, and a well-functioning market for corporate control can be thought of as the three pillars that keep managerial objectives aligned with those of the firm's stockholders. Where do Leveraged Recapitalizations (LRs) and LBOs fit into this scheme of things? It turns out that for certain types of firms, the changes in ownership and financial structure brought about by extreme leverage are an efficient mechanism for aligning the interests of the firm's owners and managers. LRs and LBOs have been found to increase corporate focus and productivity, reduce wasteful use of free cash flow, enhance the tax shield provided by the deductibility of interest payments, and result in substantial increases in shareholder wealth. The objective of this essay is to provide an understanding of these two forms of leveraged restructuring, and to present some evidence on the valuation consequences of LRs and LBOs. Critical elements underlying deal design are presented in the subsequent section.

LBO AND LR: BASIC CHARACTERISTICS

The US tax code permits deductibility of corporate interest payments, providing a substantive and highly quantifiable benefit from debt financing. Debt financing reduces taxes, and leverage increases enhance the equity values by increasing the magnitude of the wealth transfer from the Government to a firm's stockholders. Other advantages associated with leverage flow through its impact on ownership structure, managerial incentives, monitoring costs, and reductions in value losses arising from information asymmetries between the corporate insiders and the investment community. The downsides to debt use include potential costs associated with increases in the probability of default and reductions in the flexibility available to the management in the way of capital market access in successive time periods.

In this chapter, the author I explores the benefits and costs associated with extreme leverage, where extreme is thought of as debt to capital ratios approaching and at times exceeding 60%–70% in book-value terms. There are two broad categories of leverage increasing transactions that fit this bill. These are called **Leveraged Recapitalizations** and **Leveraged Buyouts**. Both these forms of restructuring involve raising a large amount of debt capital. In an LBO, the debt is used to purchase all the outstanding common stock of the firm and the security is delisted from the stock exchanges. The firm, in other words, goes private. In an LR, the firm generally pays out a large debt financed dividend to the firm's stockholders. The immediate result of such a payment is a steep decline in the stock price, and the common stock following an LR is commonly known as a 'stub'.

Both LRs and LBOs represent highly leveraged restructurings. Other similarities between the two types of deals include substantial increases in managerial ownership, which can serve to mitigate stockholder-manager conflicts of interest. High debt levels also put pressure on the management to run the firm efficiently, and reduce the likelihood of internally generated cash flows being used for non-value enhancing investments. In addition, leverage-induced tax savings can be substantial in both types of transactions. Potential negatives associated with high leverage also apply to both LRs and LBOs. Examples of these include foregoing risky investments (Myers 1977), and an incentive to emphasize investments that generate high levels of current cash flows (Peyer and Shivdasani 2001).

A major difference between LBOs and LRs is that while with the former the firm becomes privately held, the firms that execute LRs remain publicly traded. The use of strip financing in LBOs, if utilized, results in creditors becoming stockholders in the restructured firm, which can have important implications in situations where the firm experiences financial distress in the period following the LBO. This is not the usual pattern in LRs, where stockholders and bond holders tend to be separate entities. LBOs also result in a high degree of ownership concentration, a situation that is quite different from the diffused ownership holdings in LRs. Concentrated ownership in LBOs can serve to reduce monitoring costs, in addition to reducing the level of shareholder servicing costs typically incurred by a publicly held corporation. What are the advantages to such dramatic restructurings? Why do firms do this? What types of firms could benefit from such large changes in capital structure? Is there some particular advantage to private ownership that can only be achieved through an LBO? Does the significant increase in default risk associated with massive leverage negatively impact the risk level of the economy as a whole? In the following sections the author tries to sort out these matters and see what one can learn from the experience of firms that have undergone these forms of financial restructuring.

THE GENESIS OF HIGHLY LEVERAGED RESTRUCTURINGS

An understanding of the benefits and costs associated with highly leveraged transactions requires some insight into the nature of corporate America in the period following the Second World War. The US economy was an economic powerhouse through most of the 1950s and 1960s, and the latter decade witnessed a large wave of conglomeration through heightened Merger and Acquisition (M&A) activity. The stock market generally responded positively to the types of diversifying acquisitions that created conglomerates, a form of corporate organization that added value largely through the creation of 'internal capital markets', which facilitated the allocation of financial resources among the various divisions of diversified firms under the guidance of the staff at corporate headquarters. Such organizations performed quite well, providing investors with a steady stream of returns on their investment.

The impetus for change came from two distinct sources. One was the oil shock of 1973, and the second was technological progress*. The oil shock of 1973 had a dramatic impact on the economic strength and future prospects of a large segment of American industry. Industries as diverse as automobiles, steel, paper, oil, food, and tobacco experienced huge increases in operating costs, with associated declines in profitability. The economies of the industrialized nations were, and are still, driven by fossil fuels, and a steep increase in the price of basic energy led to a sharp rise in inflation and interest rates, followed by a deep recession in the late 1970s and early 1980s. The Japanese economy performed well over this period, particularly in the automobile sector. Smaller, more fuel-efficient cars found a ready market in western economies, and Japanese automakers stepped in to fill this need. The US automakers were slow to respond, and lost competitive position in world markets. It appears clear with hindsight that the American industry needed to change, to do things differently. Highly leveraged transactions facilitated a lot of this change.

Technological progress played a role in the transformation of industry by creating pockets of excess capacity in various sectors. The introduction of radial tyres, for example, dramatically increased the expected life of tyres and created excess capacity in the industry. Technological progress thus created a need for some industries to shrink, which in turn required individual firms to exit the industry. Managers who invested in such sectors with large amounts of human capital clearly did not have any incentive to do this and permitted a continuing misallocation of economic resources within the economy as a whole.

Viewed in this historical context, the problems facing western economies were multifaceted and complex. Large sectors of the economy were bureaucratic in form, insulated from the capital markets, and not competitive. Internal governance system were poorly structured, and largely failed in their responsibility to the firm's stockholders. Incentive systems for corporate management were designed to encourage growth rather than shareholder value, and a way to change this situation was not immediately evident.

---

* See Jensen (1993) for a discussion of these and related issues.

The impetus for change was triggered by substantive changes in federal regulatory, fiscal, and monetary policies starting in the early 1980s. Steep declines in tax rates served to rejuvenate the entrepreneurial spirit of the nation, and regulatory changes supporting free markets led to the creation of new types of securities that helped facilitate the restructuring of corporate America. Massive deficit spending by the Federal Government added fuel to the economy, and contributed to a sustained increase in the stock market through the 1980s. One of the key events of this period was a substantial expansion of the high-yield debt market, which provided the fuel needed to accomplish the level of restructuring required to restore competitive strength to the American industry.

THE ROLE OF LEVERAGE

The root cause of the problems facing the American industry in the early 1980s was managerial incentives that did not encourage the movement of resources to their highest valued use. This permitted the continuation of large bureaucratic organizations, low levels of managerial shareholdings, and sub-optimal use of corporate cash flows. Highly diffused shareholdings made the capital markets an ineffective disciplinary tool, and entrenched management groups with poor incentives continued to make less than optimal resource allocation decisions. The high-yield debt market presented a resource pool that could be used to force the types of restructuring that were needed for a return to competitive strength. It suddenly became possible for individual 'corporate raiders' such as Carl Icahn and Boone Pickens, among others, to raise enough capital to buy large holdings of individual corporations, and to force these firms to implement the types of restructuring needed to move resources to higher valued uses. Groups specializing in LBOs, such as Kohlberg, Kravis, Roberts (KKR) raised large amounts of debt to buy out corporations, split up diversified conglomerates and inefficient single product firms, and enhance economic efficiency. The contributions of high-yield debt to the restructuring process include the following:

- Creating a pool of capital that can be used to buy firms where managerial policies are destroying value.
- Permitting significant concentrations of managerial equity holdings, with the associated upside potential for large increases in personal wealth.
- Improvements in managerial incentives due to the large debt overhang created by highly leveraged restructurings.
- Reduced monitoring costs, which follow naturally from a concentrated ownership structure and tremendous upside potential.
- Substantial reductions in the wasteful use of free cash flows for diversifying acquisitions and managerial efforts at empire building.

Efficiently executed leveraged restructurings can thus serve to restore corporate focus, reduce waste, and enhance work incentives by creating both a threat of failure and a large upside potential if successful.

Leveraged Recapitalizations

A leveraged recapitalization entails the payment of a large debt financed dividend to existing shareholders of the firm. In addition to the dividend, shareholders can also receive subordinated notes and other forms of paper. Each shareholder in the Colt Industries leveraged recap, for example, received $ 85 in cash and one new share of stock. The retirement savings plan got additional shares in lieu of cash. The deal was financed using bank loans, subordinated debt, and cash in hand. The firm's debt to capital ratio increased from 19% before the LR to 64% post-recap, and the managerial stockholdings increased from 5.9% to 11.5% following the recap. Owens Corning followed a somewhat different approach. In this transaction each shareholder received $ 52 in cash, one new share of stock, and a junior subordinated debenture valued at $ 35. The management and corporate employees received additional shares in lieu of cash, resulting in managerial shareholdings increasing from 0.1% before to 3.4% after the recap. Bank loans and debentures were used to finance the deal, and led to an increase in debt to total capital from 27% before the recap to 84% post-recap.

As illustrated by the above examples, a leveraged recap entails distributing a substantial amount of cash and/or securities to the firm's stockholders. New debt issues are used to finance these distributions, resulting in dramatic increases in corporate leverage. Managerial shareholdings increase substantially on average, helping to align managerial incentives with those of the stockholders of the firm. Empirical evidence on the impact of such restructurings on the wealth of various stakeholders and the sources of such wealth gains are discussed in the following paragraphs.

At the time of the recap, shareholders should decide whether to accept the offer or not. In other words they must evaluate their net position after the recap and compare it with what they currently have. Assume that you have accepted an offer of recap in which you will receive $ 35, a junior debenture and a share in exchange for each share held. Your position after the recap depends on the value of the stub and the junior debenture. Given the high leverage level after the recap, we would expect the value of debentures to be highly uncertain. Assume that its value is equal to its face value. The value of the stub is estimated as follows:

- Forecast capital cash flows for the company*.
- Discount capital cash flows at pre-tax WACC.

---

* Capital cash flow valuation is discussed in the last section. CCF = FCF + Interest tax shields.

- Estimate the terminal value assuming an appropriate growth rate and its present value using pre-tax WACC.
- The sum of these two components gives firm value.
- Deduct post-recap debt.

The result is the value of equity after the recap. That is, Value of firm – Value of post-recap debt = Value of stub equity. Dividing the value of equity by the total number of outstanding shares after the recap gives you the value of one share.

The sum of these components—cash, debenture and share—gives the total wealth. If the debenture has a face value of \$ 10, the value of the stub estimated as above is \$ 7, and the total worth of the deal = \$ (35 + 10 + 7) = \$ 52.

Though less accurate than the DCF methodology, one may also undertake a valuation analysis on the basis of comparable transactions. That is, apply average market/book ratio and price/earnings ratio of comparable firms to arrive at the post-recap value of the company. For example, if the average P/E ratio of comparable firms is 12 and the post-recap earnings per share of the company in question is \$ 2.50, the post-recap value of equity is \$ 30, i.e. 12 * 2.50.

The Empirical Evidence

The empirical evidence on the valuation consequences of LRs comes in two forms. The *first* approach uses an event study framework to estimate the stock price reaction to the announcement of an LR. This approach permits the estimation of abnormal returns accruing to stockholders of firms that execute this type of restructuring. Under the assumption of semi-strong form of market efficiency, event study residuals can be interpreted as the market's estimate of the value gains expected from the restructuring. Abnormal returns estimated using the event study approach provide an *ex-ante* estimate of the present value of cash flow changes expected to follow from the restructuring.

Larger values of the estimated abnormal returns indicate greater expected value gain from the LR. Denis (1990), Gupta and Rosenthal (1991), and Handa and Radhakrishnan (1991) document abnormal gains to stockholders of firms announcing LRs. Given that many of these firms were either targets of ongoing takeover bids and/or considered to be 'in play', the announcement period of abnormal return probably does not capture the full wealth impact of the recap announcement. For firms that were 'in play', Gupta and Rosenthal (1991) report an abnormal return of 48% over a period starting 30 days before the start of the takeover activity and ending 150 days after the completion of the LR. The corresponding wealth increase for firms that were not 'in play' is reported to be 34% on average. These findings suggest the unambiguous conclusion that LRs result in substantial gains to the firm's stockholders. In addition, Denis (1990) reports that wealth gains to firms that were eventually taken over are comparable in magnitude to those that remained independent following the restructuring. These findings confirm that LRs are value-creating changes in organizational form, and that such value creation occurs even in the absence of changes in corporate control. LRs result in very substantial increases in the leverage, averaging between 20% and 70%. This suggests that one possible source of shareholders gains in these recaps is a wealth transfer from the existing bond holders.

The findings of Handa and Radhakrishnan (1991) and Gupta and Rosenthal (1991) yield no evidence to support this possibility. Both studies report small changes in bond holder wealth at the time of the LR, and Gupta and Rosenthal report a value gain of 5% to the bond holders over the period spanning the start of takeover activity to 150 days after the completion. These findings indicate that the increases in the stockholder wealth reported in these transactions are driven by the more subtle effects of debt financing on corporate focus and managerial incentives, among others. Managerial stockholdings, for example, increase between 9% and 24% on an average, and can substantially reduce the value losses arising from stockholder-manager conflicts of interest. Studies of firms announcing LRs indicate that in a significant proportion of cases, the LR is a response to a takeover threat. For example, in October 1988 Kraft announced a leveraged recapitalization in response to a hostile bid from Phillip Morris. While Kraft ended up being acquired by Phillip Morris, the announcement of an LR in response to the hostile bid greatly improved the bargaining position of Kraft in the takeover negotiations, largely because it suggested an alternative course of action that was available to Kraft. Following the recap announcement, Phillip Morris had to raise its bid from $ 90 per share to $ 106 per share, which added over $ 2 billion to the wealth of Kraft stockholders.

The Phillip Morris–Kraft experience describes a transaction in which an LR did not finally occur. In contrast, Burlington Northern, Harcourt Brace, and Revlon are examples of firms that fended off hostile bids by recapitalizing the firm using high-yield debt. These transactions created large wealth gains for existing stockholders, provided the management with substantial equity stakes in the restructured firm, and created an incentive system designed to break-up the firm into its most efficient parts, thus adding to aggregate productivity and economic value. The extremely high levels of debt in LRs result in substantial increases in the probability of default in the period following the recap. Denis and Denis (1995) examined the default experience of 29 firms that completed LRs over the years 1985 through 1988, and report that 31% of these firms experienced financial distress. An interesting aspect of their findings, however, is that this high rate of distress was largely a consequence of unexpected adverse changes in regulatory and economic conditions, and not to characteristics suggesting that these were poorly structured deals.

The second approach to estimating valuation gains from LRs entails comparing post-LR cash flows against pre-LR cash flows. This approach provides, in principle, evidence on the actual cash flow benefits resulting from recapitalization, and is thus an intuitively appealing research methodology. The problems associated with this body of work are the empirical problems associated with obtaining a well-defined firm that can be compared before and after the LR. Such problems arise largely because of the nature of the transaction. One of the first things firms do in the post-restructuring period is reduce the scope of the firm's activities and restore focus. This requires shedding parts of the firm through divestitures of divisions that are unrelated to the primary focus of the firm.

Divestitures are also used to raise cash for paying off shorter-term mezzanine financing provided by banks, and to ensure a rapid reduction in the aggregate debt burden created by the recapitalization. Such changes in the firm's activities and scope make comparisons of pre- and post-LR cash flows difficult to interpret. Several case studies have examined changes in the operating performance of firms completing LRs (see, for example, Healy and Palepu 1995, and Wruck 1994). These studies find improvements in operating performance following LRs, evidence that is consistent with the monitoring and disciplining effects of a large debt overhang.

LEVERAGED BUYOUTS

As described earlier, the *typical* LBO entails using a large amount of debt financing to purchase all the outstanding equity of a publicly traded firm (or division, in a divisional LBO), taking the firm private. Consider, for example, the experience of Congoleum Corporation. On 16 July, 1978, selected officers of First Boston Corporation, together with Prudential Insurance Company, proposed an LBO of Congoleum at a price of $ 38 per share, which implied a 50% premium over Congoleum's closing price on the previous day. The proposed financing package included $ 125 million in bank borrowings, $ 246.1 million in strip financing from Prudential, and $ 80 million in excess cash holdings of Congoleum itself. The 'strips' consisted of senior notes in the amount of $ 113.6 million, $ 89.8 million in subordinated notes, $ 26.2 million in cumulative preferred stock, and $ 16.5 million of common stock. First Boston and Congoleum management received common stock in the amount of $ 4.5 million, and $ 4 million, respectively. Congoleum's Board voted in favour of the restructuring, and the firm was taken private in an LBO. One of the interesting features of this deal is the use of strip financing to raise capital. Given that LBOs entail a large amount of leverage, financial distress in the post-restructuring period is not an unlikely circumstance. The use of strip financing combines both debt and equity securities in the lender's portfolio (in this case Prudential Insurance), thus creating an incentive structure that allows for more efficient restructuring if and when needed.

Another feature is the large amount of equity held by the management and First Boston. The upside potential created by substantial equity holdings in a highly levered firm provides an effective incentive structure and reduces costs associated with monitoring management behaviour and investment policy.

The Congoleum experience is interesting because it serves as a good example of how an LBO unfolds. By 1983 the debt was substantially reduced, and in 1984 the firm was relevered in a new buyout. First Boston and institutional investors were bought out, and the management ended up with 50% of the outstanding equity. The firm underwent piecewise liquidation in 1986, and the cash flow accruing to the management was estimated at over $ 400 million.

The above example suggests that the mechanics of a typical LBO entail a four step process. In the *first* stage, the LBO team obtains lines of credit from a group of financial institutions, called 'mezannine financing', and assurances from investment bankers that it can raise the amount of high-yield debt needed to complete the restructuring. The LBO team can be individuals or LBO groups like KKR (RJR-Nabisco for example). In the *second* stage, the LBO group makes a bid for all the outstanding shares of the target firm. In the cases where the LBO succeeds, the acquiring group obtains control and takes the firm private. The *third* stage usually involves asset sales and can include a break-up of the acquired firm, with different parts sold to the highest bidder. The objective at this stage is two-fold; **raising cash to reduce leverage**, and **carving up the firm into focused entities** that can enhance value through productivity gains. The *fourth* stage of the LBO process is when the new owners take the firm public in an IPO, enabling them to take money out of the firm.

There are several characteristics of LBOs that have the potential to enhance value. *First*, the high level of leverage in the firm's capital structure provides a tax shield. The change in ownership structure generally leads to greatly enhanced shareholdings for the new management team. Substantial equity holdings serve to focus managerial incentives on value creation and efficient use of cash flow, and success offers a significant upside potential for the personal wealth of management. Improvements in managerial incentives, coupled with the default risk arising from high leverage serve to reduce the monitoring costs associated with the governance system in public corporations. Savings can also arise from declines in shareholder servicing costs once the firm becomes privately held. Agency costs associated with wasteful use of free cash flow are effectively eliminated in an LBO, and also contribute to value enhancement.

THE EMPIRICAL EVIDENCE

Several studies have examined the stock price reaction to an LBO announcement (see, for example, DeAngelo, DeAngelo, and Rice 1984, Lehn and Poulsen 1988, and Muscarella and Vetsuypens 1990), and report abnormal returns of approximately 20% in the period immediately preceding and including the announcement date. Kaplan (1989a) documents that in the typical management buyout, the pre-buyout shareholders receive a premium of 40% over the prevailing market price to take the firm private. For divisional management buyouts, Hite and Vetsuypens (1989) find small, statistically significant gains to parent company stockholders, a finding that is consistent with such transactions moving resources to higher-valued uses.

The findings reported in the above studies confirm that existing shareholders make substantial gains in going private transactions. As described earlier, the possible explanations for the observed gains include tax savings, improved managerial incentives, wealth transfers from existing bond holders, efficiency gains and improvements in operating performance, and reductions in underpricing due to asymmetric information. The author discusses some of the evidence on these possibilities next.

The potential value of tax benefits depends on several factors, including the tax rate and the maturity of the debt used to finance the buyout. Kaplan (1989b) estimates such benefits to range between 0.26 and 1.29 times the buyout premium. In addition, firms electing to step up the tax basis of their assets obtain tax benefits of 0.30 times the buyout premium. Lehn and Poulsen (1988) find that the premium paid in these deals is positively related to the pre-LBO tax liability to equity ratio, which also suggests that tax benefits arising from leverage increases can be substantial in going private transactions. Improved managerial incentives resulting from substantial increases in managerial equity holdings can also be a source of gain. Kaplan (1989a) reports a threefold increase in the ownership interest of the CEO, all managers and directors following a management buyout. Muscarella and Vetsuypens (1990) report that 69 out of 72 firms in their sample introduced at least one form of incentive-based compensation system following the buyout.

Evidence on changes in operating performance indicates improvements in operating margins and the ratio of sales to operating assets and employees in the two years following the buyout, relative to comparable firms in the same industry. Kaplan (1989a) reports that in the three years following the buyout, sample companies experienced increases in operating income, decreases in capital expenditures, and increases in cash flows. He estimates that the market value of the firm increased by 96% on an average over this three-year period, and that operating improvements primarily drove this increase in the market value. There is little evidence to support cutbacks in R&D expenditures, advertising, and maintenance expenditures in the post-buyout period.

Smith (1990) found significant improvements in operating results from the year before to the year following the buyout, and subsequent improvements indicate that such gains are sustained. Improvements in the working capital contribute to the gains, and the observed gains are not a result of employee layoffs, or declines in R&D and property, plant and equipment

(PP&E). The received evidence is also consistent with the free cash flow hypothesis of Jensen (1986). Lehn and Poulsen (1988), for example, found a strong relationship between the undistributed cash flow to equity ratio and the premium paid in going private transactions.

The evidence on valuation consequences for the bond holders of firms that go private in an LBO is mixed. Marais, Schipper, and Smith (1989) and Lehn and Poulsen (1988) did not find significant losses to the firm's bond holders. In contrast, Asquith and Wizman (1990), Cook, Easterwood, and Martin (1992), and Warga and Welch (1993) documented losses of 3%–7% at the LBO announcement, although the magnitude of the bond holder losses appears sensitive to the presence or absence of restrictive covenants. These findings are consistent with the argument that at least a small portion of the wealth gains to stockholders in LBOs are the consequence of a wealth transfer from the firm's bondholders. The mixed findings of different studies, coupled with the relatively small values of bond holder losses indicate that the primary sources of the large shareholder gains observed in LBOs are more fundamental in nature than wealth transfers from other security holders.

In the cases where an LBO is successful, buyout investors can make a secondary public offering and take the firm public. Muscarella and Vetsuypens (1990) reported that the change in value from the time of the LBO to the time the firm is taken public is 169% on an average, and the annualized rate of change is 37%. Observed gains are highly correlated with changes in managerial holdings, suggesting that improved incentives play an important role in ensuring success. Kaplan (1991) reports that for a sample of 21 buyouts, total return to all capital was 26% higher than the benchmark return on the S&P index. These studies indicate very substantial gains to investors in successful going private deals.

Muscarella and Vetsuypens (1990) examine the operating performance of firms that return to public ownership, called 'reverse LBOs', and document significant improvements in profitability and declines in leverage. Mian and Rosenfeld (1993) found that the firms undergoing reverse LBOs obtain significant cumulative abnormal returns over the three-year period following the going public decision. These findings indicate that the changes in governance structure resulting from the LBOs have positive longer term effects on corporate performance.

LBO IN THE LATE 1980S

Leverage buyout transactions in the late 1980s were a lot less successful than those in the 1970s and early 1980s, and many of these firms later experienced financial distress. By 1990, the market for LBOs experienced a precipitous decline; the dollar value of LBOs in 1990 is estimated to be approximately 10% of 1989 value. Financial distress occurred even though, as documented by Opler (1992), and Kaplan and Stein (1993), firms that were taken private in the late 1980s continued to experience sharp increases in operating earnings.

The root causes of the problems faced by these firms are twofold. The *first* is changes in the structure of deals consummated in the late 1980s. The early successes of LBOs attracted large number of investors into the market, and new LBO funds were formed. Deal promoters paid higher prices for deals in the late 1980s, and often withdrew money upfront. Public high-yield debt became a larger proportion of total financing, relative to participant equity and private subordinated debt. Such changes in deal structure weakened both the incentive effects that contributed to the success of LBOs in the earlier time period, and heightened the problems associated with restructuring the firm in the event of distress. The second problem was the general economic downturn and recession of 1990 and 1991. Legislative actions, including passage of the Financial Institutions Reform, Recovery, and Enforcement Act in August 1989, placed stringent restrictions on the financial holdings of federally insured financial institutions, and many banks and S&Ls had to dispose off their holdings of high-yield debt in the public markets. Such actions worked to aggravate the financial problems of firms that had gone private in the highly leveraged transactions.

Some highly leveraged restructurings have reappeared in the later 1990s, although the volume of such transactions is nowhere near the level seen in the 1980s. Given the lessons learned from the poorly structured deals in the late 1980s, it is expected that these firms will be better positioned to ride out economic downturns and reap the value gains that can be obtained from the new organizational form.

REVERSE LBO

Leverage buyout firms do not remain private forever. They issue shares publicly after a few years and become public once again. That is, they *reverse* the LBO. Kidder, Peabody & Co. reports that between 1 January, 1983 and 30 June, 1988, there were 90 initial public offerings for buyout companies of $ 10 million or more. The median period between the completion of the LBO and the launch of the IPO was 22 months. More than 70% of the companies were taken public within three years of their LBO dates*. If high leverage and concentrated ownership lead to improvements in performance, we would expect the performance to decline after the LBO because of diffused ownership due to selling of shares and decrease in leverage. To the extent that these firms have higher leverage and concentrated ownership than other similar firms, these firms might continue to outperform their industry. Academic studies of reverse LBOs in the USA found that the operating performance of

* Rappaport, Alfred, The staying power of the Public Corporation, *Harvard Business Review*, Jan–Feb, 1990.

reverse LBOs is significantly better than that of the median company in their industry in the year before and in the year of the IPO*. Further, these companies tend to outperform their industry for at least four years after the IPO.

Cao and Lerner (2006) collected a comprehensive sample of 496 RLBOs between 1980 and 2002 and examined three- and five-year stock performance of these offerings†. They found that:

- RLBOs appear to consistently outperform other IPOs and the stock market as a whole, with economically and statistically meaningful positive returns.
- There is no evidence of a deterioration of returns over time, despite the growth of the buyout market; RLBOs performed strongly in the late 1980s, the mid-1990s, and the 2000s.
- Large RLBOs that are backed by private equity firms with more capital under management perform better.
- The so-called 'quick flips'—when private equity firms sell off an investment within a year after acquisition—underperform.

When is High Leverage Appropriate?

Leveraged restructurings such as LRs and LBOs create a large overhang of debt, and are clearly not appropriate for all the firms. Since debt service is of prime importance, firms with volatile operating cash flows are not good candidates for such restructurings. Once the recapitalization is completed, firms must commit a large portion of the internal cash flow towards debt service. This reduces the volume of cash flows available for wasteful investment in R&D, product development and capacity expansion. The ideal candidate for a leveraged restructuring is in a stable, mature industry, generates steady cash flows, and has limited growth opportunities. Single product firms that meet these characteristics can obtain the myriad benefits of high leverage outlined above, and create value through a leveraged restructuring. Diversified firms where the whole is less than the sum of the parts also present opportunities for leveraged restructurings. Recall that corporate diversification reduces cash flow volatility, and can be attractive for managers interested in protecting their human capital. Corporate diversification also helps with managerial empire building, and can be a consequence of managerial attempts at maximizing growth as opposed to shareholder value. A lack of corporate focus, coupled with limitations in the

---

* Another study has arrived at contradictory results. See DeGeorge and Zeckhauser (1993). This study finds that reverse LBOs do well before the IPO, then disappoint.

† Cao, Jerry and Joshua Lerner, The performance of reverse Leveraged Buyouts, NBER Working Paper No. 12626, 2006.

set of available managerial skills can result in the so-called 'diversification discount', where the whole is less than the sum of the parts.

For the shareholders holding diversified portfolios, such corporate diversification is of little value, and breaking up the firm into its focused parts can represent a value-enhancing restructuring. Good candidates for leveraged restructurings are firms that have at least one division in a mature industry, with relatively high free cash flows and low leverage. High levels of stable, free cash flows can aggravate the manager-shareholder agency conflicts, and present the management with ongoing opportunities to pursue policies that do not maximize value; included in these are efforts at geographic expansion, diversifying acquisitions, and the pursuit of market share as opposed to shareholder value. The governance, managerial ownership, and monitoring consequences of a leveraged restructuring can yield substantial gains to stockholders of such a firm. Finally, it is quite evident that the advantages of highly leveraged restructurings are not available to all the firms. The primary advantages of high leverage include a tax shield, and significant changes in ownership structure and managerial incentives. The latter leads to reduction in monitoring costs; efficiency increase, and virtual elimination of wasteful use of internal cash flow. The downside to high leverage is a potentially large increase in the probability of default. High leverage is thus clearly not appropriate for firms in a large number of sectors where the operating income displays periodic volatility.

In addition, high leverage represents a somewhat blunt approach to aligning managerial incentives with those of stockholders, and ensuring levels of managerial stock ownership that create the upside potential needed to obtain efficiency gains. Such shortcomings of extreme leverage suggest the need for other forms of corporate restructuring that could yield benefits similar to high leverage, without simultaneously creating a large debt overhang. One such approach, promoted by Stern Stewart and Company, is an Economic Value Added (EVA)-based financial management system that incorporates a leveraged stock ownership plan for corporate management (see Stern, Stewart, and Chew 1999). The intuition underlying such thinking is that if we could implement a system that includes a financing mechanism to facilitate substantial increases in managerial stockholdings, the incentive conflict problem will be reduced. This approach, combined with an EVA-based measurement system, could, in principle, result in increases in efficiency and reductions in wasteful expenditures, while simultaneously creating the upside potential needed to ensure a managerial focus on maximizing value. The idea thus is to try create ownership, measurement and reward systems that can yield results similar to those obtained in highly leveraged restructurings, while at the same time allowing the retainment of the financial flexibility needed by firms that are not in mature, stable sectors of the economy.

Changes in Restructuring Activity During the 1990s

It has been argued that the wave of highly leveraged restructurings during the 1980s was driven by an emerging dominance of the capital markets, deregulation, and the growth of information technology (see Holmstrom and Kaplan 2001, for example). These changes created the potential for substantial improvements in corporate performance, to which managers were slow to respond. The takeover wave of the 1980s worked to reverse value-reducing corporate diversification, helped with eliminating excess capacity in different sectors, and disciplined underperforming managers. A large portion of the M&A activity during this period was hostile, and large volume of debt financing facilitated changes in corporate control. The huge restructuring wave led to several fundamental changes in corporate governance systems, including recognition of shareholder value maximization as the appropriate goal of corporate managers.

Hall and Liebman (1998) report that equity-based compensation increased from less than 20% in 1980 to over 50% of managerial remuneration in 1994. The structure of board compensation in the 1990s also includes significantly larger levels of incentive-based compensation. These changes have served to reduce the managerial-stockholder incentive conflict problem, which can in principle improve corporate performance and reduce the need for hostile restructurings. New financial management systems such as EVA have led to an increasing recognition of the idea that equity capital is expensive, which has also led to improvements in resource allocation and corporate performance. In addition, as reported by Gompers and Metrick (2001), stockholdings of institutional investors have increased from less than 30% in 1980 to over 50% in 1996. These investors are less loyal to management than individual investors, and add to the value creation potential of an improved monitoring system. The highly leveraged restructuring movement of the 1980s can be said to have contributed to all of these changes in the corporate governance system, with positive implications for shareholder wealth.

Finally, after experiencing a steep decline in 1990–1991, the market for corporate control has resurfaced in recent years. Total M&A activity was at a level of about 10% of the total stock market capitalization during the mid-1980s, declined to 2%–3% in 1990–1991, and has been running at approximately 10 percent in the late 1990s (see Holmstrom and Kaplan 2001). In contrast to the 1980s, when incumbent management contested approximately 40%–50% of takeover bids, hostile bids in the late 1990s averaged between 10 and 15 of all the bids. These changes in the market for corporate control are consistent with the argument that changes in board structure and compensation, incentive compensation plans for senior management, and more active monitoring by market participants have resulted in an overall improvement in managerial incentive systems. The highly leveraged restructurings of the 1980s, it can be argued, played a significant role in bringing about a renewed focus on maximizing shareholder wealth as the driving objective of corporate policy.

Practical Consideration in Deal Design

The critical elements of a successful, highly leveraged acquisition include the following:

- Buyout pricing
- Exit strategy
- Incentive structure
- Monitoring
- Post-restructuring cash flow potential
- Reorganization potential in the event of financial distress

Buyout pricing: The price paid to the target shareholders is the starting point for the design of any deal. There are two approaches to estimating the premium that could be paid for target shares: **free cash flow valuation** and **multiples:** The author provides some parameters that can be used to implement these approaches below.

Exit strategy: This must be an integral part of the decision process. This implies determining the time frame over which the leverage will be reduced and the asset sales that could be used to affect a rapid reduction in the debt load following the buyout. The objective is to manage the firm for cash flow, which can be used to pay down debt. Buyout sponsors must also have a clear vision of the possible ways in which to dispose off the firm once the debt has been substantially reduced. Possible avenues include an IPO, sale of the firm to a corporate buyer, or piece-wise liquidation.

Incentive structure and monitoring: Successful transactions require generating large cash flows that can be used to retire the debt used to finance the buyout. Substantial ownership stakes for the management are the best ways to ensure the creation of an incentive structure that will focus managerial energies on taking the actions necessary to achieve this goal.

Post-restructuring cash flow potential: This is clearly the crux of the matter. Conservative estimates of the amount of cash that can be raised by returning the corporate focus to the core business serve as the starting point. A second variable to focus on is the possibility of increases in cash flows from operating improvements, and reductions in expenditures on non-critical activities. The latter include potential savings in labour costs, advertising, and wasteful research and development expenditures.

Reorganization potential in the event of financial distress: The potential for reorganization in the event of distress depends on the type of debt financing that is used to finance the acquisition. The potential is lowest if the primary source of leverage is publicly issued high-yield debt. As described in the following paragraphs, the use of senior bank debt, privately issued institutional debt and the use of strip financing are approaches that improve the likelihood of reorganizing the debt structure in the event of distress.

Decision Variables

While designing a deal, the managers and investment bankers need to decide on the price paid, amount of leverage, ownership stake of buyout sponsors, and managerial equity stake.

Price paid: The use of conservative assumptions in estimating future cash flow potential is a simple starting point. When using multiples, a common rule of thumb is to limit the price paid to between five and six times EBITDA.

Amount of leverage: Higher leverage allows for larger tax savings and greater ownership concentration. Two critically important drivers of this decision are: (i) the amount of cash that can be raised from asset sales, and (ii) the cash flow that will be generated from the post-restructuring operations. As a general rule, debt to capital ratios exceeding 70% should be thought of as excessive.

Ownership stake of buyout sponsors: Determining the cash flow generated by asset sales and operating improvements is the starting point for the analysis. This should be used to determine the volume of leverage used in the transaction, and, consequently, the amount of equity financing that will be used. The evidence on successful deals suggests that an equity stake of 20% to 30% provides an adequate equity cushion.

Managerial equity stake: Substantial managerial equity ownership is a critical element driving deal success. High leverage creates a need for reducing wasteful expenditures, creating corporate focus, improving operating efficiency, and running the firm for cash flow. Substantial managerial ownership provides the upside potential needed to limit the requirement for monitoring managerial decisions, and enhancing the probability of success. At the time of the buyout, providing senior management with equity stakes of 10% to 15% in lieu of cash is a simple way to achieve these objectives.

SOURCES OF DEBT FINANCING

Financing a buyout requires substantial intermediate and long-term debt financing, which is usually provided by banks and insurance companies. Banks also finance receivables and inventory. In a typical LBO, there will be more than one layer of debt—senior debt secured by assets and subordinated debt. The subordinated lenders receive equity kickers (warrants) because of their junior status. The warrant allows them to share the upside potential with the shareholders. Subordinated debt is also called **mezzanine capital**. Due to the upside potential afforded by the warrants, the yields on subordinated debt are lower than that on similar high-risk venture capital investment. The lenders in an LBO must obtain protection primarily via the cash flow of the borrowing entity. So they require a stable cash flow history and the amount lent is typically a multiple of that proven cash flow. Further, the loan is amortized over a specified period of time. They may also base the amount to be advanced on the basis of value of assets. A typical buyout in the USA is funded with 50% of senior bank debt, 30% of subordinate debt (mezzanine), and 20% of equity (with management holding 5%–10%).

Cash flows in the initial period of an LBO frequently are not sufficient to meet the debt service. If a company misses interest payments, it can be forced into bankruptcy. Consequently, deferred interest securities like step-up coupon debentures and pay-in-kind debentures are used in recaps and buyouts. In the case of deferred coupon, payment debentures are sold at a deep discount, and no interest accrues for a specified time period after which the interest is paid in cash. In the case of step-up coupon debentures, coupon increases over a period of time. PIK debentures give borrowers the choice of paying the coupon in cash or paying with some more of the security. If the latter is chosen no cash payment is necessary to meet the interest payments until the end of the PIK period, typically 5–10 years. These securities give the *issuers* the *option* to either pay in cash or in kind. Further, these securities have little or no call protection. When the market interest rate goes up, the issuer can put a certain amount of debt in lieu of cash to the investors each semi-annual period. When the interest rates fall, the bond will be called. That is, the issuer has a series of European-type put options*.

The choice of the type of debt must be made within the context of (i) interest rates, (ii) maturity structure, and (iii) reorganization potential in the event of financial distress.

Bank Debt and Institutional/Privately Placed Debt

Non-public debt has the advantage of greater flexibility in the event of distress, in that it is easier to restructure than is public debt. The downside is greater monitoring of corporate activity by the lending entity. Bank debt is generally used for shorter-term financing needs, and will have to be reduced first. A general rule of thumb is to limit the senior bank debt to three to four times EBITDA, and maintain an interest coverage ratio of at least two times EBITDA. An attractive avenue for raising debt from private sources is to use strip financing, such that the lender also has an equity position in the restructured firm. The obvious advantage of strip financing is to align the incentives of the buyout sponsors with those of the lenders, such that the debt contracts can be renegotiated in the event of financial distress.

Public Debt

The volume of public debt financing depends, among other things, on the state of the high-yield debt market. In the United States, for example, this market

* Valuation of the option component and the PIK is beyond the scope of the book. Interested readers may refer to Goodman and Cohen (1989), Black, Derman and Toy (1990).

pretty much collapsed in the early 1990s, contributing to a steep decline in the number and dollar volume of highly leveraged transactions. Public debt offers all the advantages of arms length transactions, including investor liquidity and low levels of monitoring. The downside is the low probability of debt restructuring in the event of financial distress. Debt issues with detachable equity warrants can also be used as a sweetener, particularly in more risky transactions.

Following is the leveraged lead arranger league table in 2006.

Rank	Bank holding company	Volume ($)	No. of deals	Market share
1	J.P. Morgan	122,348,766,153	347	20%
2	Bank of America	94,984,743,734	374	16%
3	Citigroup	65,584,248,000	117	11%
4	Credit Suisse	56,519,813,579	149	9%
5	Deutsche Bank	37,295,514,777	82	6%
6	Wachovia Securities	26,751,775,000	151	4%
7	Goldman Sachs & Co.	25,584,134,861	73	4%
8	General Electric Capital Corp.	18,743,314,433	159	3%
9	Lehman Brothers	17,508,721,680	57	3%
10	Merrill Lynch & Co.	14,084,051,000	70	2%

Source: Loan pricing corp.

Valuation of High Leverage Transactions Using Equity Cash Flow Valuation

Valuation and pricing are two critical steps in the design of an LBO. The managers must estimate how much their stake is worth at the time of the LBO. Similarly, outside investors would also want to evaluate their position. The discounted cash flow methodology is widely used in the valuation of LBOs.

In the DCF methodology, free Cash flow to firm (i.e. Net operating profit after tax + Depreciation – Capital expenditure – Increases in working capital) is discounted at the weighted average cost of capital to determine the value of the firm.

To arrive at cash flows, interest charges are not deducted although they are real. The reason is that the discount rate (WACC) already considers debt financing. The WACC is calculated by taking weighted average after-tax costs of equity and debt. The cost of debt in the WACC formula already accounts for firm/division specific debt financing. Deducting the interest from the EBIT would lead to double counting.

$$\text{WACC} = K_d(1 - T)\left(\frac{D}{D+E}\right) + K_e\left(\frac{E}{D+E}\right)$$

A firm can be analysed from the perspective of all the investors or just equity investors. In the former case, the cash flows do not consider interest charges and the discount rate is the WACC. While analysing from the equity investors' perspective, some changes need to be made. The initial investment would be equity investment and not total investment; the discount rate would be the cost of equity and the cash flow would be the residual cash flow to equity investors.

Cash flow to equity = EBIT – Tax + Depreciation – Capital expenditure – Increase in working capital – After-tax interest payment – Principal repayment + New borrowing.

Cash flow to equity is the residual cash flow after meeting the investment requirements and contractual payments. It should be noted that cash flow to equity is more meaningful for a growing firm that borrows all the time to invest. For a typical growing firm, the cash flow from operations would be negative.

Valuing equity cash flows would be more meaningful when leverage changes dramatically from year to year. The usage of constant discount rate (i.e. WACC) in the free cash flow valuation gives erroneous answers. When leverage changes, the risk of cash flows also changes. So we would expect the discount rate to increase whenever leverage rises and decrease whenever leverage falls. In the case of high leverage transactions like Project Finance or Leveraged Buyout the leverage increases from 0% to about 60%–90%, and then again falls back to 0 or more normal levels. The free cash flow to firm approach is cumbersome to implement because both the cost of debt and the cost of equity have to be recalculated each year. Under the equity cash flow valuation, the cost of equity has to be recalculated each year using the estimates of equity beta each year according to the formula:

$$\beta_A = \beta_E(E/V)$$

This estimate of equity beta can be plugged into the CAPM to arrive at the cost of equity.

It should be noted that the estimate of asset beta itself is constant as it depends on business risk and not financial risk.

THE CAPITAL CASH FLOW VALUATION APPROACH

In FCF valuation, the WACC is used to discount cash flows. An algebraically equivalent, yet superior, method is the Capital Cash Flow Valuation*. FCF valuation excludes interest tax shields because the discount rate, WACC, incorporates the tax advantage of debt. In the capital cash flow valuation, FCF

* Ruback, Richard S., Capital cash flows: a simple approach to valuing risky cash flows, *Working Paper*, Harvard Business School, March, 2000.

plus interest tax shields are discounted at *pre-tax* WACC (i.e. expected asset return). Since the asset return does not change when the capital structure changes, it is easier to implement capital cash flow valuation.

Capital cash flow = Net income + Depreciation – Capital expenditure – Δ working capital + Cash interest

or

Capital cash flow = EBIT (1 – *T*) + Depreciation – Capital expenditure – Δ working capital + Interest tax shields

It is easier to implement the former approach because it incorporates corporate estimates of taxes that reflect the special circumstances facing the firm rather than mechanically finding the product of tax rate and taxable income*.

The appropriate discount rate is a before-tax rate because the tax benefits of debt are already included in the capital cash flows. The correct discount rate is the pre-tax WACC.

$$\text{Pre-tax WACC} = \text{Weighted average costs of debt and equity}$$

$$= (D/V)K_D + (E/V)K_E$$

where D/V and E/V are debt-to-value and equity-to-value ratios respectively; K_D and K_E are costs of debt and equity.

$$\text{Cost of debt} = K_D = R_f + \beta_D \text{ (risk premium)}$$

$$\text{Cost of equity} = K_E = R_f + \beta_E \text{ (risk premium)}$$

$$\text{Pre-tax WACC} = \frac{D}{V}(R_f + \beta_D * R_P) + \left(Rf + \frac{E}{V}\beta_E * R_P\right)$$

$$= R_f + \left(\frac{D}{V}\beta_D + \frac{E}{V}\beta_E\right)R_P$$

$$= R_f + \beta_A(R_P)$$

Since

$$\beta_A V = \beta_D D + \beta_E E$$

or

$$\beta_A = \beta_D\left(\frac{D}{V}\right) + \beta_E\left(\frac{E}{V}\right)$$

Note that the discount rate depends on R_f, β_A and risk premium, and does not incorporate D/V or E/V. That is, the pre-tax WACC is independent of capital structure and, hence, can be applied to all cash flows regardless of the capital structure in existence. In other words, pre-tax WACC, which is a

* In other words, in many instances it does not reflect the actual tax paid.

function of asset beta, is constant. Both FCF valuation and capital cash flow valuation provide the same answer. Capital cash flow valuation, however, is easier to implement.

The capital cash flow valuation methodology is especially appropriate when the company in question is being restructured, and has high leverage and complicated tax status resulting from net operating losses, which is usually true of bankrupt firms. In a restructuring situation, all the concerned parties would be interested in estimating the value of their claim after the transaction. Typically, creditors get equity in exchange for debt; promoters (majority shareholders) invest equity to keep the company alive. So they would be interested in estimating the value of equity after the transaction. To get an estimate one should forecast the capital cash flow and discount it using pre-tax WACC. The **terminal value** is calculated assuming that capital cash flows grow at a constant rate in perpetuity, starting with the last year of the projections. Many bankrupt firms will have unused Net Operating Loss (NOL) carry forwards at the end of the projection period. These NOLs are not forecasted to continue in perpetuity (Gilson et al., 2000). Therefore the terminal value is estimated in two parts. The first part extends the financial projections and simulates a firm's use of NOLs until the NOLs are used up or expire. During this extended projection period, the capital cash flows are calculated as

([EBIT – Interest) ∗ Tax rate] + Cash flow adjustments + Tax shield due to NOLs = Capital cash flows

In the second part of the terminal value calculation, the value of the firm is estimated as a growing perpetuity of capital cash flow in the year following the extended forecast period. This cash flow does not include any NOL benefits. The present value of this portion of the terminal value is added to the present value of the capital cash flows during the extended forecast period to estimate the total terminal value.

The result of this exercise is the value of the *firm*. Subtracting the value of post-transaction debt yields the value of equity.*

CONCLUDING REMARKS

Leverage buyouts result in efficiency gains. But they are not without a cost. The probability of distress increases substantially because of high leverage. LBO funds and sponsors recognize it. KKR, for example, targets companies that have strong and predictable cash flows, readily separable assets or businesses available for sale, products with well-known brand names and

---

* One may also use the adjusted present value methodology to value the firm.

strong market positions that are not subject to rapid technological change, status as a low cost producer, and limited sensitivity to cyclical swings.

Due to a substantial increase in leverage in an LBO, we would expect a decrease in the bond holders' wealth. In other words, are the gains in an LBO a transfer of wealth from the bond holders? Some academic studies have documented losses of 3%–7% at the time of the LBO announcement, which supports the notion that at least a part of the wealth gain in the case of an LBO is due to wealth transfer from the bond holders.

When doing a leveraged buyout, be prepared to the following:

- Raise and negotiate terms of senior, subordinated, and equity financing.
- Find strategic and financial partners for these transactions.
- Organize business plans.
- Hire needed management personnel, where applicable.
- Structure new employee benefit plans.
- Communicate effectively with employees.
- Negotiate long-term supply and use agreements.

REFERENCES

1. Asquith, P. and T. Wizman, Event Risk, Covenants, and Bondholder Returns in Leveraged Buyouts, *Journal of Financial Economics*, 1990.
2. Cook, D., J. Easterwood, and J. Martin, Bondholder Wealth Effects of Management Buyouts, *Financial Management*, 1992.
3. DeAngelo, H., L. DeAngelo, and E. Rice, Going Private: Minority Freezeouts and Shareholder Wealth, *Journal of Law and Economics*, 1984.
4. Denis, D., Defensive Changes in Corporate Payout Policy: Share Repurchases and Special Dividends, *Journal of Finance*, 1990.
5. Denis, D. and D. Denis, Causes of Financial Distress Following Leveraged Recapitalizations, *Journal of Financial Economics*, 1995.
6. Gompers, P. and A. Metrick, Institutional Investors and Equity Prices, *Quarterly Journal of Economics*, 2001.
7. Gupta, A. and L. Rosenthal, Ownership Structure, Leverage, and Firm Value: The Case of Leveraged Recapitalizations, *Financial Management*, 1991.
8. Hall, B. And J. Liebman, Are CEOs Really Paid like Bureaucrats?, *Quarterly Journal of Economics*, 1998.

9. Handa, P. and A. Radhakrishnan, An Empirical Investigation of Leveraged Recapitalizations with Cash Payout as a Takeover Defense, *Financial Management*, 1991.

10. Healy, P. and K. Palepu, The Challenges of Investor Communication: The Case of CUS International, Inc., *Journal of Financial Economics*, 1995.

11. Hite, G. and M. Vetsuypens, Management Buyouts of Divisions and Shareholder Wealth', *Journal of Finance*, 1989.

12. Holmstrom, B. and S. Kaplan, Corporate Governance and Merger Activity in the U.S.: Making Sense of the 1980s and 1990s', *Working Paper*, Department of Economics, MIT, Boston, MA, 2001.

13. Jensen, M., The Modern Industrial Revolution, Exit, and the Failure of Internal Control Systems, *Journal of Finance*, 1993.

14. ———, Agency Costs of Free Cash Flow, Corporate Finance, and Takeovers, *American Economic Review*, 1986.

15. Jensen, M. and W. Meckling, Theory of the Firm: Managerial Behavior, Agency Costs, and Ownership Structure, *Journal of Financial Economics*, 1976.

16. Kaplan, S., The Effects of Management Buyouts on Operating Performance and Value, *Journal of Financial Economics*, 1989a.

17. ———, Management Buyouts: Evidence on Taxes as a Source of Value, *Journal of Finance*, 1989b.

18. ———, The Staying Power of Leveraged Buyouts, *Journal of Financial Economics*, 1991.

19. Kaplan S. and J. Stein, The Evolution of Buyout Pricing and Financial Structure, *Journal of Applied Corporate Finance*, 1993.

20. Lehn, K. and A. Poulsen, Free Cash Flow and Stockholder Gains in Going Private Transactions, *Journal of Finance*, 1988.

21. Marais, L., K. Schipper and A. Smith, Wealth Effects of Going Private for Senior Securities, *Journal of Financial Economics*, 1989.

22. Mian, S. and J. Rosenfeld, Takeover Activity and the Long-run Performance of Reverse Leveraged Buyouts, *Financial Management*, 1993.

23. Muscarella, C. and M. Vetsuypens, Efficiency and Organizational Structure: A Study of Reverse LBOs, *Journal of Finance*, 1990.

24. Myers, S., Determinants of Corporate Borrowing, *Journal of Financial Economics*, 1977.

25. Opler, T., Operating Performance in Leveraged Buyouts: Evidence from 1985–1989, *Financial Management*, 1992.

26. Peyer, U. and A. Shivdasani, Leverage and Internal Capital Markets: Evidence from Leveraged Recapitalizations, *Journal of Financial Economics*, 2001.

27. Smith, A., Corporate Ownership Structure and Performance: The Case of Management Buyouts, *Journal of Financial Economics*, 1990.

28. Stern, J., G. Stewart III, and D. Chew, Jr., The EVA Financial Management System, D. Chew (ed.), *The New Corporate Finance*, McGrawHill/Irwin, New York, 1999.

29. Warga, A. and I. Welch, Bond holder Losses in Leveraged Buyouts, *Review of Financial Studies*, 1993.

30. Wruck, K., Financial Policy, Internal Control, and Performance, *Journal of Financial Economics*, 1994.

EXERCISES

1. A company is in the process of setting up a paper division with projected cash flows as follows: the new operation requires an initial investment in plant and equipment of \$ 100 million, plus an infusion of \$ 7.5 million of working capital (=10% of first year sales). The division's sales are projected to be \$ 75 million during the first year of operation. Sales are expected to increase at 12% p.a. over the next two years with growth stabilizing at a 4% rate thereafter. The management estimates that the cash costs will constitute 60% of revenue. New investments in plant and equipment will match depreciation each year, starting at 10% of the initial investment (\$ 100 million) and growing in tandem with sales thereafter. The firm plans to maintain working capital levels at 10% of the following year's projected sales. With the division in the 35% tax bracket, unlevered free cash flow would approach \$ 16 million in three years and grow at 4% p.a. thereafter. Assume that the division arranges to borrow \$ 77.5 million initially. The firm agrees to repay \$ 8.5 million of principal at the end of the first three years of the contract, bring debt outstanding at the end of the third year to \$ 52 million. From that point on, the division will increase debt outstanding by 4% p.a., in line with the expected growth of operating cash flows. Because of the firm's highly levered position in the early years, assume that the borrowing rate is 11% initially, falling to 9% once it re-achieves a stable capital structure after year 3. Assume that the cost of unlevered equity is 18%. What is the division's worth? Use Adjusted Present Value.

2. A LBO fund has received an offer to sell from the founder of a company. The company manufactures paper that is not seasonal. In 2000 the company had a market share of 26% of the industry. The recent financial statements of the company are given as follows:

Income statement

($, m)

	1998	1999	2000
Sales	17.7	19.1	20.2
Cost of goods sold	12.7	14.1	14.2
Gross profit	5.0	5.0	6.0
Operating expenses	1.4	1.5	1.8
PBT	3.6	3.5	4.2
Taxes	1.3	1.2	1.5
Net profit	2.3	2.3	2.7

Balance sheet

($, m)

31 March 2000			
Equity	14.2	Net fixed assets	6.3
Current liabilities	1.9	Current assets	9.2
		Other assets	0.6
	16.1		16.1

The company's sales are expected to increase at 10% p.a. for the next five years. EBIT as a fraction of sales is expected to be 16% of sales. The company's tax rate is 35%. Capital expenditure each year is expected to be equal to the annual depreciation expense of 500,000. Further, working capital investment is expected to be 11% of sales. The terminal growth rate is expected to be 4%. The LBO involves heavy usage of debt carrying an interest rate of 15% repayable in 10 equal annual instalments. The company has a cash balance of $ 6 million out of which only $ 1 million is sufficient to carry out the operations.

Assuming a discount rate of 12%, what is a fair price for the company? How much debt would be required for the LBO? What level of debt can the company be able to service?

3. An LBO firm has tentatively agreed to pay $ 1.1 billion to acquire a certain business. The managers of the business anticipate EBIT of $ 100 million for the first year. EBIT is expected to grow at 5% p.a. for the next five years. The LBO sponsors are confident that they can raise $ 900 million in debt financing provided they contribute $ 200 million of equity and that all the excess cash generated by the business is used to pay down debt. The sponsors expect to divest their holdings after five years. Should they invest the $ 200 million and acquire the business? Assume the following:
Tax rate = 36%
Interest rate on debt = 7%
Capital expenditure equal depreciation and both grow at 5% p.a.

Additions to net working capital start at $ 10 million in year 1 and grow at 5%.

Risk free rate = 5%

Asset beta = 0.7
Risk premium = 8%
Perpetuity growth rate after year 5 = 8%

The company is likely to achieve a stable capital structure after year 5 at the time of which the discount rate is expected to be 12%.
(*Hint:* Value *equity* cash flows. The cost of equity is to be estimated for each year. To arrive at the value of equity in year 0 start with the value of equity in year 5, discount it back to year 4, 3, etc. to year 0 using different costs of equity for each year. The value of equity in year 5 is Value of firm – Value of debt outstanding at the end of year 5.)

4. Compare and contrast the organizational structure of a typical corporation with that of a LBO association.
5. Corporate managers generally do not disgorge cash unless they are forced to do so. In 1988, the 1000 largest firms generated total funds of $ 1.6 trillion. Yet they distributed only $ 108 billion as dividends and another $ 51 billion through stock repurchases*.
   (a) What are the incentives for managers to retain excessive cash balances in lieu of payment to shareholders?
   (b) In what way do high debt levels resolve the agency cost of free cash flow?
   (c) Equity is soft, debt hard. Equity is forgiving, debt insistent. Equity is a pillow, debt a sword. Interpret the meaning.
6. A firm is in the process of investing $ 100,000 in a project†. The project is expected to generate $ 50,000, $ 60,000, and $ 70,000 in the three years of operation. The investment will be depreciated over three years on a straight-line basis. Other relevant data are given as follows:

   Asset beta = 1.0
   Debt beta = 0.3
   Risk-free rate = 10%
   Risk premium = 8%
   Tax rate = 33%

   Beginning debt = $ 100,000, $ 65,000 and $ 20,000 in the first three years. Calculate capital cash flows and the value of the project ignoring the terminal value.

   (*Hint:* Expected interest rate is calculated using the CAPM equation, $R_f + \beta_D\ (R_p)$).
7. Capital cash flow valuation and free cash flow valuation yield same results. Explain.
8. The discount rate for tax shields in the case of CCF valuation is —.

* Drawn from Cooley, Philip L. (ed.), *Advances in Financial Management*, 2nd ed., Dryden Press, Fortworth, TX, 1986.

† This is based on Richard Ruback, Capital Cash Flows: A Simple Approach to Valuing Risky Cash Flows, *Working Paper*, Harvard Business School, March, 2000.

CHAPTER

12

An Overview of Bankruptcy Procedures Around the World*

LEARNING OBJECTIVES

After reading this chapter, you should be able to:

- Introduce a type of restructuring.
- Provide an overview of bankruptcy procedures in select countries.

INTRODUCTION

As pointed out in Chapter 10 restructuring debt contracts is one of the types of corporate restructuring. International managers need to have a broad understanding of insolvency codes around the world. This chapter provides an overview of bankruptcy code in some countries.

The way in which business firms are structured and financed has important implications in finance. While Franco Modigliani and Merton Miller demonstrated in 1961 that the capital structure of a firm is irrelevant under specific assumptions, finance professionals have always known that this irrelevance does not hold in practice. An important reason for this is that when a firm is financed partly with debt, it can be thrown into bankruptcy. The theoretical irrelevance of capital structure depends on the

* This chapter is contributed by P.V. Viswanath.

P.V. Viswanath is grateful for helpful comments from Robert Rauch.

assumption that firms can be restructured costlessly if the firm's cash flows are insufficient to make promised payments to creditors; this, however, is rarely the case in reality. As a result, firms that use financial leverage can find themselves in costly bankruptcy. As has been pointed out over and over, it is not bankruptcy, per se, that is the issue; rather it is the fact that bankruptcy can be expensive and redirects the firm's cash flows from its security holders to parties, such as lawyers and other legal professionals. Appropriate structuring of the laws that apply in bankruptcy can, however, mitigate these costs so as to increase the social efficiency of the corporate form.

There are two aspects to the question of efficiency—*one*, ensuring that the firm is run efficiently prior to bankruptcy; and *two*, that a firm is not sub-optimally forced into liquidation or kept longer in reorganization than required, once bankruptcy does occur. There is a tension between these two aspects. The former objective requires that the firm takes seriously the fact that mismanagement and excessive risk-taking might lead to loss of control to bond holders. The latter objective, on the other hand, suggests that a bankrupt firm's management should be given incentives to get back on its feet. Legal systems in different countries emphasize these two aspects to different degrees. Countries that emphasize the first objective are described as being **creditor oriented**, while those that favour the second objective are called **debtor oriented**.

Legal systems can also be categorized in another way. There are two broad law systems—civil law and common law. Civil systems require all laws to be written in a code or written collection. Common law, on the other hand, has been referred to as the "common sense of the community, crystallized and formulated by our ancestors". The common law systems tend to be more debtor-friendly and focused on efficiency to a greater degree, while the civil law systems tend to be more creditor-oriented and focused on equity. While this is not a rigid association, it is certainly valid to a great extent from an empirical point of view.*

In this chapter, we will present outlines of how bankruptcy law systems in different countries around the world attempt to deal with these problems. As countries cope with the increasing level of globalization and interdependence in the world economy, they are also being forced to deal with bankruptcy laws. Consequently, it is very difficult to provide an up-to-date survey of bankruptcy law in several countries, unless one is an expert in all those systems. The emphasis in this chapter will, rather, be on providing a feel for the basic elements of the systems in different countries, and how they are changing in response to the events in the world around them. Needless to say, anybody intending to conduct business in any of these countries should make sure that they have access to a legal expert specializing in that country.

---

* La Porta et al. (1998) document that German civil-law countries are strongly pro-creditor. Sixty seven percent of them have no automatic stay, and secured creditors.

OVERVIEW OF BANKRUPTCY PROCEDURES IN DIFFERENT COUNTRIES

The US Bankruptcy Code

Bankruptcy is the legal process of settling claims between debtors and creditors. There are two types of bankruptcy procedures in the USA: Chapter 7 and Chapter 11, and the laws are enforced through bankruptcy courts, which are divisions of district courts. The bankruptcy judges are appointed to preside over the bankruptcy cases. Chapter 7 provides for liquidation of the company. Either the debtor (the company) or the creditor may initiate the bankruptcy process. Once the bankruptcy petition is filed an automatic stay comes into effect that prevents pre-petition creditors from collecting debt and it remains in effect till the end of the bankruptcy case. Soon after the petition is filed, the bankruptcy judge appoints a trustee (an attorney or accountant or a business person) to oversee the bankruptcy process. The creditors then hold a meeting to assess the problem, determine the types of debt and the location (and perhaps quality) of debtor's assets. The trustee may seek outside expertise (legal/tax/accounting) to work on the case. The trustee then gathers debtors' assets and liquidates them by auction or by private sale. The proceeds of the liquidation are disbursed on the basis of priority: secured claims, administrative claims, employee compensation, customer claims, tax, general unsecured claims and equity claims in that order.

Chapter 11, in contrast, allows a firm to remain in operation while a plan of reorganization is being worked out. Unlike Chapter 7, the company's management remains in charge (called **debtor-in-possession**). Although the company's management remains in charge, they are required to seek approval from the court as far as certain actions such as asset sales or new credit are concerned. During the 120 days after filing for Chapter 11, the debtor is given the exclusive right to formulate a plan of reorganization and during the same period, the debtor may invite creditors for a meeting to negotiate a plan. The plan is put into action when a certain fraction of shareholders and creditors (two-third the dollar amount of claims and a majority of the class) vote in favour of the plan. The court accepts the plan only if all the classes vote in favour or if the plan is considered fair and equitable to those who did not vote in its favour.

The US Chapter 11 provisions provide the most protection for bankrupt firms' assets and result in a greater likelihood of successful reorganization, than is found in other countries where liquidation and sale of the assets for the benefit of creditors are more likely the result. But the US Code's process is usually lengthy (averaging close to two years, except in the case of a 'pre-packaged' Chapter 11) and expensive; furthermore, the reorganized firm often ends up re-filing under Chapter 11 (Altman, 2000). Chapter 11 case may also get converted into Chapter 7. Pan American World Airways and Eastern Airlines had initially filed for Chapter 11. However, significant operating losses during bankruptcy and inability to attract new funding forced the companies to liquidate (Fenster 1993).

Bankruptcy Code in the United Kingdom

There are three possible routes to reorganization in the UK.

1. Liquidation
2. Receivership
3. Voluntary arrangements

The Insolvency Act of 1986 is different from the Chapter 11 US procedures in several ways:

- Creditors run the show, by and large.
- Tax claims are first, in many cases (argued that this reduces the incentive for creditors to agree to reorganization plans).
- Floating charge agreements that allow banks to act as bankruptcy administrators (unique to the UK).
- Liquidation is encouraged, as opposed to reorganization.
- Preserving employment is not a policy objective. (But this might be changing).
- More attention is paid to directors' actions before the bankruptcy to see whether they made sound business judgement.

Liquidation involves sale of company's assets to repay creditors. Receivership involves appointment of a receiver by a creditor who has a specific lien on the firm's assets and is not subordinate to other creditors. He has full powers to run the firm on behalf of the creditor. This would not be permitted under Chapter 11 because of automatic stay. Voluntary arrangement involves formal arrangement between the company and its creditors with a minimum of court involvement, similar to Chapter 11.

China

The most comprehensive bankruptcy law is the Enterprise Bankruptcy Law; this was adopted in December 1986 and governs State-Owned Enterprises (SOEs). There are also other bankruptcy-related statutes, such as the Rules Concerning Bankruptcy of Foreign Related Companies in the Shenzhen Special Economic zone, promulgated in 1986, which applies solely to the Shenzhen zone. Non-SOEs, such as joint ventures, wholly foreign-owned enterprises and stock companies are governed primarily by the amended Chapter 19 of the Civil Procedure Law (CPL), which became effective in 1991; the CPL is also, in practice, applied to SOEs.

There are some special problems that arise with bankruptcy in China, given its status as a communist state. For example, enterprises may be subject to more than one court; furthermore, the laws are more in the nature of guidance for the courts, rather than statutes that must be followed (Flaxer 1994). China also lacks a system for registering assets and a comprehensive valuation system, which enables debtors to conceal their assets. Again, when dealing with SOEs, it is also often unclear as to who is the debtor— for example, is it the parent company alone, or its subsidiaries. Also, what are the assets of the company—does it, for example, include employees' living quarters?

Petitions for bankruptcy may be filed by a debtor or by a creditor. The People's Court determines within seven days whether or not to accept the case. If the case is accepted, other suits and enforcement proceedings against the properties of the debtor are stayed. If the governmental agency supervising the debtor is agreeable, the creditor may petition for reorganization. A creditors committee consists of all unsecured creditors, with a chairman appointed by the Court. This committee creates a conciliation agreement, which is, in effect, a plan of reorganization that lays out measures to improve the management/ productivity of the firm and proposes a repayment plan. The plan is accepted if approved by half of the claimants representing the two-thirds of the claims.

Existing bankruptcy law is applied primarily to liquidations, with little of corporate rescue. Liquidation is undertaken by a liquidation committee set up by the court. However, even liquidation is not easy to achieve, since with an undeveloped market system, it is difficult to convert assets into cash. Priority is given to employee claims and then bank loans; non-bank creditors come last. Even though banks have second priority, very often there is little money left after paying the employees—as a result, banks are often willing to accept the bankruptcy status for a firm, since then its losses will have to be officially and explicitly recognized. It must be noted that employee claims represent a prior claim, even on land; this means that there are no secured debts, where the creditor has the first priority on the assets (Li 2002)*. In any case, since the accounting system is amorphous, it is difficult to even evaluate the creditors' rights and liabilities.

What must be obvious from this description is that bankruptcy in China is a very uncertain affair. This is particularly so for foreign investors, as it became clear with the 1999 case of the Guangdong International Trust and Investment Company (GITIC) bankruptcy.

Japan†

There are five different schemes relating to insolvency in Japan; two, which

* However, Flaxer (1994) states otherwise—"Property pledged to secured creditors, whose rights are not well developed under Chinese law, are excluded from property of the estate".

† While Japan cannot be described as a developing country, still from the point of view of bankruptcy law, it is backward compared to Western European countries or the United States.

are liquidation type—bankruptcy and special liquidation; and three, which are reconstruction type—company reorganization, company arrangement and civil rehabilitation. Liquidation relates to the compulsory administration, collection and realization of a debtor's assets, and the equitable distribution thereof amongst the creditors.* The purpose of reconstruction is the rehabilitation of the company rather than bringing about its liquidation. However, in contrast to many other countries, informal negotiations among the parties, known as **private arrangements** are much more common in Japan.

The rights of secured creditors differ according to which of the five procedures are involved. Under the liquidation-type schemes, the secured creditor is entitled to enforce its collateral security without regard to the bankruptcy proceedings; in contrast, under the reconstruction-type schemes, the secured creditors are restricted from foreclosing on their security; in return, they are given the right to participate in reorganization proceedings. The two kinds of liquidation may be described as follows; the formal description of the two procedures leaves the reader very unclear as to the true differences between them. In fact, this is true of the entire legislation. One reason for this might be that, as mentioned in the previous paragraph, most distressed firms opt for informal arrangements; further, even if there are judicial proceedings, there seems to be an effort to allow for a lot of flexibility, leaving everything to be done on a case-by-case basis. One example of this informality is the provision that if the debtor files a voluntary petition, the National Treasury is required to defray the payment of advance money that will be used to defray the costs of the bankruptcy procedure. However, the Court usually requires the petitioner to make the payment, and it is, in fact, usually paid by the latter.

Under bankruptcy, the petition may be filed by the debtor or by the creditor; grounds for filing are essentially that the debtor is unable to make payments to its creditors. The filing of a petition does not result in an automatic stay. Hence, the debtor normally files for an injunction at the same time, in order to protect the bankruptcy estate. An injunction consists of a prohibition against disposition of the debtor's assets, and collection and payment of debts. The court appoints a trustee, who is expected to manage and dispose of the assets of the estate, and ultimately distribute the proceeds among the creditors. A creditors meeting is also usually convened; the creditors have the power, in principle, to dismiss the trustee, and to receive explanations from the trustee for his explanations.

Under a special liquidation, which is only open to stock companies, the petition may be filed by the creditors or by the shareholders of the company. Special liquidation seems to be called for if the firm is insolvent or expected to be insolvent, and further, when the situation is very complex—for example,

* Insolvency overview—Japan (2001). What follows is mostly based on this source.

there are many creditors, or their interests in the debtor are very complicated. Here, too, there is no automatic stay, and it is necessary to file separately for an injunction. The court appoints a special liquidator, whose functions are similar to those of the trustee in a bankruptcy case. However, in this case, he may also make individual settlements with creditors for waiver of claims or establish a settlement plan reducing the creditors' claims. In contrast to bankruptcy, the court may provide a stay on secured creditors right to exercise their security interest. A creditor meeting is usually convened to obtain the approval of a settlement plan to reduce creditor claims. Non-judicial liquidation is also possible, as explained above. In this case, the court is not involved; sometimes the initiative is taken by the debtor, and sometimes by a creditor. The three kinds of reconstruction are as follows. (i) Under company reorganization, the debtor loses control of the company. A reorganization plan is formulated whereby the debts of the company are discounted and rescheduled. However, the reorganization plan cannot be implemented until the plan is approved by both the creditors and the Court. (ii) Creditors representing two-thirds or more of the unsecured creditors' aggregate claim amount must agree to the plan; secured creditors representing three-fourths of the aggregate secured debt claim amount must also agree; if secured creditors rights are affected in a major way, the required ratio is four-fifths. (iii) Under the company arrangement, the debtor may remain in control. The procedure itself is much more flexible than company reorganization.

Civil rehabilitation proceedings may be commenced if a debtor cannot pay its obligations without affecting the continuation of the firm's operations; or when an event that may give rise to bankruptcy is likely to occur. In this case, too, the debtor normally retains control. The debtor company prepares the rehabilitation plan and submits it to the creditors for their approval. Only a majority of the creditors need to accept the plan for it to be approved. Secured creditors may enforce their security interest on the assets of the rehabilitation; they are relevant for creditor approval only to the extent to which their claims are not covered by the security interest.

India

Provincial Insolvency Act, 1920 and Presidency Towns Insolvency Act, 1909 are the two Acts that govern personal in solvency law in India. The philosophy behind these two Acts is threefold—penal, distributive and rehabilitative, depending on the context and the firm. As an example of the penal content of the Acts, if an insolvent seeks to obtain credit without disclosing the fact of his insolvency, he may be imprisoned. The distributive aspect is the clearest one—for example, an adjudication order under Provincial Insolvency Act is directed towards the realization of the bankrupt's assets and distribution of the proceeds among his creditors. As for rehabilitation, the same Provincial Insolvency Act also allows for schemes of arrangement to secure rehabilitation of the debtor.

The Companies Act of 1956 provides for three different corporate insolvency procedures. However, all of them are directed towards liquidation or winding up of the insolvent firm. The winding up may be by the Court, voluntary, or subject to the supervision of the Court.

There is neither provision for informal negotiations in the Companies Act before formal insolvency proceedings are initiated nor is there anything similar to the US Chapter 11 proceedings. Filing under the Act may be done either by the debtor or by a creditor. Normally, the creditors try and obtain an attachment before judgement, so that the insolvent's assets are not frittered away. In this connection, any doubtful payments made by the Corporation six months before the filing of the bankruptcy petition may be set aside. Secured creditors may use the proceeds from their secured assets for the satisfaction of their claims. Furthermore, debts due to workers and to secured creditors; and taxes have priority over other claims.

The Sick Industrial Companies (Special provisions) Act (SICA), 1985 was enacted with a view to the timely detection of sick companies, so that preventive, ameliorative and remedial measures might be taken. The procedures under this Act are comparable to Chapter 11 proceedings, in that the debtor may stay in control of the firm. A firm is defined as a sick firm if it has been registered for at least five years, and it has had cumulative losses which wipe out its entire net worth. The SICA is implemented through the Board for Industrial and Financial Reconstruction (BIFR). In principle, the BIFR may use any restructuring package that it chooses—mergers, sale, workers co-operative, asset restructuring, etc. However, in practice, firms are in very bad shape by the time the BIFR gets to them; consequently, rehabilitation is very difficult.

The procedure followed is this: As soon as a firm is identified as being sick, it is required to petition the BIFR. At this point, the BIFR conducts a preliminary hearing attended by representatives of the company, trade unions, financial institutions and banks, to decide whether the firm is indeed sick, as per the definition. If the company is declared officially sick, all claims are automatically stayed. Then the firm, itself, can propose a reorganization scheme; if it can convince the BIFR that it can turn its net worth positive within seven to ten years, and if all the parties agree, the scheme will be sanctioned under Section 17(2). Most 17(2) schemes are formulated in conjunction with financial institutions even before the firm is formally declared *sick*. If there are no feasible 17(2) proposals, the BIFR will appoint an operating agency, which might be a financial institution or bank to examine the turnaround possibility of the firm and submit a report. If neither of these approaches works, the BIFR can recommend liquidation to the High Court or it may conduct the liquidation itself and submit the proceeds to the Court.

While this procedure is potentially promising, it has not worked very well. The main problem seems to be the fact that the BIFR is not willing to use the threat of liquidation to move the process along. This has led to lengthy bankruptcies and excessive favouring of the debtor-in-possession. Furthermore, there are no provisions for a cram-down—unanimity in decision-making is required, which provides each participation with a veto and bogs the process down. This also leads to violations of the absolute priority rule, with workers and secured creditors getting much less than their fair share.

South Korea

South Korea has dealt with troubled firms on an informal basis since the Second World War, although the Civil Procedure Act did exist for debt collection on an individual basis. In 1980, for the first time, the South Korean government implemented executive orders to save insolvent firms that had been affected by the oil shock; these orders were to include industry rationalization measures as well, but no real steps were taken until the 1997 crisis. In 1997, the Financial Supervisory Commission took steps that were meant to liquidate ailing firms, and to consolidate struggling firms. Currently, there are three bankruptcy statutes on the books—(i) the Bankruptcy Act, which deals with liquidation; (ii) the Composition Act, which deals with compositions; and (iii) the Corporate Reorganization Act, which deals with corporate reorganizations. In 1998 these statutes were modified.

A bankruptcy petition may be made by the debtor, or by a creditor. A receiver is appointed, who distributes the estate according to priority rules. Composition is for individuals, who face insolvency and are seeking an opportunity to adjust their debts. Corporate reorganizations are normally initiated by the debtor corporation; however a qualified creditor or a qualified shareholder may do so as well. As there are no automatic stays, the debtor corporation files for a temporary protection order, which stops enforcement orders and suspends the debt payments. Creditors are required to file their claims in order to protect themselves.

In a corporate reorganization, a trustee is appointed, who drafts a reorganization plan, which must be approved by the creditors and by the Court. Four categories of stakeholders are recognized—(i) creditors of common benefits, (ii) secured creditors, (iii) unsecured creditors and (iv) shareholders. The first category has the highest priority in terms of repayment; furthermore, shareholders get nothing before all the creditors are paid. However, absolute priority is not enforced between junior and senior creditors. Only stockholders and bond holders are taken into account; employees and other stakeholders are not allowed to be considered.

The 1998 amendment to the statutes established the creditors' conference, which constitutes a channel between the creditors and the court. As mentioned before, formally, it is the trustee who drafts the reorganization plan. However, there is a series of three meetings, where the reorganization plan is presented and discussed. The admission of the plan requires approval of two-thirds of general creditors, three-fourths of secured creditors and a majority of shareholders. However, there is a cram down procedure in the Corporate Reorganization Act; the court can approve a plan even if any category of claimants rejects the proposed plan, provided the plan is considered by the Court to be in the best interest of the parties. If a corporate reorganization cannot be agreed upon, the Court can order bankruptcy.

Workout procedures exist, and are based on the Financial Institutions Agreement for Promotion of Corporate Restructuring, signed on 25 June, 1998. The key aspect of the workouts in the Korean context is that all financial institutions are expected to participate. This increases the probability of success of the workout, and provides a source of capital for the debtor firm as well. The Government is also often involved. There has been a lot of criticism that the current procedures are very slow. Hopefully, the Government will propose a unified insolvency act in the near future.

Singapore

Singapore's insolvency rules are governed by the Bankruptcy Act of 1995. There are four different procedures:

1. Scheme of arrangement
2. Receivership
3. Liquidation
4. Judicial management

The first alternative is provided for in the Companies Act, and essentially allows for a reorganization of the share capital. A majority of affected creditors representing 75% of the claims must agree to the arrangement. Once the court's approval is obtained, the scheme is binding. Receivership is meant to look after the interests of secured creditors, similar to the provision in the UK law. The meaning of liquidation is self-evident.

Judicial management is a means whereby a company in distress obtains some breathing room. However, since the management is vested in an appointed judicial manager, and the existing management loses control, this is an unlikely option for debtors to choose. Creditors may, however, view this as a reasonable way of ensuring payment of their debts in the face of an incompetent management. Independent of who files for judicial management, only creditors are allowed to vote on the plan; on the other hand, the court has wide latitude in whether to accept or reject a judicial management plan. Finally, private workouts are also possible.

There are some important differences between a scheme of arrangement and a judicial management scheme. In the former, there is no automatic stay, while in the latter, no steps can be taken to enforce any charge on the company's property or even to repossess goods. A judicial management scheme does not automatically involve a rearrangement of the company's liabilities—rehabilitation of the company from an operating standpoint is what is intended; arrangement, on the other hand, could involve rescheduling of debts, conversion of debt to equity, and even infusion of new capital into the distressed firm.

CONCLUDING REMARKS

Several things should be clear from the overview of bankruptcy systems presented in this chapter. *First*, there is no overwhelming commonality of features—different countries have adopted systems, based somewhat on the systems that their erstwhile colonial history has bequeathed them. *Second*, they are systems in development and evolution. *Third*, while business interests, creditor interests, and governmental interests are nudging the systems in various directions, one might venture to say that they are all headed towards greater workability. Whether a system is efficient or not, the most important thing is that all the parties are aware of what their rights and responsibilities are.

It is also interesting to note that many of the countries surveyed in this chapter have debtor-friendly elements in their bankruptcy procedures. This seems to be the case with the BIFR in India, for example. In most of the countries reviewed, informal procedures seem to work better than court procedures. This is not too surprising since courts have a tendency to be more bureaucratic and punctilious, rather than pragmatic. In the USA, too, out-of-court settlements and pre-packaged bankruptcies have helped reduce reorganization costs. In the ultimate analysis, it will be the potential for gains for all the parties in the process that will lead to workable solutions.

REFERENCES

1. Altman, E., Predicting Financial Distress of Companies: Revisiting the Z-score and Zeta Models, *Working Paper, Stern School of Business*, July, 2000.
2. Fenster, S.R., Note on International Comparisons Concerning Troubled Companies, *Harvard Business School Case No. 9-293–090*, November, 1993.
3. Flaxer, J., International Insolvency News: Bankruptcy in China, *American Bankruptcy Institute Journal*, pp. 1–12, 1994.
4. Insolvency Overview–Japan, Global Insolvency Law Database, The World Bank Group, 2001 (http://web.worldbank.org/WBSITE/EXTERNAL/TOPICS/LAWANDJUSTICE/GILD/GILDCOUNTRIES/GILDJAPAN/0,,contentMDK:20111761%7EmenuPK:215612%7EpagePK:157658%7EpiPK:157731%7EtheSitePK:215112,00.html)

5. Porta L., R. F. Lopez-de-Silanes, A. Shleifer and R. Vishny, Law and Finance, *The Journal of Political Economy*, **106** (6): 1113–1155, 1998.

6. Li, Shuguang, Bankruptcy Law in China: Lessons of the Past Twelve Years, *Harvard Asia Quarterly*, 2002 (http://www.fas.harvard.edu/~asiactr/haq/200101/0101a006.htm)

SUGGESTED FURTHER READING

Fitzpatrick, D., Country Report for the Philippines, in *Insolvency Systems in Asia: An Efficiency Perspective*, *OECD Proceedings*, Paris, France, 2001.

Goswami, Omkar, Corporate Bankruptcy: A Comparative Perspective, Development Centre Studies, *Organization for Economic Co-operation and Development*, 1996.

Insolvency Service, Singapore. Country Report for Singapore, *Insolvency Systems in Asia: An Efficiency Perspective*, *OECD Proceedings*, Paris, France, 2001, (InsolvencyAsia, Asian Development Bank Website http://www.insolvencyasia.com/insolvency_law_regimes/singapore/index.html.)

Johnson, D., Country Report for Indonesia, *Insolvency Systems in Asia: An Efficiency Perspective*, *OECD Proceedings*, Paris, France, 2001.

Koh, P. T.N., Country Report for Malaysia, *Insolvency Systems in Asia: An Efficiency Perspective*, *OECD Proceedings*, Paris, France, 2001.

Miller, M. and F. Modigliani, Dividend Policy, Growth, and the Valuation of Shares, *Journal of Business*, **34**: 411–33, 1961.

Nam Il, C. and S. Oh, Asian Insolvency Regimes from a Comparative Perspective: Problems and Issues for Reform, *Insolvency Systems in Asia: An Efficiency Perspective*, Organization for Economics Co-operation and Development, 2001.

Nam Il, Chong; S. Oh and J.-K. Kim, Country Report for Korea, in *Insolvency Systems Asia: An Efficiency Perspective*, *OECD Proceedings*, Paris, France, 2001.

Omar, P.J., Insolvency in Private International Law: The Rule in Malaysia and Singapore, http://www.mlj.com.my/articles/P.Omar2.htm.

Phelan, R., Report of the Indonesian Private Business Initiative Regarding the Indonesian Insolvency Law, *International Insolvency Institute*, June 11-12, 2001.

Wisitsora-At, W., Country Report for Thailand, *Insolvency Systems in Asia: An Efficiency Perspective*, *OECD Proceedings*, Paris, France, 2001.

PART VII

COORDINATION AND CONTROL

CHAPTER

13

Corporate Governance*

LEARNING OBJECTIVES

After reading this chapter, you should be able to:

- Define and highlight issues in corporate governance.
- Describe how ownership structure affects governance.
- Summarize empirical findings on governance.
- Provide a summary of Cadbury committee and Sarbanes Oxley Act recommendations.

INTRODUCTION

High profile corporate failures and scandals like those at Enron, and WorldCom have shaken investor confidence because of which regulatory authorities around the world are tightening corporate governance norms. This chapter highlights all the issues in corporate governance and provides an introduction to Sarbanes Oxley and Cadbury Committee recommendations.

The term 'governance' refers to the exercise of power, authority, direction and control. A firm is a collection of physical assets that are jointly owned. Corporate governance refers to the allocation of ownership. It explains how power is shared, contracts are written and enforced, the role of Board of Directors and Chief Executive, management compensation and so on. Corporate governance is of concern not only in the industrialized economies like the UK and the USA but also in developing

* This chapter is contributed by S.R. Vishwanath.

countries. Modern societies depend on corporations for employment, goods and services, for international trade and growth in the standard of living. So, how companies are governed and run is a matter of concern to all. The starting point is the classic **principal-agent** problem. Shareholder wealth maximization rule is based on the assumption that other investor groups in the company are unaffected by the company's decisions. There could be potential conflict of interests between shareholders and bond holders, managers and shareholders, majority and minority shareholders.

Investment in projects generates cash flows that can either be reinvested in the business or returned to shareholders in the form of dividends, who in turn can decide where to invest their money. Managers, as agents of shareholders, have discretion over the investment of residual cash flow. Increasing dividends reduces the resources under the manager's control and limits growth. It is likely that managers may pursue unprofitable projects leaving the shareholders in a lurch.* In theory the shareholders elect the Board to oversee the Chief Executive on their behalf. But, in practice, the Chief Executive, who, sometimes, chairs the Board, exercises considerable influence on the Board, including directors' remuneration! Typically the Boards are populated with friends and relatives of the Chief Executive. Undisciplined managers may be replaced if the market for corporate control is active. The threat of acquisition keeps the managers on their toes. But takeovers are an expensive disciplining tool entailing large administrative and legal costs.

OWNERSHIP STRUCTURE AND GOVERNANCE

In all but few advanced economies such as the US, the UK and Japan, most publicly traded firms are closely held with the majority shareholders playing an active role in the management. The majority shareholders often serve as the chairman of the Board. A study of the world's top 27 stock markets suggests that only 36% of the largest publicly traded firms are widely held, i.e. with no shareholders holding more than 20% of the votes (La Porta et al. 1999). Most of the widely held firms are concentrated in the US, the UK and Japan. Most large publicly traded firms have a controlling shareholder, which may be a family, a state or another company. The 10 largest families in Indonesia, Philippines and Thailand control half the corporate structure in terms of market capitalization while the 10 largest families in South Korea and Hong Kong control about a third (Claessens, Djankov and Lang 1999). In Philippines and Indonesia, the control of about 17% of market capitalization can be traced to a single family. The Suharto family of Indonesia led by Suharto's children, relatives and business partners control 417 listed and unlisted companies.

* This is the agency cost of free cash flow identified by Michael Jensen.

Control is defined as 20% of voting rights and a widely held company is one in which no owner has significant rights. In many East Asian countries control is enhanced through pyramid structures and cross holdings. Exhibit 13.1 presents the control of publicly traded companies in East Asia in 1996.

EXHIBIT 13.1

Control of Publicly Traded Companies in East Asia in 1996

			Corporations with ultimate owner			
Economy	*No. of Corp.*	*Widely held Corp.*	*Family*	*State*	*Widely held financial institution*	*Widely held corp.*
Hong Kong	330	7.0	71.5	4.8	5.9	10.8
Indonesia	178	6.6	67.3	15.2	2.5	8.4
Japan	1240	85.5	4.1	7.3	1.5	1.6
Korea	345	51.1	24.6	19.9	0.2	4.3
Malaysia	238	16.2	42.6	34.8	1.1	5.3
Philippines	120	28.5	46.4	3.2	8.4	13.7
Singapore	221	7.6	44.8	40.1	2.7	4.8
Taiwan	141	28.0	45.5	3.3	5.4	17.8
Thailand	167	8.2	51.9	24.1	6.3	9.5

Source: Claessens, Djankov and Lang (1999)

Exhibit 13.2 presents the complex ownership structure of Fiat S A.

Managerial expropriation of funds can also take more elaborate forms than just taking the cash out. A share is a share in the share capital of the company. Each share entitles the holder to exercise one vote at the annual general meeting. If this is true, then the value of the share should be the same for all the shareholders irrespective of how many shares one is holding—one million or 100 shares. A glance through the financial dailies and magazines shows that companies after companies are acquired for hefty premiums. The majority shareholders control many of these companies. Why do they pay such hefty premiums? In other words, why do people value being in control? The answer lies in the benefits of being in control that accrues to majority shareholders but not to minority shareholders.

The next logical question to ask would be what those benefits are and how are the minority shareholders affected. The obvious benefits are the status bestowed on the head of the company by the society, love and affection bestowed by family and friends, the ability to buy larger than optimal size computers to play with, plush carpets, corporate jets etc. The sum of these benefits does not add up to the premium paid. The less obvious benefits are the value of benefits arising out of access to information in related businesses,

EXHIBIT 13.2

Ownership Structure of Fiat

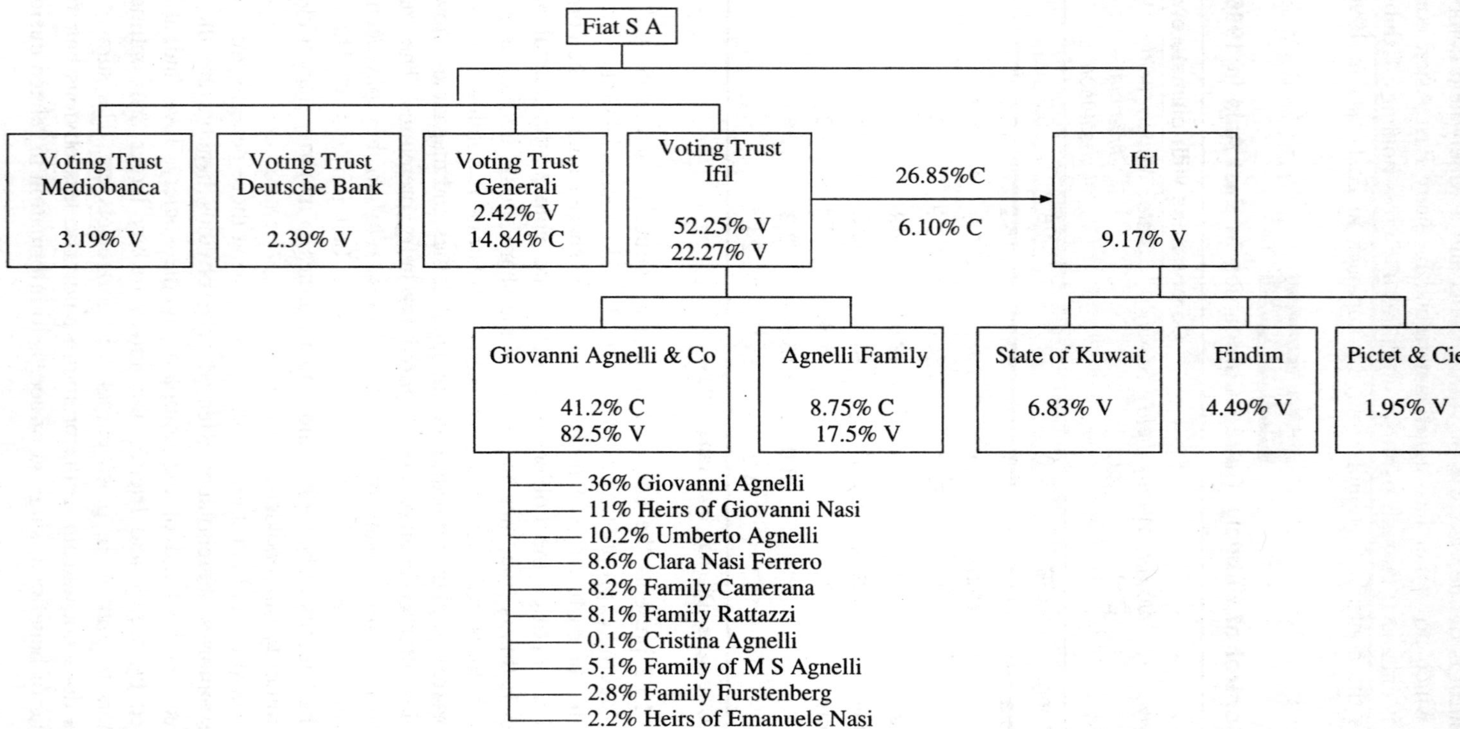

Note: Principal shareholders in Fiat Spa are shown. Ownership stakes are denoted with C and Voting stakes with V. A voting trust formed by Mediobanca, Deutsche Bank, Generai, Ifil, and Ifil controls 39.44% of the votes in Fiat . Members of the Agnelli family control 100% of the votes in Ifil, Fiat's shareholder.

Source: La Porta et al. (1999)

and the ability to fix transfer prices between the company and its suppliers and customers. An example will clarify the point. Assume that a company has a 51% and a 100% subsidiary. If the parent transfers profitable brands and businesses from a long established 51% subsidiary to a newly formed 100% subsidiary at low prices, the minority shareholders of the 51% subsidiary suffer a loss. Another form of rip off is collecting royalties for the use of a brand that the subsidiary has built through years of advertising. The parent takes the earnings pie away leaving the shareholders in dismay. Yet another form of rip off is to acquire a more or less related business where the promoter has business interest through the holding company and furthers his/her interest without sharing any of those benefits with the minority shareholder. Academic studies suggest that the value of control is about 30% of the market value of equity in Italy, 10–20% in Switzerland, the UK and Canada, and 4% of firm value in the USA.

When the risk of expropriation is high, investors either refrain from investing in closely held firms or demand a discount on the company's securities. When the risk of expropriation is very high, the discount can be as high as 60%. But concentrated ownership in itself is not a bad thing. An obvious advantage of concentrated ownership is that it gives the owners better incentives to monitor firms and make necessary changes in management. Diffused ownership, in contrast, does not provide adequate incentives. If concentrated ownership indeed leads to better oversight by managers, we would expect positive correlation between ownership concentration and profitability and firm value. This is indeed the case in some central and Eastern European countries*. A study of 700 Czech firms between 1992 and 1995 found that the more concentrated the ownership of a firm, the higher is its market value and profitability.

INVESTOR PROTECTION

Shareholders provide equity in exchange for dividend and voting rights. Likewise creditors lend money in exchange for interest and principal payments, and the right to possess collateral when the company defaults on its payments. The differences in governance in different parts of the world are partly due to the differences in the rights of the shareholders and creditors (La Porta et al. 1997, 1998; Shleifer and Vishny 1997). A shareholder, as a residual claimant, has the right to attend annual general meetings and vote on various corporate matters such as asset sales, mergers and acquisitions, election of directors, etc. Often widely dispersed shareholders do not actively take part in the governance process. In those countries where voting by mail is not

* Classens, Stijin, Simeon Djankov, and Gerhard Pohl, Ownership and Corporate Governance –Evidence from the Czech Republic, Private Sector, May, 1997.

allowed, the company's management can get away uncontested. In some countries like Italy and Belgium whose legal systems are based on the French Civil law, shareholders are not allowed to vote by mail. In general, countries following the common law tradition (the US, the UK, Australia, Canada, etc) provide the best investor protection.

Likewise, the creditor rights vary from country to country. Some countries allow possession of collateral whereas some do not. Again, the common law tradition provides the best protection to creditors. Further, in many countries the companies can issue shares with different voting rights. The one-share, one-vote rule is followed in the US, the UK and many other countries. But it is common in countries such as Brazil and Chile to issue shares with different voting rights. Some companies restrict the voting rights of foreign investors. For example, some companies from Latin America and Europe have issued (depository) shares with differential voting rights*. The shareholders of B class shares of Saga Petroleum, a Norwegian company, have no voting rights but holders of A-shares have full voting rights. Mexican companies have issued L shares, which provide limited rights to elect the number of directors and such other matters. Two Swedish firms—Astra and Scania—have issued two classes of shares, A and B. The A class shares have one vote each and B shares carry 1/10 vote each. ABB has 24,345,619 shares with 0.1 vote per share and a par value of 5 SEK, as well as 66,819,757 shares with one vote per share and a par value of 5 SEK. Investors, in general, are better protected in countries where the one-share, one-vote rule is enforced. In the absence of such a law, the insiders of the company can have disproportionate control on the company in relation to their investment.

DOES GOVERNANCE MATTER?

Do good governance practices lead to an increase in market value of the firm? One set of studies conducted in the USA found that the correlation between corporate governance attributes and firm performance is either weak or zero. For example, the proportion of independent directors on a company's Board has no significant effect on performance. Likewise, other attributes like institutional shareholding or a firm's committee structure are not correlated with performance. This weak correlation between governance attributes and performance is probably because the differences in practices between firms (in the sample) are negligible. But we would expect the correlation to be much higher in a country where investor protection rights are weak, expropriation by insiders the maximum and so on.

A study of the correlation between performance and corporate governance in Russia suggests that a one-standard-deviation improvement in governance

* Pinegar, Michael and R. Ravichandran, The Idiosyncratic Nature of Sibling ADRs Issued by Mexican Firms: A Clinical Study, *Unpublished Working Paper*, Northern Arizona University, May, 2001.

ranking* leads to eight fold increase in firm value and a worst-to-best improvement in ranking leads to 600-fold increase in firm value†. While individual governance attributes are not correlated with firm performance in the USA, a *group* of attributes are. Gompers et al. (2001) constructed a governance index from 24 factors for 1500 firms per year, and then they studied the relationship between this index and several forward looking performance measures during the 1990s. The index is a proxy for the balance of power between shareholders and managers. In order to construct the index they added one point for every provision that reduces the shareholder rights. Firms in the highest decile of the index were placed in the *management portfolio* (firms with the highest management power or weakest shareholder rights); firms in the lowest decile of the index were placed in the *shareholder portfolio* (firms with strongest shareholder rights). They then analysed the relationship between governance and stock returns. They found that shareholder portfolio outperforms the management portfolio by 8.5% every year. The factors they considered for constructing the index are shown in Exhibit 13.3. They found that, in 1990, a one-point increase in the index is associated with a 2.4 percentage point lower value for Tobin's q. By 1999, this difference level increased significantly with a one-point increase in the index associated with an 8.9 percentage point lower value for Tobin's q.

EXHIBIT 13.3

Governance Factors

Anti-greenmail provision	Poison pills
Blank check preferred stock	Secret ballot
Business combination laws	Severance agreements
Bylaw and charter	Silver parachutes
Classified board	Special meeting requirements
Compensation plans	Unequal voting rights
Director indemnification contracts	
Control—share cash out	Limitations on action by written consent
Cumulative voting	
Fair price requirements	Limitations on director liability
Golden parachutes	Pension parachute
Super majority requirements for approval of mergers	

* The ranking takes into account factors like transparency, asset stripping, limits on foreign ownership, dilution through share issuance to construct an index and rank companies.

† Bernard Black, Does Corporate Governance Matter? A Crude test Using Russian Data, Stanford Law School, Working Paper No. 209.

Recently, Standard & Poor's conducted a survey of corporate governance practices in Asia, Latin America, Central and Eastern Europe*. The survey used latest available annual reports to assess the level of transparency and disclosure of companies in emerging and developed markets. Transparency and disclosure are evaluated by searching company annual reports for the inclusion of 98 possible information items (attributes) divided into three sub categories.

1. Ownership structure and investor relations (28 attributes).
2. Financial transparency and information disclosure (35 attributes).
3. Board and management structure and process (35 attributes).

Companies are ranked in the decile order. The governance score ranges from 1 to 10. Exhibit 13.4 gives the ranking of some companies.

EXHIBIT 13.4

Corporate Governance Scores

Decile rank	Company	Country	Industry	Sub categories 1	2	3
7	China Eastern Airlines	China	Industrials	6	9	5
	Infosys Technologies	India	Information Technology	5	8	7
6	Bank of Asia	Thailand	Finance	5	7	5
	Dacom Corp	Korea	Utility	6	7	4
	IJM corp	Malaysia	Industrials	6	6	7
	Siam Commercial Bank	Thailand	Finance	7	6	6
5	Engro Chemical	Pakistan	Materials	4	7	3
	John Keels Holdings	Sri Lanka	Industrials	9	5	4

Source: Euromoney

Another survey by McKinsey of Institutional Investors from around the world suggests that investors are willing to pay a premium of up to 28% for good governance†. The results of the survey are presented in Exhibit 13.5.

* *Euromoney*, October, 2001.

† Coombes, Paul, and Mark Watson, Three Surveys on Corporate Governance, *The McKinsey Quarterly*, No. 4, 2000.

EXHIBIT 13.5

The value of Good Governance around the World (Premium, in%)

Asia		Europe/USA		Latin America	
Indonesia	27	Italy	22	Venezuela	28
Thailand	26	France	20	Colombia	27
Malaysia	25	Germany	20	Brazil	23
South Korea	24	Spain	19	Mexico	22
Japan	20	Switzerland	18	Argentina	21
Taiwan	20	UK	18	Chile	21
		US	18		

Ranking of Investors' Priorities, (in %)

	First priority		Second priority	
	Latin Am. investors	Foreign investors in Latin Am.	Latin Am. investors	Foreign investors in Latin Am.
Shareholder rights	36	71	28	22
Disclosure	56	48	39	36
Board of directors	42	12	26	57

In the context of the separation of ownership and control, management compensation is one of the important tools for reducing the conflict. The other tool is the market for corporate control, which disciplines underperforming managers through the threat of takeover. These are discussed in the following paragraphs.

Management Compensation

The objective of incentive compensation is to make managers behave like owners. They should identify themselves with the fortunes of the company. A potential source of conflict between the managers and the shareholders lies in their risk tolerance. Shareholders would want managers to take riskier projects because of larger up side potential whereas managers would want to limit downside because their career would be jeopardized in the case of a failure. Another source of conflict lies in the time horizon of investments. If managers are rewarded on the basis of current profits, they would have little incentive to invest in long-term projects even if it is desirable. The objective of the compensation plan is to reduce such conflicts. Awarding stock options is one way to achieve this. Options limit the downside while at the same time allowing participation in the upside because stock options are sensitive to the volatility of the stock price.

The higher the volatility, the more valuable is the option. But higher volatility makes the pay off riskier. The value of the option depreciates when the stock price falls as quickly as it appreciates when the stock price rises. A disadvantage of stock options is that they reward *all* the managers whether they perform or not when the market rises. An executive who gets the option during a bull run can make money by just showing up. This is the drawback of fixed exercise price option contracts. One solution is to tie the exercise price to some benchmark index (say, a stock market index or an index of peer companies). The strike price rises and falls along with the benchmark index*. Most executive pay packets contain four components—a base salary, an annual bonus, stock options and long—term incentive plans. Exhibit 13.6 presents the CEO compensation in the S&P 500 companies.

EXHIBIT 13.6

1996 CEO Compensation S&P 5000 (thousands of 1998 USD)

Salary + Bonus	2043
Benefits	149
Performance-based long term	381
Restricted stock	399
Options	2887

Source: Abowd and Kaplan (1999)

Exhibit 13.7 presents the level and composition of CEO pay in OECD countries. It depicts the estimate of pay for a typical CEO in an industrial company with approximately $ 250 million in revenues. The use of stock options is more common in the USA than in other countries. Indeed stock options are non-existent in many countries. Stock options are non-tradable and are to be forfeited if the executive leaves the company before vesting. The exercise price is usually set at the fair market value on the grant date. Some stock options are offered at a discount or premium. The Black—Scholes option valuation formula modified to incorporate continuous dividend payments is given by the following:

$$\text{Option value} = Pe^{-\ln(1 + d)T} N(z) - Xe^{-\ln(1 + r)T} N(z - \sigma\sqrt{T})$$

* Alfred Rappaport, New thinking on How to Link Executive Pay with Performance, *Harvard Business Review*, March-April, 1999. Also see Akhigbe, Aigbe, Jeff Madura and Alan Tucker, Market Controlled Stock Options: A New Approach to Executive Compensation, *Journal of Applied Corporate Finance*, **9** (1), Spring, 1996.

where

P = stock price

X = strike price

T = expiration term (years)

d = annualized dividend yield

σ = annual stock price volatility

r = risk-free interest rate

EXHIBIT 13.7

Level of CEO Pay (in Firms with at least $ 500 million in Sales) around the World ($)

Country	Total compensation
Argentina	879,000
Canada	787,000
Hong Kong	736,500
Germany	455,000
Japan	508,000
Mexico	866,000
Spain	430,000
UK	668,500
USA	1.9 million

Source: Towers Perrin

$$z = \frac{\ln(P/X) + (\ln(1+r) - \ln(1+d) + \sigma^2/2)T}{\sigma\sqrt{t}}$$

$N(\ ) =$ cumulative normal distribution function

The annualized yield on treasury, a security maturing on the option's expiry date is taken as the risk-free rate. Dividend yields are measured as the annualized yield over the past one, two or three years.

Since stock options are non-tradable, their values are somewhat lower than standard options traded on exchanges. Since managers are undiversified, they are exposed to the total volatility of the firm whereas an investor is exposed to the systematic component of risk. The value of stock option, therefore, is less than its market value.

Studies that have documented the stock market reaction to introduction of new stock-based compensation plans by companies report positive abnormal return (2.4%). See Tables 13.1 and 13.2.

Table 13.1 List of Highest Paid CEOs of the US and their Option Grants

Year	Highest Paid US CEOs Company/ CEO	Amount ($, m)	Largest Options Grants Company/ CEO	Amount ($, m)
1990	Time Warner Steven Ross	75	Time Warner Steven Ross	215
1991	Coca-Cola Roberto Goizueta	61	U S Surgical Leon Hirsch	170
1992	Bear Sterns Alan Greenberg	16	Merck Roy Vagelos	35
1993	Eastman Kodak George Fisher	29	Eastman Kodak George Fisher	67
1994	Allied Signal Lawrence Bossidy	34	Allied Signal Lawrence Bossidy	63
1995	GreenTreeFinancial Lawrence Coss	66	GAP Millard Drexler	79
1996	Walt Disney Michael Eisner	194	Walt Disney Michael Eisner	506
1997	Cendant Henry Silverman	194	Cendant Henry Silverman	570
1998	Dell Computer Michael Dell	94	Dell Computer Michael Dell	272
1999	Computer Associates Charles Wang	507	Quest Comm. Joseph Nacchio	257
2000	Apple Computer Steven Jobs	381	Apple Computer Steven Jobs	872

Source: Fortune, 25 June, 2001

Table 13.2 Highest Paid CEOs in 2005

Terry Semel Yahoo	230.6
Barry Diller InterActiveCorp	156.2
William McGuire United HealthGroup	124.8
Howard Solomon Forest Labs	92.1
George David United Technologies	88.7

Source: Forbes

Market for Corporate Control

Changes in ownership through mergers and acquisitions generally lead to an increase in shareholder value. Many academic studies in America report increases in shareholder returns of target companies. Mergers and acquisitions enable transfer of assets to owners who value them the most. The gain in well-planned acquisitions comes from better governance and improved efficiency. In a market-oriented economy like the USA, companies making value-destroying investments are disciplined by capital markets. The takeover wave of the 1980s in the USA was largely due to deconglomeration. That is, companies sold off unrelated businesses and acquired related businesses. In many countries the market for corporate control is either weak or non-existent. In some Asian and European countries, the market is restricted because of complex cross holdings, pyramid structures and anti-takeover laws. For instance, one of the fiercest takeover battles in Europe was fought between Nestle and the Agnelli family over the control of Perrier, a mineral water company*.

As in other parts of continental Europe, networks of power elites play important roles in the French corporate and financial worlds. Factors such as political position, cultural and social capital are as important as economic capital in shaping power structures. Takeovers are extremely difficult when strong personalities and institutions are involved. Furthermore, shareholdings are so complex that it is almost impossible to acquire (see the ownership structure of Fiat, for example, given in Exhibit 13.2).

Companies may resort to anti-takeover tactics such as poison pills, crown jewels or heavy debt. Poison pills enable a company's management to buy shares at a discount when any person owns more than a specified percentage of equity. This dilutes the interest of the bidder. Companies may take on disproportionately large amount of debt or sell off key assets making the acquisition unattractive. All of them have the same effect of retarding governance reforms.

The Role of Active Investors

Any large corporation is dependent on a large number of small investors for capital as it is not possible for any single investor or a small group of investors to provide the necessary capital because, by definition, large companies have large requirements. Further, the law in some countries prevents financial institutions (e.g. banks) from holding equity or cross a certain threshold (e.g. mutual funds are prevented from holding more than a certain percentage of shares in any one company). Due to the wide dispersion of shareholding no single investor will have an incentive to monitor a company. Since

* Dau, Hans and Anant Sundaram, Perrier, Nestle and the Agnellis, *Thunderbird Case No.* A06-98-0016, 1998.

diversification can be achieved by holding a dozen stocks it is possible for institutional investors to hold a small number of stocks and actively monitor the portfolio companies.

Shareholder activism comes from two sources: institutional shareholders and wealthy individuals. Activism may take on two following approaches:

- Presenting a proposal at a shareholders' meeting.
- Prod the company's management to change strategy and/or CEO.

Studies conducted in America find that a small number of institutional investors spend a trivial amount of money on activism efforts. They do not conduct proxy fights or elect their own candidates for the Board.[*] Further, it is not clear whether institutional activism leads to better performance. The results are mixed. One study, however, reports positive long-term stock price returns to firms targeted by CalPERS, a large state pension plan[†].

Particular institutional or individual investors may have the skill to improve the performance of their portfolio companies. For instance, USX corp., when it decided to issue a tracking stock, was being pressurized by Carl Icahn to restructure and improve performance. In the 1980s US Steel acquired Marathon Oil and Texas Oil & Gas, and changed its name to USX in recognition of its hybrid status. Gradually USX became an energy company as a large portion of its revenues came from the energy business. But investors, apparently, did not welcome this diversification move. USX's stock price steadily declined. This attracted Carl Icahn's attention and he started accumulating USX's stock. He had no intention of taking over USX. His intention was to force USX to take a relook at its structure and strategy, and spin off its steel business to unlock value. What followed was a bitter war between the two camps. Both the camps presented their analysis and proposal. Eventually USX won the war and issued tracking stocks. Though Carl Icahn did not win the proxy contest, he did succeed in provoking a corporate change. Likewise, Harold Simmons waged a year long campaign at Lockheed pressing for several reforms in the governance process while Robert Monks, a wealthy investor and founder of Lens, a private company, waged a successful campaign against Sears, Roebuck and Company to sell off its interest in financial businesses and concentrate on the retailing business.[‡]

In another interesting episode, Gulf Oil was under attack by Boone Pickens Jr, the Chief Executive Officer of Mesa Petroleum who had a long string of successes in targeting oil companies. Boone Pickens, with the support

[*] Bernard Black, Shareholder Activism and Corporate Governance in the United States, in Peter Newman, ed., *The New Palgrave Dictionary of Economics and the Law*, 1998.

[†] Nesbitt, SL, Long Term Rewards from Shareholder Activism : A study of the CalPERS effect, *Journal of Applied Corporate Finance*, Spring, 1994.

[‡] Pozen, Robert, *Institutional Investors: The Reluctant Activists, Harvard Business Review*, Jan-Feb, 1994.

of an experienced investors group, called Gulf investors group, would put himself on the Board of the target company, effect changes in policy and cash out. Even if the bid failed, the group would make substantial profits by selling the stock back to the target at a premium or in the open market at a higher price (the stock price would go up due to announcement of takeover attempt). For obvious reasons Boone Pickens was considered a corporate raider and some kind of a shorttermer who cannibalized companies. Is shareholder activism good? Probably yes. Most chief executives of underperforming companies would attribute the discount on their company's stock to irrationality of stock markets, and portray shareholder activism as short-termist while portraying themselves as long-term visionaries.

The Case of Leveraged Buyouts

In a LBO, a group of investors use debt financing to purchase a company or a division. The erstwhile public company becomes a private company. Buyouts are arranged by specialists like Kohlberg, Kravis, Roberts & Co. The LBO specialist arranges debt and equity financing. Buyouts are structured in such a way that the management's equity interest increases substantially. The equity investors join the company's board and run the company along with the company's managers. LBOs are often accompanied by substantial improvements in value and operating performance of the company/division. This improvement is usually attributed to concentrated ownership and better oversight by the investors (Palepu 1990; Jensen 1989; Kaplan 1989). Critics of LBOs claim that the heavy debt burden makes the organization short sighted and vulnerable to bankruptcy.

The gains in an LBO need not come from (tax shields arising out of) leverage alone. One LBO firm Clayton, Dubilier and Rice (CD&R) is known for its expertise in adding value by improving governance and operations[*]. In 1986, O M Scott & Sons was taken private by its management and Clayton & Dubilier in an LBO transaction (Baker and Wruck 1989). Scott's performance improved dramatically between 1986 and 1988. Sales increased by 25%, EBIT by 56% and capital spending by 23%. The improvement in performance was largely due to changes in incentives, monitoring and governance.

An important insight from LBOs is that companies can enforce the same discipline one finds in an LBO situation even in the absence of an LBO. In other words, companies can simulate the LBO environment to generate superior returns to shareholders by optimizing capital structure, investment decisions and better compensation practices.

---

[*] Kester, Carl and Timothy Luehrman, Rehabilitating the Leveraged Buyout, *Harvard Business Review*, May–June, 1995.

The Role of Boards

The Board's responsibility is to hire top-level managers, monitor them and fire them if they do not perform. Increasing shareholder activism is exerting pressure on the Boards to be more active. The usual practice is that the company's management team briefs the Board on the competitive developments and the company's strategy. Often the Board members lack experience in that industry and knowledge of the company.

Typically Board members (outside directors) are provided with reports that the Board and the company's management discuss at annual meetings. Many directors not only lack knowledge and experience of the industry, but also do not spend much time in understanding the reports. Consequently, most meetings are essentially necessary rituals. It is also possible that the Board members may not suggest major changes in strategy or leadership wary of unpleasant consequences even when a significant change is required. A company would do well to involve the Board more actively by letting the Board perform a strategic audit*. The Board may set up a committee to provide strategic oversight. The company's management must maintain and provide necessary data to perform the same. The role of the Board is to monitor the company and not manage. There is a thin line between the two. An emerging practice in some American companies is to plan a strategic retreat in which the directors take part in no-holds barred discussion of the changes in their industry†. The debate on governance has centred on the separation of ownership and control and the resulting power imbalance. The focus, instead, should be on the decision-making process. In other words, the managers and the Board should collaborate. Many companies have annual calendars for the different activities of the Board. Strategy meeting may be held in January; audit committee meetings may be held in February/March; the compensation committee meetings may be held in November/December and so on. Exhibit 13.8 presents the *Business Week* rankings of best and worst Boards of directors in 2002.

THE BALANCED SCORECARD AND CORPORATE GOVERNANCE

The balanced scorecard popularized by Kaplan and Norton recognizes the fact that executives do not focus on one set of measures, as no single measure can provide a clear performance target, or focus attention on the critical areas of business (Kaplan and Norton 1992, 1993, 1996). The balanced scorecard

---

* Gordon, Donaldson, A New Tool for Boards : The Strategic Audit, *Harvard Business Review*, July-August, 1995.

† Lorsch, Jay, Empowering the Board, *Harvard Business Review*, Jan-Feb., 1995.

EXHIBIT 13.8

The Best and Worst Boards of Directors in the US in 2002

Best boards of directors	Worst boards of directors
3M	APPLE
APRIA HEALTHCARE	CONSECO
COLGATE-PALMOLIVE	DILLARD'S
GENERAL ELECTRIC	GAP
HOME DEPOT	KMART
INTEL	QWEST
JOHNSON & JOHNSON	TYSON FOODS
MEDTRONIC	XEROX
PFIZER	
TEXAS INSTRUMENTS	

Source: Business Week

allows managers to look at their business from the perspective of customers, shareholders and employees. A typical balanced scorecard shown in Exhibit 13.9 considers goals and measures from various perspectives, and tries to bring all the elements of the business together in a single management report. The balanced scorecard could serve as the focal point for the organization's efforts communicating priorities to managers, employees, investors and customers. It is important to understand that performance measurement is an important aspect of strategy. What gets measured, gets managed. The balanced scorecard tries to measure the capital allocation efficiency of executives from various perspectives. From a purely financial perspective, ROI, cash flow, project profitability and sales booking might be the relevant measures whereas from a customer's perspective, customer satisfaction index, customer ranking survey, market share might be the relevant measures. A company can start by assesssing its current position on these perspectives, and arrive at the priority areas where attention is required. The balanced scorecard is an excellent tool that can help managers track the many factors that influence performance.

The balanced scorecard can be used as a central document for a Board review. Companies may use a three-part BSC programme—the enterprise scorecard, executive scorecards and Board balanced scorecards*. CEOs can use the enterprise scorecard to foster constructive discussions with their Board. The executive scorecards can be used to select, evaluate, and reward senior executives, and, finally, the Board can develop a scorecard for itself to define its strategic contributions.

* Kaplan, Robert and David P. Norton, Aligning the Board of Directors, *Balanced Scorecard Report*, March-April 2006. Also see Kaplan, Robert and David P. Norton, *Alignment*, HBS Press, Boston, MA, 2006.

EXHIBIT 13.9

The Balanced Scorecard

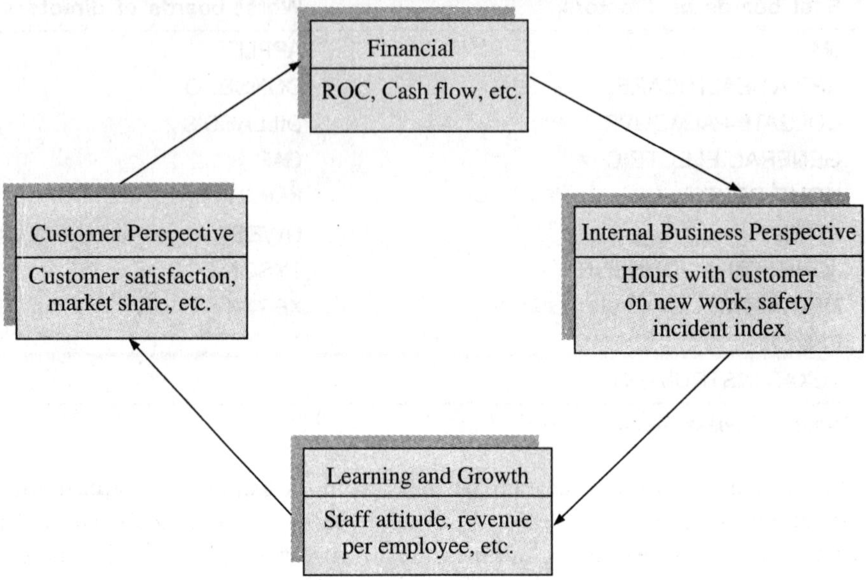

CORPORATE GOVERNANCE REGULATIONS

High profile corporate failures like that of Enron and accounting scandals like that of WorldCom have shaken investors' confidence. Regulators around the world have come up with new corporate governance norms and (stock exchange) listing standards. Two such corporate governance codes—Cadbury Committee Recommendations (UK) and Sarbanes Oxley (US) are discussed here.

The Cadbury Committee Recommendations

The report of the committee on the Financial Aspects of Corporate Governance (the Cadbury report) recommends that Boards should comply with 19 items contained within the code. The committee also recommends that the companies make a statement about their compliance with the code, and identify and give reasons for any area of non-compliance.

The Cadbury disclosure requirements require the directors to the following:

- State whether they have complied with the code.
- Give full and clear disclosure of directors' total emoluments.
- Give a balanced and understandable assessment of the company's position.

- State their responsibility for preparing the financial statements.
- Review the effectiveness of internal control.

All the corporate governance disclosure requirements may be dealt with in a single integrated statement in the annual report, separate from the financial statements.

The committee recommended that:

- statements of compliance be reviewed by auditors before publication;
- the review by the auditors should cover only those parts of the compliance statement which relate to provisions of the code where compliance can be objectively verified; and
- the auditors should draw attention to any area of non-compliance, which is not properly disclosed, in their report on the financial statements.

The Cadbury committee requires the directors to report on the effectiveness of the company's system of internal control. The directors' statement should contain the following:

- Acknowledgement by the directors that they are responsible for the company's system of internal financial control.
- A description of the key procedures that the directors have established and which are designed to provide an effective system of internal financial control (including how the directors review the effectiveness of that system).
- Confirmation that the directors have reviewed the effectiveness of the system.

The term 'internal control' encompasses the following:

- The safeguarding of assets against unauthorized use or disposition; and
- The maintenance of proper accounting records and the reliability of financial information used within the businesses or for publication.

The action plan for the directors is as under:

- Risk analysis
- Setting minimum control standards
- Monitoring
- Review by the Board
- Public report

Risk analysis

The Joint Working Group guidance summarizes the process of risk identification and evaluation under three heads:

1. Timely identification of key business risks.

2. Consideration of the likelihood of risks crystallizing and resulting financial impact.
3. Establishment of priorities of allocating resources to the control of risk.

Minimum control standards

Having set minimum control standards there should be some monitoring to ensure that they are met. Monitoring may make use of one or more of the methods given as follows:

- Independent review
- Internal audit
- External audit
- Self-certification

Review of the board

The audit committee is required to review the Board statement on internal control. The audit committee should also review the company's statement of internal control prior to endorsement by Board.

The public statement

The statement on internal control will be topical and subject to much attention. It must be credible, and properly reflect the ethos of the organization. Readers will be interested not only in what it tells them about the way the company is controlled, but will also examine to see what it reveals about the Board's attitude to corporate governance and disclosure in general.

The central recommendations to the Boards regarding their roles, responsibilities are given as follows.

The Board should meet regularly, retain full and effective control over the company, and monitor executive management. There should be a clearly accepted division of responsibilities at the head of the company, which will ensure a balance of power and authority, such that no individual has unfettered powers of decision. When the chairman is also the chief executive, it is essential that there should be a strong and independent element on the Board with a recognized senior member. The chairmen should make certain that their non-executive directors receive timely relevant information tailored to their needs, that they are properly briefed on the issues arising at the Board meetings, and that they make an effective contribution as Board members in practice.

The Board should include non-executive directors of sufficient caliber and number for their views to carry significant weight in the Board's decisions. Non-executive directors bring an independent judgement to bear on issues of strategy, performance, resources, including key appointments and standards of conduct. The majority should be independent of management and free from any business or other relationship which could materially interfere with the exercise of their independent judgement, apart from their fees and shareholding. Non-executive directors should be appointed for specified terms and should not be automatic. They should be selected through a formal process, and both this process and their appointment should be a matter for the Board as a whole.

Executive directors' service contracts should not exceed three years without shareholders' approval. There should be full and clear disclosure of directors' total emoluments and those of the chairman including pension contributions and stock options. Separate figures should be given for salary and performance–related elements, and the basis on which performance is measured should be explained. Executive directors' pay should be subject to the recommendations of a remuneration committee made up of wholly or mainly non-executive directors.

It is the Board's duty to present a balanced and understandable assessment of the company's position. The Board should establish an audit committee of at least three non-executive directors with written terms of references that deal clearly with its authority and duties. The Board should be formally constituted as a subcommittee of the main Board to whom they are answerable and to whom they report regularly.

The committee also recommends that all the directors should undertake some form of internal or external training. This is particularly important for directors, whether executive or non–executive with no previous board experience.

Provisions of the Sarbanes Oxley Act*

The Sarbanes Oxley Act of 2002, commonly called SOX, is a United States Federal Law passed in response to a number of high profile corporate scandals including those affecting Enron, Tyco, Peregrine and WorldCom. These scandals resulted in a decline of public trust in accounting and financial reporting. The legislation is wide ranging and establishes new, enhanced standards for all the US company boards, management and accounting firms. The Act contains 11 titles, or sections, ranging from additional corporate board responsibilities criminal penalties, and requires the Securities and Exchange Commission (SEC) to implement rulings on requirements to comply with the new law. Given are the following provisions of the Act:

* The details of the Sarbanes Oxley Act can be found at: http://www.sarbanesoxley.com/section.php?level=1&pub_id=SOA-Manual

The OECD Principles of corporate governance can be found at: http://www.oecd.org/document/19/0,2340,en_2649_34727_36989779_1_1_1_1,00.html

A list of corporate governance codes can be found at: http://www.ecgi.org/codes/all_codes.php

I. **Public company accounting oversight board:** It is a non-governmental, non-profit board to oversee auditors of public companies to protect investors.

II. **Auditor independence:** It prohibits auditing firms from performing certain other activities for clients, such as book keeping and financial information systems work. Requires the rotation of lead audit partners.

III. **Corporate responsibility:** It requires audit to be overseen by independent Board members of the company and the company officers to certify company financial statements.

IV. **Enhanced financial disclosures:** It addresses the accuracy of financial reports and transparency regarding off-balance sheet accounting and limits personal loans to officers. Further, it requires reporting on the effectiveness of internal controls and addresses codes of ethics for financial officers.

V. **Analyst conflicts of interest:** It addresses conflicts of interest involving securities analysts writing research reports and investment banking activities within the same firm.

VI. **Commission resources and authority:** It provides funding for the SEC and also increases the federal courts' and SEC's authority to censure certain individuals and prohibit activities.

VII. **Studies and reports:** Commissions study regarding the role of credit rating agencies, violation of securities laws, etc.

VIII. **Corporate and criminal fraud accountability:** It increases penalties for improper destruction or alteration of documents and statute of limitations for securities fraud. It makes personal debts non-dischargeable if incurred during fraud.

IX. **White collar crime penalty enhancements:** According to it, individuals who attempt to commit securities crime will be treated as if the crime was actually committed. Prison terms and fines for certain securities fraud are also increased.

X. **Corporate tax returns:** This means federal income tax returns will be signed by the corporate CEO.

XI. **Corporate fraud and accountability:** This creates additional penalties for the destruction or alteration of documents and allows the SEC to prohibit individuals from serving as officers or directors.

Much of the research on governance is on the differences in practices among the USA, Japan and Germany. The rest of the chapter is devoted to governance in Germany and Japan.

GOVERNANCE IN JAPAN

Unlike the Anglo-Saxon model of governance, the Japanese governance system does not require the management to pursue the interests of shareholders. The Japanese governance system is characterized by allegiance to inside stakeholders (not shareholders), weak institutional shareholders and absence of market for corporate control. Inside stakeholders in Japanese companies often hold substantial equity (36% in 1996) and outside shareholders are a minority. Institutional investors control just 16% of household assets compared with 33% in the USA[*]. The large institutional investors like life insurance companies play a passive role in governance. In the USA, and now in some parts of Europe, dominant shareholders often discipline companies making value-destroying investments. Minority shareholders would take necessary action to discipline erring managers if the cost of disciplining were to be small. The primary way shareholders contribute to effective governance is by tendering shares when there is a takeover attempt. Hostile takeovers are rare in Japan. Through complex cross shareholdings, Japanese companies can often escape the discipline of the stock market or so they say. But a casual study of some of the large business groups does not support this hypothesis[†]. Among the 48 non-financial firms of the Mitsui group and the 36 of the Sanwa, only six pairs exchange 1% stakes. Among the 46 Mitsubishi non-financial firms, four pairs do, among the 45 Fuji firms three pairs, and among the 29 Daiichi firms two pairs.

The practice of granting stock options to executives is relatively new in Japan. In 1998 only 70 large companies had instituted stock option programmes. In contrast, 93% of a similar group of the US firms had stock option plans in 1996.

The Japanese corporate governance model consists of a dual structure: the Board of directors, which carries out the functions of strategy formulation and oversight, and, the Board of corporate auditors, which audits management's execution of strategy. In practice, the Board of directors consists primarily of in-house directors who are loyal to *shacho* (president, who is the top management executive). The Japanese style of management has been criticized for its obsession with preserving inefficient businesses for the sake of providing lifetime employment. While downsizing is quite common in the USA, lay offs are a rarity in Japan. The difference in the two approaches is partly due to the fact that Japanese firms invest heavily in *contextual skills* whereas the US firms invest in *functional skills*. Since contextual skills are

---

[*] Gibson, Michael, Big Bang Deregulation and Japanese Corporate Governance: A Survey of the Issues, Board of Governors of the Federal Reserve System, *International Finance Discussion Papers*, Number 624, September, 1998.

[†] Miwa, Yoshiro and Mark Ramseyer, The Myth of the Main Bank: Japan and Comparative Corporate Governance, *Discussion Paper No. 333*, Harvard Law School, September, 2001.

firm specific they are not readily transferable to other firms or industries. But the fact of the matter is that Japanese companies never offer long-term contracts explicitly. Further, the courts in Japan do not allow them to fire employees even if they wish, and it is almost impossible to prove in many situations that a lay off would do good to the company. Since they cannot fire employees in troubled times, companies do not hire in good times: they outsource from small suppliers.

In Japan, firms tend to have strong business relationships with one or a few banks. These banks often belong to the same group of companies, the *keiretsu*. So these institutions stand behind the companies when they get into financial trouble and also take active interest in investment decisions. As a result, the bankruptcy costs are lower for these companies, while the benefits of debt remain thereby giving them a competitive advantage. The companies in bank-oriented economies like Japan and Germany can therefore, it appears, add more value than their counterparts in market-oriented economies like the US and the UK. Although a firm may have relationships with many banks, one of them acts as the main bank. The main bank, apparently, acts as a monitor on behalf of all other banks. Again, it is not clear if one bank has explicit agreements and there is evidence to prove that Japanese firms are no more highly leveraged than the US firms.

GERMAN CORPORATE GOVERNANCE

One of the special characteristics of the German governance is the two-tier Board structure—the **Vorstrand** (management board) and **Aufsichstrat** (supervisory board). The management board consists of inside directors only and manages the affairs of the company. The supervisory board consists solely of outside directors and the membership of the two boards does not overlap. Although the supervisory board monitors the management board, the day-to-day functioning of the company is the responsibility of the management board.

The supervisory board consists of 3–21 members with an average of 13 members. One person can hold up to 10 seats on supervisory boards of other companies. Shareholders and employees appoint the members of the supervisory board. Under the Industrial Constitution Act, the employees and two-third by the shareholders appoint one-third of the members of the supervisory boards of stock corporations and limited liability companies with more than 500 employees. In corporations and limited liability companies with more than 2000 employees, shareholders elect half the members; the employees and the trade unions elect the other half.

Special Position of Banks in German Governance

The German governance is more close to the Japanese system than the Anglo-Saxon model. A company, in the German system, is required to fulfil its obligations towards other stakeholders such as employees, creditors and society at large even if it is not in the interest of the shareholders. One of the distinguishing characteristics of the German governance is the dominant role played by banks. The big banks control a large chunk of equity stake in numerous public companies and are represented on the Boards of many large companies. Banks have substantial influence on the exercise of voting rights in publicly held corporations. Even if banks hold relatively small fraction of stock, they can still exercise substantial influence because Boards apparently consult substantial shareholders, including banks, before making major corporate decisions. But is this necessarily bad? In other words, is a bank-oriented system an adequate proxy for a market-oriented system? Let us rephrase this question. While the practices in the three countries are different, are the outcomes of the practices also different? A recent study suggests the following*:

- The fortunes of both German and Japanese managers, like those of the US managers, are tied to stock performance and cash flows.
- The bank and inter-corporate relationships in Germany and Japan play a monitoring and disciplinary role. The relationships do appear to substitute for the market-oriented control mechanism in the USA.

CONCLUDING REMARKS

The goal of corporate governance system is to control value-destroying behaviour of managers. This can be achieved by shareholder activism, developing an active market for corporate control and healthy Boards. Whether one governance system such as the US system is better or worse than the rest (say, German or Japanese) is a debatable issue. The reason why institutional investors do not normally involve themselves in the governance of a portfolio firm is that the returns from such an activity are less than the costs involved. Further, the benefits from monitoring accrue not only to them, but also to other investors. That is, other, investors can free ride on the efforts of one investor. In this chapter, the author outlined the salient features of alternate governance systems, the reasons for shareholder activism and its impact on the companies. Managers are much more focussed on stock prices and shareholder value now than two decades back.

A summary of the characteristics of alternate governance systems is given as follows:

---

* Kaplan, Steven, Corporate Governance and Corporate Performance : A Comparison of Germany, Japan, and the US , *Journal of Applied Corporate Finance*, **9**(4), Winter, 1997.

	USA	Germany	Japan
Executive compensation	High	Moderate	Low
Board of directors	Primarily Outsiders	Dual Board	Primarily Insiders
Ownership	Diffused	Concentrated	Less Concentrated
Capital markets	Very liquid	Relatively illiquid	Moderate
Takeover market	Major	Minor	Minor
Banking system	Fragmented	Universal banking	Main bank system

The characteristics of an empowered board are as follows:

- The CEO and the Board's chair should be different.
- The Board members should come from a wide range of industry groups and business experience.
- The size of the Board should be small enough to be cohesive.
- The Board must meet in the absence of the CEO to discuss sensitive issues, both formally and informally.
- The CEO must evaluate his or her performance, and discuss it with the Board members. The evaluation may be done annually.

APPENDIX A: GLOSSARY OF CORPORATE GOVERNANCE TERMS

Given here is a glossary of terms that is commonly encountered in corporate governance literature.

1. A *board member* (or director) is one who serves on the board of a company, including executive board members, independent board members, and non-executive board members.
2. *Executive board members* are members of executive management.
3. An *independent board member* is one who meets the qualifications of independence. Independence refers to the degree to which members are not subject to control by company management.

   Some companies, (say, a bank)/countries may define independence this way: a 'Voting Director' will be considered independent if not a member of management and if he/she meets the following criteria:

   (a) Is not a substantial shareholder of the company or of a company holding more than 5% of the company's voting stock or an officer of or otherwise associated directly or indirectly with a shareholder holding more than 5% of the company's voting stock.

(b) Has not within the last three years been employed in an executive capacity by the company or another group member or been a director after ceasing to hold any such employment.

(c) Is not a principal or employee of a professional adviser to the company and its entities whose billings exceed 5% of the adviser's total revenues. A Voting Director who is a principal or employee of a professional adviser will not participate in any consideration of the possible appointment of the professional adviser and will not participate in the provision of any service to the company by the professional adviser.

(d) Is not a significant supplier or customer of the company or its entities or an officer of or otherwise associated directly or indirectly with a significant supplier or customer. A significant supplier is defined as one whose revenues from the company exceed 5% of the supplier's total revenue. A significant customer is one whose amounts payable to the company exceed 5% of the customer's total operating costs.

(e) Has no material contractual relationship with the company or any of its associates other than as a director of the company.

(f) Is not a director of any of the company's subsidiaries or responsible entities.

(g) Has not served on the Board for a period exceeding the company's agreed tenure rules (including transitional arrangements).

(h) Has no other interest or relationship that could interfere with the Voting Director's ability to act in the best interests of the company and independently of management.

With good cause, the Board Corporate Governance Committee may at its discretion determine that a Voting Director is independent, notwithstanding that not all of the above criteria are satisfied. Correspondingly, the Board Corporate Governance Committee can in appropriate circumstances, determine that a Board member has lost their independence notwithstanding that they continue in a formal sense to satisfy all of the above criteria.

4. *Non-executive* board members are those who are neither executive nor independent board members.
5. The *audit committee's* primary objective is to ensure that the financial information reported by the company to shareowners is

complete, accurate, reliable, relevant and timely. Audit committee members are usually independent directors.

6. The *compensation committee* is responsible for ensuring that compensation and other awards encourage executive management to act in ways that enhance the company's long-term profitability and value. The compensation committee also consists of independent directors.
7. The *nominations committee* comprising independent directors is responsible for recruiting board members with appropriate qualities and experience to suit the company's business needs.

APPENDIX B: CORPORATE GOVERNANCE AT THE WALT DISNEY COMPANY*

Given here are the board composition and the policy statement of The Walt Disney Company:

The Certificate of Incorporation of The Walt Disney Company provides that the Board of Directors shall consist of not less than nine or more than 21 Directors, with the exact number being determined from time to time by resolution of the Board. The Board believes that a desirable target number of Directors is 12 to 15, allowing, however, for changing circumstances that may warrant a higher or lower number.

It is the policy of the Board of Directors that the Board at all times reflects the following characteristics:

1. Each Director shall at all times represent the interests of the shareholders of the company.
2. Each Director shall at all times exhibit high standards of integrity, commitment and independence of thought and judgment.
3. Each Director shall dedicate sufficient time, energy and attention to ensure the diligent performance of his or her duties, including by attending shareholder meetings and meetings of the Board and Committees of which he or she is a member, and by reviewing in advance all meeting materials.
4. The Board shall meet the standards of independence from the Company and its management set forth under 'Director Independence' below.
5. The Board shall encompass a range of talent, skill and expertise sufficient to provide sound and prudent guidance with respect to all of the company's operations and interests.

---

* This section is reproduced from the company's statement in its website http://corporate.disney.go.com/corporate/governance.html

6. The Board shall reflect the diversity of the company's shareholders, employees, customers, guests and communities.

FUNCTIONS OF THE BOARD OF DIRECTORS

The responsibility of the Board of Directors is to supervise and direct the management of the company in the interest and for the benefit of the company's shareholders. To that end, the Board of Directors shall, acting directly or through committees, have the following duties:

1. Overseeing the conduct of the company's business to evaluate whether the business is being properly managed;
2. Reviewing and, where appropriate, approving the company's major financial objectives, plans and actions;
3. Reviewing and, where appropriate, approving major changes in, and determinations of other major issues respecting, the appropriate auditing and accounting principles and practices to be used in the preparation of the company's financial statements;
4. Assessing major risk factors relating to the company and its performance, and reviewing measures to address and mitigate such risks;
5. Regularly evaluating the performance and approving the compensation of the Chief Executive Officer and, with the advice of the Chief Executive Officer, regularly evaluating the performance of principal senior executives; and
6. Planning for succession with respect to the position of Chief Executive Officer and monitoring management's succession planning for other key executives.

The Board of Directors has delegated to the Chief Executive Officer, working with the other executive officers of the company and its affiliates, the authority and responsibility for managing the business of the company in a manner consistent with the standards of the company, and in accordance with any specific plans, instructions or directions of the Board.

The Chief Executive Officer shall seek the advice and, in appropriate situations, the approval of the Board with respect to extraordinary actions to be undertaken by the company, including those that would make a significant change in the financial structure or control of the company, the acquisition or disposition of any significant business or the entry of the company into a major new line of business.

DIRECTOR INDEPENDENCE

It is the policy of the Board of Directors that a substantial majority of

Directors be independent of the company and of the company's management. For a Director to be deemed 'independent', the Board shall affirmatively determine that the Director has no material relationship with the company or its affiliates or any member of the senior management of the company or his or her affiliates. This determination shall be disclosed in the proxy statement for each annual meeting of the company's shareholders. In making this determination, the Board shall apply the following standards:

- A Director who is, or has been within the last three years, an employee of the Company, or whose immediate family member is, or has been within the last three years an executive officer, of the company may not be deemed independent. Employment as an interim Chairman or Chief Executive Officer will not disqualify a Director from being considered independent following that employment.
- A Director who has received, or who has an immediate family member who has received, during any 12-month period within the last three years, more than $ 100,000 in direct compensation from the company, other than director and committee fees and pension or other forms of deferred compensation for prior service (provided such compensation is not contingent in any way on continued service), may not be deemed independent. Compensation received by a Director for former service as an interim Chairman or Chief Executive Officer and compensation received by an immediate family member for service as a non-executive employee of the Company will not be considered in determining independence under this test.
- (A) A Director who is, or whose immediate family member is, a current partner of a firm that is the Company's external auditor; (B) a Director who is a current employee of such a firm; (C) a Director who has an immediate family member who is a current employee of such a firm and who participates in the firm's audit, assurance or tax compliance (but not tax planning) practice; or (D) a Director who was, or whose immediate family member was, within the last three years (but is no longer) a partner or employee of such a firm and personally worked on the Company's audit within that time may not be deemed independent.
- A Director who is, or whose immediate family member is, or has been within the last three years, employed as an executive officer of another company where any of the Company's present executive officers at the time serves or served on that company's compensation committee may not be deemed independent.
- A Director who is a current employee or general partner, or whose immediate family member is a current executive officer or general partner, of an entity that has made payments to, or received payments from, the Company for property or services in an amount which, in

any of the last three fiscal years, exceeds the greater of $ 1 million or 2% of such other entity's consolidated gross revenues, may not be deemed independent.

- Further to the provision above that applies to goods and services generally, a Director who is, or whose immediate family member is, an executive officer, general partner or significant equity holder (i.e. in excess of 10%) of an entity that is a paid provider of professional services to the Company, any of its affiliates, any executive officer or any affiliate of an executive officer, and which received payments with respect to such services in an amount which, in the preceding 12 months, exceeds $ 60,000 (but does not exceed the greater of $ 1 million or 2% of such other entity's consolidated gross revenues) may not be deemed independent.
- A Director who is, or whose immediate family member is employed as an executive officer of a tax-exempt entity that received significant contributions (i.e. more than 2% of the annual contributions received by the entity or more than $ 200,000 in a single fiscal year, whichever amount is lower) from the Company, any of its affiliates, any executive officer or any affiliate of an executive officer within the preceding 12-month period may not be deemed independent, unless the contribution was approved in advance by the Board of Directors.

For purposes of these guidelines, the terms:

- 'affiliate' means any consolidated subsidiary of the Company and any other Company or entity that controls, is controlled by or is under common control with the Company, as evidenced by the power to elect a majority of the board of directors or comparable governing body of such entity;
- 'executive officer' means an 'officer' within the meaning of Rule 16a-1(f) under the Securities Exchange Act of 1934; and
- 'immediate family' means spouse, parents, children, siblings, mothers- and fathers-in-law, sons- and daughters-in-law, brothers- and sisters-in-law and anyone (other than employees) sharing a person's home, but excluding any person who is no longer an immediate family member as a result of legal separation or divorce, or death or incapacitation.

The Board shall undertake an annual review of the independence of all non-employee Directors. In advance of the meeting at which this review occurs, each non-employee Director shall be asked to provide the Board with full information regarding the Director's business and other relationships with the Company and its affiliates and with senior management and their affiliates to enable the Board to evaluate the Director's independence.

Directors have an affirmative obligation to inform the Board of any material changes in their circumstances or relationships that may impact their designation by the Board as 'independent.' This obligation includes all business relationships between, on the one hand Directors or members of their immediate family, and, on the other hand, the Company and its affiliates or members of senior management and their affiliates, whether or not such business relationships are subject to the approval requirement set forth in the following provision.

BOARD LEADERSHIP

The Board of Directors shall designate one of its members to serve as Chairman of the Board. The powers and responsibilities of the Chairman of the Board shall be set forth in the Corporation's By-laws, as supplemented from time to time by resolution of the Board of Directors.

The Chairman of the Board shall serve for such term as the Board shall determine. The identity of the Chairman shall be set forth in the proxy statement for the Company's annual meeting, together with a method for interested parties to communicate directly with the Chairman or with the non-management Directors as a group.

The Chairman of the Board shall be an independent director unless the Board concludes that the best interests of shareholders would be otherwise better served. In such circumstances the Board shall (a) provide a written statement in its next proxy materials discussing why the different arrangement is in the best interests of shareholders, and (b) designate one independent Director to serve as Lead Director, with the duties and responsibilities described in the following paragraph.

In the event the Board makes a determination that it is in the best interests of shareholders for a non-independent Board member to serve as Chairman, the Board shall designate an independent director to serve as Lead Director, with the following duties and responsibilities: preside at all meetings of the Board of Directors at which the Chairman is not present, including executive sessions of non-management or independent directors; call meetings of the independent or non-management Directors; serve as liaison between the Chairman and the independent and non-management Directors; approve information sent to the Board of Directors; approve meeting agendas for the Board of Directors, including assurance that there is sufficient time for discussion of all agenda items; be available for consultation and direct communication upon the reasonable request of major shareholders; advise Committee Chairs with respect to agendas and information needs relating to Committee meetings; provide advice with respect to the selection of Committee Chairs; and perform such other duties as the Board may from time to time delegate to assist the Board in the fulfillment of its responsibilities.

MANAGEMENT SUCCESSION AND REVIEW

At least once a year, the Chief Executive Officer of the Company shall meet with the non-management Directors to discuss potential successors as Chief Executive Officer. The non-management Directors shall meet in executive session following such presentations to consider such discussions. The Chief Executive Officer shall also have in place at all times a confidential written procedure for the timely and efficient transfer of his or her responsibilities in the event of his or her sudden incapacitation or departure, including recommendations for longer-term succession arrangements. The Chief Executive Officer shall review this procedure periodically with the Chairman of the Board and the Governance and Nominating Committee.

The Chief Executive Officer shall also review periodically with the non-management Directors the performance of other key members of the senior management of the Company, as well as potential succession arrangements for such management members. Any waiver of the requirements of the Company's Standards of Business Conduct with respect to any such member of senior management shall be reported to, and be subject to the approval of, the Board of Directors.

BOARD MEETINGS

The Chairman of the Board, in consultation with the other members of the Board, shall determine the timing and length of the meetings of the Board. The Board expects that six regular meetings at appropriate intervals are in general desirable for the performance of the Board's responsibilities. In addition to regularly scheduled meetings, unscheduled Board meetings may be called upon appropriate notice at any time to address specific needs of the Company.

The Chairman shall establish the agenda for each Board meeting. Each Director shall be entitled to suggest the inclusion of items on the agenda, request the presence of or a report by any member of the Company's senior management, or at any Board meeting raise subjects that are not on the agenda for that meeting.

The agendas for Board meetings shall provide opportunities for the operating heads of the major businesses of the Company to make presentations to the Board during the course of the year. At one meeting each year the Board shall be presented the long-term strategic plan for the Company and the principal issues that the Company expects to face in the future. Sufficient time shall be allocated for this presentation to allow for questions by and full discussion with the members of the Board.

The non-management Directors shall meet regularly, in executive session, without the participation of the Chief Executive Officer or other members of the Company's management, to review matters concerning the relationship of the Board with the management Directors and other members of the Company's management and such other matters as the Chairman and participating Directors may deem appropriate. The Board shall not take formal actions at such sessions, although the participating Directors may make recommendations for consideration by the full Board. Additional executive sessions may be scheduled from time to time as determined by a majority of the non-management Directors in consultation with the Chairman. In addition, at least once a year, the independent Directors shall meet in executive session without members of management or the non-independent Directors present.

BOARD COMMITTEES

Committees shall be established by the Board from time to time to facilitate and assist in the execution of the Board's responsibilities. Committees may be standing or ad hoc. Generally, a Committee shall be constituted to address issues that, because of their complexity, technical nature, level of detail, time requirements and/or sensitivity, cannot be adequately addressed within the normal agenda for Board meetings.

There are currently four standing committees:

1. Executive Committee
2. Audit Committee
3. Compensation Committee
4. Governance and Nominating Committee

Each Committee shall have a written charter of responsibilities, duties and authorities, which shall periodically be reviewed by the Board. Each Committee shall report to the full Board with respect to its activities, findings and recommendations after each meeting.

Each Committee shall have full power and authority, in consultation with the Chairman of the Board, to retain the services of such advisers and experts, including counsel, as the Committee deems necessary or appropriate with respect to specific matters within its purview.

COMMITTEE MEMBERSHIP

The Chairman of the Board, after consideration of the desires, experience and expertise of individual Directors and after consultation with the Chief Executive Officer, shall recommend to the Governance and Nominating Committee the assignment of Directors to Committees, including the designation of Committee Chairs. The Governance and Nominating Committee shall review such recommendations and report to the Board thereon.

In acting upon such recommendation and report, the full Board shall give consideration to the following objectives:

- The target size of each Committee should be three to five members, unless circumstances call for an exception;
- Committee membership should be rotated, on a staggered basis, at five-year intervals, subject to any applicable legal, regulatory and stock exchange listing requirements; and
- Committee Chairs should also be rotated at reasonable intervals, taking into account any applicable legal, regulatory and stock exchange listing requirements.

The Audit, Compensation and Governance and Nominating Committees shall be composed entirely of Directors who are independent under these guidelines and any applicable regulatory requirements or listing standards. The Executive Committee shall include the Chief Executive Officer of the Company. At least half of its members shall be independent Directors.

If any Director ceases to be independent under the standards set forth herein while serving on any Committee whose members must be independent, he or she shall promptly resign from that Committee.

BOARD TENURE POLICY

The Board recognizes that it is important for it to balance the benefits of continuity with the benefits of fresh viewpoints and experience. Therefore, the Board will not nominate for re-election any Director if the Director shall have completed 15 years of service as a member of the Board on or prior to the date of the election as to which the nomination relates.

Each non-management Director shall submit to the Board a letter of resignation upon resignation or retirement from, or termination of, the Director's principal current employment, or other similarly material changes in professional occupation or association. The Board shall be free to accept or reject this letter of resignation, and shall act promptly with respect to the letter and promptly notify the Director concerned of its decision.

COMMITTEE CHARTERS—AUDIT

The responsibilities of the Board of Directors of The Walt Disney Company include oversight of the Company's systems of internal control, preparation and presentation of financial reports and compliance with applicable laws, regulations and Company policies. Through this Charter, the Board delegates certain responsibilities to the Audit Committee to assist the Board in the fulfilment of its duties to the Company and its shareholders. As more fully set forth below, the purpose of the Committee is to assist the Board in its oversight of:

- the integrity of the Company's financial statements;
- the Company's compliance with legal and regulatory requirements;

- the qualifications and independence of the Company's independent auditors; and
- the performance of the Company's independent auditors and of the Company's internal audit function.

Authority

The Committee shall be given the resources and assistance necessary to discharge its responsibilities, including appropriate funding, as determined by the Committee, unrestricted access to Company personnel and documents and the Company's independent auditors. The Committee shall also have authority, with notice to the Chairman of the Board, to engage outside legal, accounting and other advisors as it deems necessary or appropriate.

Membership

The Committee shall consist of three or more directors, who shall be appointed annually and subject to removal at any time, by the Board of Directors. Each Committee member shall meet the independence requirements established by rules of the Securities and Exchange Commission and listing standards of the New York Stock Exchange, as well as the independence standards set forth in the Company's Corporate Governance Guidelines.

All Committee members shall be financially literate, having a basic understanding of financial controls and reporting. At least one Committee member shall also have accounting or related financial management expertise, including at a minimum the expertise required by rules of the Securities and Exchange Commission and listing standards of the New York Stock Exchange.

No member of the Audit Committee shall receive directly or indirectly any compensation from the Company other than his or her Directors' fees and benefits.

Procedures

The Committee shall meet at least four times a year and may call special meetings as required. Meetings may be called by the Chair of the Committee or the Chairman of the Board. The presence in person or by telephone of three members shall constitute a quorum. Meetings may be held at any time, any place and in any manner permitted by applicable law and the Company's bylaws. Minutes of the Committee's meetings shall be kept. To the extent practicable, the meeting agenda, draft minutes from the prior meeting and supporting materials shall be provided to Committee members prior to each meeting to allow time for review. The Committee shall have authority to create and delegate specific tasks to such standing or ad hoc subcommittees as it may determine to be necessary or appropriate for the discharge of its responsibilities. The results of the meetings shall be reported regularly to the full Board.

Responsibilities

The Company's executive management bears primary responsibility for the Company's financial and other reporting, for establishing the system of internal controls and for ensuring compliance with laws, regulations and Company policies. The Committee's responsibilities and related key processes are described as follows. From time to time, the Committee may take on additional responsibilities, at the request of the Board.

Financial reporting

The Committee shall monitor the preparation by management of the Company's quarterly and annual external financial reports. In carrying out this responsibility, the Committee shall:

- review with management the significant financial reporting issues, judgments and estimates used in developing the financial reports, including analyses of the effects of alternative GAAP methods on the financial statements;
- review the accounting and reporting treatment of significant transactions outside the Company's ordinary operations;
- review with management and the Company's independent auditors significant changes to the Company's accounting principles or their application as reflected in the financial reports;
- review with management and the Company's independent auditors the effect of regulatory and accounting initiatives, as well as off-balance sheet structures, on the financial statements of the Company;
- meet periodically with the Company's independent auditors (in private, as appropriate) (a) to review their reasoning in accepting or questioning significant decisions made by management in preparing the financial reports; (b) to review any audit problems or difficulties and management's response; (c) to review any outstanding disagreements with management that would cause them to issue a non-standard report on the Company's financial statements; (d) to examine the appropriateness of the Company's accounting principles (including the quality, not just the acceptability, of accounting principles) and the clarity of disclosure practices used or proposed; (e) to determine if any restrictions have been placed by management on the scope of their audit, and (f) to discuss any other matters the Committee deems appropriate;
- meet periodically in private with the Company's management;
- review earnings press releases, as well as financial information and earnings guidance provided to analysts and rating agencies and discuss their appropriateness with management and the Company's

independent auditors, paying particular attention to any use of 'pro forma' or 'adjusted' non-GAAP information; and

- review draft quarterly and annual financial statements and discuss their appropriateness with management and the Company's independent auditors, including the Company's disclosures under "Management's Discussion and Analysis of Financial Condition and Results of Operations".

Relationship with independent auditors

The Committee shall bear primary responsibility for overseeing the Company's relationship with its independent auditors. In carrying out this responsibility, the Committee shall:

- be directly responsible for the appointment, compensation, retention and oversight of the work of the Company's independent auditors, in consultation with the full Board;
- review the scope and extent of audit services to be provided;
- review the overall audit plan, including the risk factors considered in determining the audit scope;
- review the independent auditors' annual letter pursuant to Independence Standards Board Standard No. 1, outlining all relationships that may impact their independence;
- review with the independent auditors the extent of non-audit services provided and related fees, and pre-approve any non-audit relationships;
- determine whether the Committee believes the outside auditors are independent;
- review the responsiveness of the outside auditors to the Company's needs;
- at least annually, obtain and review a report by the Company's independent auditors describing the independent auditor firm's internal quality-control procedures; any material issues raised by the most recent internal quality-control review, or peer review, of the firm, or by any inquiry or investigation by governmental or professional authorities, within the preceding five years, respecting one or more independent audits carried out by the firm, and any steps taken to deal with any such issues; and (to assess the auditors' independence) all relationships between the independent auditors and the Company;
- at least annually evaluate the auditors' qualifications, performance and independence and present its conclusion with respect to the auditors to the Board of Directors;
- resolve any disagreements between management and the auditors regarding financial reporting; and
- set clear hiring policies for employees or former employees of the Company's independent auditors.

Internal control

The Committee shall have responsibility for overseeing that management has implemented an effective system of internal control that helps promote the reliability of financial and operating information and compliance with applicable laws, regulations and Company policies, including those related to risk management, ethics and conflicts of interest. In carrying out this responsibility, the Committee shall:

- inquire of management, management auditors and the Company's independent auditors concerning any deficiencies in the Company's policies and procedures that could adversely affect the adequacy of internal controls and the financial reporting process and review any special audit steps adopted in light of any material control deficiencies and the timeliness and reasonableness of proposed corrective actions;
- review significant management audit findings and recommendations, and management's responses thereto;
- meet periodically with management auditors in private session (without the participation of management or the independent auditors);
- review management's responses to recommendations for improving internal controls in the independent auditors' management letters;
- review the Company's policies and practices with respect to risk assessment and risk management;
- review the Company's policies and practices related to compliance with laws, ethical conduct and conflicts of interest;
- review significant cases of conflicts of interest, misconduct or fraud;
- review significant issues between the Company and regulatory agencies; and
- review as appropriate material litigation involving the Company.

Relationship with management auditors

The Committee shall have responsibility for determining that the Management Audit department is effectively discharging its responsibilities. In carrying out this responsibility, the Committee shall:

- review and approve the Management Audit department's charter;
- review the appropriateness of the funding, staffing and operational independence of Management Audit; and
- review and approve the appointment or dismissal of the Vice President of (or corresponding officer responsible for) Management Audit.

Receipt of complaints

The Committee shall establish procedures for:

- the receipt, retention and treatment of complaints received by the Company regarding accounting, internal accounting controls and auditing matters; and

- the confidential, anonymous submission by employees of the Company regarding questionable accounting or auditing matters.

Preparation of reports

The Committee shall prepare and approve the Committee's report included in the proxy statement for the Company's annual meeting of shareholders, and such other reports as may from time to time be necessary or appropriate.

Annual performance review

The Committee shall conduct an annual evaluation of its performance in carrying out its responsibilities hereunder.

As amended and restated by the Board of Directors on 2 December, 2003.

COMMITTEE CHARTERS-COMPENSATION

The Compensation Committee (the 'Committee') is a committee of, and reports to, the Board of Directors of the Walt Disney Company (the 'Board'). Through this Charter, the Board delegates certain responsibilities to the Committee to assist the Board in the fulfilment of its duties to the Company and its shareholders.

Membership

The Committee shall consist of two or more directors, all of whom shall meet the independence standards set forth in The Walt Disney Company's Corporate Governance Guidelines, the listing requirements of the New York Stock Exchange, the requirements for non-employee directors in Rule 16b-3(b)(3)(i) of the rules and regulations promulgated under the Securities and Exchange Act of 1934, as amended (the 'Exchange Act'), and the requirements for 'outside directors' set forth in Treasury Regulation 1.162-27(e)(3). Each Committee member shall be appointed annually, subject to removal at any time by the Board. Each Committee member shall serve until his or her Committee service is terminated by the Board.

Procedures

The Committee shall hold at least four regular meetings each year, and such additional meetings as may be required. Meetings may be called by the Chair of the Committee, the Chairman of the Board or any two members of the Committee. Meetings may be held at any time, in any place and in any manner permitted by applicable law and the Bylaws of The Walt Disney Company. The presence in person or by telephone of the lesser of two members or a majority of the Committee shall constitute a quorum. The Committee may also act by unanimous written consent. Any member of the Board of Directors who is not a member of the Committee may attend any Committee meeting with the concurrence of the Committee Chair or a majority of the members of the Committee.

To the extent practicable, the meeting agenda, draft minutes from the prior meeting and supporting materials shall be provided to members of the Committee prior to each meeting to allow time for review. The Committee shall have authority to create and delegate specific tasks to such standing or ad hoc subcommittees as it may determine to be necessary or appropriate for the discharge of its responsibilities, as long as the subcommittee contains at least the minimum number of directors necessary to meet any regulatory requirements. The results of the meetings shall be reported to the full Board.

Purposes

The Committee shall have direct responsibility to:

- review and approve corporate goals and objectives relevant to the compensation of the Company's Chief Executive Officer, evaluate the performance of the Chief Executive Officer in light of those goals and objectives, and, either as a committee or together with the other independent members of the Board of Directors (as directed by the Board), determine and approve the compensation level for the Chief Executive Officer based on this evaluation;
- make recommendations to the Board of Directors with respect to non-Chief Executive Officer compensation, incentive-compensation plans and equity-based plans; and
- produce a report of the Committee on executive compensation as required by the Securities and Exchange Commission to be included in the Company's annual proxy statement or annual report on Form 10-K filed with the Securities and Exchange Commission.

Responsibilities

To carry out these purposes, the Committee shall have the responsibilities set forth as follows:

- **Overall policy:** The Committee shall conduct a periodic review of the Company's general executive compensation policies and strategies and report, and make recommendations to the Board with respect thereto.
- **Executive performance:** The Committee shall review and approve corporate goals and objectives relevant to compensation of the Chief Executive Officer, the Chief Operating Officer and/or the President and any other executive officers, and periodically evaluate their respective performances in light of such goals and objectives. The Committee shall have authority, either as a committee or acting

together with the other independent members of the Board of Directors (as directed by the Board) with respect to all matters relating to compensation of the Chief Executive Officer, to determine the compensation of the Chief Executive Officer, the Chief Operating Officer and/or the President based on this evaluation.

- **Section 162(m) executives:** The Committee shall identify, in consultation with the management of the Company, persons subject to Section 162(m) of the Internal Revenue Code and/or Section 16(b) of the Exchange Act ('162(m) Executives').
- **Executive salaries:** Subject to the terms of any existing employment contracts, the Committee shall establish the salaries of the Chief Executive Officer, the Chief Operating Officer and/or the President and approve the salaries of (a) those persons who report directly to the Chief Executive Officer, the Chief Operating Officer and/or the President and (b) any other executive officers.
- **Bonuses:** Subject to the terms of any existing employment contracts, the Committee shall (a) set performance targets for eligibility for bonuses, in the case of 162(m) Executives, and (b) approve bonus awards, including any equity-based bonus awards, to 162(m) Executives and all other eligible executive officers.
- **Other incentives, benefits and plans:**
    - The Committee shall conduct a periodic review of the Company's benefit programmes, individually and in the aggregate, for the Chief Executive Officer, the Chief Operating Officer and/or the President and all other executive officers.
    - The Committee shall review and approve all grants of equity-based compensation to executive officers.
    - The Committee shall review, approve, amend, and/or make recommendations to the Board relating to (i) all incentive, performance-based and equity-based plans and (ii) such other compensation, benefit, pension or welfare plans or programmes as may be submitted to the Committee by the Chief Executive Officer, the Chief Operating Officer and/or the President (all of the foregoing being referred to collectively as 'Plans').
- **Contracts:** The Committee shall review and approve employment contracts, or compensation arrangements, for each of the following:
    - Corporate officers who are members of the Board, regardless of salary;
    - All executive officers, and the head(s) (chairman and/or president) of each division or subsidiary reporting to the Company's Chief Executive Officer, Chief Operating Officer and/or President, regardless of salary; and
    - Such other employees of the Company and its subsidiaries as the Committee shall determine from time to time.

- **Director compensation:** The Committee shall recommend to the Board compensation policies for outside directors.
- **Professional development policies:** In connection with its executive compensation responsibilities, the Committee shall review and make recommendations to the Board regarding the Company's policies and practices with respect to the professional development of executive personnel, including policies and practices with respect to professional training and executive succession within the Company's business segments. Notwithstanding the foregoing, executive succession planning with respect to the principal senior executives officers of the Company shall remain within the direct purview of the Board of Directors as a whole, as provided in the Board's *Corporate Governance Guidelines*.
- **Annual report:** The Committee shall prepare an annual report on executive compensation for inclusion in the Company's annual meeting proxy statement, in accordance with applicable rules and regulations.
- **Additional assignments:** The Committee shall perform such other functions as the Board may from time to time assign to the Committee.

Authority

The Committee shall be given the resources and assistance necessary to discharge its responsibilities, including unrestricted access to Company personnel and documents. The Committee shall also have the authority to engage outside advisers as it deems necessary or appropriate. The Committee shall have sole authority to retain and terminate any consultant or firm retained to advise the Committee on matters within its sphere of responsibility, including sole authority to approve the firm's fees and other retention terms.

COMPENSATION COMMITTEE CHARTER

The Committee shall review this Charter periodically for adequacy and recommend to the Board any necessary changes.

Annual Performance Review

The Committee shall conduct an annual evaluation of its performance in carrying out its responsibilities hereunder.
(As amended and restated 2 May, 2006.)

Charter of the Governance and the Nominating Committee of the Board of Directors*

The Governance and Nominating Committee is a committee of, and reports to, the Board of Directors of The Walt Disney Company. Through this Charter, the Board delegates certain responsibilities to the Committee to assist the Board in the fulfilment of its duties to the Company and its shareholders.

Authority

The Committee shall be given the resources and assistance necessary to discharge its responsibilities, including unrestricted access to Company personnel and documents. The Committee shall also have authority, in consultation with the Chairman of the Board, to engage outside advisers as it deems necessary or appropriate. The Committee shall have sole authority to retain and terminate any search firm to be used to identify Director candidates, including sole authority to approve the search firm's fees and other retention terms.

Membership

The Committee shall consist of three or more Directors, who shall be appointed annually, and subject to removal at any time, by the Board of Directors. Each Committee member shall meet the independence standards set forth in the New York Stock Exchange listing standards and the Company's Corporate Governance Guidelines. Each Committee member shall serve until his or her Committee service is terminated by the Board.

Procedures

The Committee shall hold at least two regular meetings each year, and such special meetings as may be required. Meetings may be called by the Chair of the Committee or the Chairman of the Board. The presence in person or by telephone of two members shall constitute a quorum. Meetings may be held at any time, any place and in any manner permitted by applicable law and the Company's Bylaws. Minutes of the Committee's meetings shall be kept. To the extent practicable, the meeting agenda, draft minutes from the prior meeting and supporting materials shall be provided to Committee members prior to each meeting to allow time for review. The Committee shall have authority to create and delegate specific tasks to such standing or ad hoc subcommittees as it may determine to be necessary or appropriate for the discharge of its responsibilities. The results of the meetings shall be reported to the full Board.

* As amended and restated by the Board of Directors on 6 January, 2004.

Responsibilities

The Committee's responsibilities shall be the following:

1. To monitor the implementation and operation of the Company's Corporate Governance Guidelines.
2. To review from time to time the adequacy of the Corporate Governance Guidelines in light of broadly accepted practices of corporate governance, emerging governance issues and market and regulatory expectations, and to advise and make recommendations to the Board with respect to appropriate modifications.
3. To identify and review measures to strengthen the operation of the Corporate Governance Guidelines, and to advise the Board with respect thereto.
4. To prepare and supervise the implementation of the Board's annual reviews of (i) director independence and (ii) the Board's performance, as contemplated by the Corporate Governance Guidelines, and to oversee the Board's processes for evaluation of the management of the Corporation and make recommendations to the Board with respect to such processes.
5. To identify, review and evaluate candidates for election as Director who meet the standards set forth in the Corporate Governance Guidelines, including such inquiries as the Committee deems appropriate into the background and qualifications of candidates and interviews with potential candidates to determine their qualification and interest, and to recommend to the Board of Directors nominees for any election of directors in compliance with the Corporate Governance Guidelines (including the policy that a substantial majority of Directors be independent of the Company and of the Company's management).
6. To advise the Board with respect to such other matters relating to the governance of the Company as the Committee may from time to time approve, including changes to terms or scope of this Charter and the Committee's overall responsibilities.
7. To carry out such other tasks as the Board may from time to time delegate to the Committee for action consistent with this Charter.

Annual Performance Review

The Committee shall conduct an annual evaluation of its performance in carrying out its responsibilities hereunder.

REFERENCES

1. Abowd, J.A. and D. Kaplan, Executive Compensation: Six Questions that Need Answering, *NBER Working Paper No. 7124*, May, 1999.

2. Baker, G.P., and K.H. Wruck, Organizational Changes and Value Creation in Leveraged Buyouts: The Case of the O.M Scott & Sons Company, *Journal of Financial Economics*, **25**, 1989.

3. Classens, S., S. Djankov and L.H.P. Lang, Who Controls East Asian Corporations?, *Policy Research Working Papers 2054*, World Bank, Washington D C, 1999.

4. Fram, E., Are Professional Board Directors the Answer?, *MIT Sloan Management Review*, Winter, 2005.

5. Gompers, P.A., J. Ishii and A. Metrick, Corporate Governance and Equity Prices, *Unpublished Working Paper*, July, 2001.

6. Jensen M.C., Eclipse of the Public Corporation, *Harvard Business Review*, Sep–Oct., 1989

7. Kaplan, R.S. and D. Norton, Linking the Balanced Scorecard to Strategy, *California Management Review*, **39** (1), 1996.

8. ________, The Balanced Scorecard—Measures that Drive Performance, *Harvard Business Review*, Jan-Feb., 1992.

9. ________, Putting the Balanced Scorecard to Work, *Harvard Business Review*, Sep-Oct., 1993.

10. Kaplan, S., The Effects of Management Buyouts on Operations and Value, *Journal of Financial Economics*, **24**, 1989.

11. La Porta, R., F. Lopez–de-Silanes, A. Shleifer, and Robert Vishny, Which Countries Give Investors the Best Protection?, *Private Sector*, April, 1997.

12. ———, Law and Finance, *Journal of Political Economy*, **106** (6), 1998.

13. La Porta, R., F. Lopez–de-Silanes, and A. Shleifer, Corporate Ownership Around the world, *Journal of Finance*, **54**, 1999.

14. Palepu, K., Consequences of Leveraged Buyouts, *Journal of Financial Economics*, **27**, 1990.

15. Shleifer, A. and R.W. Vishny, A Survey of Corporate Governance, *The Journal of Finance*, **LII** (2, June), 1997.

SUGGESTED FURTHER READING

Anders, G., The Barbarians in the Boardroom, *Harvard Business Review*, July-August, 1992.

Andrade, G., M. Mitchell and E. Stafford, New Evidence and Perspectives on Mergers, *Journal of Economic Perspectives*, **15**(2, Spring), 2001.

Aoki, M. and H. Patrick, (ed.), *The Japanese Main Bank System*, Oxford University Press, New York, 1994.

Barclay, M. and C.G. Holderness, Private Benefits of Control of Public Corporations, *Journal of Financial Economics*, **25**, 1989.

Baums, T., Corporate Governance in Germany: System and Current Developments, *Working Paper*, Universitat Usnabruck, Undated.

Black, B.L., Institutional Investors and Corporate Governance: The Case for Institutional Voice, in Joel Stern and Donald Chew, (ed.), *The Revolution in Corporate Finance*, Blackwell, Oxford, 1992.

Brickley, J.S. Bhagat and R. Lease, The Impact of Long Range Managerial Compensation Plans on Shareholder Wealth, *Journal of Accounting and Economics*, **7** (1–3), 1985.

Charny, D., The German Corporate Governance System, *Paper Prepared for the Cross-border Conference on Comparative Corporate Governance,* sponsored by Columbia Law School, Undated.

Conger, J.A., D. Finegold and E. Lawler III, Appraising Boardroom Performance, *Harvard Business Review*, Jan-Feb., 1998.

Dyck, A., The Hermitage Found: Media and Corporate Governance in Russia, *Harvard Business School Case No.* 9-703-010, October, 2002.

Fama, E., and M.C. Jensen, Agency Problems and Residual Claims, *Journal of Law and Economics*, **XXVI**, (June), 1983.

Franks, J. and C. Mayer, Corporate Ownership and Control in the UK, Germany and France, *Journal of Applied Corporate Finance*, **9**(4, Winter), 1997.

Gibson, M.S., Big Bang Deregulation and Japanese Corporate Governance: A Survey of the Issues, Board of Governors of the Federal Reserve System, *International Finance Discussion Papers*, Number 624, September, 1998.

Grossman S.J. and O. Hart, The Costs and Benefits of Ownership: A Theory of Vertical and Lateral Integration, *Journal of Political Economy*, **94**, 1986.

Hall, B. and K.J. Murphy, Stock Options for Undiversified Executives, *Harvard NOM Research Paper No.* 00-05, Harvard Business School, October, 2001.

Hermalin, B.E. and M.S. Weisbach, Boards of Directors as an Endogenously

Determined Institution: A Survey of the Economic Literature, *Unpublished Working Paper*, 15 June, 2000.

Holmstorm, B. and S.Kaplan, Corporate Governance and Merger Activity in the United States: Making Sense of the 1980s and 1990s, *Journal of Economic Perspectives*, **15** (2, Spring), 2001.

Jensen M.C. and W.H., Meckling, Theory of the Firm: Managerial Behavior, Agency Costs and Ownership Structure, *Journal of Financial Economics*, **3**, 1976.

Jensen M.C., Agency Costs of Free Cash flows, Corporate Finance and Takeovers, *American Economic Review*, **76**, 1986.

———, The Modern Industrial Revolution, Exit and the Failure of Internal Control Systems, *Journal of Finance*, **48**, 1993.

Jansen, M.C. and R.S. Ruback, The Market for Corporate Control: The Scientific Evidence, *Journal of Finance*, **11**, 1983.

Corporate Governance Committee, Corporate Governance Principles—A Japanese View, *Working Paper*, Corporate Governance Forum of Korea, May 26, 1998.

Kester, C., Japanese Takeovers: The Global Contest for Corporate Control, *Harvard Business School Press*, Boston, MA, 1991.

Kester, C., Koito Law/Acting Ltd., *Harward Business School Case No.* 9-291-027, April, 1991.

Leechor, C., Reviving the Market for Corporate Control, *Private Sector*, September, 1999.

Lightfoot, R.W. and C.W. Kester, Note on Corporate Governance Systems: The United States, Japan, and Germany, *Harvard Business School Case No.* 9-292-012, December, 15, 1992.

Macey, J., Measuring the Effectiveness of Different Corporate Governance Systems: Toward A More Scientific Approach, *Journal of Applied Corporate Finance*, **10** (4, Winter), 1998.

Miwa, Y. and M. Ramseyer, The Myth of the Main Bank: Japan and Comparative Corporate Governance, *Discussion Paper No.* 333, *Harvard Law School*, September, 2001.

Meulbroek, L., The Efficiency of Equity Linked Compensation: Understanding the Full Cost of Awarding Stock Options, *Financial Management*, Summer, 2001.

Murphy, K.J., Executive Compensation, Ashenfelter, Orley and David Card, (ed.), *Handbook of Labor Economics*, **3**, North Holland, 1999.

Pickens, T. B. Jr., Professions of a Short-Termer, *Harvard Business Review*, May-June, 1986.

Pound, J., Beyond Takeovers: Politics Comes to Corporate Control, *Harvard Business Review*, March-April, 1992.

Pozen, R., Institutional Investors: The Reluctant Activists, *Harvard Business Review*, Jan-Feb., 1994.

Rajan, R. and L. Zingales, The Governance of the New Enterprise, in X Vives, (ed.), *Corporate Governance*, Cambridge University Press, Cambridge: 2000.

Salmon, W., Crisis Prevention: How to Gear up your Board, *Harvard Business Review*, Jan-Feb., 1993.

Scott, K., The Role of Corporate Governance in South Korean Economic Reform, *Journal of Applied Corporate Finance*, **10**(4, Winter), 1998.

Useem, M., How Well Run Boards Make Decisions, *Harvard Business Review*, November, 2006.

Wagner, S. and L. Dittmar, The Unexpected Benefits of Sarbanes—Oxley, *Harvard Business Review*, April, 2006.

Zingales, L., The Value of the Voting Right: A Study of the Milan Stock Exchange, *Review of Financial Studies*, **7**, 1994.

———, What Determines the Value of Corporate Votes?, *Quarterly Journal of Economics*, 1995.

Index